Radical Origins to Economic Crises

Henri Savall

Radical Origins to Economic Crises

Germán Bernácer, A Visionary Precursor

palgrave
macmillan

Henri Savall
ISEOR
ECULLY CEDEX, France

ISBN 978-3-030-06647-5 ISBN 978-3-319-93366-5 (eBook)
https://doi.org/10.1007/978-3-319-93366-5

Softcover re-print of the Hardcover 1st edition 2018

Cover illustration: GettyImages/Dougal Waters

This Palgrave Macmillan imprint is published by the registered company Springer Nature Switzerland AG
The registered company address is: Gewerbestrasse 11, 6330 Cham, Switzerland

Foreword

Henri Savall asked me to present Germán Bernácer's works (1883–1965), which he analyses here better than anyone. The intellectual affinities between the Spanish economist and Sir Dennis Robertson, my teacher at Cambridge, are the reason why I surveyed the meticulous and penetrating research of Henri Savall. Thanks to his research, French-speaking economists have discovered Germán Bernácer. Indeed, who knew about this senior official at the Bank of Spain, cursed by a degree of disgrace and by the isolation of Hispanic culture from Anglo-Saxon culture? However, Sir Robertson admitted he was subconsciously impressed by the article on disposable funds that Bernácer sent him in 1923.

Posterity is often unfair: Keynes eclipsed both Robertson and Bernácer, even though the latter two have offered a much more dynamic concept of the circulation period of active money, while Keynes adopted a comparatively static method. Bernácer, like Robertson, proposes a much more accurate concept of interest rates in which the difference between the actual and the monetary components explains the cycle, while Keynes' *General Theory* contradicts the *Treatise on Money*. Bernácer and Robertson see that hoarding dormant and speculative money does not coincide with true savings, while Keynes rejects this notion.

Certainly, Bernácer and Robertson are divided on the subject of the productivity of legal capital and the time preference. Bernácer rejects those concepts, while Robertson's Marshallian background forbade him from questioning them. We can imagine their discussions strolling in the streets of Granada, where they met in 1954. Despite their differences, Bernácer and Robertson criticized the general equilibrium theory in a less paradoxical way than Keynes but with more objectivity and nuance.

Therefore, it would be a mistake to qualify Bernácer as pre-Keynesian. On the contrary, he is very modern, a follower of the value of labour, experienced in macroeconomic accounting, a supporter of companies' self-management, an opponent of the private ownership of unearned income-yielding assets, and convinced that the government's role includes the satisfaction of collective needs. Should Germán Bernácer—a mind whose self-taught training ensured originality, whose contact with monetary reality fed scientific induction, and whose doctrinal options led to a unity of thought that could inspire the envy of contemporary technocrats—earn, through Henri Savall, his rightful place among the pantheon of economists?

Colette Nême, Professor at the University of Law, Economics and Social Sciences (University of Paris II), Paris, 1974

Preface to the First Edition

In the history of economic thought, 1883 was a momentous year: Karl Marx died and Keynes and Schumpeter were born. Additionally, Germán Bernácer, the subject of this book, was born in Alicante. In 1951, when I wrote my book on economic fluctuations, I read Bernácer's ideas on cycles, and I was inspired by his thoughts and those of Sir Dennis Robertson. In truth, Bernácer was barely known in France, but Louis Baudin, André Piatier, François Perroux, and later Jacques Rueff contacted him. In 1965, the Revue d'Économie Politique (Political Economy Review) published a tribute written by one of his compatriots, José Pozuelo (1965).

Unfortunately, the famous saying that no one is a prophet in his or her own country has been proven. Among Spanish economists, there was a conspiracy of silence against Bernácer. It was not until 1973, eight years after his death, that the Spanish press finally paid homage to him.

Even so, it is now a young French author who, through this incisive book, definitively takes Bernácer out of the shadows. Given his Spanish background, Henri Savall had the privilege of knowing the family of the late master, and thus went directly back to Bernácer's origins. He told us that Professor Jacques Monteil guided him towards this research, and this topic was the subject of his Ph.D. in Economics at the University of Paris II.

We should highlight the subtitle chosen by the author: "A general theory of employment, income and hoarding". Noteworthy, isn't it? Will

Bernácer, who had been so long disregarded, therefore emerge as the Spanish Keynes? The two thinkers do not appear similar, although there are points of convergence in their scientific agendas. Keynes devoted himself to probability, while Bernácer became dedicated to physics when he was 22 years old. While Bernácer never belonged to the University, he was a professor at the Écolesupérieure de Commerce d'Alicante for many years and served as an industrial technology chair at the École des Hautes Etudes Commerciales de Madrid. He also led the Research Department at the Bank of Spain in times of the Republic and even after Franco's victory. He was also interested in art, painting, and even classical music.

From a demure family without a fortune, Bernácer was unpretentious and shy, constantly attracted by the landscape of his small hometown of Alicante, where solitude among the pines, watching the sea, inspired his deepest writings; he passed away there at 82 years of age.

Henri Savall considers Bernácer as the implicit author of a general theory, but Bernácer himself was too modest to make such a claim and considered it to be risky. In an incomplete world, there will always be an opportunity to generalize a theory that still seems general.

All of Bernácer's writings impress, and they cover almost all modern problems. However, we must limit our focus to the key works.

The title of his book published in 1916—Science and Happiness—reminds us of recent works by Philippe D'Iribarne and Louis Leprince-Ringuet (1973). Even so, the subtitle is even more evocative: "Social mechanical essay". It suggests Pareto, an engineer, was also concerned with the transformation of solid matter equilibrium to economic action equilibrium.

A second theme is related to monetary problems. Bernácer does not talk about cash, but in a 1922 paper, he constructed a theory of disposable funds, which was similar to the Keynesian notion to which he would return in his excellent 1945 book, *The functional theory of money*, where we find outlines of Nogaro, Aftalion, and, more similar to us, B. Schmitt.

Finally, Bernácer's last book—*A free economy without crisis and without unemployment*—was published in 1955. This resembles the general theory proposed by Savall, and the title is, antithetically so, current.

How can we express our gratitude to Henri Savall? Indeed, without him, who could say that he or she knows Bernácer? Obviously, despite the convincing attempts to paint him as a new Keynes—almost a Keynes precursor—Bernácer will never be among the pantheon of economists.

Could this reality be consistent with Bernácer's vocation?

Is it not also valuable to honour the memory of a self-taught man (is the lack of a teacher a merit?), a solitary researcher who, without the knowledge of the rest of the world, touched the deepest roots of economic problems?

Should we regret the lack of Bernácer's influence during his lifetime, recalling André Piettre's malicious opinion: "he missed being Anglo-Saxon"? From his place in the heavens, which he shares with Daniel Villey, to whom he wrote on January 17, 1955, because he too was a Christian humanist, Bernácer must give to Henri Savall the homage I just attempted to express.

Paris, France
Christmas 1974

Henri Guitton

Preface to the Third Edition

The work of Spanish economist Germán Bernácer is largely unknown in English language scholarship despite the publication of the first edition of this book in French in 1974. Bernácer's legacy is an inspired and original theory of economic fluctuations and crisis that provides a dramatic and useful contrast to better known and more commonly used economic theories of Marx, Keynes, Schumpeter, and liberal economists.

The search for new theories that can prevent and manage economic crisis is a common and timely theme in contemporary discussions of social and economic crises. Yet an innovative and uncommon theory can be found in Bernácer's work on economic crisis and unemployment written over half a century ago. This theory is important and unique because it provides an alternative to prevailing macro-economic theories that posit the need for high rates of interest to attract investment and savings, speculative markets that produce high interest and return on investment, and high levels of unemployment to allow for frictional economic adaptations. In contrast, Bernácer's theory shows how the presence of income from speculative investments (income without work) and high interest rates that allow for unearned wealth produce unemployment by removing money from the productive circuit of the economy and relegating it to the more profitable circuit of speculative investments. This move restricts economic activity by taking value added from past production out of circulation. Thus Bernácer's theory recommends against the very solutions to economic crisis that prevailing theories endorse. The current volume is especially significant because it presents Bernácer's important ideas to the English-speaking audience of scholars for the first time.

Bringing these ideas to light in English has taken some time. Fortunately, Professor Savall, no longer the "young French scholar" referred to in the preface to the first edition of this book, has been persistent and has once again taken Bernácer's ideas out of the shadows. One reason for this may be the many discussions of Bernácer's ideas I have had with Dr. Savall over the last decade. These discussions were rather one-sided as there were no English-language translations of Bernácer's works to inform my side of this conversation! So I repeatedly encouraged Dr. Savall to arrange the translation of this work into English. And I am delighted that this fine translation of Dr. Savall's treatise on Bernácer has finally been accomplished and Bernácer's ideas are now revealed to the English-speaking world.

The most direct relevance of Bernácer's work lies in the economic domain, but important sociological implications need to be noted as well. These implications can be highlighted by brief discussion of two key sociological theories of economic crises. First, consider Habermas's theory of Legitimation Crisis (1973). In this theory, the crisis cycle begins when economic activity transforms natural resources into commodities and encounters the countervailing process of falling profit that can limit the ability of the political administration to steer the economy toward more profit. Consequently, the social system can experience motivational crises where citizens lack the motivation to work due to low (or no) wages, poor working conditions, or a sense of unfairness in the work place. Together these cascading crises can become triggers of legitimation crisis where the state and its institutions are threatened by loss of mass support, disintegration, and/or the rise of authoritarian leadership. Here, Bernácer's theory exposes the fact that the underlying cause of crisis in advanced capitalism is not labor resistance to management demands but the removal of the surplus value extracted from labor from the circuit of production. This removal of value and its retention in speculative investments that create income without work reduces the financial resources available for wages and investments in production. These limitations on production exacerbate the problem of unemployment and can be addressed through Bernácer's theory.

Bernácer's theory of economic crisis also speaks to Ulrich Beck's (1992) theory of Risk Society. Risk society is the successor to the wealth generation society and is organized around the problem of managing the unintended side effects (e.g. pollution, disparities in wealth) of decades of wealth production. Wealth has become highly concentrated in certain sectors of the economy alongside high unemployment as financial resources are shifted out of the productive economy to the speculative economy. This value added is lost to production and wages and thus creates a of demand in production market. So long as this value added is outside of the sphere of production, unemployment will remain a serious social problem that wage adjustments, better working conditions, and other actions cannot correct. This is an issue that Bernácer's theory anticipates and addresses.

These few examples point to the significance of the presentation of Bernácer's work by Henri Savall. Perhaps now that the work of Bernácer is available in English, the theory will become better known and used to understand how economic crises are grounded in speculative markets that produce unearned income and unemployment. If the adoption of Bernácer's theory into practice occurs, we will all be indebted to the perseverance of Henri Savall's contributions to our understanding of alternative theories of crisis and unemployment in advanced capitalist economies.

Edmonton, Canada   Robert Gephart
June 19, 2018

Acknowledgements

This book is a distillation of our dissertation for a doctorate in Economics defended at the University Paris II on September 27, 1973, entitled: *Bernácer Germán, Spanish Economist (1883 to 1965). A General Theory of Employment, Unearned Income and Hoarding*, Ph.D. dissertation in Economics, offset, 602 p. (Paris University, 1973, Best Dissertation Award).

With few exceptions, the text body was respected. Annexes were cut in accordance with the requirements of the scientific edition and to reduce the amount of materials included. In particular, we exclude here a synopsis of economic thoughts and facts throughout history, which had been based on the table at the end of the manual of history of thought by Professor Piettre, which includes Bernácer's life and main publications, as well as events in Spain. Several elements of the complete bibliography of Bernácer and the summaries of his major works have been removed. We regret the omission of more detailed testimonies from world-renowned economists, especially the translation of the basic article published in 1922 on the theory of disposable funds as an interpretation of economic crises and social problems, which Robertson references. Scholars will find all these sacrificed elements in our original Ph.D. dissertation.

We should recognize here our debt to those who have followed our journey first in discovering Bernácer's theory and then in distributing it in France. We are indebted to Jacques Monteil for guiding us, several years ago, towards a study that proved fertile: research on Germán

Bernácer's economic thought. We owe Bernácer's widow and children a double debt of gratitude; without them, we would have had great difficulty in finding Bernácer's early writings, which have long been out of print. It is mainly through Bernácer's private correspondence, kindly sent to us by his family, and the testimonies collected from his wife, his children, and his friends and colleagues that we have been able to reconstitute each trait of his personality. With this help, we have better understood some of the author's original views and, potentially, some incarnations of his thoughts.

We strongly thank Colette Nême for the various remarks she offered throughout the writing of this book. We also thank all those who encouraged us to publish this book and, among them, in particular, the members of our thesis committee chaired by Colette Nême, André Piettre from the Institute of France, Luc Bourcier de Carbon, Maurice Bernadet, and Pierre Dockès, as well as the members of the Centre National de la Recherche Scientifique who, under the chairmanship of Henri Guitton, judged this book worthy of public funds.

Last but not least, we offer our gratitude to François Perroux, Professor at the Collège de France, the only economist who succeeded in securing Bernácer's presence at a conference outside his country—a conference in Paris in 1952. Perroux testified once more his high esteem of Bernácer, asking us to honour the memory of the Spanish economist in a short article published in June 1974 in the journal of the Institut de Science Economique Appliquée (ISEA): *Mondes en développement*.

Contents

List of Figures

Part I

A Pre-Keynes Founder of Modern Economics: Germán Bernácer

1

Why Publish This Work on Germán Bernácer, the Great Pioneering Spanish Economist, Now?

1.1 Understanding the Crisis in Order to Return to Prosperity

The current crisis is not transitory—it is a profound upheaval that will upset our economic and social benchmarks for a long time to come. The structures and behavioural patterns of tomorrow must be created today because the road to durable prosperity will be long and difficult. This reality presents an exceptional opportunity. Fortunately, the profound effects of the current crisis, such as bankruptcies, frauds, and dismissals, were attenuated by financial first aid. Although the fire is out, it is still smouldering, as the basic causes of economic and social imbalance have not been addressed.

Expert voices are increasingly emerging, encouraging us to think deeply about this mega-crisis. Sociologist Alain Touraine (2010) analysed the crisis and the double death of all that is social, while Guy Sorman (2010) invoked the parable of Saint-Simon or the Disillusioned States. A recent book by Nobel Economy Prize winner Joseph Stiglitz (2010) highlights the current triumph of cupidity, and another work by philosopher Michel Serres (2009) is called *Times of Crises*. Opinions on the crisis are expressed daily in the media, popular works, and erudite publications,

H. Savall, *Radical Origins to Economic Crises*,
https://doi.org/10.1007/978-3-319-93366-5_1

with critical opinions sometimes accompanied by proposals that deserve the attention of public and private industry decision-makers, company directors, management, personnel, and—last but not least—citizens. In our recent research on the worrying phenomenon of *tetranormalization*, which heralded the current crisis (Savall and Zardet 2005), we conclude that thought trends are strong signals of a vast decennial movement and a host of innovations that will impact all aspects of economic and social life within all organizations, markets, and territories and, in fact, society as a whole. Tetranormalization refers to the avalanche of contradictory standards that are grouped into four principal themes and that disturb the operations of the economic and social universe and delay the decisions needed to protect business and citizens.

This forecast is also a result of the numerous experiments that the Institut de Socio-économie des Entreprises et des Organisations (ISEOR) researchers in firms and organizations have conducted over the last 44 years on the beneficial and encouraging results of an innovative management system that integrates social variables and economic performance.

Our very first study led us to an extraordinarily original pioneering theory by a somewhat unknown Spanish economist, the neglected inspiration for the world-renowned Keynes (Savall 1973, 1975b). In a 1922 article, Germán Bernácer proposes an explanation for recurring crises that is congenital with the existence of speculative markets, such as property and works of art, long-term money markets, and commercial trading (materials and energy). These speculative markets abound in financial capital, attracting and capturing it. This capital then becomes scarce in production industries where real value is created, thereby *draining these industries' financing*.

History repeats itself: 1929, 2007–2008, and 2012.

The most recent economic crisis, which was of an unexpected acuity and magnitude and was worse than any previous crisis, calls for major reflections and actions to avoid global catastrophe or an economic and social meltdown in the countries that intensely experience the effects of a global economy.

Supported by many years of research and observation as the Research Director for the Bank of Spain, Germán Bernácer offers a luminous, basic, and original explanation for the origin of crises and how to avoid them.

Currently, no one dares to advocate for a return to a planned, centralized economy, as it failed with the fall of the Berlin Wall in 1989. Instead, all members of society currently feel the ferocity of the aberrant attacks that destroy jobs, economic prosperity, and social well-being. These attacks are dangerous for political democracy and are caused by the uncontrolled excess of the financial hurricanes that periodically wreak havoc on the real economy. This reality reveals the cynical arrogance of the excesses of chaotic speculative markets. Currently, given that most States are bankrupt (with recurring deficits and over-borrowing), we are occasionally tempted to rely on the illusory Keynesian promise of a Welfare Government that can help poor, defenceless citizens. In this context, it is important to shine light on the robust theory forged by Germán Bernácer regarding the structural and chronic explanation for crises, which calls for more radical and more durable economic and financial policies than vain monetary manipulations or ineffective gesticulations aimed at polemically regulating financial markets' outrageous speculative activities.

A visionary equipped with a rigorous scientific method inherited from his training as a physicist (he taught Physics throughout his life), Bernácer published a book entitled *Society and Happiness. An Essay in Social Mechanics* in 1916. A few years later, in 1922, he published a famous article that proposed *the theory of availabilities* to explain economic crises and the social problem of unemployment. This article inspired several reputed Anglo-Saxon and German economists. Long before Keynes' *The General Theory of Employment, Interest and Money* (1936), Bernácer laid the foundations for modern macroeconomic theory: the functional theory of money, a synthetic and functional theory of interest rates and a basic theory of economic crises, which, according to him, are attributable to the existence of *speculative markets for unearned income yielding assets*, that is, goods that provide incomes without the counterpart of work, entrepreneurial risk, or the creation of real value-added—that is, the revenue to be shared between the economic and social parties.

At first sight, certain aspects of Bernácer's economic policy recommendations may seem utopian or too radical, such as the elimination of stock markets and interest. Nevertheless, Bernácer's prolonged demonstration of the inevitable chronic instability and under-employment that results from the existence of these *unearned income yielding assets*, which are recurrently impacted by speculation and are typically found in the financial, real estate, art, raw materials and energy markets—particularly in long-term markets—could be meaningfully explored to create more effective and efficient economic and financial policies at the national and international levels after the 2012 crisis.

Bernácer shows that interest rates are a chronic cause of inflation and artificially increase the cost of financing the real economy without contributing any effective counterpart to economic and social activity. He recommends interest rates that are lower than observed inflation rates—and even zero interest rate for some activities privileged by national or international social policies or for financing structural projects. In addition, based on Bernácer's very convincing demonstration of the origin of the succession of chronic, recurring, and cyclic crises, the most disastrous effects of which are unemployment and latent under-employment, we suggest abolishing or strongly restricting medium- and long-term financial markets—as well as the raw materials and energy trading markets—from being excessively speculative. In short, eliminating speculation would significantly contribute to supporting economic and social development and enable resources to be directed towards activities that create true value-added to be shared between all participating parties. Eliminating speculation would also prevent the recurring financial bubbles that accompany global business cycles at increasingly frequent intervals.

Before Maurice Allais, Bernácer (1916, 1922, 1945, 1955) proposed *The General Theory of Employment, Unearned Income and Double Hoarding* based on the idea that rigorous financial management of economic and social activities, a balanced budget, and price stability contribute to durable economic prosperity, safeguard employment levels, and encourage the creation of new jobs, new products, and new wealth. Allais, the first French Nobel Economics Prize Winner before Jean Tirole, was also shunned by academics before he received the Swedish Academy Award.

In the current debate, some experts prefer demagogic facility and "short-term action" with the recourse of increasing the money supply, which worsens the debt position of States and public administrations and increases companies' finance charges as they resort to expensive day-to-day borrowing to finance working capital.

Additionally, a demagogic recourse to the Mint (systematic budget deficits) is added. States and national and international central banks have acknowledged their incapacity to explain to their citizens the need for good housekeeping with balanced budgets, which is the source of ethical behaviour, social justice, and confidence by savers both large and small.

What we currently call austerity plans are only palliatives applied with detrimental brutality, given the accumulation of long periods of inaction and repeated drifts. For many years, even several decades, budgetary and monetary carelessness was privileged by States and many players in the economy who preferred easy living and speculation rather than the occasionally risky innovation that creates wealth to be shared between participating parties.

We do not advise brutal rigour here, but rather—based on the theory suggested by Bernácer—a rigour integrated into the reflexes of everyday life and the recurring operation of the economic and social systems and built into decision-making models and tools on both the macro- and microeconomic levels. This behaviour would allow a dynamic financial balance in relations between stockholders to be maintained.

Inflation is a very dangerous mirage and misleading mask because it tends to hide the harmful effects of *an effective rate of interest*, that is, the nominal rate of interest after deducting the inflation rate. Nevertheless, this advantage is illusory because unstable prices and interest rates caused by continuous and ephemeral adjustments make it difficult to discern the path that should be followed among those suggested by traditional economic decision-making models.

As soon as Keynes published his *The General Theory of Employment, Interest and Money* in 1936, Bernácer denounced its chronic inflationary nature that was generated by the imprudently systematic recourse to Government intervention in the event of private venture failure. Indeed, private ventures cannot continually finance with their own capital the infinite needs of all economic players or ensure the growth and qualitative development of their shared economic and social prosperity.

In the panic caused by the economic slump in 1929 and the rise of Fascism and Nazism in Europe, which seized the world between the two world wars in the twentieth century, Keynes's proposals logically found support from politicians, who found their role enhanced as a result. Indeed, due to citizen strong fears and politician complicity and occasional cowardice, this period was the beginning of the logical and popular belief in the almost unlimited capacity of Government to pay for the financing, investment, and economic drive needed to ensure national prosperity. Keynes thus found "customers" for his national economic policy ideas and was to some extent a very effective marketer of his own theory: in a time of distress and disorder, his ideas inspired the structural works policies, particularly in Italy and Germany, providing a conceptual framework that justified the relevance of government intervention, which thereby became an *operator* with the other economic players. The authorities assumed the initiative and regulation that the private industry failed to provide and questioned private industry's ability to undertake creative and responsible initiatives, thereby indiscriminately incriminating very small, small, medium, large, and very large businesses.

The decisive role of private industry in economic buoyancy was demonstrated by the major Austrian economist Joseph Schumpeter, a contemporary of Keynes and Bernácer (all three were born in 1883, the year Marx died). Schumpeter became a professor at Harvard University just before World War II.

The doubt that resulted from the combination of speculative and entrepreneurial capitalists, the perverted speculative market, and the real market, that is, the healthy conflict between the supply and demand for goods and services, was a very damaging historical mishap.

Bernácer deplored this state of affairs in the interwar period, followed by François Perroux and Maurice Allais in France after World War II; all criticized the chronic inflation caused by Keynesian policy. Additionally, Keynes's recommendations were attractive because, following the Yalta Conference, they offered an alternative to Marxism and centrally run national economies such as the USSR and Eastern Europe. These ideas were believed to threaten Western society and the "liberal" economy. The renewal of the economies destroyed by World War II also played a very significant role in the prosperity experienced during this long period, called the "30 glorious years" in France, Germany, the UK, and other European countries that were severely affected by the war.

The combination of renewal and Keynesian easy financing policies was likely the main driver of these three decades of prosperity and economic growth without major crises and with no cyclic reversals. Unfortunately, however, this period was accompanied by habituation to permanent inflation, which reached very high levels at certain times during the post-war period. The consequences of the oil crisis in 1973 caused unemployment to increase in France from 500,000 to over 3 million, and it has remained at this level ever since.

1.2 The Influence of Bernácer on Our Work in Economics and Management Science

The strength of Bernácer's pioneering works between 1916 and 1962 (he died in 1965) had a considerable influence on my own work and on that of ISEOR. From an anecdotal perspective, I have personally never bought a single share on the stock market, and I have always been deeply mistrustful of excessive fluctuations in prices, interest rates, and speculative ventures. More basically, I acquired the reflex from Bernácer to systematically reason in terms of traditional dynamics, dating all economic and organizational analysis data and their variables by *breaking down time into successive periods*. This process makes it possible to consider *the learning effect,* that is, the rules of knowledge acquired during a previous period and integrated into the simulation for a subsequent period. This *heuristic* logic process can improve forecast quality when making decisions. This successive period approach, which is a constant in all Bernácer's works, also inspired British economist Dennis Robertson, who acknowledged this influence on his works published after 1926 and, very explicitly, in an article entitled "*A Spanish Contribution to the Theory of Fluctuations*", which was published in the English journal "*Economica*" in February 1940. Bernácer's works are hallmarked by a remarkable independence of mind with regard to the established ideologies that inevitably inspired mainstream economic thought, namely, the traditional school and its three antagonistic affiliates: Marxist criticism, the liberal neo-classical school, and its Keynesian alternative.

This independence of mind has hallmarked our works and encouraged us to adopt a deliberately *heterodox posture.* As in physical, life, and natural sciences, this approach consists of privileging rigorous observation and the integration of powerful epistemological reflexes in the scientific process, the essential source of reconstructive criticism of existing theories and scientific progress. This approach ensures a suitable level of intrinsic quality, societal utility, and the academic credibility of the research. Our research on Bernácer's theory, the main results of which are provided in this document, led us to conclude that we should refute the cogency of theories imputing the cause of the creation of value and economic growth to the two traditional production factors: the accumulation of capital and the quantity of labour.

I devoted the eight years between 1965 (the year of Bernácer's death) and 1973 to researching Bernácer's *General Theory of Employment, Revenue and (Double) Hoarding* in the fields of macroeconomics, history of economic thought, and theory of crises, including my doctoral thesis in economic sciences at the University of Paris 2 Pantheon- Sorbonne.

Then, for about 30 years, I abandoned my macroeconomic research and turned to research on the value creation factor, which has not been addressed by established theories. To do so, I used an extremely thorough and longitudinal investigatory method to research inside organizations, private firms, and public and associative industries in terms of their activities and the *observable* behaviours of all participants in the production of *real economic value.* The method developed consisted of research programmes, with most lasting over two years and often over ten years—the longest lasted 34 years—to *observe, measure,* and *analyse* in detail *how and in what conditions* generally held beliefs—capital and labour—generate economic value added. We aimed to observe and study the mystery of economic value creation and the process of its *partial destruction by dysfunctions* (Savall 1974b, 1975a, 1981, 2010). At that time, the destruction of economic value had not been researched through *in-depth observations* and robust analyses, nor through measurements of these misunderstood phenomena. I abandoned this macroeconomic analysis level for a time in order to pursue management sciences research, which allowed me to find more evidence to question the simplistic theory of the two factors of production traditionally suggested by classical theory and its three prolongations (neoclassic, Marxist, and Keynesian) and their inability to account for the complexity of the economic value-creation process.

Certainly ambitious but enlightening, the objective was to build a theory of the phenomena that lead to wealth creation. This innovative theory was called the *Socio-Economic Theory of Organizations.* An *organization* is any human and social grouping producing economic value, regardless of the analytical level adopted. The first level is a business company or a public, semi-public, or private organization; it can also be an industrial industry, local communities, or departmental, regional, national, or transnational territories that constitute tangled sets of organizations. Territories and organizations are characterized by the existence of systems of governance and the finalization of their activities by its active members, participants in governance, directorial and management teams, and personnel at all levels. In particular, the *Socio-Economic Theory of Organizations* contains *a* theory of hidden costs and performances, which we originated in 1973 (Savall and Zardet 1987, 2008a, b, c; Savall, Zardet & Bonnet, 2000, 2008). This theory includes elements, data, and variables that had not been previously measured and were even said to be unmeasurable by the economic and management literature dedicated to the well-established theories of these two disciplines.

In 1972, the in-depth research of the Malinvaud econometrics team, following other authors, showed that two traditional factors—capital and labour—explain only about 50% of economic growth. In 1969, Solow referred to a figure of 18%. The relevance of the two-factor (capital and labour) theory is called into question by the existence of a remainder equal to or greater than the portion of value creation these factors explain. Indeed, in the production function Y = f (K*L) + r, the "remainder" r represents the difference between the economic value of production and the portion explained by capital and labour. Our aim was to identify the less-understood contents of this remainder. My ISEOR research team's programme aimed to detect and calculate the costs and performances that have remained unidentified by traditional analytical methods and models and that were not shown in private or national industry accounting information systems or in decision-making assistance tools. We called these elements the hidden costs and performances of organizations. The analysis of the causes of the loss of value unexplained by the mainstream theories made it possible to construct an interpretative and operational theory of the way organizations operate and generate their economic performance. Hidden costs can be very high—from *€20,000 to €70,000 per person per year*—and include historical costs, which do not create value-added and opportunity costs unmeasured by experts in these organizations and by existing theoretical models designed to assist with decision-making. Applying this theory in a large number of firms and organizations has shown that these hidden costs are not inevitable because according to the database we constructed for the last 45 years through experimenting with the socio-economic model in over 2000 firms and public and private industry organizations, in more than 72 different branches of industry (industries, profit-making services, public services) and of many different sizes (employing from 5 to 30,000 people) in 45 different countries on 4 continents, we can convert a significant proportion of these hidden costs (from 35% to 55%) into value-added.

Analogously with the principle of energy saving, we conclude that firms and organizations generate a chronic destruction of value-added, of which a part can be avoided by organizational methods and activity control methods that mobilize corporate human resources to a greater degree. This database makes it possible to show that the established economic value creation theories are erroneous and do not resist more robust and in-depth investigations than those usually used in economics and management research, which are more superficial and use very rudimentary observation techniques that distort the research results. Our innovative measurement of the hidden costs of dysfunctions opens significant research horizons. It is analogous with research on energy saving, which has shown remarkable progress over the last 30 years thanks to the attention paid to the causes and measurement of energy loss, followed by a quest for alternative operating modes. The analogy between energy saving and saving in human resources in the economic value production process makes it possible to clarify the scope of the hidden costs and performance theory, also called the *Socio-Economic Theory of Organizations*. Indeed, the use of real resources in the production of goods and public and private services and the non-creation of potential resources can be compared to the evaporation of value into "the economic and social atmosphere", which is of no use to any of the participating parties.

The failure to create value-added is a loss of earnings in the form of opportunity costs, which would be useful in the economic and social universe. This evaporation of resources is unreasonable if we accept that the finality of economic activity, particularly in a democratic regime, aims to ensure social progress for the well-being of the greatest number of people.

The implication of these discoveries is considerable since the *Socio-Economic Theory* shows that any organization can *finance* a significant part of *its* development except for large-scale new investments—structural projects or the implementation of breakthrough innovations—which require considerable capital investment from private savings either through stockholder equity or debt. Recourse to the cash money market would be sensible in this latter case because it would contribute to a macroeconomic development stripped of excess inflation and toxic speculation, which would also ensure better financing of SMEs, which create most new jobs and real value-added. These firms are often badly treated by the money market, which prefers the massive financing of large companies or speculative investments.

The mixed financing of the growth of SMEs is possible. One part of this mixed financing is the self-financing enabled by hidden cost recycling, a possibility neglected by the management methods most frequently used by organizations because of ignorance of *the disposable funds* of hidden resources, which can be valued at between €20,000 and €70,000 per person per year and should be partially recycled.

The other part of mixed financing is *reasonable borrowing* from banks or the Stock Exchange, increasing the reimbursement capacity of SMEs due to the recycling of the hidden costs of their dysfunction. After these discoveries in the field of management sciences, our research has led us back to the meso- and macroeconomic levels over the last 15 years, particularly within the framework of our new research programme on "*tetra-normalization*". This programme mobilizes a network of approximately 30 research teams in France, Spain, Portugal, Romania, the United States, Mexico, Argentina, and Lebanon.

Our assumption of *isomorphism* was born out of the observation of identical or analogous phenomena at different levels of analysis: within an organization or at the level of increasingly vast territories, such as a municipality, a region, a nation, or a set of nations. The value creation model at the level of the firm, industrial industry, job catchment area, region, nation, or set of nations is isomorphic. The *value-added over variable cost* calculated from a firm's accounts is of a comparable nature to the *GDP* of a region or a nation. In the same way, the principle of isomorphism seems to indicate that the theory of the hidden costs and performance makes it possible to trace and clarify new paths for policies not only for firms but also for industries and nations by reducing the dysfunctions that absorb a significant portion of resources without creating comparable value-added. Experience shows that it is possible to recover a significant portion (35% to 55%) of economic value, which is invaluable for development and job creation.

In 1975, the *macroscopic framework* that guided our research and experiments of organizational *socio-economic management* (SEAM) for the past 42 years was published under our innovative concept of *Socially Responsible Capitalism and* then published in English by Routledge in 2017 (Savall, Péron, Zardet & Bonnet, 2015, 2017). Socially and sustainably responsible capitalism goes in the direction of what Bernácer proposed, yet nonetheless is confronted by speculations tied to excesses of *financial capitalism* so that it should be qualified as *Socially Irresponsible Capitalism.*

"*Creative* innovation in matters of financial instruments has largely contributed to economic development, but *perverse* innovations, as the *hedge funds* and *subprimes' crisis* demonstrated, are producing a predatory value. The financial economy is siphoning resources from real economy needs and is locking itself into a sphere that Petty and his contemporaries would judge as more and more unattainable"… "That is why we name *human potential* as the prime factor of economic value creation in the socio-economic theory (SEAM), in order to distinguish it from the traditional concept of labor used in classical approaches of economics and management theories and their substitutes whether they be Keynesian or Marxist criticisms."… "Social responsibility is incumbent upon the Schumpeterian entrepreneur and those espousing all other forms of governance with the essential finality of stopping the exclusive primacy given to financial domain". The *discarnate financial,* disterritorialized, uncontrolled, and *speculative* type of capitalism is not assimilated to any system, but it can be considered as an obstacle to an intelligent growth and to the establishment of a *responsible and democratic* development model… It is therefore not surprising that Joseph Stiglitz (2012, p. 200) emphasizes that "bankruptcy is a crucial characteristic of capitalism" (Savall, Péron, Zardet & Bonnet, 2015, 2017).

The French economic press has begun to discuss the "macro hidden costs" of prescription drugs that are financed by French Medicare and go unconsumed, which are worth several billion euros. Our research in the field of macroeconomics provided us with a reading grid based on Bernácer's very innovative, remarkably heterodox theory, which disparages the more established theories. François Perroux, our second inspiration in the field of economics, introduced Bernácer to France at a conference in Paris in 1952. He suggested the subtitle of my book on Bernácer, published in the collection *Les grands économistes* by Dalloz in 1975: "*Heterodoxy in Economic Science*". Thanks to this heterodox attitude acquired from studying Bernácer's work and comparing it with the works of his famous contemporary economists in different streams of thought, we had the strength and audacity to brave the risks of refuting the "historic monument" theories, such as the production function and the two-factor (capital and labour) theories, which are always explicitly or implicitly present in all classical, neo-classical, and Keynesian schools of thought. For example, although stated in different terms, Marxist thought embraces the two-factor theory. We must thank Bernácer, who taught physics all his life, for having devoted most of his scientific research to economics. He believed that economic and social activity needed his contribution as a researcher more than the physical sciences, on which so many scientists were already focused. Perhaps it is no coincidence that French Nobel Economics Prize winner Maurice Allais was also an eminent physicist.

Appointed research director of the Bank of Spain during the second Spanish Republic, Bernácer headed an economy observatory and laboratory that were able to nourish, support, refine, and validate the theory he forged by combining his career as a physics teacher and his position at the bank, as he was in direct contact with the economic and social environment of his time between 1931 and his retirement from 1956 to 1965.

The reason for the re-publication of this book on Bernácer's pioneering theory is to avoid futile disputes between old ideologies, outrageous liberalism, failed Marxism, and imprudent and stalled Keynesianism. This introduction highlights the very current nature of Bernácer's work in the context of an acute crisis that has completely upset the economic and social universe and our own innovative work, which has extended, deepened, and rendered his theory operational.

Professor Henri Savall

IAE Lyon, University Jean Moulin

President founder of ISEOR (Institut de Socio-économie des Entreprises et des Organisations).

Chevalier de la Légion d'Honneur.

Awarded, with *Véronique Zardet*, of the Académie des Sciences Morales et Politiques (INSTITUT DE FRANCE) prize "*for their work on the integration of social variables in corporate strategies*".

Presentation of Plan

We exclude from our study the reports drafted under Bernácer's authority in the Department of Studies of the Bank of Spain, as well as popular articles published in certain non-theoretical journals. Therefore, our sources include Bernácer's books, doctrine articles, and correspondence with contemporary foreign economists.

Because Bernácer's work is little known in France, a synthetic presentation of his thought and his biography seemed necessary in this first section. To focus on his forerunner position, we situate his work into various schools of thought. Then, we highlight his contribution to the modern economics which makes it still current in the international context.

The second part is aimed at explaining Bernácer's model and ideas on money and interest. Chapter 3 introduces the elements of Bernácer's economic analysis and critics of the actual capitalism. His analysis leads to focus on the concept of money and its role in the overall economic theory. Then, the interest rate as a factor of crises is detailed. The last section analyses Bernácer's contribution to economics. Through a comparative study of Bernácer's positions on several major issues with those of economists who marked the history of the field, we hope to enlighten the reader about the importance of Bernácer's theoretical contribution.

Our conclusion will illuminate our motivation, thus far unacknowledged in our thesis, namely, that the evaluation of Bernácer's work must place him among the pantheon of great economists, and may our clumsiness be forgiven in this regard: not all Jean Moulins have the good fortune of finding a Malraux.

Germán BERNÁCER
(1883-1965)

Playa de San Juan (Alicante) Agosto 1946

Querido Prof Robertson:

Recibo aquí en mi residencia veraniega su grata del 30/7 acompañándome el prefacio para la edición ~~española~~ temática, que me parece muy adecuado, y una nota biográfica, que utilizaré en una breve introducción acerca de su obra económica. Espero todavía una fotografía suya que el editor Aguilar desea absolutamente incluir en el libro. Acostumbra a ponerla en toda esta serie de obras de primera fila.

A mi regreso a Madrid le escribiré acerca de esta cuestión difícil, pero general, del cómputo de beneficios. Para mí se halla arraigada la ahí el punto crucial de una teoría dinámica del mercado. Ha sido uno de mis temas fundamentales, y creo que mi solución es satisfactoria, aunque me explico perfectamente su dificultad, todo por lo que yo mismo he dudado y me han dado mucho trabajo.

Muy sinceramente suyo.

Germán Bernácer

References

Allais, M. (1947). *À la recherche d'une discipline économique* (In search of economic discipline), t. 1, « Économie et Intérêt » (Economy and interest). Paris: Imprimerie nationale.

Bernácer, G. (1916). *Sociedad y felicidad – Ensayo de Mecánica Social* (Society and happiness – Essay on social mechanics). Madrid: Ed. Beltrán.

Bernácer, G. (1922). La teoría de las disponibilidades como interpretación de las crisis y del problema social (The theory of disposable funds as interpretation of crisis and social issues). *Revista nacional de economía* (40).

Bernácer, G. (1945). *La teoría funcional del dinero* (The functional theory of money) (2nd ed., 1956). Madrid: Consejo Superior de Investigaciones Científicas.

Bernácer, G. (1955). *Una economía libre sin crisis y sin paro* (Free economy without crisis nor unemployment). Madrid: Aguilar.

Keynes, J. M. (1936). *Théorie générale de l'emploi, de l'intérêt, de la monnaie* (General theory of employment, interest and money), French translation. Paris: Payot, 1959.

Marx, K. (1859). *Contribution à la critique de l'économie politique* (Contribution to the criticism of political economy). Paris: Éditions sociales.

Marx, K. (1927). *Le capital* (The capital). Paris: Éditions Molitor.

Marx, K. (1962). *Le capital* (The capital). Paris: Éditions sociales.

Marx, K. (1963). *Œuvres de K. Marx*: « Économie I » (Marx's works by: "Economics I"), Bibliothèque de la Pléiade, Paris: Gallimard, especially: « Introduction générale à la Critique de l'économie politique » (Including: "General Introduction to the criticism on political economy").

Savall, H. (1973). Germán Bernácer, économiste espagnol (1883–1965). Une théorie générale de l'emploi, de la rente et de la thésaurisation (General theory of employment, unearned income and hoarding). PhD dissertation, University of Paris II, 602p., mimeographed.

Savall, H. (1974a). Avant Keynes et au-delà: Germán Bernácer, économiste espagnol (Before Keynes and beyond: Germán Bernácer, Spanish economist). *Mondes en développement, 5*.

Savall, H. (1974b, 1975a, 1981, 2010). *Enrichir le travail humain: l'évaluation économique* (Enriching human work: the economic evaluation). PhD dissertation at the University Paris IX-Dauphine; integral text published at Dunod; 4th edition increased, Economica, 1989. Translated in English: *Work and people: an economic evaluation of job enrichment.* New York: Oxford University

Press (1°.Ed 1981); 2°Ed Charlotte, NC: IAP (2010); in Spanish: *Por un trabajo más humano*, Madrid: Tecniban, (1°Ed 1977); 2° Ed, Charlotte, NC: IAP (2011).
Savall, H. (1975b). *G. Bernácer: L'hétérodoxie en science économique* (G. Bernácer: The heterodoxy in economics). Paris: Dalloz, Collection Les Grands Économistes.
Savall, H. (2001). *Origine radicale des crises économiques: Germán Bernácer, précurseur visionnaire* (Radical origin of economic crises: Germán Bernácer, a visionary precursor). Charlotte: IAP.
Savall, H., & Zardet V. (1987, 2008, 2015). *Maîtriser les coûts et les performances cachés. Le contrat d'activité périodiquement négociable.* Prix Harvard l'Expansion de Management Stratégique (Harvard-L'Expansion award in strategic management, 6th edition, 2015). Paris: Economica. Translated in English *Mastering hidden costs and performance.* Charlotte: IAP (2008).
Savall, H., & Zardet, V. (2005). *Tétranormalisation, défis et dynamiques* (Tetranormalization, challenges and dynamics). Paris: Economica.
Savall, H., Zardet, V., & Bonnet, M. (2000). *Releasing the untapped potential of enterprises trough socio-economic management* (2nd ed., 2008). Genève: ILO-BIT.
Savall, H., Péron, M., Zardet, V., & Bonnet, M. (2015, 2017). *Socially responsible capitalism and management.* New York: Routledge.
Serres, M. (2009). *Temps des crises.* Paris: Ed. Le Pommier.
Sorman, G. (2010). Le déplacement du pouvoir vers l'économie-monde, Le Monde, 2 mars.
Stiglitz, J. (2010). *Le triomphe de la cupidité.* Paris: Les liens qui libèrent.
Stiglitz, J. E. (2012). *Cost of inequality.* Luxemburg City: Babel.
Touraine, A. (2010). La crise et la double mort du social, Le Figaro, 1 mars, p. 12.

2

Biography and Testimonies

2.1 Bernácer's Life and Career

The Child and the Student

Germán Bernácer was born on June 29, 1883, in Alicante, to a humble family. His father owned a shop selling almost everything, which was common in the Mediterranean—it was part grocery store, part bazaar, and part haberdashery. His mother, a modest, intelligent, and cheerful woman, instilled in Germán various values and qualities, and he worshipped her.

From his terrace, the young Germán loved contemplating the sea and the movement of merchant ships that moved Alicante wine overseas. Thus, his love of nature and his curiosity for all human activity remained linked throughout his life.

At the business school where he began his studies, Germán was a diligent learner. Beginning at the age of 14, he had to assist his family financially because his father's business had declined. He gave private lessons during the day and studied at night by the light of an oil lamp, as Alicante had not yet received electricity at the end of the nineteenth century. At dawn, when the sun began to loom on the Mediterranean horizon, the

H. Savall, *Radical Origins to Economic Crises*,
https://doi.org/10.1007/978-3-319-93366-5_2

young Bernácer went to bed, earning a little rest before undertaking another laborious day.

At the end of his studies, Germán Bernácer earned the rank of "profesor mercantil". He then assisted his physical chemistry professor at the High School of Commerce of Alicante. During these years of assistantship, he learned and perfected French, English, German, and Italian, which were to serve him throughout his career in reading foreign economic journals and works and in writing articles for foreign journals.

In Madrid, in 1905, he applied to become an industrial technology teacher at the country's business schools. He was chosen immediately, and rather than opting for a chair in Madrid, the young Bernácer—who was then 22 years old—accepted an appointment to the Business School of Alicante because his family still needed financial assistance and his attachment to his homeland was resolute.

His Life in Alicante

Germán Bernácer remained in Alicante for 26 years. This long, fertile time enabled him to develop his abilities, which today we would call multidisciplinary. Indeed, Bernácer showed a strong curiosity in all subjects throughout his life. After marrying, he became Secretary of the Chamber of Commerce of Alicante.

This multidisciplinary approach first began at an intrapersonal level: he devoted most of his energy to studying economics and yet he continued to teach his core disciplines—physics and chemistry—at the Graduate School of Commercial Studies in Madrid until his retirement in 1953. At the interpersonal level, we will emphasize his cultural thriving in what we call the humanist circle of Alicante and his contribution as an economist—through his relations with great Spanish mathematicians at the beginning of research in mathematical economics and econometrics in Spain.

The Humanist Circle of Alicante

Bernácer had three friends in Alicante: a great writer, a great musician, and a painter in the famous School of Sorolla. First, Gabriel Miró had an important role in the Spanish literature of the first 30 years of XXth century. At the time of Miró's death, Bernácer published a literary tribute to him in the review Sigüenza. Second was Oscar Esplá, who, despite his age, still lived between Alicante and Madrid, in 1973, leading the foundation of the music award bearing his name. Emilio Varela did not reach the fame of his master Sorolla. Excursions to the beautiful nature surrounding Alicante, as well as literary, philosophical, and artistic discussions, linked the four men; they formed the editorial board of a local literary magazine that had some national resonance, particularly because of Gabriel Miró's fame.

Bernácer actively participated in the cultural life in Alicante. As a great lover of classical music, he was interested in all manifestations of art and knowledge. During the Spanish Civil War (1936–1939), while the majority of children did not attend elementary school, Bernácer, at over 50 years old, taught his own children at home. He even learned Latin.

The Physicist

At age 22, Bernácer was a young professor of physics. He was struck by the shortcomings around him: difficulty in documentation, a lack of qualifications among many of his fellow citizens in technical fields, and a lack of infrastructure of all kinds. He brought books to Alicante and committed himself to the difficult and exciting task of training young people. He created the first laboratory of experimental physics and chemistry. He was also eager to participate more directly in the active life of his country and his city: he created a department of product analysis in his laboratory to study industries and insurers, and his young disciples participated. At that time, he published two works on technology.

The additional resources procured by this activity allowed Bernácer to provide the Graduate School of Commerce with the only teaching laboratory of the city. Until then, the study of chemistry and physics was purely bookish.

He received a travel scholarship in 1911 and undertook a year-long journey across Europe. He lived and studied in France, Germany, Belgium, The Netherlands, Italy, and England. The physicist discovered some very interesting elements, but what he observed in the economic and social field grieved the economist, confirming his belief that it was likely more important to focus on studying the problems of the political economy and to try to solve them. Upon his return, he finished the manuscript for his first book, *Society and Happiness*, and after some laborious effort, published it in 1916.

From then on, his studies' domain was the vast field of economics, but he remained a physics professor until he was 70 years old.

In 1926, at the age of 43, Bernácer married Maria Guardiola, who was 20 years his junior and the daughter of his friend, the biographer of Gabriel Miro. They had four children.

His Life in Madrid

While the second Spanish Republic (which began in 1931 after the electoral victory of the leftist party) called for the famous painter Pablo Picasso to manage the renowned Prado Museum, Germán Bernácer was asked to create and manage the Studies Department of the Bank of Spain in Madrid in 1931. This important position did not fulfil him, and Bernácer aimed to become chair of industrial technology at the Graduate School of Commercial Studies in Madrid. To do so, he had to compete once again in the physics aggregation competition and, in this effort, he wrote a manuscript on a treaty of methodology in physics that was never published. Ranked second in the competitive exam of 1932, he settled in Madrid and established a laboratory at the Graduate School of Commercial Studies in Madrid at a time when the Faculty of Sciences did not have one. He later published a manual.

Bernácer had to remove the strictness in observation and scientific analysis acquired from his training in physics for his work as an economist; additionally, we noticed a very discreet kind of frustration in his economics work because of his inability to engage in experimentation, without which science is only half science.

The Vocation of the Economist

Upon reaching adulthood, Bernácer noticed a difference between, on one hand, the flow of scientific and technical progress, which he considered to be much more advanced than industrial reality and, on the other hand, that of economic progress, which rightly seemed very late due to mysterious chronic diseases, unemployment, and cyclic crises.

We believe that Bernácer's travel in Europe strengthened his idea that advancing economics rather than physics was more important for social well-being. His first economics book, a youth work, includes all the seeds of his future thought generously and without scientific concessions. It appears that this book had an impact in Germany. Bernácer's family often heard him speak about letters written to him by German economists following the publication of *Society and Happiness.*

At that time, Madrid attracted Bernácer in every sense of the term, as his recent fame led to contacts with popular thinkers and scholars. The great sociologist and philosopher José Ortega y Gasset, who had a large audience even outside academic and intellectual circles, wrote to Bernácer on May 29, 1931, at the dawn of the Second Republic: "I have always believed that one of the great crimes of the defunct regime was not to create a serious and great Graduate School of Economics". This call led Bernácer to pursue the position of Director of the Department of Studies at the Bank of Spain rather than to create graduate studies in Spain, which was the work of some of his friends who were politically engaged in the new regime after the Spanish Civil War.

Bernácer's task was scientifically ambitious. Despite his mutual contact with great foreign economists, he was poorly received by his fellow economists. His desire to stay out of politics—especially after 1939—may have motivated the ostracism to which he was victim. His temper was also certainly decisive in determining his situation. According to interviews with or written testimonies of those who had met Bernácer, all were unanimous in recognizing his great modesty, his intellectual and moral probity, and his shyness in daily interactions. His love of nature coincided with solitary studies in the pine forests near his home on the beach of San Juan in Alicante. He died there in May 1965 at 82 years of age.

The Vicissitudes of His Career at the Bank of Spain

According to our interviews, Bernácer took effective action until the explosion of the Spanish Civil War in 1936. Afterwards, his work was interrupted first by military events that distressed Spain and then by political events that established a particular political and social order.

Between 1936 and 1939, while the "nationalists"—under a military junta led by General Franco—and the legal Government of the Republic entered a civil war that some qualified as a massive and tragic prelude to the Second World War, the government left Madrid and settled in Valencia and Barcelona. The Bank of Spain followed the government, and Bernácer moved his family to Alicante. The economist travelled there every week from Valencia, where he held office, to be with his family. In 1938, the central bank moved to Barcelona. A few months before the end of the war, the troops of the nationalist movement blocked communications between Valencia and Barcelona. Then, Bernácer was then stuck at home in Alicante, and his work was temporarily interrupted.

The end of the war in Spain almost ended Bernácer's career at the Central Bank. Indeed, the victory of General Franco's "movement" was followed by a washout period that impacted—to varying degrees—leaders at all levels who had not spontaneously joined the "movement". Bernácer was not free from investigation, but the intervention of well-placed colleagues eliminated his republican inclinations. After some time in "purgatory", the intervention of the statistician Olegario Fernández Baños and Ramón Artigas, deputy governor of the Bank of Spain, Bernácer managed to restart his work in Madrid.

Nevertheless, his discreet opposition to the regime, which occurred due to the incompatibility of his liberal ideas with the country's political, social, and economic structures, condemned him. The reform of the Bank of Spain in 1947, when the politically oriented Sebastián Mariano Herrador was appointed as the director of the Studies Department—produced an opportunity to limit Bernácer's influence. He stepped between the administration board and Bernácer, who was appointed deputy director. However, Bernácer's full influence within the organs of the Central Bank vanished with the Spanish Republic: he basically served as a civil servant on probation since 1940. The 1947 reform was only one episode in his declining influence. The government of General Franco left Bernácer to pursue his studies but, in fact, dismissed him from his role as senior officer and limited his functions.

During the 1940s, the BA in economics in Spain was created and the faculty of economics in Madrid was opened, but Bernácer was not among the founders, who included, among others, Emilio Figueroa, Sebastián Mariano Herrador, and Olegario Fernández Baños.

Bernácer and Economics Research

Nevertheless, Bernácer's discretion, shyness, and lack of social ambition suited his situation because what mattered to him was not only staying in touch—thanks to his position—with publications and men who wrote or visited him from abroad but also having the infrastructure and environment for research (library, translation services, competent staff, etc.). Bernácer spent a third of his life at the Central Bank; he left in 1955 at the age of 72.

Several important moments punctuated the last part of his life.

During World War II, he met Dr. Schacht, Minister of Finance of the Third Reich, when he visited Madrid to preach the virtues of the gold standard during a memorable conference. Although Bernácer was not invited to participate in the conference, Schacht knew Bernácer by reputation and summoned him there. The exchanges between the two men during a heated debate persisted in the memory of those present.

Several years later, Bernácer met Jacques Rueff and, the Swede, Johan Ackermann several times in Madrid.

Bernácer spoke at a conference at the ISEA in Paris on April 1, 1952, at the invitation of François Perroux. The conference was covered in the journal *Applied Economics* in the same year. Many French economists attended his speech.

Two years later, in 1954, Bernácer finally met Robertson on the outskirts of an international bank conference in Granada. The two men decided to meet there, isolated themselves in the surrounding countryside, and their long walks offered opportunities for scholarly conversations. Finally, we found a 1959 letter from the faculty of economic sciences of Buenos Aires that documented him an offer to become chair of political economy, despite his age—he was 76 years old at the time.

Bernácer and Mathematics

Although he often denied it, Bernácer gradually integrated the mathematical method into his economics research. His young friend, José Antonio Fuentes, a professor of analysis at the faculty of sciences of Madrid, offered him valuable resources in this regard.

Furthermore, Bernácer had two prestigious mathematicians as longtime friends: Julio Rey Pastor, who lectured in Madrid and at Harvard before dying in exile in 1962, and José Gallego Díaz, who taught at the Graduate Engineering Agronomists School of Madrid and the University of Stanford before dying in exile in Caracas in 1965.

With these mathematicians and his colleague from the Graduate Business School, Antonio Estrugo, an actuary mathematician, Bernácer founded the "Sociedad Española de matematicas aplicadas" in 1954, which published studies of mathematical economics and econometrics in the Arquímedes review and sat on the Consejo Superior Calculation Institute of Investigaciones Cientificas, the Spanish national centre of scientific research.

His Ending

After retiring from the Graduate Business School in 1953 and from the Bank of Spain in 1955 and publishing his last book in 1961 and his last article in 1962, Bernácer retired permanently to his house on the hill on the beach of San Juan in Alicante. He rediscovered the pines close to his house, under which he read books that formed his background as a self-taught economist and constituted sketches of his future works.

He died on May 22, 1965, surrounded by his family and old friends, such as the musician Oscar Esplá.

His family received sympathy from all major surviving foreign economists and his Spanish friends. It seemed for a time that the steps made at the suggestion of his popular colleagues in Madrid and the glowing stories on Bernácer in the local press, such as the newspaper Información of Alicante on June 4 and 5, 1965, and the Verdad de Murcia, June 16, 1965, and June 1966, would result in him receiving a tribute in the form of a bust in his hometown. In the article on June 4, 1965, Óscar Esplá cites the opinion of the philosopher Ortega y Gasset on Bernácer as "one of the first thinkers of Spain".

Bernácer Prize

The Prize was created in 2001 by the European Central Bank Observatory (ECBO) and is financed by Bank of Spain. ECBO is a non-profit association focusing on watching the European Central Bank and promoting the public debate on issues related to the Eurozone economy and with the aim of improving the quality of economic policy.

The Bernácer Prize is awarded annually to European economists under the age of 40, who have made outstanding contributions in the fields of macroeconomics and finance.

The 2012 Bernácer Prize was awarded to the British economist Nicholas Bloom (currently professor at Stanford University, California) for his influential research contributions on "the sources, dynamics and effects of good management practices". The award ceremony took place in Madrid on September 24, 2013 (Wikipedia, Bernacerprize.com). The 2016 Bernácer Prize has been awarded to Prof. Ricardo Reis (LSE) "for his influential research on the transmission of shocks in the presence of sticky information and the analysis of automatic stabilizers during the business cycle".

2.2 Testimonies

An Important Story Background: Robertson

Robertson published an article in February 1940 in the journal *Economica* under the title "*A Spanish Contribution to the Theory of Fluctuations*", pages 50–65:

> "Sixteen years ago, I received from Germán Bernácer, then professor at the Business School of Alicante, a Spanish article entitled 'The theory of disposable funds as an interpretation of economic crisis and social problems". (Barcelona 1923)

"I read the French summary accompanying the brochure without much attention. But I must have given it more subconscious attention than I thought because there is obviously a close resemblance between the successive periods analysis method used by Bernácer (see II, 3, infra) and the method I used some time later in my work, *Banking policy and price level.*

Later, in successive archiving, these documents resurfaced. When rereading the summary in French, it seemed to me, in light of recent controversies, to be of greater interest than I had initially assessed.

My attempts in recent months to personally connect with Bernácer were unsuccessful. I therefore propose a summary of his article with extensive excerpts of passages that seem the most interesting to me and make several comments. If, as I hope, he is still alive and this review reaches him, I hope he will give me permission to do this review retrospectively and claim the modest reward *Economica* can offer its colleagues!

I used a translation conducted by Joshua Saens. Nonetheless, two expressions raise some difficulties: the word *disponibilidades*, which I have translated as *disposable funds* and the expression *valores de renta*, which I have translated as *unearned income-yielding assets*. However, the latter term does not include the 'a functional' pattern that I believe emerges from the original expression…".

The second part of Robertson's article consists of large excerpts of the Bernácer article, translated into English. We found our comprehensive French translation of Bernácer's original article in the report on the works of Bernácer (A-222) from our thesis entitled *Germán Bernácer, a Spanish Economist (1883–1965). A General Theory of Employment, Unearned Income and Hoarding*, University Paris II, 1973, 602 pages, offset; and in the introduction to this new edition, in 2012, which was re-inserted into the entire Bernácer article (1922) we translated…

"I propose to briefly comment on only two aspects of the work of Mr. Bernácer: his theory of interest rates (II, 2 and 5) and his experience with successive period analysis (II, 3).

1. There is an obvious resemblance, in some respects, between Bernácer's theory of interest and that of Keynes. The interest rate is considered to be determined primarily outside the production circuit as the result of

a game between a mass of cash and a mass of *unearned income-yielding assets*. The interest rate is therefore a barrier to the use of disposable funds in an industry. If money is subtracted from speculative use, the interest rate will fall, and the industrial system will tend towards full employment.

Until then, the two authors seem to be in the same direction, but their paths diverge as soon as they more precisely formulate the foremost origin of interest.

Both, I think, make the same mistake, namely, refusing to recognize the productivity of funds that could be invested, the direct determinant of interest on the demand side. Nevertheless, their errors differ. By his own admission, Keynes stuck to a purely monetary theory with shortcomings I attempted to denounce. Bernácer recognized that physical productivity is the real source of interest, but by refusing to recognize productivity of capital or funds likely to be borrowed ('loans are not in themselves the cause of interest'), he was forced to seek refuge in the productivity of nature. In this piece of neo-physiocracy, I'm afraid he was late for our time, although he was a few centuries ahead of Keynes and his neo-medievalism!

2. I have already paid my tribute of respect and even gratitude to Bernácer's attempt to dynamically reason in terms of periods. Even so, in my opinion, we cannot say he reached perfect clarity with his simplistic equations. Subsection (b) gives an additional explanation of paragraph (a). In reality, it is a different question. In paragraph (a), we presume a source of confusion in the inequality of two successive intervals: one between the time work is completed and monetary income is perceived and another between the time work is completed and the product obtained through this work is sold.

We may simplify by assuming that the first interval is virtually zero. In this case, it seems to me that Bernácer tries to demonstrate that an imbalance can arise if the rate of input (related to the monetary income circulation velocity) increases or decreases in relation to the output rhythm. A more developed analysis in this direction would have led him to a pattern similar to Hawtrey's, in which an excess of expenditure over income leads to lower stocks, while an expenditure shortfall leads to higher stocks. Nonetheless, I do not think he did this because, in paragraph (b), we proceed to a third interval that had not been demonstrated before, between the perception of income and income expenditure.

In the following passages, it is clear that Bernácer offers generally positive and concrete results on the hoarding and dishoarding process, but his algebra is incomplete, as he does not really explain how, for the whole community, the income received (I) may not vary along with total demand (D), that is, how can a discrepancy appear between these two quantities? I believe it does not seem that Bernácer considers, like Hawtrey, a disparity between expenditure and income associated with a variation in stocks levels. He also does not explicitly adopt, as Keynes did in his *Treatise on money*, a definition of income including only 'normal' profits. He no longer strives, as I did, to make a distinction between 'perceived income' and 'disposable income' in the same period, although he seems to have touched all these concepts.

I feel I must apologize to English-speaking economists for not having shared Bernácer's essay with them earlier. Given the language difficulties and the many monetary literature manuscripts sent to us, it was difficult to distinguish the good papers from the bad, so I may have an excuse.

Without diminishing the merits of Bernácer's works, we can say that this essay may not ultimately be as interesting as it first seems. According to legend, before 1930, almost all orthodox economists thought and wrote exclusively in terms of overall equilibrium, leaving it to a few inspired amateurs to scribble in their ivory tower on issues dealing with idle money and unused resources. This legend does not reflect reality. If Bernácer's essay were better known by his fellow economists in 1923, I think the ideas in it would be newer to them than modern students believe. Even so, I believe that it is well worth reprinting, and I sincerely hope that this author is still alive."

This article was included in the appendix of the Spanish edition of *Essays on monetary Theory* published by Aguilar in 1961. In the preface to this book, Robertson cites Bernácer among the economists who directly inspired his works, such as Keynes, Hicks, and Hawtrey.

Following the publication of this article in 1940, Robertson had an extensive exchange of correspondence with Bernácer. These epistolary relations culminated in Granada in 1954, when the two men met on the outskirts of an international conference. Robertson's letters to Bernácer dated from the Treasury in London on June 14, 1944 (shortly before his departure to the Bretton Woods conference), and Trinity College, Cambridge (December 20, 1945, and May 16, 1947). Robertson also refers (his letter to Bernácer dated February 26, 1946) to contacts he had with Hayek. He met Bernácer on several occasions in Madrid, especially towards the end of World War II and was responsible for Bernácer's article submission to Robertson. In another letter (see Bibliography), Robertson alluded to a correspondence between Bernácer and Domar about Bernácer's book *Functional Theory of Money*. The book certainly strongly interested Robertson, as this letter was accompanied by a long summary and comments in English by the English economist.

Nevertheless, Bernácer never had any correspondence with Keynes, but he met him once before 1936. "Keynes visited Spain in 1930, invited by the Spanish English Committee to host a Master Conference in the Students Residence (*La Residencia de Estudiantes*). On Tuesday, 10th June, at 7 pm, the British economist dictated the conference 'The possible economic situation of our grandchildren'". In the "Residencia de Estudiantes", J.M. Keynes was received with great expectation by Spanish economists, among whom Germán Bernácer was present… Keynes, hearing the name of Germán Bernácer, who remained discreetly apart, reacted effusively embracing him and calling him "Master" at the same time he commented aloud to those present that the work of the Spanish economist "had illuminated and opened new paths to his thought" (Sánchez Monllor 2014: 74).

In his article "The Spanish and the Economic Science" (El Español y la Ciencia Económica)—Boletín Económico de ICE 2746 editado por el Ministerio de Economía y Competitividad—Arturo Pina González related a brief encounter between Keynes and Bernácer, mentioning the story the eyewitness gave him, José Antonio Piera Labra (Professor of Economics at the Faculty of Political Science and Economics of the University of Madrid, Flores de Lemus's disciple and early member of the Economics Section of the Institute of Political Studies), who in 1950 published, at the same time as Bernácer, a work on the studies on the economic unit of Europe. "Don Mariano Alonso-Burón has confirmed to me not only the fact that Keynes

> and Bernácer greeted each other in the Residence but also the compliments terms used by Keynes, which passed on to the oral memory of the people of the Free Educational Institution (Intitución Libre de Enseñanza) who transmitted it to him". (Pina 2002: 14)

We conclude that Robertson did not understand the theory of unearned income that underlies Bernácer's theory of interest, as illustrated in his article in which Robertson (1940) presented *unearned* income-yielding assets as "income-yielding assets". This confusion is allowed given the vagueness of the Spanish word *renta*, which is taken to mean *unearned income*. Furthermore, Bernácer replied to Robertson's various objections in his 1941 article, "The monetary theory and market equation".

It appears that Robertson has not truly entered the crux of Bernácer's temporal analysis. As for the theory of interest, both authors' positions are too entrenched to really understand each other.

Testimonies from Other Contemporary Economists

Bernácer maintained extensive correspondence with contemporary economists from different countries, especially after 1945. We examined his correspondence with Howard Ellis from the Federal Reserve Board, Washington; Arthur W. Marget from the University of Minnesota, Minneapolis; Per Jacobson, from the International Monetary Fund; James W. Angell, from Columbia University, New York; F. Machlup from Washington; Montgomery D. Anderson from the University of Florida; Gottfried Haberler from Harvard University; Virgil Salera from the University of Miami; Henry C. Wallich from the Federal Reserve Bank of New York and Yale University; and Jorge Freyre. The four authors in this group quoted Bernácer's works. Haberler did so in the preface to the Spanish edition of his book *Prosperity and Depression* (1942) published in Mexico. He recommended Bernácer to François Perroux. A few years later, Salera reported on Bernácer's book, Functional Theory of Money, in the *American Economic Review*, 1947. Wallich wrote a report of the same book for the Review of Economic Statistics in 1947. Finally, Freyre (1957) wrote a report on Bernácer's *Free Economy Without Crises and Without*

Unemployment in the American Economic Review, 1956. Bernácer was also in contact with Italian scholars. Camilo Supino (1923), from the University of Milan, wrote a glowing review of the article "*The theory of disposable funds as interpretation of economic crisis and social problem*". This is the only response that we recorded following Bernácer's 1922 article sent to the 150 best-known economists in the world, with the exception of Robertson's 1920 article and a glowing, but laconic and anonymous, commentary from the International Labour Organization in 1924.

Particularly after 1940, Bernácer had to maintain epistolary relations with several famous economists, including the Italians Marco Fanno from the University of Padua; Giovanni Demaria and Aldo Scotto from the University of Genoa; Francesco Vito from the University of Milan; and Ferdinando di Fenizio, who cited Bernácer in his Manual of Political Economy. Bernácer also corresponded with the Germans Predohl and Walter Hoffmann from the Institute of World Economy at Kiel; the Swede Johan Ackermann, who met Bernácer several times in Madrid; the Dane Erich Schneider from the University of Aarhus; the Swiss Emile Kung from the University of Zurich; the Argentinians Rafael Olarra Giménez from the University of Buenos Aires, who summarized Bernácer's main ideas in his book on money and monetary structures; as well as Oreste Popescu (1961), who quoted Bernácer several times in his book *Introducción a la ciencia economica contemporánea*.

In France, Bernácer met Louis Baudin from the Institut de France; Henri Guitton from the University of Paris and the Institut de France; François Perroux from the Collège de France; André Piatier from the École Pratique des Hautes Études; and Jacques Rueff, Chancellor of the Institut de France. Louis Baudin (1964) had Bernácer's article translated into Italian and published in the Milanese magazine Rivista Bancaria under the title, "*Stabilità monetaria contro pieno impiego*". The translation was completed under the leadership of Jean-Claude Dischamps and published in France (Figueroa 1965). Henri Guitton paid tribute to Bernácer's works in his book *Les fluctuations économiques* (Economic fluctuations), Sirey Éditions, Paris, 1951, page 390; and André Piatier quoted Bernácer's works in his book *Statistics and Economic Observation*, PUF, Themis, Paris, 1961, Volume I, page 34. François Perroux invited Bernácer to Paris to give a lecture at the ISEA in 1952. He published two articles in the journal Economie appliquée (Applied Economics) and recommended in 1954 that Bernácer become a foreign corresponding member in the Institut de Science Économique Appliquée (Applied Economic Science Institute).

Shortly after Bernácer died in 1965, the Revue d'économie politique (Journal of Political Economy), Paris, published a tribute from Bernácer's compatriot José Pozuelo, who superficially summarized outlines of Bernácer's works without demonstrating that he understood them well. In his own country, Bernácer was little known or even despised by academic economists (Pozuelo and Barnuevo 1965).

Nevertheless, Emilio Figueroa, professor at the University of Madrid and Deputy Director of the Department of Studies of the Bank of Spain, celebrated Bernácer. He wrote that the publication of Robertson's article in the journal *Economica* on February 1940, which caused leading economists around the world to rave about Bernácer, aroused among "academic" economists in Spain no positive criticism but rather absolute disdain. On one hand, he celebrated the intellectual and scientific qualities of the author, quoting J. Rueff's private opinion on Bernácer and, on the other hand, he noted his moral qualities, which formed his thought to include not only cold analysis of economic realities but also a regular humanistic orientation that inspired all of his works.

Quoting Bernácer, Emilio Figueroa categorized the "pillars" of Germán Bernácer's socio-economic thought as freedom, efficiency, justice, and peace. Figueroa discusses Bernácer from a place of authority: he was his student at the Graduate Business School of Madrid and then his colleague at the Bank of Spain before being entrusted with the Chair of Economic Policy at the Faculty of Economic Science of Madrid, and succeeding, in 1955, to recommend Bernácer in the Department of Studies at the Bank of Spain. Nevertheless, strictly speaking, he has never been Bernácer's disciple, even though he liked to claim he was; we believe he was his disciple through sympathy and respect rather than through scientific conviction.

Fabian Estapé, professor at the Faculty of Economics of Barcelona, quotes Bernácer at length in his translation of Ferdinando di Fenizio's *Manual of Political Economy*, published in Bosch Editions (Barcelona,

2nd ed. 1958), pages 184, 526, 527. Indeed, referencing Robertson's 1940 article, Professor Estapé evokes the work of his compatriot: nobody is a prophet in Spain, let alone elsewhere.

The Wall of Silence in Spanish Academia

In our interviews, those close to Bernácer all discussed a conspiracy of silence, referring to how Bernácer was neglected by academic economists in his own country. Political and ethical reasons are certainly behind this wall of silence around Bernácer's work in Spain. We cite only two examples: the economist Flores de Lemus was the ignored originator of the input-output table; and the mathematician Rey Pastor, who died in 1962, taught at Harvard University in the United States. However, Bernácer maintained personal relationships with a few Spanish economists, such as his colleague from the Academy of Economic and Financial Sciences, Professor Ramón Perpiñá, Fuentes Quintana, professors José Larraz (former Minister of Finance), Luis Olariaga, Olegario Fernández Baños, Sebastián Mariano Herrador (former Secretary general of the Bank of Spain), Higinio París Eguilaz (former secretary of the National Council of the Economy), Ildefonso Cuesta Garrigos, and Wenceslao Millán. However, these colleagues' political orientation and/or commitment to and speciality in theoretical economics made these private relations professional, given that they did not favour true scientific dialogue. Marcial López Moreno, former Dean of the Faculty of Madrid, was his pupil.

Nevertheless, in the Spanish economic literature published to date, we did not find comments, debate, or even a single reference to Bernácer's work, with the exception of the Emilio Figueroa tribute and a citation by Fabián Estapé. There are also illustrations of such injustice against other Spanish scholars who benefited abroad from the merited prestige that Spain did not offer them. We will not speak here of the many scholars, academics, great artists, and literary giants who, for political reasons, were forced to settle abroad.

Finally, in 1973, the prestigious Spanish press twice echoed favourable testimonies of Bernácer's work. The great Spanish newspaper ABC of Madrid, in its March 2, 1973, issue, devoted a whole page to Bernácer's ideas, entitled "A free economy without crises and without unemployment". This newspaper took advantage of the international speculation outbreak in February 1973, which offered a true sounding board for Bernácer's ideas.

We found a sentence that illustrates the audacity—as perceived by a layman—of erasing the *financial market*: "Had some bold and humanitarian Greek ever advocated the abolition of slavery during Antiquity, the economic foundation of the society at that time, they would have been considered crazy". On January 30, 1973, the inauguration of the Faculty of Economic Sciences, the ABC of Seville devoted a series of articles to studies of economics in Spain. The paper interviewed Professor Manuel Berlanga from the University of Madrid, who stated: "Nevertheless, the figure in Spanish Economics was a teacher of Graduate Business School, who also passed away, Germán Bernácer Tormo, who combined all the qualities of a scientist: humility, simplicity, serenity and tireless taste for study and for the spirit of observation… Spain has to do a national tribute to Bernácer".

The tribute took place in November 1983 in Madrid, under the patronage of the Ministry of Economy and the Bank of Spain, as well as in Alicante, with the support of the University and the Caja de Ahorros. A street in Alicante now bears Bernácer's name. Salvador Almenar Palau, Marcial Jesús López Moreno, Alicia Martínez Sánchez, Gumersindo Ruiz, Henri Savall, Velarde Fuertes, and José Villacís González presented the main papers (see references). In the 2000s, many articles and some books were published about Bernácer, Boianovsky, John Presley, H. Dar, Brañas Garza, Cid, Jorge Hurtado Jordá, Martín-Aceña, Enrique Martínez García, Pina, Manuel Sánchez Monllor, Martín Sevilla, Teresa Torregrosa, Bernard Yvars, and Zeghni.

2.3 Bernácer as a Visionary Forerunner

We will attempt to clarify two points in history: was Bernácer's thought influenced by Swedish thought, recognized as an antecedent of Keynes, and could Bernácer have influenced Keynes's thought?

Bernácer and Swedish Thought

Knut Wicksell published his first books in German between 1893 and 1906. It was not until 1934 that the first English edition of his works appeared under the title *Lectures on Political Economy*, and *Interest and Prices* was published in 1936. Meanwhile, in 1907, Wicksell published in the Economic Journal an unnoticed article at that time: "*The influence of the rate of interest on prices*". James (1963) wrote that Wicksell was "unknown until 1930", including in his country, where "the dominant influence around 1920 was that of Professor Cassel". As for the other economists from the school of Stockholm, including Davidson, Lindahl, Myrdal, and Ohlin, their first Swedish publications date from 1927 (Myrdal) and 1929 (Lindahl), with English editions appearing in 1932 and in 1939, respectively.

Recall that in 1916, Bernácer published *Society and Happiness;* in 1922, his seminal article on the theory of disposable funds; and in 1925, *Interest of Capital*. His later works particularly intended to refine his thought and to put it into debate with that of his contemporaries or predecessors. Therefore, only Wicksell's works published in German preceded those of Bernácer, and if there was Swedish influence on Bernácer's thought, it was due to Wicksell.

Even so, we know that Wicksell was unknown in his own country—and a fortiori abroad—until about the 1930s, and his works in German did not have an audience until the followers of his thought cited them. Moreover, according to Émile James, Bernácer extensively quotes Böhm-Bawerk, the Viennese teacher of Wicksell, and Cassel, the most prominent Swedish economist at the time, in his 1925 book, but he did not refer to Wicksell. Bernácer's first contact with the Wicksellian thought was through Hayek, who Bernácer knew in Madrid. It is therefore unlikely that Bernácer knew Wicksell's theory before publishing his seminal works on interest, money, and fluctuations.

Moreover, at the beginning of the twentieth century, the media were even more limited on the Iberian Peninsula than on the mainland; therefore, if Bernácer only quotes Cassel, and knowing that Wicksell became known in Europe only around 1930, we can presume that Bernácer ignored Swedish authors' publications, especially when working on his writings published in 1916, 1922, and 1925.

Bernácer and Keynes

Keynes's first publication appeared in 1919. Nevertheless, except for an article published in 1923, most of his thought can be found in his two books published in 1930 and in 1936, respectively. There is no doubt that Bernácer published before Keynes, but the question of whether Keynes came into contact with Bernácer's thought remains. In this regard, we will first report some interesting facts.

A Precedent Story: Keynes and Wicksell

It seems that Keynes contradicts himself regarding Wicksell; sometimes he affirmed "only knowing Wicksell's works very late, after his own thought had already taken its final form", while other times, he explicitly recognized knowing them, as Marchal and Lecaillon (1966) quoted Keynes, writing on page 196 of his *Treatise on Money*, Volume I, published in 1930—before the English translation of Wicksell's works—"According to Wicksell, we should call the rate of interest… the natural rate of interest and the current rate: the market rate of interest". The authors of *Cash Flows* commented, "As noted, the author (Keynes) expressly refers to Wicksell's works, which contradicts a commonly held view according to which he would ignore Swedish works".

We may conclude that Keynes was not truly concerned with recognizing his precursors and that he could have also known of Bernácer's thought directly without admitting it.

Keynes and Robertson's Article About Bernácer's Influence on Both Authors

It is curious that Keynes, as directly implicated by Robertson—his colleague from Cambridge—in an article published in the journal

Economica in February 1940, did not try to study or to contact Bernácer. Given that Keynes acknowledged Robertson's influence on his own thought, shared with him public responsibilities for the British Government during the World War, and worked with him at Bretton Woods, it is inconceivable that Keynes did not have conversations with Robertson about Bernácer.

Although world events caused economists from all countries to write about their friendly admiration of Bernácer, we are struck by the silence of Keynes and Hawtrey after the publication of that article. Keynes nevertheless played an important role during the 40 years until his death; the fact remains that this silence was undoubtedly to avoid admission, especially since Bernácer's article "*Theory of Disposable Funds*", written in Spanish and accompanied by a summary in French, was sent in a brochure to 150 of the most prominent economists of the time (1923) from all countries—particularly Keynes, Robertson, Hawtrey in the United Kingdom, Gide in France, Supino in Italy, Seligman in United States, and all economists of the School of Vienna. We know that Robertson received it, as did some other economists.

Therefore, our reasoning is simple. Robertson was struck by the similarity between the method used by Bernácer in his 1922 article and the method in his own book published in 1926, *Banking Policy and the Price Level.* He admits to likely having been influenced by Bernácer "subconsciously", as he says. Should we assume that Keynes also read this article—since he likely received it by the same messenger—and that his subconscious worked similarly to Robertson's? Would this process prove the direct influence of Bernácer's thought on Keynes?

We can also accept that Bernácer had an influence on Keynes through intermediaries since Keynes wrote, "As for me—and I think it is the same for the other Anglo-Saxon economists—I owe the good guidance of my thoughts to Robertson's works, *Banking policy and the price level,* published in 1926". Keynes had previously announced, "Robertson led a powerful light on some basic matters, and this book would not have covered its present form without the help of his ideas".

Still, with or without influencing Keynes's works, Bernácer emerged as a precursor of Keynes's thought, or rather as a founder of modern economic thought. Indeed, we believe that Bernácer would not have found it valuable to compare his thought with Keynes's, which was very ambiguous and linked to the circumstances of the Great Depression Theory.

2.4 Bernácer's Contribution to the Foundation of Modern Economics

Rejection of Economic Dogmatism

Bernácer considerably advanced analysis with his negative attitude towards the dogmas he inherited from classical economists, like his contemporaries, and the new dogma of the political economy of the mid-twentieth century: "the" Keynesian theory. He refuted the first set of dogmas because they were unable to satisfactorily account for the economic reality of his time. He rejected the second for its shortcomings and serious gaps.

Repudiation of Conventional Dogmas

Facilitated by the self-taught nature of his economic training, Bernácer's rejection of conventional dogmas consists of accepting no ideas from classical and neoclassical conceptual inventory except those that corroborated social and economic facts with positive and timely analysis. He therefore a priori, rejects the individual approach, the static approach, interest, value-utility, economic equilibrium, and absence of unemployment in classical economic panorama, the "evil" institutions of the world—the so-called "liberal" institutions, including the "financial market", monopoly, and capitalism, dissociating both active and complementary factors of production: labour and capital. He retains, under certain conditions, elements of economic policy that he considers to ensure social well-being through economic efficiency: profit, money, and the market.

His analysis, free from conventional ideas, is all the more scientific.

Refusal of a New Dogma: Keynesianism

Bernácer sought to highlight the shortcomings of Keynesian analysis. He was among the first to do so, and his criticism is important not because of its earliness in the great debate between Keynesian and anti-Keynesian thought but because of its immanence. Bernácer saw the shortcomings and especially the inconsistencies within the Keynesian analytical framework. His criticism, despite the firmness of its form, does not have the same characteristics as that of Rueff, for example. Bernácer's criticism of *General Theory* is more thoughtful and, therefore, has a broader scope. One of the many elements of Keynes's theory that Bernácer often criticized is the multiplier mechanism. In one of his later articles, Bernácer demonstrated in 1956 that, in fact, it is not the propensity to save that limits the multiplier effect from initial investment but rather the propensity to hoard, unlike what Machlup (1944) affirms when lamenting that many criticisms of the multiplier cannot interpret filtrations other than hoarding. This argument seems to confirm our interpretation of Bernácer's criticism of Keynes when he reproaches Keynes for his excessively brief distinction between demand for consumption and savings. From Keynes's point of view, the latter has a decidedly fruitless or even pernicious role in the multiplier mechanism. Bernácer proposes differentiating aggregate demand (consumption + investment) on one hand and double hoarding on the other. We are ready to accept this point of view.

This is just one example of Bernácer's basic criticisms of Keynes; we consider it important, given the place of the multiplier in the "pure" theory of Keynes as it applies to his policy proposals for public expenditure.

Economic Fact Approach

Among the characteristic elements of Bernàcer's contribution that we identify in our analysis, we highlight three: dynamics, macroeconomics, and synthetic conception.

Bernàcer's analysis has double spatial and temporal content. We particularly highlight the temporal component of the analysis because the author specifically assigns an important role to the time factor in all his theoretical writings. Nevertheless, the spatial aspect is inseparable from time, and we can summarize his conception in the following way. The dynamic explanation of economic activity is based on the following observation. The production and distribution process that is the core economic activity implies a sequence and a circuit in which agents produce goods and receive incomes and then spend their incomes and acquire assets. Bernácer not only reproaches Keynes's static analysis; he also shows that the introduction of time would distort Keynes's theory. Later—and in the same spirit—Denizet (1958) shows, for example, that the expansionary effects that Keynes expects from initial investment can be achieved only at the cost of renewed investment in successive periods.

Bernácer (1945), we believe, attaches more importance to time than any other economist: "How do we cross this mysterious river that separates Statics from Dynamics? That's an open question for research and criticism. Nevertheless, unless we are crossing the Rubicon, whether we like it or not, we will remain in Static and we must admit in all logic and against all evidence that the price level is unchangeable". By evoking the absurdities to which static analysis can lead, he concludes with the urgent need for a dynamic analysis, which is the only possible method to analyse social facts.

He suggests reviewing successive static states to ensure a correct analysis and then transposing discrete analysis and on-going analysis to be more similar to reality. Future methodological research should strive to perfect this approximation; he does not claim to have discovered everything but rather only guiding the way. Thus, statistics, which are so essential to economic analysis, are only to reality what the images of a film are to reality; the trouble is that we have no projector for statistics that gives the illusion of movement to the "photographed" facts!

Bernácer studies the economic circuit through an analogy with hydraulic analysis. Again, his conceptual contribution is innovative, and once again, he precedes Keynes, who was praised Ullmo (1967) as follows: "the concept (of the economic system), however, should come back to it to emphasize its innovativeness over conventional conceptions. It is in fact the main instrument of thought and action that left us with what may be called Keynes's heritage… To grasp the singular characteristic of this notion of the economic circuit, it is necessary to contrast it with the traditional market concept".

Bernácer would not agree with the end of this postulation, as the market is a fixed point in space, while a circuit consists of all inter-structural and inter-agent relations that evolve in space and in time. Why should we exclude markets from the circuit? Such exclusions sterilize the analysis and lead to monistic conceptions that are not to Bernácer's taste. It seems that Keynes did not place as much importance on the dynamic circuit as Bernácer did.

Quesnay, his board, and other physiocrats created the first macroeconomic approach. Classicals did not ignore it, especially in the quantity theory of money. Nevertheless, their analysis is based primarily on individual behaviours. For this reason, historians of economic thought generally trace the birth of macroeconomics back to Wicksell and then to Keynes. We would agree with Bernácer, who, inspired by physiocrats and as an admirer of Turgot (1914), defined overall variables and the perceived economy as a whole.

Nevertheless, Bernácer assigns more importance than Keynes to the differentiated behaviours of agents. However, he clearly observes the heterogeneous nature of these overall quantities. Therefore, he often breaks them down into relatively homogeneous subsets. For example, he does not grasp the money supply as a whole; rather, he distinguishes the kinds of disposable funds within it. Likewise, he seeks to differentiate fixed incomes from random incomes. Finally, he is very attentive to tensions and not just to equality relations. Keynes made the mistake of handling quantities he assumed to be homogeneous. For example, he assumes a fluidity of labour that does not exist in reality.

Given his macroeconomic approach that dates to his first book, Bernácer naturally tends to extensively use the resources of the accounting method. It is striking to note the analysis at the social level in *Society and Happiness*, 1916; the neoclassical perspective is almost entirely absent from Bernácer's analysis beginning with his earliest writings. The author, therefore, argues for aggregates that have accounting relations. He establishes a close link between dynamic analysis, accounting analysis, and the positive method. Thus, regarding the accounting of revenues in a short time period—conducive to the cycle analysis—Bernácer opts to account for actual payments through successive balance sheets using the real money supply method, that is, the sum of agents' balance sheets, with disposable funds counted as positive terms and debts as negative terms. Then, he studies the changes in aggregates over successive periods. Similarly, in the normative order of the reform he advocates, he assigns great importance to national accounting, especially in the statistic seizure of cash and money movements.

Bernácer's concepts are rich because they are *synthetic*, and he integrates multiple elements in his theories. His theory of value incorporates both labour as a privileged factor of production and the market to give a similar theory of both labour value and exchange value. His conception of money is dynamic, both functional and integrationist. In contrast to the quantity theory of money, which is based on two identical expressions of demand, Bernácer's functional theory strives to integrate supply. His theory of interest is highly synthetic and includes many components.

Therefore, in the history of economic thought, Bernácer is far ahead of his contemporaries, even most pioneers. Indeed, we can conclude that Bernácer's theoretical thought reached its fullness—but not its completion—in 1945 with the publication of his *Functional Theory of Money*.

Nonetheless, Bernácer's theory sometimes presents insufficiently synthetic aspects, and we could accuse him of a certain monism in explaining disequilibria based primarily—though not exclusively—on the "financial market", unearned income, and double hoarding. He might also attach importance to money to an extent that we would currently consider excessive. Nevertheless, does not he belong within a school of thought that judged precisely that it was necessary to deepen monetary theory in order to advance economic science?

Bernácer's Thought Normative Aspect

Bernácer's thought is going beyond a lucid descriptive analysis. Several authors criticize classicals for wanting to change the course of economic history through their theories; they consider neoclassicals to somehow be scientifically superior, renouncing the need to inspire action and merely explaining observable reality. Nonetheless, we might wonder the extent to which this reality was correctly observed by these critics and how Walras and Pareto, who are symbolic in this regard, gave up on what we call economic action. It seems that some historians of economic thought, minimizing the importance of policy propositions with Walras and of the sociological analysis with Pareto, have unfairly distorted the prevailing opinion on their works. Nevertheless, we may believe that the twentieth century is characterized by the advent of praxis as an instigator of the element of scientific research. Economics do not escape this trend, which was driven by authors such as Bernácer and Keynes and, in the previous century, precursors such as Marx and, to a lesser extent, Wicksell.

Bernácer brilliantly combines descriptive analysis and normative construction, creating a kind of *dialectic relation* between these two views such that each guides the other. Bernácer strives, of course, to remain lucid and "objective" when observing reality. Nevertheless, we must recognize that any theory is built on a choice of materials and tools and that this choice is *sui generis* the result of a more conscious or less conscious guidance from the author. From this point of view, is it not the case that authors who claim to reject the analysis of action choose to justify, in a way, a pre-established economic and social order?

The normative content of Bernácer's economic thought is not only social, aiming at improvement, but also has a technical system aspect. According to Bernácer, economic systems, once ethical dominants are defined, must follow certain rules, the convergence of which must ensure the good operation of the whole system.

The New Economic Regime he advocates is a vast cybernetic for which a *self-control* element is national accounting—especially money—and a *self-correction* element is the money issuance operation, given its various assignments in production units. Recognizing the importance of minimizing *correction delays*—for this, he condemns authoritarian government planning—he stresses the need to improve the statistical system and claims that, in this way, the theory of economic information is somehow essential for the cybernetic system to work well. He recommends, for instance, that statistics on money supply are centralized and published weekly in order to allow for corrective action on the controlled compensatory issue. In this area, he is inspired by his practical experience at the Bank of Spain. It is one of the few points in which the practitioner emerges from within the theorist he is and seeks to remain.

Bernácer's General Crisis Theory

We emphasize that Bernácer's analysis coherently synthesizes ideas on the basic problems of the universal economy. We claim that his theory is general, as the implications of his analysis are related to all areas of activity and economic analysis and the various issues studied: employment, money, interest, fluctuations, and growth. However, because of his extreme humility, Bernácer never uses the word "general" to describe his theory. We highlight the seraphic title in the first presentation of his theory—*Society and Happiness*; what a big agenda! His analysis of structures justifies our classification.

The first presentation of Bernácer's theory appears in his first book, written in 1905 and published in 1916.

His article published in 1922 marks a significant advance over his previous book: his monetary theory is refined, and it is much shorter. It constitutes an insightful presentation of the political economy.

His 1925 book, devoted to the theory of interest, is monolithic in the sense that the analysis is focused entirely on demonstrating that interest is pernicious, economically speaking, which is one of the major themes of Bernácer's general theory. After this book, a series of articles marked the author's progress, specifically in the monetary field. His 1945 book synthesizes these studies. Finally, in 1955, after about 50 years of research and after retiring from his life as a teacher and as Director of the Studies Department at the Bank of Spain, Bernácer synthesized all his investigations in his book, *Free Economy, Without Crisis and Without Unemployment*.

This last book is as comprehensive as the first, and it actually contains a general theory. From a certain point of view, it cleanly uncovers what we are tempted to call the extra-economic "gangue" that encumbers his first essay. In this book, the language is more current in the broad sense, and his ideas benefit from time and maturity, as well as Bernácer's communications with leading contemporary economists.

With some exceptions, we will highlight that his key ideas are the same. The theory he offered at the age of 73 is the same that had germinated in this physicist mind at the age of 33, at the dawn of his career as an economist. For various reasons, we chose to start with his 1955 book. First, the book makes some allusions to the Keynesian contribution, and the current reader inevitably addresses Bernácer's theory from a Keynesian and post-Keynesian knowledge base. Therefore, within this knowledge base, there is an antecedent of Keynes's thought that opposes the chronological anteriority of Bernácer's ideas (see Guitton 1969, questions on page 5: "*Are Not We All a Bit Keynesian*?" We might express grief about the sometimes-excessive impact of Keynesian thought on our generation, but it would be useless to study Bernácer as if Keynes's general theory had not yet been published (see Wallich's correspondence with Bernácer). In this regard, the 1955 presentation is more assertive in its expression than that of 1916. Therefore, the 1955 book is more developed than the first and shows the author's increased mastery of economics. It even contains a mathematical appendix that we will use for certain demonstrations. Therefore, it is necessary to reconcile the clarity of Bernácer's theory in its zenith—at the end of his career—and one of the themes of our thesis, namely, the precedence of some of Bernácer's ideas over those of Keynes.

For this reason, we chose to use the following method: built on the 1955 book—the synthesis—our presentation contains quotes and references to pre-Keynesian works (in a chronological sense) by Bernácer: *Society and Happiness*, 1916; *The Theory of Disposable Funds*, 1922; *The Interest of Capital*, 1925; and, in the post-Keynesian period, *The Functional Theory of Money*, 1945. These references may mark the evolution of Bernácer's ideas.

References

Ackermann, J. (1957). *Structures et cycles économiques* (Structures and economic cycles), t. 1 and 2. Paris: P.U.F.

Baudin, L. (1964). *Textes choisis: problèmes monétaires* (Selected writings: Monetary problems). Paris: Dalloz et Sirey.

Bernácer. Wikipedia.com

Bernácer, G. (1916). *Sociedad y felicidad—Ensayo de Mecánica Social* (Society and Happiness—Essay on social mechanics). Madrid: Ed. Beltrán.

Bernácer, G. (1922). La teoría de las disponibilidades como interpretación de las crisis y del problema social (The theory of disposable funds as interpretation of crisis and social issues). *Revistanacional de economía, 40*, 535–562.

Bernácer, G. (1945). *La teoría funcional del dinero* (The functional theory of money) (2nd ed. 1956). Madrid: Consejo Superior de Investigaciones Científicas.

Bernácer, G. (1955). *Una economía libre sin crisis y sin paro* (Free economy without crisis nor unemployment). Madrid: Aguilar.

Bernácer, G. (1961). Preface to the Spanish translation of Robertson D. H. *Essays in monetary theory: Ensayossobre la teoria monetaria*. Madrid: Aguilar.

Bernacerprize.com

Denizet, J. (1958). La part des phénomènes monétaires dans le modèle de Keynes etdans les modèles de comptabilité économique (The part of monetary phenomena in Keynes model and in economic accounting models). *Économie Appliquée, 3*, 112–133.

Estapé, F. (1958). Preface and translation in Spanish of Ferdinando Di Fenizio *Political Economy* (2nd ed.). Barcelona: Bosch.

Figueroa, E. (1965). Germán Bernácer in memoriam. *Moneda y crédito, 2*, 96–102.

Freyre, J. F. (1957). Review of Bernácer's book (1956) "*A free economy without crisis and unemployment*". *American Economic Review, 47*(3), 436–438.

Guitton, H. (1951). *Les fluctuations économiques* (Economic fluctuations). Paris: Sirey.

Guitton, H. (1969). *La monnaie* (Money). Paris: Dalloz.

James, E. (1963). *Problèmes monétaires d'aujour d'hui. Étude des fondements d'une théorie et d'une politique monétaire modernes* (Current monetary problems. Analysis of theory and modern monetary policy foundations). Paris: Sirey.

Keynes, J. M. (1919). *The economic consequences of the peace*. Cambridge: J. M. Keynes.

Machlup, F. (1944). Period analysis and multiplier theory. In G. Haberler (Ed.), *Readings in business cycle theory.* Philadelphia: The Blakiston Company.

Marchal, J., & Lecaillon, J. (1966). *Les flux monétaires* (Monetary flows). Paris: Cujas.

Piatier, A. (1961). *Statistiques et observation économiques* (Statistics and economic observations) (Vols. 1 & 2). Paris: PUF.

Popescu, O. (1961). *Introducción a la ciencia económica contemporánea.* Spain: Ariel, Esplugas de Llobregat.

Pozuelo, Y., & Barnuevo, J. (1965). Hommage à Bernácer (Tribute to Bernàcer). *Revue d'Économie Politique, 4,* 312–321.

Robertson, D. H. (1940, February). A Spanish contribution to the theory of fluctuations. *Economica, 16*(1), 50–65.

Salera, V. (1947). Review of La doctrina funcional del dinero (Review on Bernácer's book *The functional theory of money). The American Economic Review, 37*(1), 221–223.

Savall, H. (1973, September). *Germán Bernácer, économisteespagnol (1883–1965). Une théorie générale de l'emploi, de la renteet de la thésaurisation* (General theory of employment, unearned income and hoarding). PhD dissertation at the University of Paris II, 602p. Mimeographed.

Savall, H. (1975). *G. Bernácer: L'hétérodoxieen science économique* (G. Bernácer: The heterodoxy in Economics). Paris: Dalloz, Collection Les Grands Économistes.

Savall, H., Zardet, V., & Bonnet, M. (2000). Releasing the untapped potential of enterprises through socio-economic management (2nd ed. 2008). Genève: ILO-BIT.

Savall, H., Péron, M., Zardet, V., & Bonnet, M. (2017). *Socially responsible capitalism and management.* New York: Routledge.

Sánchez Monllor, M. (2014). Estampas con un ilustre alicantino. *CANELOBRE Review, 63*(Verano), 190–216.

Turgot. (1914). *Œuvres de Turgot* (Turgot's works). Paris: Alcan.

Ullmo, J. (1967). *Preface to L. STOLÉRU: L'équilibreet la croissance…* (Equilibrium and growth …). Paris: Dunod.

Ullmo, J. (1969). *Le profit* (Profit). Paris: Dunod.

Walras, L. (1877). *Éléments d'économie pure* (Elements of pure Economics). Paris: Guillaumin.

Walras, L. (1883). *Théorie de la monnaie* (Theory of money). Lausanne: Storck.

Walras, L. (1889). *Éléments d'économie politique pure* (Elements of pure political economics). Lausanne: Storck.

Walras, L. (1896). *Études d'économies ociale* (Studies on social economy). Lausanne: F. Rouge.
Wicksell, K. (1934). *Lectures on political Economy.* London: Routledge and Kegan (English translation of his book published in 1913).
Wicksell, K. (1936). *Interest and prices.* (English translation). London: Royal Economic Society.

Part II

Crisis and Unemployment Theory

3

Bernácer's Critical Analysis of Actual Capitalism: "A Free Economy Without Crisis and Without Unemployment"

This chapter focuses on Bernácer's work dealing with the interpretation of different economic crisis. In the first section, we introduce the theory of disposable funds proposed by Bernácer (1922) to analyse the economic crises and social issues. In the second section, key concepts are defined to clarify Bernácer's analysis (Savall, 1973, 1975, 2012).

3.1 Using the "Theory of Disposable Funds" to Interpret Crises and Social Issues (Bernácer 1922)

Although the expression "disposable funds" is familiar to finance experts and specialists, this concept must still be refined for the economics field. Those in business know well that it is sometimes easy to raise speculative funds and that the issuance of industrial or public securities is well received on the market, while it is sometimes much more difficult to borrow or obtain money for business needs. These phenomena are commonly expressed as "disposable funds are scarce or abundant on the market". What scientific concept reflects this intuitive notion by business

H. Savall, *Radical Origins to Economic Crises*,
https://doi.org/10.1007/978-3-319-93366-5_3

practitioners? I propose a method to develop this subject in the following paragraphs.

This concept shares commonalities with "capital" and with "money", but it should not be confused with either. In financial terms, there are types of capital that should not be confused with disposable funds, including houses, factories, and commodities. Additionally, there are disposable funds that cannot be considered capital, such as the credit equilibrium of a bank account. Money, such as money intended for expenditures or peremptory payments, is not always a disposable fund. There are also non-money disposable funds, such as lines of credit.

The introduction of this concept in economics theory appeared for the first time in my book *Society and Happiness*, but because it appeared spontaneously, I could not develop the subject further. A preliminary analysis of the monetary mechanism is the only way to create a rigorous foundation for this concept, and therefore it will be the subject of my next book, *Dynamics of Wealth*. I think it would be useful for readers to have a preview of the broad lines of a research programme that crosses the threshold of an unexplored field of the physiology of our economic system but can provide singular clarification on some basic phenomena of our social order: business fluctuations, unemployment, and poverty, among others.

Concept of Disposable Funds

General Concept

In the legal sense, we can only dispose of things over which we have total property. Therefore, it is obvious that any economic good we use in full and free property is a disposable fund. The owner may allocate the good—as is or through its virtual equivalent on the market—to meet his or her needs or others' according to his or her will or to carry out his or her plans in the context of the relevant economic opportunities. Through exchange, any valued heritage property—anything valued by humans and that can be transferred—allows us to obtain objects, services, and advantages from others. Nevertheless, from this point of view, all properties are different. It will be more difficult to find someone willing to exchange something for a diamond or a house than for wheat or wool; some goods have easier outlets than others because they meet usual and common needs.

First Restriction of the General Concept

Among goods with ready outlets, none has an easier outlet than money. Almost all are willing to accept money in exchange for goods or valuables; this is the characteristic and essential quality of money. Whether as a useful material (such as metal) or as a fiduciary sign, such as refundable credit equity, money is a specific commodity that is usually not different from others. However, it has acquired a very singular characteristic in that it has a universally conceded special use, with the greatest guarantee that the market will provide when someone desires it: the fair equivalence of what he or she had alienated in exchange for this sign. This quality is consubstantial with the creation of disposability, in the economic sense.

If the object that we would like to dispose in order to achieve our economic purposes is not money but property, jewellery, a commodity, or a public debt security, we must evaluate it in terms of money, find the person who needs this particular object, discuss the price, and, finally, exchange it for money, all of which are not very easy to achieve. Hence, among commonly held assets, only money is generally considered to be a disposable fund; other objects are not, regardless of their value or their price—even if they are of greater value than the money itself.

Even if a businessperson does not have less capital than before, he or she may be in a difficult situation. He or she may even be forced into bankruptcy if his or her disposable funds do not regenerate as a result of a paralysis of sales, considering that money is and has always been the symbol of wealth, though, in truth, it has less value than any other object.

Whatever form it takes, money essentially marks a society's credit; it symbolizes the extent of a society's right to claim—given its social heritage—assets that the market considers equivalent to that amount of money. Indeed, the possession of this money is in itself evidence that some value or effort has been achieved, evaluated, and remunerated by a certain amount equivalent to the value of social goods. Thus, when he or she wishes, the owner can claim a right reward in the equivalent of this money in the form of goods. Bringing goods onto the market implies increasing supply, while bringing money onto the market means increasing demand; in this sense, money and other goods are contradictory. Under this principle, what is accepted as money acquires the power to generate, through the market, economic forces that produce what the owner desires. Someone who possesses this object because he or she owns it manages the implementation of productive energies. If those desires and intentions change, a shift in production activities occurs later, similar to the change in orientation of a magnetic needle due to variations in electric current.

Second Restriction of the General Concept

Can we consider all money in the same way and to the same extent as disposable funds?

Let us consider the monetary capital owned by an individual. The portion required to meet one's most urgent needs until further income is earned is a certain amount that cannot be disposable for other purposes. Even if there is an opportunity to assign this amount elsewhere or even to invest it in a profitable business, the most elementary prudence prevents its use because subsistence is every individual's most important concern. Other needs can easily wait, and a very slight instigation makes us postpone their satisfaction or offset it in other ways. Nevertheless, most people always have extra money to spend for non-essential purposes.

The maximum degree of disposable funds is represented by money that we are not willing to spend because we hope that we will obtain future profit or benefits from its use or possession. This profit would not be sufficiently compensated by an immediate placement. This money, with no incentive for its use or compelling need to spend it, constitutes what is disposable with maximum freedom for investment at any time in a placement that seems judicious or in a business that seems profitable.

In principle, real disposable funds—in the financial sense—include money subtracted from current expenditures; that is, money that we do not need to face inescapable commitments and that therefore remains reserved, suitable for any use. There is no precise delimitation between absolutely disposable money and non-disposable money. On one hand, there is money that is totally unnecessary for essential purposes, and on the other, there is money that strictly must be spent. However, there is always an intermediate area: money that we are more or less willing to reserve for consumption and that will be consumed or saved, depending on the circumstances.

Third Restriction of the General Concept

Again, we must discern what portion of money we are not willing to devote to current expenditures and, from this point of view, can be considered disposable funds. Cash that traders, industrialists, or speculators possess to meet their business needs is undoubtedly disposable in the generic sense. Nevertheless, if these disposable funds are required for normal business operations—all businesses require a certain amount of disposable funds to operate—they are very relative in practice because their absence would cause real difficulties for the business.

In contrast, newly accumulated savings—that is, a trader's money stock that exceeds his or her normal needs and that he or she can devote to expenditures, the growth of his or her or another business, or to lucrative non-trade tasks—are disposable funds in the full sense of the term and in all regards.

Levels of Monetary Disposable Funds

In summary, there are three levels of monetary disposable funds.

> First: The productive wages that constitute consumers' normal income, whether directly productive or not. Those are generally designed to meet these consumers' usual needs (minimum level of disposable funds).

Second: The amount of money owned by industrialists, traders, bankers, and speculators that constitutes the monetary funds necessary for business operations. It cannot be decreased without causing major harm to business growth (the relative or average level of disposable funds).

Third: The excess between recent gains or the received income and personal expenses, as well as recent savings that owners do not intend to spend on current expenditures and for which they have no useful or lucrative use at hand (an absolute or maximum level of disposable funds).

For the purposes of our research, it seems judicious to particularly differentiate the first and last two forms of disposable funds. When using the expression "disposable funds", we refer mainly to the second and third types of disposable funds, while we refer to the first type as income.

Physiology of Disposable Funds

Application of Disposable Funds to Individuals

What can disposable funds be used for? Of course, they can be used for luxury consumption.

Nevertheless, let us ignore this specific situation, which constitutes a simple shift of the demand between the time when savings are generated and the time they are spent. Instead, let us consider another situation where disposable funds definitely constitute savings that we plan to allocate for purposes of profit.

We can acquire goods that generate unearned income, such as public debt securities, land properties, industrial equities, businesses, and working industrial companies. We can also lend this unearned income to people willing to pay interest that is at least as much as what we would gain from any of the previous uses and under the same security or guarantee conditions. In such cases, we expect to generate income from savings.

We can buy any of the aforementioned commodities or the right to use any advantage with the hope to resell it at a higher price. Then, any profit is the result of our speculation.

Finally, there is the possibility to use this money to offer something that is useful to others or to complete a service for which people are willing to pay in regard to either effort, attention, or invested capital, as is the case when creating and setting up a business, implementing a trade, constructing buildings, or developing any other company, for example. These cases imply a demand for products that may be generated or replaced by a production process, as well as a demand for machines that transform them. In this case, disposable money is gradually converted into wages, salaries, interest, unearned income, profits, and payments generally for those who work or collaborate to promote the creation of the new product, which no longer represents a disposable fund.

The Function of Disposable Funds

Of course, the economic effect of a disposable property depends on its implementation. Selling goods is about exchanging a non-disposable property for disposable funds; buying is about the opposite. Selling is a transfer of disposable funds from the buyer to the seller. In the hands of the seller, money maintains the same characteristic as it has in the hands of the buyer: the possibility to demand a certain quantity of goods, values, or services, even if this quantity is still undetermined. However, the effect of money on the product market is non-existent and unpredictable as long as its owner will neither decide nor fulfil where to allocate this money. The same situation occurs in the case of a loan or transfer of disposable funds. It is a simple transmission, and the effect depends on how the receiver will use it. For the government, this transmission is then transformed into a demand for materials and labour to carry out public works, to buy weapons and supplies for the army, and to constitute civil servant assets, among others.

If the borrower is an industry, it will demand raw materials, machinery, wages, and interest on capital, among other factors. Even so, as long as it does not occur, the simple transmission of disposable funds as payment for a previous debt, as an acquired good, or as a loan does not alter the function and the nature of these disposable funds. It represents a powerful economic strength, an element of reserve maintained as speculation or as a loan. On one hand, its economic function is to support and balance the prices of unearned income-generating properties, the prices of products sold in bulk, and the prices of anything that can be an object of speculation. On the other hand, it aims to balance and determine the relative unearned income of various capital uses. It requires specific attention because it explains numerous equilibrium economic indexes.

Disposable Funds and Unearned Incomes

Let us suppose that the amount of disposable funds on the market increases in relation to the goods that might be the subject of speculation and to money demanded in the form of loans. Then, the value of securities—including land and stock market securities—that are the subject of speculation rises due to the classic law of supply and demand.

Nevertheless, the price of unearned income-yielding goods is related to the relative unearned income these goods produce. If their prices increase without increasing their productivity, the relative unearned income will decrease and the owners of disposable funds who are willing to confer these funds to a lucrative use will avoid exchanging them for low, unearned income securities.

In contrast, an increase in unearned income from variable income securities, such as land and industrial shares, will make these securities more attractive because of their greater relative profitability. Disposable funds will flow, their values will increase, and their less desirable uses will be avoided. These funds will therefore undergo cost depression that tends to balance the relative income.

This relation creates a balance between the mass of disposable funds, seekers of unearned income-yielding assets, and the amount of each category of assets on the market.

This relation also determines the unearned income relative to the average value of the unearned income unit; however, this opinion is not the current one in our field about the origin of interest. However, the usually supported opinion cannot withstand serious scrutiny, and an analysis would involve too much digression. The doctrine that I support seems to be more rational and fruitful, and it is the cause of the so-called interest rate. Nevertheless, if it is true that the interest rate arises from the possibility to use the disposable funds to acquire rent-producing assets, it has the same effect on the other uses of disposable funds. These disposable funds will be allocated to a particular use to the extent that they will create a benefit at least equal to that of other uses of the same security. Conversely, the least favourable uses of these disposable funds are avoided until their scarcity leads to an increase in the unearned income rate either because of a decrease in the transfer value or because of the choice to increase benefits to attract enough disposable funds.

The following is the path of a loan. The borrower endeavours to obtain the best possible conditions. Nevertheless, if he or she offers less than what disposable fund owners may obtain by buying unearned income securities at the market rate, the borrower will not receive the loan. If he or she encounters opportunities to obtain loans at a lower rate than the market rate, loan demand swells inordinately as soon as borrowers recognize a good deal, borrow money, and use it to acquire securities they can pledge.

The increase in money demand will inevitably increase interest loans, and the demand for income-yielding and rent-producing assets will increase the price and lower the unearned income rate until equilibrium is restored.

Loans are not the cause of capital interest in themselves. Loan interest reflects the unearned income phenomenon produced by values that can be exchanged for money. Since these values—except that of land—also become loans, we must conclude that the origin of this phenomenon must be sought in the unearned income of land and the interchangeability between land ownership and other values. We also consider that money is never lent without interest because it is never transferred for any other purpose—whether for production or speculation—without a proportional benefit.

Speculation and Speculative Profit

The growth of disposable funds tends to raise the prices of speculative assets, including consumer products and unearned income-yielding assets. Conversely, a decrease in disposable funds tends to lower the prices.

Nevertheless, when prices increase, speculation is very profitable because the margin between production cost and the selling price to consumers—which represents the index for speculative opportunities—increases. Therefore, speculation profits exceed the capital gains from unearned income-yielding assets and tend to be allocated to the purchase of increasing cost commodities and values. Nonetheless, the rise in unearned income-yielding asset prices is limited by the decrease in generated relative unearned income and is therefore less elastic than consumer goods. If the speculation profit margin is insufficient, disposable funds evade commercial speculation.

Given that disposable funds are to some extent necessary for the current organization of production, their relative lack generates difficulties for producers in finding outlets for their production and for consumers and retailers in stocking up. In the first case, the cost of manufacture or prices on the production market decreases. The second case leads to a higher consumer sale price and results in an increase in profit margins, and the owners of disposable funds begin to consider this speculative use attractive. Indeed, the margin sufficiently compensates for the interest they may earn from using unearned income assets, as well as the specific risk involved in speculation and the compensation that the profession provides.

The differential margin between unearned income and speculative profit is attributed to these latter causes. Nevertheless, this margin is independent of the fact that the first cause—the real interest rate—is larger, smaller, or even non-existent. To some extent, the speculative profit rate is still greater than the real interest rate, similar to how the water of the river always rises above the level of an obstacle opposed to it, enough to unleash its flow, regardless of the height of the dam. Without the ability to receive a free benefit by acquiring land or unearned income securities, the rate of industrial or commercial profit would start from zero. In reality, this rate starts from a positive value, like two electric generators mounted in tension, which add their potential because each of them, instead of producing electrodynamic effects from the neutral zero tension—like they would when working alone—produces them from a power decrease generated by the other generator.

Metabolism of Disposable Funds

While the loan, speculation, and acquisition of unearned income-yielding assets do not affect the disposable funds' objectivity, independent of their owners, industrial use leads to a noticeable change in their condition. In this case, they are used to pay salaries, assets, interest, and land unearned incomes, among other payments, and they are turned into revenue. They move from the condition of maximum or medium disposable funds to the state of minimum disposable funds because they constitute the normal income of many individuals. This income is generally intended to meet immediate needs and to create new demand for subsistence, comfort, and leisure items. This flow will then restore real disposable funds to the hands of these product manufacturers, and from their sales, they will recover the disposable funds speculatively invested in these products and profit from commercial compensation.

There is always a certain amount of disposable funds transformed into income. Conversely, there is a certain mass of income constrained for restoring disposable funds or semi-disposable funds to the hands of traders at the same time, creating a mass of savings that is subtracted from consumers' regular income and added as maximum disposable funds to those that already exist.

Owners will devote a certain portion of this mass of savings to their individual expenses or to borrowers such as the government, thereby increasing the demand for consumer products. Thus, what appears from the outside to be equilibrium with slow oscillations is actually a very active dynamic state similar to the material equilibrium of living beings that survive only through constant assimilation and dissimilation, where reserve tissues—represented here by disposable funds—increase or decrease depending on the equilibrium of two opposite aspects of the metabolism. From this point of view, we must note that industrial use is identical to unproductive consumption, such as the government's consumption or individuals' luxury consumption. Both generate a demand for products. Then, the products' value becomes compensation for production or constitutes direct compensation (civil servant salaries) immediately allocated to the demand for consumer goods.

Disposable Funds and Production

Compensations and Product Value

It is necessary to ascertain a series of simple but no less important quantitative relations between the components of disposable funds and those of production. These relations were perhaps unclearly defined by economists from the classical school in their approach to the stagnationism that has never been clearly or suitably defined.

It is logical and necessary that the amount of all revenues from production is the same as the created value. The production entrepreneur may be limited to distribute in the form of wages, salaries, raw materials prices, and interest, for example, more money than he or she earns in return for the product on the market. Thus, he or she works at a loss—or in mathematical terms, has negative earnings.

Considering all the interest in production, including negative equity, there is no doubt that the algebraic sum of interest is exactly equivalent to the product's value, or more precisely, the price obtained by exchanging the product on the market.

This situation will also be true when, instead of considering one particular production, we consider all productions in a given period. Representing by P the value of these productions and by I all income from them,

$$P = I(a)$$

Nevertheless, we must ensure, by totalling production on one hand and revenue on the other, that we do not omit any component of the product value and avoid duplication in accounting; otherwise, we could falsely interpret the equation.

If the value of production encompasses all the incomes received by all participants from production, it should also represent the final price of the products. If we take the factory price, we will eliminate the profits of speculators and traders who later sell them. Those profits also represent revenues born from the product. If we take the wholesale price, it will lack retailers' profits. Thus, the consumer public selling price fairly and accurately includes all the incomes born from the product.

We easily note that P should be formed by all sales to real consumers for consumption outside the production cycle. It should exclude all goods transactions made by industrial users to meet their industry's needs, such as purchases of coal, raw materials, chemicals, and fertilizers, among other products, because the value of these goods is then covered in the finished product. If the number of such transactions were taken into account, the same item would be accounted for twice. The same situation applies to speculative operations, in the broadest sense, for a product, which should, therefore, be excluded. The current trade statistics and domestic production are very far from expressing, by volume, the industrial importance of a country. A nation that organizes production as vertical trusts integrating all stages of product development—from production of raw materials to consumer outlets—will have a lower transaction volume and potentially greater real production than that of a nation with highly specialized industries, which would leave a product on the market in its various stages of processing and would record the value each time, counting the same value several times.

Since the production value should cover only the prices of the ultimate finished products, the total value of income R must include only the income directly generated by material production. It should include the income from the product value and exclude the specific services intended for producers. In fact, these transfers of part of their income are provided in exchange for a useful service they receive. Nonetheless, this service is not productive in the economic sense. For example, doctors' fees are obviously not generated by production. Those who need these services and pay for them actually transfer the right to receive a portion of production in exchange for these services, which does not depend on the nature of the service but rather on how it is used. In the case of a doctor employed by an industrial firm, the same medical services constitute remuneration derived directly from production by healthcare staff because these fees will be counted as general costs of production.

The tax paid by the firm to the government is part of the product's value because the firm accounts for it as a cost. However, if one includes in income the compensation from government services, income that the state distributes to its officials should not be taken into account because it would double-count a payment for the same service, as the state is a mere intermediary that transfers and distributes to its officials what it has received from producers.

The simple equation we have just established is important because incomes are redistributed after the product is created, according to the assessment of all parties' collaboration. Thus, the sum of these revenues can neither be greater nor less than the price of the product; the alternative case would result in an anomaly in which—as consumers—participants in production would be entitled to a greater or lower amount than what has been produced. It would result in a deficit or a residual, which would harm some individuals and/or favour others. This paradox can occur in reality and merits explanation.

Considering the production from which revenues are generated, equation (a) expresses a tautology.

Nevertheless, a certain amount of time elapses between the realization of production and the product's release on the market, which may be different from the time that elapses between the realization of production and the payment of revenues upon their processing into product demand by the collectors of such revenues. As a result, we can assume that the supply and demand that arise from same production operations do not always coincide in the market. This situation should therefore be followed by disequilibrium because more revenues appear on the market in the form of demand for consumer goods than in the form of produced (and therefore offered) consumer goods or vice versa.

This process is of the utmost importance for interpreting economic phenomena. Thus, it is necessary to examine how it occurs.

Income and Demand

It is obvious that each individual's demand during a period can only be met at the cost of the funds that he or she disposed early in the period. The revenue he or she receives over the current period will be added to these funds. The total sum represents his or her maximum demand capacity, and it is also likely that he or she will not fully use this capacity because he or she will maintain residual disposable funds at all times.

This case will hold for all the individuals of a territory. This assertion is even more rigorously established by considering the whole because there is no need to consider the transmission of disposable funds between individuals due to loans, repayments, and speculative buying since transmissions increase the disposable funds of some and, thereby, decrease those of others.

Consider that at the beginning of the period, A is the existing disposable funds and R the total income earned by all producers during this period. The quantum of effective demand, quantified in monetary units (the cash offer for consumer product or personal use), may not exceed the sum (A + R).

Normally, this value will be lower because at the end of this period, a certain amount of disposable funds A′ will remain equal to or higher or lower than A but still positive, will reduce the maximum demand, and will represent effective demand D; therefore, we can write the following:

$$A + R = D + A'(b)$$

This equation can also be shown in the form:

$$R + (A - A') = D(c)$$

Given that (A – A′) represents the positive or negative variation in the disposable funds, we can interpret this formula as follows: the effective demand in a certain period is necessarily equal to the amount of revenue plus the decrease in disposable funds or minus the increase in disposable funds. Disposable funds can increase only thanks to revenues and vice versa.

Equations (a) and (c) provide the following equation:

$$P + (A - A') = D(d)$$

This equation shows that production is equal to demand provided that the difference (A–A′) is zero, but there is no equality when this difference has a positive or a negative value.

There is no doubt that the effects of such disequilibrium are of utmost importance for the dynamics of our economic system; for this reason, we will analyse the two cases that may occur.

Case When Disposable Funds Decrease

In addition to the income received by producers during the considered time interval, a portion of previously saved disposable funds is used to acquire products.

Therefore, the sum of incomes represents the amount required only to purchase the issued production at its valued price. If, in addition to income as a whole, other amounts are added to demand and compete to acquire the products, the price of production will exceed the total budget considered normal. Then, the prices of consumer goods are likely to rise.

It is of utmost importance to know how value increase is distributed. Production income takes two forms: fixed income and random income. The first includes wages and salaries, while the second includes the profits of business owners, traders, and speculators. The immediate effect of a price increase is that production obtains higher sale value than expected, which increases business owners' and traders' potential profits and creates an incentive to engage in speculation and production. If this effect is constant enough, businesses and existing companies grow and new factories are created to meet new demands. Industry and trade activities attract jobs and capital, demand labour, and provide new jobs. The increased funds, distributed as incomes, imply a greater mass of buyers in the market for consumer goods and lead to new demand growth.

Nevertheless, because of the imperatives of our economic system—that is, because the sum of income and disposable funds is invariable (formula (a) 29)—these incomes must be taken out of disposable funds. It is therefore impossible for the increased demand to be indefinitely satisfied by these inelastic funds, particularly because speculation on products, stimulated by higher prices, also requires disposable funds, in the same way that industry creation and business development.

As disposable funds are in greater demand, they become scarce. This phenomenon leads to an increase in the discount rate and, generally, an increase in the interest rate because the prices of unearned income-yielding assets consequently fall. Savings are likely to be stimulated by possibilities for higher profit. Nevertheless, savings represent a decrease in demand. Thus, given that interest rate increases are an obstacle for production expansion, market expansion slows down from both the production and the demand sides since increased prices reduce the purchasing power of consumers who receive income.

What is the fate of our economic system? Any expansion of production simultaneously requires effective market demand and the creation of new capital (capital in the economic sense, i.e., means of production). However, both must be made at the expense of disposable funds; inelasticity absolutely halts production.

The means to obtain new disposable funds are savings. However, savings specifically reduce demand in the market and eradicate the largest industry stimulus, including price increases and possibilities to increase industrial profits. Conversely, the major causes of demand increases—such as large government loans for financing public works, for military expenditures, or for other major national goals that collect savings and release them onto the market as requests for materials and services—decrease the disposable funds to be used to produce goods to meet this demand and, second, to increase the interest rate, as a result of which firms can acquire financial resources.

By reducing the price of production, technical inventions and industrial progress that should facilitate an increase in consumption decrease the disposable funds in the market initially required for their implementation. They reduce the amount of labour and, therefore, the volume of income used to create demand. Therefore, when production capacity increases, consumption capacity decreases, and most of the benefits that should arise from progress are lost in vain.

To a certain extent, some individuals obviously benefit from the effect of these progress-generating savings when acquiring certain products. Even so, if these savings are spent to increase the sterile amount of disposable funds, social benefits are not likely to reach a high level. Even if this specific case is not discussed here, it merits a thorough analysis in every way.

Case When Disposable Funds Increase

If disposable funds increase, demand inevitably decreases. Therefore, a depression in the prices of the least popular items occurs because producers can only achieve savings by creating a relative deprivation. If the decrease in demand coincides with a decrease in the production cost, a decrease in consumption may not result, but rather only a restraint on the expansion that we would expect as a result of a decline in prices. Prices affected by the decline cease to create profits because the industry has adapted to production at the previous price. Since depression is likely to persist for a certain amount of time, manufacturers are forced to cut production, to dismiss workers, to demand fewer raw materials, and to inject savings. All these measures represent an income decline, and those incomes were previously on the market in the form of demand for consumer goods. Since this demand may no longer be found there, a new depression occurs, which cannot be balanced even by equivalent savings that will increase disposable funds because it decreases production, which in turn leads to new depressions, leading new industries to unemployment dead ends, and so on.

In this way, a small initial depression that causes unemployment can affect the whole production process and a great crisis of unemployment and industrial stagnation can be generated, even if, paradoxically, needs and production capacity do not decline or are lower. Because production is to be realized from prior market demand, the demand capacity is constantly repressed by an excessive desire to accumulate savings. From a social point of view, these savings are sterile because they have no productive use, but they may still be profitable for their owner.

The serious aspect of this case is that rectification does not occur automatically, as seen in the previous case. Instead of overcoming this damage, unemployment indefinitely worsens it. The depression effect of one of these crises can only be partially absorbed because the reverse process is always automatically concealed and paralyses production expansion. Thus, our social situation is similar to that of a chronically ill person who is always on the verge of serious crises. Sickness is addressed just enough to make life bearable again but returns with increased severity, attracted by the slightest imbalance.

In the absence of any other cause, a poor grain harvest is enough to prompt disaster. Logically, all people should limit their grain consumption as much as possible.

Nevertheless, the high cost of this essential product decreases the industrial product consumption capacity of most consumers, which is enough to trigger a general explosion. The intense damage is the crisis, a chronic disease, or a continually persistent social malaise. Chronic poverty exists everywhere, despite the progress of science and the dominion of humankind.

Relative improvement—achieved slowly and painfully—is not a result of spontaneous and necessary causes but rather of accidental causes. When a crisis is too great, the effects of unemployment must be overcome by a private or public charity or by employment, even at the cost of a perfect waste of labour. We see that the acute symptoms disappear as a result of wars, which compel, through extraordinary expenses, most saved disposable funds to be collected and released as demand for food and war materials, thus addressing the production restriction at the expense of more suffering.

Although the explanation for the genesis of crisis, for social malaise, and for most characteristic phenomena of our industrial system is—in my point of view—linked to previous deductions, some aspects of economic fluctuations, including the sudden and brutal nature of certain crises, will not find full and suitable explanations if we do not take into account how some disposable funds that are not originated by savings are generated.

Creation of Disposable Funds

Coinage

When disposable funds that do not come from private savings emerge on the market, they undoubtedly grow without prejudice to demand. In the opposite case, higher demand may occur if one part is paid into the consumer products market, with overabundant disposable funds. Considering the sense that we have used to now, all disposable funds are money, while not all money is disposable funds. Therefore, when new money is created, how does it appear on the market: as income or as disposable funds? Both can occur. To adequately address these cases, we must, even briefly, study how money is created.

First, money is created through free coinage. In this system, currency is coined at the request of individuals when they see this speculation as lucrative. This means that metal prices decrease significantly in relation to the price of coinage. A trader who buys gold for coinage gives the seller disposable funds in exchange for a commodity that is not—strictly speaking—a commodity, but he immediately recovers his disposable funds through this coinage and receives profit as a reward for this speculation. The disposable funds double, fully retaining their characteristics, and more new income appears without a reduction in disposable funds.

Another system is the circulation of money whose intrinsic value is much lower than its nominal value, as in the case of divisional money. This system is represented by the coinage on behalf of the government, where the government acquires metal in exchange for cash and immediately recovers it through coinage, thus achieving a significant profit. This case differs from the previous case only by the magnitude of this profit, which, in this case, is deposited into the government treasury's reserves as a resource that, unlike taxes, is drawn neither from production nor from citizen income.

In any case, the result is an increase in disposable funds achieved without decreasing demand, as in the case of savings, and an increase in monetary forms of demand that do not reduce the mass of disposable funds. We are aware of the positive effect of this measure in regard to industrial development that makes this result possible without any difficulty.

Such favourable circumstances generate benefits only if the disposable funds obtained are exclusively allocated to the development of production. Nevertheless, the prerequisite incentive for industry, especially in countries where industrial dynamism is lacking and where capital is very restrained, is a significant and sustained increase in prices, which means that a large portion of the new, disposable funds is employed in speculation.

Nevertheless, an increase in payment instruments without a parallel production increase inevitably results in higher prices, virtually reducing consumers' purchasing power. Consumers are thus forced to abandon their less necessary expenses such that, if this price increase reaches a level that imposes very severe deprivations, workers and employees strongly protest. These actors demand increases in their fixed incomes through strikes and social demonstrations, extreme responses to an ever-present problem that arises when suffering and inequality become too stark.

Thus, the declining value of money, which is a secular and permanent phenomenon, contributes to causing and maintaining the restriction of a great mass of consumer needs at a minimum level, even though there are interruptions determined mainly by crises. It prevents nominal incomes from growing at the same rate as monetary depreciation such that actual income, far from increasing, decreases in parallel with production capacity. Nevertheless, the demand capacity is the single true stimulus of industrial development.

Monetary fusion, in contrast to monetization, occurs when the metal price increases relative to the value of minted coins, like converting disposable funds into goods. Some owners of disposable funds may find it more profitable to melt their coins in order to sell them as metal or as manufactured items.

In this way, some disposable funds are destroyed and can never be recovered by society, which causes a reduction in existing funds and generally results in a redistribution of cash between demand and disposable funds, which also diminishes the amount available to acquire production. I believe it is useless to argue the effects of this phenomenon here.

Issuance of Paper Money

The creation of fiduciary money is, in fact, a special form of coinage on behalf of the government, distinguished by quantity rather than quality. In this case, the cost of money is small and, therefore, almost all of its value represents revenue for the government treasury, except in Spain, where the Central Bank takes advantage of this amount. This revenue is provisional and refundable but generally has a lower value due to the depreciation of money caused by an increase in the money supply. Although dangerous, this creation of fiduciary money is a convenient way for the government to obtain payment and, thus, directly or indirectly increase demand. Let us take a closer look at the consequences of this practice for the private economy.

As previously shown, when attempting to increase demand at the expense of disposable funds, these funds may soon become so scarce that the discount rate must be increased, which slows the expansion of production and consumption. Nevertheless, since disposable funds can be offered in unlimited quantities, the reverse phenomenon never occurs. Unlimited disposable funds are provided by creating these funds from nothing; this is what occurs in paper money issuance. Thanks to this system of trade, industry, and speculation, issuance can easily cope with all demands, and businesses can obtain disposable funds at a relatively low rate.

In the case of coinage, this phenomenon can be seen in larger proportions. Indeed, coinage has a natural limit—the difference between the value of the money and that of the metal—while paper money issuance has no limit other than the cancellation of the money's value, as the relative cost of printing banknotes is itself likely to indefinitely decrease by including increasingly high numbers on the banknote.

We are aware of the harmful effects of creating fictitious disposable funds. Since it is difficult for production to keep up with such a rapid increase in demand, most of the funds created fall into speculation and increase prices. They are likely to reduce the consumption capacity of classes that are paid with a fixed income. Individuals who receive invariable income definitely receive less income, as in the case of traders, industrialists, and speculators. Nevertheless, because individual consumption capacity is more limited, the propensity of this class of agents to invest represents a greater limit to consumption, which appears more easily in the case of extraordinary income rather than at the expense of usual needs. This transfer of consumption capacity does not support demand but rather encourages the accumulation of unsuccessful disposable funds. Demand eventually stagnates at a rapid rate that can only be moderated by an improved income for working and employee classes.

At the end of an economic conflict, crisis inevitably erupts, driven by the inability to achieve equilibrium between supply, demand, and income. Another factor may accelerate and even increase the severity of this crisis:

the excessive withdrawal of paper money, which creates industrial and financial discomfort after a scarcity of disposable funds. This excessive withdrawal immediately leads to price depression and all its consequences: unemployment, falling demand, and industrial stagnation.

It is noteworthy that two opposing causes—expansion and contraction of disposable funds—produce the same result in different ways. These causes represent an overwhelming obstacle to the expansion of consumer needs and to industrial development. If the cause is an increase in disposable funds, the obstacle is the price increase caused by speculation, which, in return, reduces the purchasing power of the main classes. If disposable funds decrease, the obstacle originates from the price decline that leads to business bankruptcy and to industrial paralysis. It reduces workers' livelihoods and, for some, eliminates them entirely because competition in the unemployed labour force and the workers' interest in keeping their jobs force workers to be content with the minimum wage compatible with their livelihoods.

The heart of the social problem lies in the material and moral consequences of this phenomenon.

There is no reason to wonder whether a limitation of natural means of production or of the efficiency of the production system causes a nation's economic downturn. Indeed, long before this extreme case arises, an economic system is able to produce this efficiency and maintain it through greater land productivity and the potent progress of techniques.

This situation explains how the greatest waste, wars, military peace, administrative corruption, and oligarchies become parasitic; not all immoral and perverse factors produce consequences that are as ruinous as we might logically expect. In nations that experience extreme political problems, social malaise, and misery among the majority of individuals, we see that crisis never occurs, for example, during wars; wars calm persistent economic malaise because they create apparent prosperity, while discomfort returns more acutely with peace, that is, when productive energies are freed and allocated to citizens' well-being.

It can only be understood from the hypothesis that social malaise does not originate from the inability to produce but rather comes from artificial causes that paralyse the production system and prevent the expansion of needs and, hence, the effective use of social energies. Despite its evils, waste has an advantage: it boosts production by encouraging consumption; like war, it brings economic relief despite calamity. In contrast, however, savings and scientific progress, which are technical ways to save labour, often have the opposite effect, which explains workers' disdain for technological developments and other related factors.

These arguments demonstrate that our economic system continues to generate greater problems and may be no less cruel than war; waste and administrative disorder, lead to pain and suffering, and dampen the forces that could produce what is needed for a more enjoyable life. These concealed forces must find emotional release and relief to close the gaps opened by the calamities that disrupt a society's development.

Private Credit

The particularly severe characteristics of these crises cannot be fully explained if we do not consider a final source of fictitious disposable funds, which are no longer money in a material sense.

We know that in business, credit is equal to disposable funds, and being able to buy on credit prevents any trader from actually possessing cash. Especially in nations that are experiencing the greatest economic progress, credit offered by a bank is a disposable fund often used without effectively disposable money and, therefore, without diminishing the business's effective disposable funds. If the credit use is limited, the social economy of the disposable funds will certainly not be great. However, to the extent that confidence is widespread, each creditor obtains credit from his or her own creditors who, in turn, obtain them from their sellers. Thus, a long line of cashless transactions emerges that, under other circumstances, would require the existence of actual disposable funds.

Such virtual disposable funds cannot be considered identical to other disposable funds in all aspects. They are not used, for example, to pay wages; generally, they are not used for consumer goods purchases, but they do not prevent actual freed disposable funds from being used for such purposes.

All of these factors are welcome in times of prosperity because they help to soften the yoke that constrains, as an iron hand, production and trade and prevents it from freely taking off, but here, there is a seed of the most terrible problems that arise as soon as credit is suddenly contracted. Indeed, this contraction is critical—as critical as the crisis, worsening and giving it greater severity. From a business's initial financial difficulties, mistrust will arise alongside the fear of outstanding commitments, and therefore the building of imaginary disposable funds will decline. On-going operations will be liquidated and later achieved with actual disposable funds.

Then, the effect is not different from that of the contraction of any other type of disposable funds. However, in this case, the effect is even more brutal and more difficult to contain since the causes of panic are more difficult to control.

It seems pointless to dwell on the consequences of all of these situations; they are almost identical to those previously analysed. The thirst for effective disposable funds that could fill the void left by the fading fictitious disposable funds reaches its climax. Therefore, we try to import and attract these funds by any means. Moreover, I mentioned the case of the 1907 crisis in the US, where contraction was extremely severe despite the import of six hundred million dollars worth of gold from Europe.

The effect of this action was an increase in metal stocks by half, and the scarcity of disposable funds was considerable. We are aware that this thirst for disposable funds can be quenched through paper money issuance to the extent that panic has not reached a degree to which it will lead to a loss of trust in this means of payment.

Failing this situation, the need for disposable funds must be addressed slowly at the cost of attracting savings and boosted by high interest rates, which results in paralysis caused by the contraction of demand.

Solutions to Social Problems

Communist System

Consistent with our previous point of view, the question of society's economic problems is insoluble or fatal. It depends on the established production regime, which we are in a position to correct—in that case, socialist schools of thought would be correct. Nevertheless, our findings lead us to a radically different point of view about the appropriate solution than those of these schools.

Socialists focus mainly on unequal distribution. From our perspective, it is not the unfairness of distribution but the scarcity of production that lies at the origin of social impoverishment, although inequality, as the most noticeable phenomenon of suffering, is the cause of proletarian class anger.

It is certain that current production, distributed more fairly, would not sufficiently improve the situation of the lower classes, and the general state of society could even worsen. Relatively, there is not enough production, but this is not for a lack of resources: land is fertile and tools are powerful. It is because social organization does not stimulate productive forces. In contrast, it abolishes these forces by making workers' situation more precarious and that of parasites more opulent. It encourages idleness, parasitism, and vice, which is often more lucrative than work.

Socialists do not see other ways to achieve greater justice and better organization than extending the authority of the government to the economic order by socializing all means of production and converting citizens into officials. Leaving aside all biases and prejudices, those who experienced Russian socialism generally do not believe that humanity's salvation can be found in such a system.

Some believe that the Soviet economic failure is due to the poor conditions in which the experiment was conducted, that is, in a country impoverished by war and affected by the revolution. However, the value of a healthy system must be demonstrated, especially in difficult cases, and if the value of the communist system were positive, the country's renaissance would have been better achieved in this system than in any other system.

In addition, many reasons suggest that failure is inevitable, regardless of the conditions under which the socialist experiment is attempted. An economic system is always poor when it separates the work from the worker's reward, as a communist regime does. The result of this phenomenon is invariably a decrease in productivity. In fact, this problem exists under the current system because the worker does not perceive that his or her increase in production capacity is immediately reflected in the improvement of his or her economic fate. This phenomenon would be even stronger in a communist regime. Rigorous communism would only be possible with an economic morality that does not currently—and may never—exist.

It appears that this difficulty was anticipated by communist leaders, as they devised a complicated system of rewards and punishment to stimulate production. However, there is no more effective reward or fairer punishment than the reward and punishment that results from the fruit of labour, of intelligence, of the ability and interest shown by the worker in his or her work. Mutual aid is likely to overcome the contingencies attributable to chance.

Collectivism

Collectivist schools, which are less extreme than communist schools, focus on establishing a relation between production reward and effort. From the moment the socialization of means of production accompanies this system, fixing rewards can only be predicted pragmatically by specific regulations and entrusted to competent courts.

Unfortunately, implementing ways to fix fair and suitable compensation for such a complex phenomenon as human labour is a difficult task. Therefore, finer aspects of psychology and sociology should be taken into account to achieve the required social efficiency. Time is just one of several factors, but if we take only time into account, we neglect the most important factor, namely, labour quality. Physiological effort is very difficult to measure and has no connection with the social utility of labour. Psychological effort is more difficult to estimate and is essentially variable. Depending on innumerable different circumstances, this effort is a purely subjective object. The only authentic economic object is fixing a reward in accordance with created value.

Nevertheless, the notion of value is one of the most complex constructs in economics. Is anyone other than the consumer himself able to evaluate it?

This question does not imply that one or another consumer can do so, but rather that all consumers in society can. The concept of value is born from the social utility of the product and is measured by the relative need felt by the consuming public. Nevertheless, this need is so variable and so complex that only the fluctuating game of market demand can determine it. Estimating value through the market deserves criticism, but any other way to measure it would be more arbitrary and erratic, regardless of the safeguards surrounding it. In addition, an alternative method would inconveniently transform an economic issue—which happens to be the nerve of the whole economy—into a political issue.

Organizations with this mission would inevitably remain subject to the political and social influence of various corporations. This influence would not lie in the merit of their productive activity but rather in the dangers and fears that discontent could create. We observe these problems as a result of the state's economic interventions and professions or businesses that are—by nature—less conducive to creating serious conflicts with less material force and that are frustrated by their claim of stronger and better-organized forces, also concerning workers' corporations and civil servant groups. We can add to all of these phenomena the problems generated by conspiracy and favouritism that apply to all political regimes.

In the economic order, an automatic control system is always superior to a regulatory system and to arbitrary decrees. We cannot expect natural pathways to be distorted through dialectic, corruption, or relations with human laws; their fate is more efficient and more moral than the most complicated phenomenon. From this point of view, our free-market economic system has undeniable advantages, although many experts have somewhat discredited it. However, it is not possible to accept this discredit without prior critical judgement of its origin; the situation will be different if the system's failure results from the condition of the system itself and from a substantial misuse.

Freedom and Property Regime

Economic freedom currently exists in the competition between products in domestic market and is used in normal times to fix the prices of goods. Nevertheless, the majority of the free production regime does not aim to fix the relative prices of goods as a function of their economic value. This method is just one particular means to obtain something more important, namely, that the rewards that arise from the production of each agent involved in the creation of value are proportional to the value they create and to the degree of their contribution through their personal efforts and abilities to create. It is also a way to stimulate the maximum and encourage productive energies. In addition, sufficient freedom is certainly needed in order to find the most efficient application of these energies within the means disposable to humanity.

Nevertheless, does this process actually work this way? The most concise observation shows well that the unearned incomes of the wealthy, workers, plutocrats, traders, and senior and low-state officials are in no way proportionate to the social utility generated by their participation in production. There is a basic inequality between these groups, and there is no trend towards greater equity. Is this phenomenon due to the freedom of the agreement itself, or, in contrast, to the lack of full freedom and equity when realizing contracts?

Socialists lean towards the first point of view and see no other way to achieve equity than by eliminating private ownership of the means of production and exchange. Certainly, there is an element of production—land—of which ownership is very difficult to justify from an economic point of view because it is not the product of human labour but rather a natural means of work that is absolutely necessary to achieve production. Its private appropriation is therefore a formal restriction on the freedom of production. Nonetheless, this is not the case for capital. Capital is the result of private effort, and an individual's right to the private ownership of his or her production capacity seems unquestionable to me.

I do not believe that we can support—even from a simple efficiency point of view—that the government should be responsible for creating capital by absorbing the individual's savings. From experience, we know that government intervention in economics can cause disasters and spur a decrease in the propensity to save. The organization of production and the creation of social capital in a social system of public property, products, and even capital seem to be the weakest aspects of the socialist argument.

Defects of the Current System and Ways to Correct Them

From my point of view, there is currently a disturbance in the natural functioning of the instrument of production. Socially, capital is a way to help people to work. Individually, it is considered a way to not work, not because one can claim to live at the expense of previous saving, which would be indisputably legitimate, but because one can claim not to work by living parasitically at the expense of others for an indefinite time. This notion spawns the moral absurdity that wealth is considered an end in itself. Nothing is less certain than whether this notion is inherent to the condition of capital in a free-market system.

In this case, there is a seed of inequality that is incompatible with freedom. Freedom should be fair before being absolute. Capital, as an instrument for work, should be accessible to all and, as a result of labour, should be generated by all. However, it becomes monopolized by a minority because not all experience the same conditions in obtaining the reward for labour. Far from being consubstantial, this phenomenon is incompatible with freedom. The capacity to obtain the reward for one's labour is limited for a non-capitalist worker because of our current economy's tendency to limit and reduce income for actual work. Generally, capital cannot be accumulated by those who need to use it. Conversely, those who possess it can appropriate products to the capital they own, which has no theoretical limit.

Nevertheless, the notion that resorting to the turbulence of the capital socialization system helps to avoid this phenomenon does not appear legitimate if we consider the inferences we can draw from the study of economics and mechanics. To avoid the problems we previously mentioned, it is sufficient to eliminate the causes of limitations to workers' income and debilitate one's effort to improve his or her fate by placing boundaries to production. The main cause we discovered is variable disposable funds maintained by speculation—mainly and fundamentally land speculation and unearned income-yielding assets.

It would be sufficient to avoid the harmful effects of this reserve fund, which has no socially beneficial function. This process would help production to reach its natural expansion and, at the same time, help eliminate interest on capital. Thus, it would enable workers to obtain the full extent of compensation for their work, creating much more fruitful labour. Indeed, the decrease of interest on capital would remove the main obstacle to the implementation of the most effective means of production.

The most radical way to prevent speculation would be to eliminate the private ownership of unearned income-yielding assets. Nevertheless, given that this measure seems too extreme and impractical at this time, it would prove to be useless; it would be sufficient to prohibit the exchange of these assets for actual value. When disposable funds can no longer meet opportunities to be used or to be exchanged for unearned income-yielding assets, the interest on capital arising from that possibility would disappear automatically. Therefore, disposable funds without a profitable use would be devoted to consumption or investment use—the creation of authentic capital for production—attracted by a profit level that would be only slightly higher than the compensation for the incurred risk. This way, disposable funds would be minimized, and their changes would prove to be harmless.

There is still the possibility of speculation on current production commodities. Nonetheless, apart from the usual case in which speculation is essential for the circulation of goods for provision to industries and consumers, this phenomenon remains rather unusual. Speculation on goods occurs when, due to excessive financial practices by governments or to industrial fluctuation specific to the current system, sudden changes in actual or fictitious disposable funds arise. This process results in fluctuations of all kinds of goods, representing transaction items, to the extent that speculation on commodities is generated by other types of speculation. Nevertheless, regardless of the circumstances and from the point of view of the most rudimentary economy, reducing commercial speculation to the required minimum is always desirable. This process consists of ensuring that products reach consumers through the fewest intermediaries possible and at the minimal cost. When production is freed from the constraints of inelastic demand, when fluctuations in disposable funds do not prevent income growth alongside production progress, industry would grow to its full potential. It is certain that we currently do not have the slightest idea about these opportunities because current industry development is not commensurate with actual production capacity, which is potentially created by progress.

The first pulse is given by the great mass of disposable funds currently allocated to speculation. When such speculation is prevented, disposable funds are intended for either the acquisition of consumer goods or the creation of industries, which would, therefore, increase demand and generate a period of intensive industrial progress, which would not be slowed, as it is now, by the subtraction of interest, which determines the high cost of disposable funds if they can be allocated to lucrative use outside the productive system.

Conversely, upon an increase in productivity, income growth would be rapid. This increase would no longer be prevented by the aforementioned phenomena inherent to speculation on disposable funds; it would facilitate the creation of more abundant savings than today. These savings would be shared between all real producers, who could no longer aspire to a life of seeking unearned income, as there would no longer be opportunities to use these savings as unearned income. These savings would immediately turn into real capital, especially because the owners using their workforce in the industry would benefit more from using their savings in order to make their work more productive. Thus, for the first time, the social function of capital would be reconciled with its individual function.

The unearned income-yielding assets that are left out of the circuit but continue to produce unearned income for their owners, including land, will ultimately be purchased by the government because the demand increase caused by production expansion would significantly raise rents by parasitically absorbing a significant portion of production. Nevertheless, it would unduly prolong this study, in which I intend only to highlight the immediate causes of social problems. These causes should be examined within the living trap in which speculation corners the industry, like a snake whose spasmodic contractions produce painful crises of the collective organism, consume social energies in vain, and neuter the best fruits of thought and human genius.

All nations seek ways to avoid problems and suffering. They believe they have found them—at least temporarily—in customs tariffs, policy changes, new market openings, and colonial conquests. However, these attempts do nothing more than encourage hatred and rivalry between nations and between humans and promote wars, strikes, social discord, political revolutions, and other cruelties, which are all sources of further suffering and obstacles to humanity's moral progress.

ALICANTE, October 1922.

3.2 Definition of Concepts and Analysis Framework

This section gives some definitions to precise the framework in which our study takes place

Bernácer's Definition of Functionalism

Prior to conducting an analysis, Bernácer takes care to accurately define the concepts he studies. This precaution is useful in our field, given its semantic particularities (see Galbraith and his plea for specific language for economists, and Machlup's essays of economic semantics (1944, 1971).

In this regard, we observe that Bernácer always defines the concepts relative to their function and not relative to the nature or the materiality of the concept defined. This functionality goes beyond the scope of semantics because all of Bernácer's economic analyses are made from this perspective, as shown in the title of his most "technical" book: *The Functional Theory of Money* (1945).

Two examples illustrate this principle of Bernácer's vocabulary: the definitions of capital and money.

Capital is a corporal element that increases labour productivity. The ultimate function of capital is to encourage work and production activity.

Money is a signal: a sign of community debt to its holder that will be extinguished in exchange for goods. Money is, therefore, characterized by three functions: the acquisition of goods that immediately meet needs, the acquisition of goods that increase production, and, finally, the acquisition of speculative assets that provide income without work. Consumption, investment, and hoarding are thus included in the definition of money.

Premises to Illuminate the Presentation

Bernácer analysed three themes: the macroeconomic universe, the capitalist market, and the monetary system. His approach has some specifics presented in this section.

Analysis of the Macroeconomic Universe

The universe described by Bernácer is macrocosmic. We will not dwell on the innovative character attributed to Keynesian works in this respect because historians have recognized that physiocrats and Marx, for example, preceded Keynes. Similarly, does Bernácer base all his analysis on overall economic phenomena, and does he reason on aggregates?

His analysis at the agent level is exceptional. When he does not offer details, he refers to macroeconomic concepts. Therefore, instead of savings, he discusses overall savings; instead of income, he discusses national income; and so on.

Analysis of a Historically Achieved Regime: Capitalist Market Economy

Bernácer studies the capitalist system in its concrete historical reality, even though the word "capitalism" does not often appear in his writings. He rejects the fiction of such a system in a frozen equilibrium but only in his life rhythms. Economic activity is in perpetual motion, and equilibrium is in a unique position: fiction created by the observer. Therefore, he immediately seizes the system with all its imperfections but never refers to another perfect system a priori.

Thus, Bernácer observes a real environment and then sets economic ethics, without which no judgement is possible. Finally, he proposes reforms for the analysed regime, depending on the chosen ethics.

At this level of study, these ethics must be designed in accordance with the mathematical rigor of coordinate axes in relation to which any point of space is defined. Therefore, a priori, the word "ethics" should not be given moral content a priori. Spinoza's (1632–1677) fundamental work

Ethics demonstrates the geometric method in terms of definitions, axioms, demonstrations, and corollaries, following the deductive method. More recently, this work was described in the book by S.Ch. Kolm, *Justice and Equity* (CNRS 1973), who founded what might be called scientific ethics.

Analysis of Monetary Economics

The same concern about realism is also obvious in Bernácer's consideration of monetary economics. In contrast to some contemporary economists (Robertson and Allais, for example), Keynes sometimes thinks in non-monetary terms, that is, in real wages units (*General Theory*, Book III, chapter 8). Also refusing a dichotomous analysis, Bernácer directly observes a concrete environment in which monetary phenomena are captured in their reality without the pretence of an organization from which money would be first excluded and then reintroduced in a later phase of the analysis.

Key Elements of Bernácer's Economic Analysis

To facilitate the merging of various concepts, we chose three areas to define: production factors and the law of value, money, and product distribution.

Factors of Production and the Law of Value

In the spirit of Bernácer, the three classical factors of production are categorized hierarchically according to their function. At the top of the hierarchical structure is labour. Labour is the most dynamic factor of production, consisting of designing, implementing, and accomplishing tasks. The second factor is capital, which is a passive element that is nonetheless a valuable tool since it improves the productivity of the production system, all things being equal. The last factor is land, which is an essential component; production and life would be impossible without it.

It acts as an inert element and cannot itself create an economic good. This analysis naturally led Bernácer (1916, 1955) to adopt a law of value, similar to the law of labour-value.

Work

Considering that labour is the most important factor of production, the need to define it requires some meaningful quotations about the nature and specificity of labour. "Work, in the broad sense, is the active agent of production" (Bernácer 1916, p. 3). Concerning working capacity, the need for reserves and unemployment, "It is difficult to understand why, considering the working capacity and all the unsatisfied existing needs, labor, which is the only factor to meet them, is paralyzed, and why unemployment has become the great spectrum of the modern world" (Bernácer 1916, p. 38). Schmitt (1966, p. 267) said that "labor is the only factor of Gross Domestic Product".

Labour and money are intangible factors that implement production; "by its potential utility character, labour is what most resembles money… Why is labour depreciated compared to money?" Bernácer (1955, p. 6) denominates this question as a "strange paradox".

Labour is a living force used in the activity to create a product. It involves efforts from people, and an economic organization should allow the efforts to create a product to be adequate with the wage scale settlement.

Labour is a specific factor of production. It has no cost and no value outside of work (Bernácer 1916). In fact, he rejects the theory of work-force maintenance. In that sense, salary is not a cost but a part of product distribution regardless of cost and, therefore, of individuals' lifestyles. "The wages depend on supply and demand for labour, except that in this case there are no subsidiary effects of the cost (the price), as there is no actual cost… If competition between workers is high, wages decrease. Persistent unemployment should strengthen the competition and decrease wages, as it has been since the earliest times" (Bernácer 1955, p. 96). This conception by Bernácer is remarkable and opposes the classical and Marxian theories generally accepted at his time.

Capital

Based on quotes from Bernácer's work, we suggest a definition of capital. "The capital itself is nothing but past work fixed on the matter...The capital, fruit of labour, is a passive instrument" (Bernácer 1955, p. 3). He rejects Adam Smith's (1961) broad notion of capital, defined as everything designed to produce income. The first condition of capital is that it is a product; the second is that this product enables other products to be obtained or at least to be used for this purpose and not to satisfy any direct human need (Bernácer 1916).

Therefore, Bernácer conceived capital similarly to the way Marx did, as expressed by S. de Brunhoff (1967): "Credit is undoubtedly the auxiliary of the real capitalist accumulation, but in its own way. No more than the right to confuse money and commodity, we cannot confuse loan capital and 'real' capital. Marx himself explains the difference to be established between money capital and real capital, taking the example of public debt 'purely illusory capital,' money-capital loaned to the government but spent by it for a long time" (Marx 1963, III, vol.2, p. 129; first published in1848).

Nevertheless, influenced by Henry George (*Progress and Poverty* 1879), Bernácer (1916) refuses the idea that the worker is sustained during the production process by previously accumulated capital. We observe that Bernácer:

(a) Rejects the idea of variable capital: the mass of goods necessary for maintaining a "workforce".
(b) Considers as capital goods only those that, through their immediate physical qualities, directly contribute to production.
(c) Implicitly denounces, by this definition, the confusion between investment and savings and between stockbuilding and fixed capital creation. Indeed, worker needs during the production process are composed of savings previously accumulated as stocks of consumer goods.

This position has social and political consequences: in no way is the worker indebted to the capitalist for subsistence in advance. To Bernácer, capital consists of reproducible goods, and its basic component is embedded labour. Moreover, it is essentially different from monetary wealth. More recently, this basic differentiation was adopted by Joan Robinson.

Referring to Robertson's error (in his 1940 article in *Economica),* Bernácer (1955, p. 3) calls Robertson neophysiocratic and states, "Nature, from an economic point of view, is also an inert element. The error of the physiocrats was not to consider it as such but to consider land as the production core".

Value

The concept of value deserves to be precise through its function and its use with the law of value and the exchange value. Bernácer also offers a functional definition of value: the natural function of value is the distribution of social products. Outside of distribution, the definition of value comes from pure metaphysics, in the worst sense of the term, as Voltaire and this Bernácer (1955, p. 3) quote (without reference) illustrate: "When a speaker no longer understands what he says and that those who listen understand absolutely nothing, metaphysics begins". Nevertheless, the value distribution has two huge difficulties: "establishing a unit of value and fixing value in this unit, and on behalf of everyone, as a reward for his or her collaboration in production". The unit of value appears as the essential common denominator of exchange: the unit of measure is both the exchange value of goods and income from production. Product prices and wages, for example, are expressed in the value unit on various individual markets. Bernácer rightly refutes the concept of utility and cost. This concept is meaningful only in microeconomics and is essentially subjective in content. Therefore, it is an inadequate concept for the baseline of an economic system.

The main argument for the rejection of monetary value is the existence of unreproducible goods or goods with prices that are not proportionate to their cost of production. The amount of work necessary to obtain a product is its cost; cost is essentially different from value. Bernácer does not always manage to overcome the dualism of macroeconomic and microeconomic analysis, particularly in the law of value.

Although Bernácer (1916, p. 27) is certainly a follower of the law of "labour" value at the macroeconomic level, he contradicts himself when he analyses the various markets (1955, p. 96): "Some schools of economists—including those of Ricardo and Marx—argue that the products' value lies simply in the quantity of incorporated labour, although they immediately contradict, admitting that profit lies in the market price or a value-added, which is different from labour. To justify this view, we must resort to a distinction between value and price, the difference would be the value-added. Even so, then, value takes very difficult sense, because we do not know what is a value different from price, that is, distinct from human relative appreciation for things through the market".

We can try to reconcile Bernácer's critical and favourable positions on labour value in two propositions. First, we note that, according to Bernácer, labour does not mean only wage labour (the element of cost in microeconomic theory) but also a broader concept of participation in production activity. Thus, the employer ensures that in the company, there is coordination work, management work, etc. Then, and most importantly, there is ambiguity in the definition of this concept. In his descriptive study, Bernácer strains to note the existence of elements of value other than labour; whereas in a normative study, Bernácer is in favour of labour-value. Nevertheless, even in this case, labour is particularly an element of distribution and not the basis of value. Therefore, profit may be compensation for effective work and may be of a residual, complementary, or stimulating nature. According to this hypothesis, the contradiction between price and value indicated by Bernácer (1916, pp. 47–57) in the quote above is no longer incompatible with the notion of labour-value.

According to Bernácer, a hierarchy of structures controls value. The market sets the price or the exchange value. In that respect, it is not necessary to refer to the subjective criterion of utility. This exchange value is a priori independent of the cost. The articulation between different markets (goods, labour, and money) thus allows us to determine the cost of various components to a certain extent. One of these margins is profit, which sanctions the company in the sense that we undertake a production. The quantum of profit controls new producers' subsequent arrival on the market and allows a fluctuating adjustment of the value into cost if there are no barriers.

If we pursue Bernácer's argument, we can reach a pragmatic and dynamic concept of value. We will attempt this briefly. The first basic requirement is the existence of innovation reserves of both goods and production techniques. The second requirement is market fluidity and, therefore, the existence of information structures and of vocational training.

At time 0, implementing several innovations on the market determines readjustments related to the price of goods (old goods and new goods, according to their degree of substitution) and the price of factors (depending on the situation in their respective markets).

At time 1, a readjustment of factor prices occurs as a result of movements triggered at time 0.

At time 2, the effects of all the foregoing result in factor reallocation.

In conclusion, we believe that, in Bernácer's mind, the macroeconomic concept of value is different from his microeconomic concept and only the first has a full meaning.

Money

Money, as general equivalent is also labour. Closely linked to value in human mindset, the concept of money is defined in this section, extending to disposable funds and hoarding "In all of this, what is there other than labour? Where is the work of money, which appears to be the deus ex machina of the economic architecture?" (Bernácer 1955, p. 4).

The Monetary Fetishism of Advanced Societies

According to Bernácer (1955, p. 4), primitive man would be naturally good; see. J.J. Rousseau.

"…If money may consist of a symbol, such is its essence, the truth is that Montesquieu was intuitive to state, 'Money is a signal'…Money is a debt of the community, the effective payment of which will be completed on the market and will consist of goods…The value of paper money is conditioned by the trust or credit instilled in the issuer, either private or public." Money is therefore an intangible signal, a measure of value, and an instrument of distribution. It influences the levels of use and production and causes two kinds of problems: scarcity and the purchasing power monetary unit.

Disposable Funds

The concept of disposable funds was forged by Bernácer in 1922 to refer to the money disposable by various agents, and we can relate it to cash. Pivoting from the entirety of Bernácer's analysis on economic dynamics, this concept in the plural form covers different forms of money, which is considered in terms of its various functions.

Overall, an analysis of disposable funds shows that there are three degrees of disposable funds, in increasing hierarchical order:

(a) Income predestined for consumption;
(b) Intermediate companies' cash, real crucibles of incomes;
(c) Finally, cash and income portions intended either for investment or for hoarding.

Beyond the study of money, this analysis leads to the Keynesian view of expenditure distribution (C + I) and to a fluctuation theory based on hoarding. In particular, it allows the mistake of confusing saving and hoarding to be avoided.

Hoarding as a Perverse Function of Money

Hoarding has a perverse effect on employment levels: unused money referees a nation's energy: it enables its possessors to live well and prevents unemployed people from working. This is a strange mystery (Bernácer 1955, p. 5).

Hoarding is defined as a retention of purchasing power from the production circuit: it can have a fixed appearance (disposable cash) but may also be in motion when financing transactions on goods that are outside current production. To cover the two concepts' unique functioning, we coined the term "double hoarding"; this term is not used by Bernácer.

Therefore, hoarding is a fraction of monetary savings that is never invested in the present production of goods.

Circulation and Distribution of the Product

Goods, market, and income are included in the process of circulation and distribution of product. The classification of goods depends on two coordinates: their time of production and their nature. Moreover, the characteristics of goods make them non-reproducible.

The function of a good is to satisfy a need. The good acquires its full value once in the hands of its user. The unsold machine tool for the producers of investment goods—as well as the consumer goods still held by the trader—has not yet fully achieved its economic function. The first and the second are meant to be transferred through the industry and the consumer, respectively. Meanwhile, their function is imperfect: economic equilibrium depends on whether the products reach their target, to use the language of marketing specialists.

The Vintage of Goods

This expression is ours. Solow illustrates this concept of vintage by different ages of capital goods. At any time, there are three kinds of goods on the market:

(a) Goods "recently" produced and that have not yet reached the user. These are stocks of goods produced during the former period.
(b) Goods produced several periods ago that are in the hands of the user and are likely to be requested again on the market.
(c) Non-reproducible goods that were created long ago.

The first category of goods represents the main portion of production. These goods are the real source of income for the period. The second have varying effects on activity. The third are the source of many problems because they will eventually be subject to speculation that disrupts productive activities.

It is important to vintage goods if we want to identify their different effects on economic activity. The issue of vintage is even more important when we note that income, estimated in value units, from production during the period is intended to acquire contemporary goods, which are estimated in the same value units. We presume that any discrepancy between these flows will lead to distortions and disequilibria.

Non-reproducible goods are those that exist before the time of production: historical artworks, historical objects, usually antiquities, and irreplaceable goods, such as historical items we could qualify as vintage in regard to current production.

The value of these goods is related to:

(a) The volumes of the huge sums spent for their acquisition; these are monetary quantitative elements.
(b) The probabilities, as proven through experience, of the value growth of these goods: speculative elements.

This value is therefore not related to the cost of these goods' production nor to the cost of their impossible reproduction, which should not be confused with their imitation.

Goods other than antiquities meet the same laws; these are the unearned income-yielding goods without the intermediary of work that we will thereafter call unearned income-yielding assets, including domains, lands, mines, forests, land ownership in general, fisheries, and private territory, which, in fact, are all monopolies. Material debt securities may also be assimilated to these goods, such as transferable securities with an economic role similar to that of real estate, due to their double content of bare ownership and usufruct. This assimilation is based on the identity function of these goods (the production of cash and speculation), not on their nature since, in a sense, securities are likely to be "reproduced" when new issuance is conducted.

These assets' essential feature is that their value is more closely related to the income they produce and the prospects of value-added they offer rather than to their production or replacement costs. We will further note the impact of this categorization within Bernácer's analysis.

Market

The market is the locus of the points of contact between consumers' desires and producers' initiatives. In Bernácer's analysis, the market has a central place. "An economy must regulate itself or be regulated from the outside. Yet it will be a free economy only to the extent that it will be able to regulate itself. The regulatory mechanism of the economy is the market" (Bernácer 1955).

The existence of the market gives value all its originality. Without the market, value is reduced to a simple subjective concept and therefore is not likely the subject of scientific treatment at the level of the entire economy.

According to Bernácer, the market is the tangible manifestation of consumers' and producers' freedoms. It is therefore logical that Bernácer makes an unconditioned apology for the market.

Bernácer's approach to the market concept is both functional and sequential.

We can summarize the author's thoughts as follows:

- Supply responds first, according to a very Schumpeterian conception of the dynamic role of the entrepreneur.
- The first demand response is to establish a value scale through the prices of goods, which depends on needs on one hand and on income on the other.
- Supply therefore calculates a cost based on the factors' prices and then develops a first production programme.
- Demand then renders a verdict by setting the price-quantity pair equilibrium.
- Supply subsequently calculates its a posteriori profit, that is, the residual: (revenue minus costs). Then, depending on the past results on one hand and on its projection on the future on the other, supply establishes a new production programme for the following sequence of periods. We propose the following diagram to illustrate this idea.

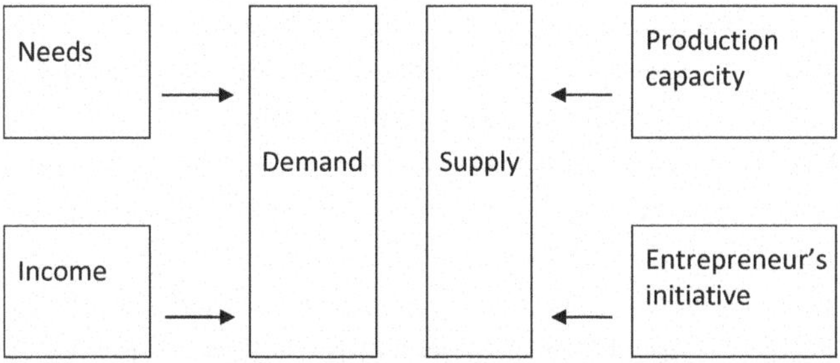

The determinant of the value is the market, which sets the scale of the relative values of different goods and labour, according to its qualifications. This mechanism is likely to bring the price of goods closer to their cost and, in turn, determines the wage scale, not according to the cost of labour—a notion rejected by Bernácer in 1916—but to its relative scarcity.

In this analysis, we note the implicit hypothesis on the market's competitive structure, which could be a vestige of classicism in Bernácer. Nevertheless, the author (1955) later explains that reality does not always reflect this perfect image of determinism. "If the reality, he says, does not meet these conditions, we must be explained why and not accept it as do those who accept the possibility of equilibrium of unemployment and those who believe in the fatality of misery."

Throughout his work, Bernácer remains faithful to the market: it is the only important element of capitalism that he keeps in the rational system he advocates. As such, for him, the market embodies freedom in the economic sense.

Incomes Other Than Salary

There are different kinds of income: unearned income, rent, interest, and profit. The differential unearned income of land is the income from monopolizing the best land. We generalize this concept by saying that all land produces unearned income, which is income, perceived without work, by the landowner, who is an absolute monopolist. There are other situations of monopoly that produce unearned income.

Rent is the price for using a property and is therefore compensation for a service. It should not be confused with unearned income. Nevertheless, rent from natural assets, particularly land and mineral resources, is unearned income that is legitimate only when the community—the only legitimate owner of the property—is the only beneficiary of this unearned income.

Conditional on the points about interest rates that we will specify in the next chapter, we can provide a few ideas to facilitate understanding of the following ideas.

(1) Bernácer condemns interest because it makes productive investment more expensive and maintains unemployment.
(2) According to Bernácer, the origin of interest is generalized unearned income.
(3) Interest is the price one must pay to generate a double dishoarding from sterile savings or speculative investments.

Profit is income that is residual, random, and stimulating. It is determined at the collective level of the production unit and is allocated through wage supplements; the entrepreneur is the primus inter pares, employee, and worker, among other roles in the business. Profit is a basic element of the dynamics of the productive system and of economic and social progress.

The Two Markets and the Production Circuit

Money has two main functions: product circulation and distribution on one hand and circulation and accumulation outside the productive channel on the other. This duality characterizes the entire economic circuit.

Production of goods and services is the primary—but not the only—source of income. There is an unproductive channel in which wealth—in monetary terms—is created. Relations between the two circuits are dialectic: there are both instantaneous and successive interactions that generate reciprocal effects. Those effects are themselves controlled by para-economic variables (psychological, sociological, historical, political, and cultural) born out of the two considered circuits. Both sources of income, production and unearned income, are co-existing.

No economic activity can exist without production. Therefore, production represents the first floor of a building on which a second floor is grafted: the financial circuit. Production is based on the concept of needs and humans' ability to satisfy them. In this market, use value prevails. This activity is restricted by the labour supply (demographic factor), by the organization and technical intensity level (technical factor). Nevertheless, these natural conditions are not the only ones; sociological and economic conditions can be added, including the ability to implement one's own work—which is a privilege of entrepreneurs—and the availability of monetary means for acquiring the necessary goods and satisfy needs during the start-up period due to the production cycle. The "product market" sets the value (purchasing power) of money, that is, the inverse of the general price level.

Bernácer published the first version of his analysis on *unearned income* and *interest rates* in 1916, in Chapters V and VI of *Society and Happiness*.

Without production, there is neither welfare nor well-being. However, at all times, some people manage to live at the expense of others' work. This domination, historically established based on factual or legal institutions, including serfdom and taxes for the benefit of certain classes under a monarchy, changed during the industrial age into practices enabled by legal, economic, and sociological institutions.

The economic substance leaking from the production circuit, namely, the use of monetary means to acquire certain goods or certain debt securities that can produce value-added, is a parasitic activity grafted on the production of goods required to satisfy needs.

Thus, at all times, these parasitic activities have been legitimized even though they represent the utter thievery of workers. They are therefore a source of income without work: through the acquisition of unearned income-yielding assets and through speculation on these goods. At all times, people have looked for unearned income, in the most perfect tradition of the *homo economicus*: incomes for which the intra-individual return on cost is highest.

The *financial market*, so named by Bernácer (or the *money and capital market*), is that in which *unearned income value* prevails. Unearned income value means the ability of an asset to produce income without work. In this market, the supply and demand of income-yielding assets determine the price and thus, at given income, the interest rate that appears as the average unearned income rate. The analysis of the financial market will be the object of the next point. Now, we will focus only on the production circuit.

The Production Circuit or the Market for Contemporary Production Includes Demand, Supply, and Market: And the Main Issue Is Equilibrium

Demand

Bernácer proposed a monetary expression of demand that implies rejection of J.B. Say lam of markets. In his 1926 article, "The Economic Cycle", Bernácer shows that the supply of a commodity does not create demand for any other commodity but money.

In a money economy, "demand does not depend on any merchandise, but only on money, and the supply depends on all other goods, since all are offered in exchange for money and only money…" (Bernácer 1955, p. 40). In fact, the law of markets makes two proposals. First, products are a source of income and therefore of demand. Second, products are exchanged against products. Bernácer acknowledges the first postulation but rejects the second, which establishes the principle of the neutrality of money. He stated in 1955 (p. 297), "What Say forgot is that we do not live in a barter system. If our economy is an exchange economy, it is also a money economy, which implies that all things will exchange through money. Money was established, among other things, such that Say's law might be fulfilled in better conditions. If it does not happen, which is obvious, there is a reason to believe that there is a fundamental flaw in the mechanism".

Bernácer thus admits that there is a dichotomy in the product distribution process. Indeed, money interferes—but plays an active role—in the trade process. As a result, according to Bernácer, demand is expressed only through money. From this point of view, he makes substantial progress over his contemporaries by definitively incorporating money into economic analysis in real terms. At the risk of exaggerating, we believe that, for Bernácer, the demand for goods is equal to money supply.

According to Bernácer, effective demand splits into consumption and investment. In his 1926 article, "The Economic Cycle", he establishes the principle that demand is a function of income, that any actual demand eliminates an equivalent amount of income, and any portion of income that does not become demand implies the existence of a stock of unsold products whose value is equal to non-demand.

Excluded from the proposed circuit are unearned income-yielding assets and intermediate consumption; their value is covered by those of goods.

According to Bernácer, consumption and investment are likewise elements of general demand that hereafter we will call aggregate demand or effective demand. There is no need to differentiate these two concepts since their effects are the same, considering equilibrium in the production market. He emphasizes only the distinction between real investment and operating capital: "Capital formation is an operation that falls under the ordinary market. The achievement of ancient capital is a neutral operation that falls under the financial market" (Bernácer 1955, p. 42). In his view, the neutrality of the operation applies to what he calls the ordinary market (market production). It would be different if we studied the effects of the implementation of capital in the financial market and its impact on the interest rate.

From Bernácer's perspective (like Keynes's), that is, with full employment as an objective, we can accept the mix of consumption and investment demands in aggregate demand. However, we cannot blame them for being included in a perspective of full employment with inflation risk. Under this hypothesis, the amounts of consumption and investment in aggregate demand are of paramount importance.

The Demand Equation

First proposed in 1916, Bernácer's aggregate demand function allows stocks to be integrated. In this way, Bernácer's concept of demand is more similar to Hawtrey's than to Keynes's, as investment, defined by Keynes as all unconsumed property in the period, is a hazy concept, according to Bernácer.

Bernácer's idea of savings is thus tautological because investment appears alongside it as a residual of goods that are produced in time—not consumed—and that are not known.

(a) If they represent authentic production goods by nature;
(b) If they are not implemented as a factor of production.

According to Bernácer, the eq. P = C + I is pure tautology.

I = (P−C) does not represent, according to Bernácer, the *demand* for investment goods. Aggregate potential demand.

As defined by Bernácer, potential demand is restrictive. It represents the maximum that can reach solvent demand during a period and not potential demand in the sense of the theory of production units.

Let

A = consumers' income from previous periods that has not yet been spent at the beginning period,
P = the income received during the period,
M = money creation in the time interval t.

$$\text{Potential demand} = A + P + M.$$

This sum represents the maximum theoretical demand likely to emerge on the goods and services market during the period. Aggregate effective demand.

At the end of the period, consumers will usually have a certain amount of unspent income. Let A′ be that sum.

During the period, private individuals loan to businesses. Let E be that amount.

During the period, a portion of E will be invested by companies in fixed capital formation (F).

The effective demand of the period becomes:

$$D = Dp - A' - (E - F)$$

If we start with our formula, Dp = A + P + M.

That is, the equation for the *aggregate potential demand*, we obtain the equation for the aggregate effective demand:

$$D = P - (A' - A) + [M - (E - F)]$$

$\Delta A = A' - A$: hoarding during the period.

$\Delta M = M - (E - F)$: money created in the period intended for consumption or fixed capital formation.

The effective demand in the period may differ from the amount of production in the period for two reasons:

- Variation in disposable funds; and.
- Creation of money allocated "to productive expenditure": consumption and investment.

We summarize this idea in the two following figures (Figs. 3.1 and 3.2):

Supply

There are two kinds of supply: potential and effective supply.

Potential Supply

According to Bernácer (1955), it is impossible to estimate supply in real terms; instead, we do so through the value of goods that compose supply. This value is defined as the sum of incomes (wages, profits, and interest) incorporated into products. Therefore,

(a) The production value in the period is the sum of the income distributed during the period, Y.
(b) The value of stocks at the beginning period is the sum of income distributed in prior periods and incorporated into goods not yet sold, Z.

USES		RESOURCES	
- Potential consumption in the period		P	Income arising from the production in the period
		+	
	Dp	A	Disposable funds (or cash) at the beginning of the period
- Potential capital formation in the period		+	
			Creation of money in the period
		M	
- Actual consumption in the period	D	P	Income arising from production in the period
Effective capital formation in the period		: ΔA	Increase in disposable cash during the period (hoarding)
		+ΔM	Money creation out of the time allocated to productive expenditure

Fig. 3.1 Balanced uses and resources

It is therefore possible to sum (a) and (b) to represent potential supply:

$$Sp = Z + Y$$

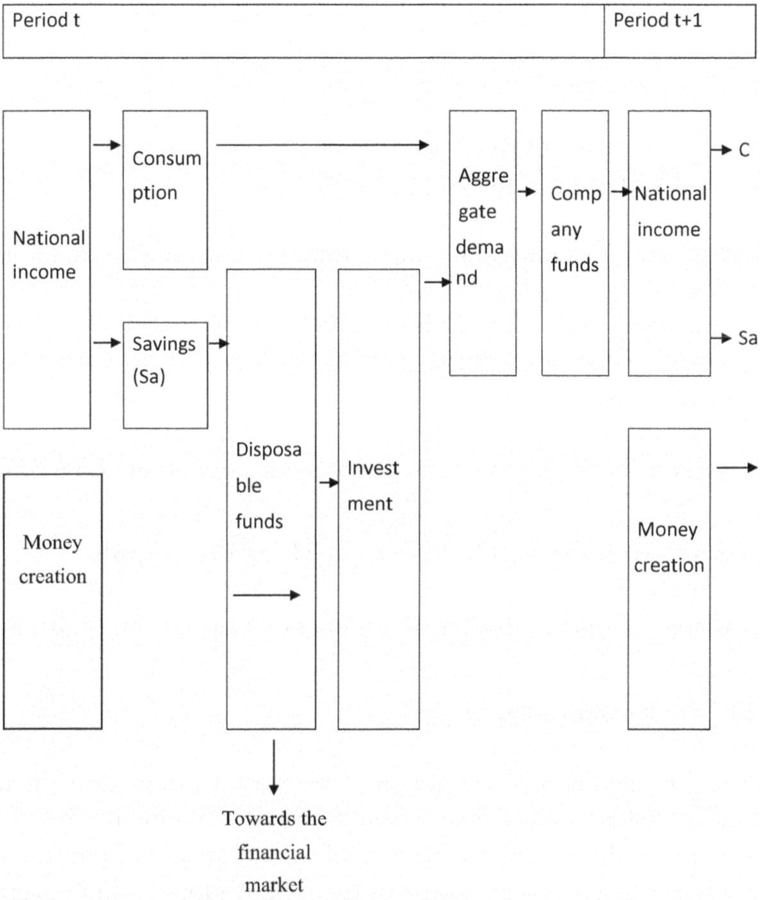

Fig. 3.2 Creation of aggregate demand

Effective supply

Effective supply is the sum of the period's income incorporated into goods sold during the period.

Let Z': stocks at the ending of the period.

$$S = S_p - Z'$$

$$S = Y - (Z' - Z)$$

$$S = Y - \Delta Z$$

With ΔZ: creation of stocks during the period.
We specify that stocks are composed of:

- Final goods (of production or consumption) not yet allocated to their final use
- Intermediate goods (semi-finished goods of consumption of production) which can't yet fulfil their final function due to their state of incompleteness

We suggest this figure to represent the market's structure (Fig. 3.3):

Variables Governing Production and, Therefore, Supply

Two variables have an influence on production: capacity and initiatives.

Physical Production Capacity

According to Bernácer, there are large reserves of production capacity. Physical capital is not as scarce as people say; the labour supply is often superfluous. In this regard, the scandal of capitalism and of political economics is to suggest that the cause of the lack of supply, which degrades purchasing power, is the scarcity of production factors. From this point of view, there is a real breach of trust. We can see the opposition between the physicist's optimism and the economist's pessimism. Nevertheless, this pessimism applies only to structures (institutional, for example) because Bernácer has faith in humans.

Production Initiatives

In capitalism, the production initiative belongs to the capitalist; in any case, production cannot occur without him or her. Nevertheless, monetary

<table>
<tr><td rowspan="2">Goods produced during the period</td><td>Consumption goods</td><td rowspan="4">Potential aggregate supply in the period on the ordinary market (or production market)</td><td rowspan="4">Aggregate demand in the period</td><td rowspan="6">Income in the period</td></tr>
<tr><td>Production goods</td></tr>
<tr><td rowspan="3">Goods produced during prior periods</td><td>Stock of consumption goods</td></tr>
<tr><td>Stock of production goods</td></tr>
<tr><td>Inheritance of sustainable unearned income-yielding assets</td><td rowspan="2">Potential supply on the financial market (or speculative market)</td><td rowspan="2">Demand for unearned income-yielding assets</td></tr>
<tr><td>Portfolio of assets</td><td>Investments in debt securities and transferable values
New issuances</td></tr>
</table>

Fig. 3.3 Market structure

or institutional constraints make these investment opportunities scarce (Bernácer 1916, p. 205).

There are several causes of this shortage; however, most are related to economic, political, social, and legal institutions, which cause market disequilibria.

Market Equilibrium

Let us note the progression of the following works: Bernácer 1916, p. 15; 1922, 1926, 1929, op. cit.

According to Bernácer (1955), admitting the possibility that there is equilibrium on the market implies admitting the principle of equality between product and income. So, the principle of equilibrium follows from an accounting approach to income and production. The brief demonstration of equality between income and product make sense in terms of two propositions (Fig. 3.4):

	PRODUCT		REVENUE	
Time 0 Period 1	Stocks = 0 Production value in the period	Sales of consumer goods Sales of capital goods	Consumption expenditure Investment expenditure	Income from production Disposable funds at the beginning of the period = 0
		Stocks formation during the time = balance	Disposable funds = final balance	
Time 1	ΣP	ΣP	ΣR	ΣR
Period 2	Initial balance = Stocks at the beginning of the period			Initial balance = Disposable income at the beginning of the period

Fig. 3.4 Market equilibrium: Product = Revenue

(a) Any income of a micro-unit distributed during the production increases the "value" of social product.

$$\Delta R = \Delta P$$

(b) If this is true for an item, it is true for the sum of the components (aggregation process).

$$\sum \Delta R = \sum \Delta P$$

Any variation in the exchange value of the aggregate product involves a variation in the aggregate income in a similar direction and amplitude. Indeed, it would be illogical and vain to seek an instantaneous balance position if income flow were permanently and definitively different from the value of goods.

Our diagram below fairly reproduces the financial perspective of Bernácer's equilibrium:

Hypothesis: overall balance at time 0.
Stocks = disposable funds.

Consequences:

- If Δ_1 Stocks = Δ_1 disposable funds: overall balance at period 1
- If Δ_1 Stocks $\neq$ Δ_1 disposable funds: imbalance

Since traded quantities are identical, the imbalance results in a "value" balance with price variation. The result of an overall imbalance on the market will be a change in the general price level. If we accept proposals (a) and (b), we postulate the existence of a potential equilibrium. Price stability, which was mentioned by Bernácer as an equilibrium condition, does not have the same status as it does in Wicksell's theory. Wicksell—as almost all non-Marxist economists before 1930—is a theorist of equilibrium, unlike Bernácer, for whom equilibrium is virtual and a simple repository. Nevertheless, history shows that, to date, there has never been a sustainable and stable equilibrium, but it does not mean there could never be. We must investigate the causes of disequilibrium. Market instability may be due to either company strategy or consumer behaviour for purely monetary reasons, such as money creation or the use of consumers' loans to businesses.

The Question of Profit

Bernácer addresses an objection made to him, namely, that equality between supply and demand proceed from simple tautological reasoning. This objection would be true if profit were not the link between ex-ante and ex-post concepts of supply and demand, which are at best implicit in Bernácer. Bernácer focuses mainly on the calculation of profit. Indeed, a priori, demand is not equal to supply. Even so, when transactions occur, saying that supply is equal to demand is like saying that the amount of assets that changed hands during the session is unique, which is factual evidence, and therefore that the sum of money representing the exchange value of this unique quantity of goods is itself unique.

Profit plays a decisive role in the equilibrium of supply and demand by matching costs and market prices. Furthermore, fluctuations in profit are very connected to those prices.

If we consider profit as income that has the same nature as other revenue arising from production and distributed during the same period, it is quite certain that supply and demand are necessarily and automatically equivalent and that equality between supply and demand is pure tautology. Indeed, profit randomness, which is essentially of a residual nature, ensures that, by definition, profit related to a given production flow balances supply and demand. The disequilibrium may therefore occur when profit determination and distribution are always a posteriori.

It is important to know at what time income should be accounted: is it due to their payable nature or due to their effective payment? In market analysis, it is appropriate to seize these incomes when they turn into demand. Observations show that, at the overall level, one can dispose of past or contemporary incomes but not of future income. Some agents can spend their future income now[2] because other agents agree to loan. This case was considered under two headings in the demand analysis: money creation and loans.

A shareholder must wait for the end of the financial year before knowing his profit share; in the same way, an employee has to wait one month to be able to spend the income gained from his or her current labour. This shift is similar—only the length of time is different.

The notion of profit should be extended to the undistributed portion: self-financing. We must consider that the shareholder has received the full benefit and that he or she lends a share in his or her own business. This case has already been considered in determining demand under the name "loans for financing companies' working capital".

A Revenue Accounting Convention

A generalization of the profit accounting method results in a permanent disparity between working capital and income variations from the previous period to the current one. This disparity arises when elements of cost are integrated into the price of sold goods or stocks.

Therefore, an imbalance between supply and demand occurs without price variations from one period to another. This imbalance consists only of variation in working capital. Indeed, working capital incorporates payable but non-liquidated elements (taxes, unearned income, and interest), while corporate debt to their collectors (government, owners, and lenders) is not counted.

This calculation would not offer many disadvantages over a longer period—at least one year—because all or most payable income would actually be distributed. Nevertheless, an analysis over such a long period would be inappropriate for highlighting the real explanation for the forces governing the market. We should use a short operational period and, hence, we need to adopt an accounting policy based on the following three elements.

(a) Considering the need to consider that profit is known only at the end of the period;
(b) Considering the accounting need to match the income paid during production and product market prices;
(c) Considering that the reference period should be as short as we like for the purposes of supply and demand fluctuation analysis on the market.

We recognize:

– That all incomes in the period are disposable at the end of the period or, if preferred,-that income from production completed during the period (t) will be spent only in the period (t + 1).

In this analysis, we observe a significant contribution by Bernácer to the dynamic economy at the conceptual level: an analysis of successive periods, where authorship is too often attributed to Robertson. Bernácer's theory appeared not only earlier but also higher than that of Robertson, thanks to Bernácer's conception of continuous time (see the chapter below, the functional theory of money).

The Nature of Equilibrium

In monetary terms, exchange is always balanced. What we refer to as disequilibrium is reflected in another area—that of all traded goods assigned with a coefficient value. The following development is not explained by Bernácer and will avoid distorting his thinking with our words.

Disequilibrium has an epiphenomenon—price change—which reveals disequilibrium between the physical quantities of supplied and demanded goods. Nonetheless, this disequilibrium would be inappropriate as an explanation for price changes if there is a mechanism for balancing the market: price. If we acknowledge that the proposed price before a transaction includes wages for employee labour directly or indirectly incorporated into the product, investment and budgeted profit (company's compensation), and all the predetermined elements of a transaction, we might assume that the exchange value of these goods is a priori equal to the cost of these factors. The price that will lead to a disequilibrium between supply and demand after the transaction will affect the only element that can fluctuate: real profit. We introduced the expression of budgeted profit to denote the expected profit in the beginning period by the contractor, given the real profit rate in the previous period. This notion, similar to that of "normal" profit for Keynes ("Treatise"), has contents that Bernácer considers more objective and less psychological.

Actual profit = budgeted profit + relative appreciation of the good by market or relative depreciation of the good by market.

Then, we can roughly conclude that disequilibrium expresses a gap between value and price. A price increase would occur because buyers are willing to give monetary compensation that is greater than the product "value" estimated ex ante.

The Conditions of Equilibrium

> ... with a certain purchasing power, we acquire the same amount of income units contained in purchased goods. This is what I call the market equilibrium, as it involves the price level stability (Bernácer 1955, p. 63).

The equilibrium stability condition results from hypotheses and their consequences. Initially, a hypothesis is made regarding overall equilibrium on the goods market. Added to this are the non-creation of money during the period and consumer loans to entrepreneurs used to finance working capital. This hypothesis has two consequences:

(a) Initially, equality between the purchasing power of disposable income and unsold production value. Prices are stable since buyers have at hand a just and strict amount of money units to buy the stocks of goods held by sellers. There is a contradiction between (a) and (b). Starting from a given level of balance, it matters that changes in stocks of goods and disposability—and not necessarily their absolute values—are equal: it is $\Delta A(t) = \Delta Z(t)$ and not $A(t) = Z(t)$ that is required as a condition necessary and sufficient for balance.

(b) Any positive or negative increase in overall income will be concomitant with the production increase with the same sign and amplitude. The condition of equilibrium, or if we prefer, of price stability, is that at any moment, the changes in stocks of goods must be equal to the changes in disposable fund volumes; disposable cash balances are unspent revenues.

(c) Introducing money and loan creation between consumers and producers does not modify the equilibrium as long as there is compensation between supply and demand.

$$\Delta M = \Delta A + (E - F) - \Delta Z$$
$$-\Delta M + \Delta A + (E - F) - \Delta Z = 0$$

As possible factors of disequilibrium, we can include those mentioned implicitly above: behaviours of consumers and entrepreneurs, money creation, hoarding, and international trade. We only evoke disequilibria here, dedicating a chapter to analyse the factors with static and dynamic order.

The Mechanism of the Financial Market and the Interest Rate

The mechanism of the financial market and the existence of the rate of interest account for the general economic activity disequilibria.

Financial Market

The first description of an unearned income-yielding assets market appears in Bernácer, Chapters III, IV, and V, *Society and Happiness* (1916), his article published in 1922, and his book *Interest of Capital* (1925). Additionally, this thesis was detailed in several articles: in 1926, "The Business Cycle"; in 1934, "On the Origin of Crisis" and "The Training and the Vicissitudes of Savings"; and in 1935, "The Theory of the Financial Market" and "Money and the Economic Cycle". Finally, in his 1955 synthesis book *Free Economy* the author perfectly fits the second largest market into the overall scheme.

Wages are generally spent to buy goods from usual production. Nevertheless, a fraction of wages is continually diverted from its "natural" use to unearned income-yielding uses that do not involve work (work in Bernácer's extensive sense, i.e., active participation in production). Bernácer calls the financial market—or the *unearned income-yielding assets market*—the place of supply and of demand for these assets. Bernácer sometimes uses the term *financial market* (mercado financiero) and sometimes the term "unearned income-yielding assets market" (mercado de rentas). Note that this expression (literally in English: unearned income market) summarizes Bernácer's view that the financial market is more of a market with the exchange of cash units for goods, although these two things are inseparable. We translate assets—the term "valores de renta"—into English as "income-yielding assets", as Robertson did; however, this translation is ambiguous or even wrong. These assets consist of real property and debt securities.

Parallel Market

The expression *parallel* is ours: it is borrowed from the vocabulary of the stock trade. Nevertheless, we should not push the analogy to the transposition of a geometric expression because, as we shall see later, this parallel market has many points of contact with the production market.

Rent and speculation are demons that tempt holders of disposable funds. These holders sometimes abandon their roles as consumers or investors to become hoarders and then speculators and unearned income-seekers either by themselves or through an intermediary. This diversion of disposable funds has a significant impact on productive activity.

Unearned Income, Speculation, and Hoarding

The *homo economicus* tries to maximize his or her satisfaction functions, including minimizing his or her cost. Among the elements of cost, one is intimately perceived and accepted by the individual: the personal work conducted to obtain satisfaction, and we might say, a wage, as work is the primary way to obtain an income. This principle of the individual economy—selfishness—originates from a historical practice that is more or less developed according to socio-political regimes, where people always look for an advantageous position in economic activity.

The conditions for the existence of unearned income are institutional. The first condition is the right to private property, which legally consecrates an individual's absolute dominion over a thing. This right goes against others' and represents a real monopoly.

The second is a condition of the prosperity phenomenon: it is the existence of a market organized on the basis of the freedom of contract and, thus, of the exchangeability of unearned income-yielding assets. In this market, the demands of the unearned income seekers and the supply of the unearned income holders willing to cede those assets—provided that sufficient value-added is granted—come into conflict. This value-added in itself is true unearned income and is the basis for a specific form of it: speculation. This second condition distinguishes unearned income from taxes and adds to unearned income a perverse effect that does not have a tax.

At all times, people have been fixed to perfect game structures: speculation is based on a betting notion. The fluctuations of speculation issues are more frequent in a game than in an economic situation. Bernácer provides a broad definition of speculation. Any investment is, in a sense, a speculative operation, at least because of uncertainty about the future (nominal or real) amount of income, of prices of the securities, or of property. A financial transaction consists of the exchange of current money against future money.

Furthermore, Bernácer argues that money supply is not homogenous: current amounts of money spent on such operations cannot be confused with those that individuals allocate to consumption or those that entrepreneurs need for their usual business operations. It is a fraction of the current money that composes financial market demand. Bernácer refers to it with the concept of disposable funds.

"In Latin countries' broker language, the word 'disponibilidad' (disposable funds) is commonly used to refer to money that is likely to be allocated, as opposed to securities, which, although converted into money, do not represent disposable funds for their holders but rather demand for disposable funds or cash, when they wish to have it. It is also used to differentiate 'free' amounts and amounts allocated to other operations. It is a useful concept for scientific terminology". I recently saw the English term of "disposability" used in a similar way (see Robertson, *Utility and All That and Other Essays*, p. 85–86).

Unearned income and speculation's effect of unearned income can be called "double hoarding". This term is ours; it seeks to avoid any vagueness with the current concept—hoarding—which is very restrictive. We use the term "double hoarding" because it corresponds to Bernácer's idea (which is broader than that of Keynes') of hoarding in the form of money in potentially lucrative operations and in the form of money in currently lucrative operations outside of production. Indeed, the prospect of unearned income attracts disposable funds (or cash balances) outside the production circuit, where they allow the product to be acquired to integrate the market for unearned income-yielding assets.

These disposable funds have two positions:

(a) A standby position outside the production circuit but within the financial circuit: this is the position that Keynes called the preference for cash (speculative motive);
(b) A position of means of payment in financial market operations: the effect is the same regardless of whether these disposable funds are in the hands of operators-buyers or operators-sellers.

Therefore, besides hoarded money, which is in the expectation of an advantageous transaction, there is a permanent stock of money used for non-production transactions. The cause of a scarcity of disposable funds on the production market—that is, a scarcity of money (so-called abusively because money is not scarce on the financial market)—is twofold, but the essential effect is the same: to maintain outside the production circuit a money supply that does not perform its natural function of the purchasing power of goods issued by contemporary production.

Bernácer (1916, p. 157) also provides an approach to hoarding in dynamic terms: "Economists have generally neglected, for simplicity, the time required for the formation of accumulations and for the implementation of all these operations that hold disposable funds on the financial market, thus fulfilling no productive work and causing no effect on the demand for real products". We perceive in this quote, on one hand, that time in itself may be an additional and immediate cause of hoarding and, on the other hand, that dynamic analysis can reveal only some perverse effects of certain phenomena.

We interpret Bernácer's thoughts on this crucial point of his theory in the following way. Bernácer creates a double generalization: that of *unearned income* and that of *hoarding*. Unearned income is due to perverse institutions and consists of all income derived from non-work, in the sense of income gains from inheritance. The immediate effect of unearned income is hoarding: all money diverted from product circulation is hoarded in cash form either because of the expectation of a speculative transaction or because of time lags between payment and cashing. Remember that, according to Bernácer, hoarding sometimes has a very broad and still functional sense: a hoarded disposable fund is a disposable fund that has not yet been used in market demand for contemporary production.

The Financial Market, a Competitor of Contemporary Production

Competition in the financial market thrives at two levels:

(a) The amount of hoarded disposable funds reduces effective demand. We will call hoarded funds those we have previously defined as disposable funds that are subtracted from the production market or that are used in speculative operations (without being considered in the production circuit), pending the completion of such operations.
(b) The financial market provides income without work (unearned income in every sense). Accordingly, any use of disposable funds must provide income at least equal to the average income of the financial market to attract disposable funds and to face the competition from the financial market.

To the extent that we denounce unearned income, it is certain that the existence of average unearned income rates distorts economic calculations for the production market.

The Perverse Effect of the Financial Market on Effective Demand: Leaks in the Contemporary Production Circuit

We will first explain production circuit leaks in terms of energy loss and potential decreases.

Any subtraction of money from the production circuit leads to a lack of purchasing power and, thus, a lack of buying decisions involving consumer goods or capital goods. In each case, depressive effects on the production system occur, which can generate income and satisfaction. Any system in which a power loss occurs loses power, and its performance decreases. We have seen that the depressing effect of hoarding is expressed through the failure of the product purchase decision of consumer goods or of capital goods. Therefore, the aggregate effective demand decreases.

We must highlight that the aggregate potential demand, whether solvent or insolvent, is not lower than the aggregate potential supply, whether effective or ineffective, because the overall real product needs are never saturated. Bernácer rejects the notion of overall overproduction and therefore the concept of sustainable overall overinvestment. Economic agents are always able to absorb the quantities they produce and generate income through that production. However, the monetary means to buy the product are lacking.

The existence of idle disposable funds at the overall level shows that scarcity does not arise from the community's powerlessness to buy all of the production but rather from a *deficit* of agents who are willing to buy but who temporarily lack of the means of payment and cannot find the money for their purchasing activity—economic activity par excellence—from agents who have excess money.

The community does not find this inter-agent *credit* because agents with excess hoard, as there are unearned income opportunities for owners of disposable funds. Eliminating these opportunities would solve the alleged scarcity of money problem.

The Effects of the Financial Market on Production, Investment, and Employment or the Problem of Non-profitability Outside Production

The financial market has a second perverse effect, and we wonder if it could be the second face of Janus. Indeed, hoarding—the financial market's monopoly over purchasing power—is due to the existence of a type of profitability specific to the financial market that acts as bait.

Nevertheless, profitability in monetary terms is itself due to the profusion of disposable funds on the money market. In fact, there is a *feedback* effect that maintains the process and that produces two forms of a unique phenomenon: unearned income.

If we examine the case of unearned income (other than that resulting from speculation, a source of value-added), we observe that someone who demands unearned income-yielding assets is willing to purchase a certain number of unearned income units per period. There is therefore a supply of and demand for unearned income (excluding unearned income-yielding assets), and at any time the market balances them through the price of an unearned income unit.

Let P_t be the price at time (t), while the ratio $\frac{1}{P_t}$ represents the profitability of a unit of unearned income-yielding assets or, if you prefer, a compensation rate of the monetary investment in unearned income. All money holders with access to a direct or indirect financial market will therefore assess all proposed investment programmes based on their profitability. They will thus rank them compared to $\frac{1}{P_t}$. Let C1, C2, and C3 be the three proposed programmes and r (C) be their productivity rate:

$$r(C_1);r(C_2);r(C_3)$$

C1: direct real estate investment.
C2: direct investment in industry.
C3: loan.

Let $\frac{1}{P(L)_t}$ be the productivity rate of more cash investment; it seems clear, then, that all r (Ci) and the net rate of productivity of any lower cash investment C_i must be $> \frac{1}{P(L)_t}$.

We can find examples of P $(L)_t$ such as the weekly interest rate of euro currency or stock exchange deferral, with the borrower taking a cash advance to defer the liquidation of a transaction to the next month. A particular case of these investments is investment financing on the productive market. Any investment in production must have greater performance than the safest investment in the financial market. Taking this requirement into account is like introducing an additional term into the investment cost, meaning that it is outbid. The profitability in the financial market leads to lower levels of investment because the equilibrium price is higher and thus prevents short-term production growth.

The effects on employment are similar because, if we admit that, at the macroeconomic level, there is primarily a complementary relation between capital and labour as a factor of production, any instance of job creation requires a parallel capital investment. At the overall level, technical progress is not incompatible with this notion of complementarity. In the long term, financial market repercussions consist of increasing growth by incorporating technological progress more slowly. All other things being equal, it is clear that lower innovation costs would allow technological progress to be incorporated at a faster rate in the contemporary production circuit.

In summary, the instant effect decreases levels of production and employment. Ultimately, technical progress, growth, and thus welfare decrease due to the competitive nature of the financial market.

Market Components

There are three main market variables: the demand for unearned income-yielding assets, the supply, and the financial market equilibrium. Even though we have so far avoided using the expression *interest rate*, it was implicit in the previous paragraphs. Bernácer assimilates the yield rate of *unearned income yielding assets* and the interest rate. From now on, we will use the second expression: *interest rate.*

Demand for Unearned Income Yielding Assets

According to Bernácer, the analysis of demand does not raise any particular problem. It is usually a direct function of the interest rate and is subject to budget constraints: the policy of the open market or of issuance.

We can add that demand analysis also includes an expression for money supply on the financial market.

The potential demand Dp consists of:

$$Dp = \text{Disposable funds} + \text{Credit}$$

$$Dp = f(i) \text{ or } f\left(\frac{1}{p}\right)$$

Supply

The current potential supply, that is, all assets likely to be traded on the financial market, is very large in absolute value in regard to the volume of disposable funds likely to be allocated. When financial panic occurs, certain assets collapse and the rate increases to extraordinary heights.

Furthermore, the current potential supply has a certain elasticity based on business prospects and on low interest rates: issuance of new securities (securities themselves or debt) can increase the potential supply.

Supply is a decreasing function of asset prices and therefore an increasing function of interest rates.

Financial Market Equilibrium

The financial market does not exist alone: there are multiple markets, such as the market for consumer goods. Financial markets therefore have a complex structure, including a varying degree of internal organization and more or less complex interconnections. For example, it is easier to move from the government funds to industrial securities on the stock market than on the mortgage market. These movements depend on agent information and habits and on cost transfers, among other factors.

Nonetheless, this complex market exhibits movement to unite the various markets within it. This movement can be promoted by such actions as arbitration or the spontaneous transfer of operations from one market to another. Nevertheless, this standardization trend does not imply the existence of a single financial productivity rate.

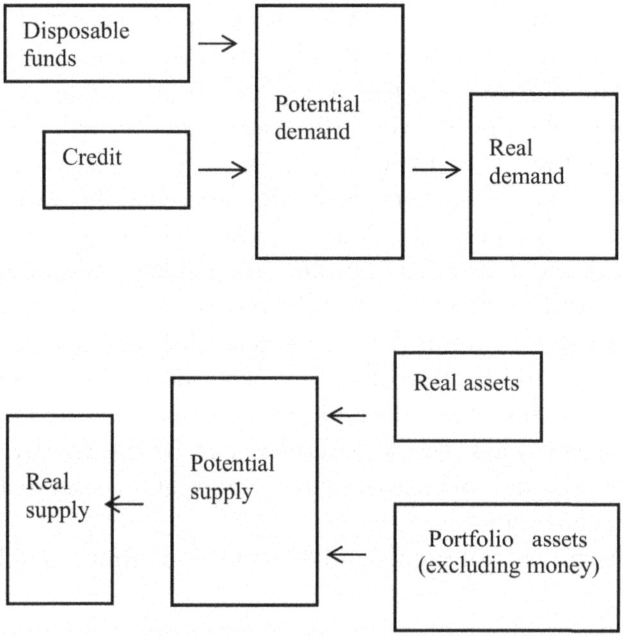

Fig. 3.5 Financial market structure

We propose the following diagram for the financial market (Fig. 3.5):

The common denominator of supply and demand to aggregate the various assets, which is the goal of a transaction, is the price of an unearned income unit, as the appropriation of unearned income is the goal of asset acquisition. However, unearned income, even expressed in value units, is not homogeneous: not all forms of unearned income have the same degree of security because some are certain and others are random. Nevertheless, it is possible to define a concept of the unity-type of unearned income because different unearned income actually observed scatter around the average value, which represents the unit.

We cannot criticize Bernácer for this simplification because any theory—particularly in economics, but not exclusively—is based on this method of analysis. Therefore, when speaking of interest rates or price, using the singular corresponds to the generic sense. Reformulating Keynesian theory, Hansen (1953) speaks of the "pure" interest rate. Nevertheless, Robinson (1953, p. 23) emphasizes the diversity of rates, "talking about the interest rate as Keynes did does not give an adequate response to the question". Gurley and Shaw (1960) agree with Robinson on this point and insist on the diversification of core assets; therefore, they do not subscribe to Marx, Bernácer, and Keynes's thesis of the uniqueness of the rate as it appears.

Non-contemporary authors apparently proceeded this way, regardless of their school. With regard to Marxists, Denis (1950, p. 438) says, "The trend towards the unification of profit rates (tendency toward the formation of a general profit rate in Marxist theory) is quite generally recognized so that we can admit that a very general theory of capital interest starts from the consideration of a profit rate expected by all capitalists".

Nevertheless, this price—the typical unit of unearned income—can be expressed in two ways: we can consider it to be the relative unearned income of a price unit of an asset or as the price of the asset that yields an unearned income unit.

We can write the real supply and demand equilibrium as follows:

$$S = D = f(i) \text{ or } S = D = f\left(\frac{1}{p}\right)$$

i = relative unearned income of a unit of asset price
p = price of unearned income-yielding asset

The transaction volume can be expressed either by the number of typical unearned income units exchanged or the total price of the assets that changed hands. This equilibrium has several characteristics: it is instantaneous and essentially unstable because transactions on this market, rather than meeting real needs, as in the production market, more often meet speculative bets. This means that in these transactions, we usually expect deviations from the previously reached equilibrium. Moreover, this market is hypersensitive to the slightest conjectures, with the particularity that in certain collective psychology circumstances, demand may be a decreasing function of the interest rate and supply a decreasing function of the price. The normal conditions for market disruption then lead to a change in the curves' shape.

The Interest Rate

Bernácer (1955) justifies the importance of researching the origin of interest for the rest of the theoretical analysis as follows: "No one can think that this is a problem of pure scientific speculation; it is instead a very practical question that leads me to ask it, to be precise, the ability to find a way to take action on economic fluctuations by radically correcting them at the base. If interest, as some authors assert, is a normal and necessary phenomenon that appears in both socialist and capitalist societies, in both natural and mercantilist economies, economic fluctuations would be an inevitable fact that we would be forced to admit and that we could at most strive to overcome... Nevertheless, if interest is an institutional phenomenon, we can find, through an appropriate reform, the stabilization of the economy".

Basic Opposition to the Theories of Interest

Bernácer first distances himself from classical theorists by stating that abstinence is not the cause of interest that effort towards savings is a myth and that savings would exist even in the absence of interest. From this point of view, Bernácer is the first post-classical theorist.

The author explains the existence of savings by factors unrelated to interest. The current saturation of needs, the future timing of satisfaction, and, we might add in general, the law of decreasing marginal utility incite people to spontaneously save, without needing to be compelled by interest. Any manager with a budget knows that expenditures should be staggered when the income perception time differs from expense completion. A priori, interest plays no role in this savings function.

The third argument is that of inflation: despite the monetary erosion phenomenon, agents save because they would ultimately rather dispose of depreciated purchasing power over having no future purchasing power at all. Bernácer summarizes his refutation of the theory of the premium in this way; we present it as a psychological theory, but the saver psychology indicates that due to savings, future satisfaction is more valuable than current satisfaction. Finally, Bernácer rejects the productivist thesis, which serves as the starting point for the classical theory of interest. For him, there is confusion between the concept of real capital and that of financial capital (or money).

This confusion was maintained by the classics, so Bernácer—before Joan Robinson—attaches great importance to this point in economic terminology. He uses the word "capital" to describe that only the physical means of production is always more precise in the case of financial capital, using the terms "financial" or "monetary". Real capital appears as the materialized product of labour, while financial capital is the result of savings.

According to Bernácer, monetary capital—an instrument for acquiring real capital—has no productivity in itself: sharing the fruits of capital between the entrepreneur and the capitalist (the provider of monetary capital) is not an intrinsic consequence of the industrial production regime but rather results from institutionalized practices.

The Foundations of the Interest Rate in Bernácer's View

Bernácer's point of view on interest rates is multiform, integrating diverse original foundations: the religious history, the historical socio-political reality, and the sales of disposable funds. Bernácer appears as a visionary. The institutionalization of interest as a legal practice would be a historic victory, similar to that of Protestant morality over Catholic morality in hegemonic countries, or if we refer to the history of thought, of the victory of Calvin's and Luther's ideas over those of scholastics such as Saint-Thomas d'Aquin.

According to Bernácer, interest proceeds from unearned income, which resulted from military, political, and social domination and corresponds to their economic emergence. Unearned income has two faces: it is a monopoly (absolute opposability between certain rights) and a theft (conscious or discreet authoritarian direct debit of the work of authentic producers). Unearned income is the product of private land ownership and, historically, owners have had to share this unearned income with other agents: the lord, the clergy, the finance steward (sometimes in the name of the king), the middle-class lender, or the foreign occupier. Despite this sharing, the ownership of unearned income-yielding assets is attractive. In a republic, middle-class citizens' loans to the government are subject to the payment of unearned income (sometimes into perpetuity).

If we accept this interpretation of the facts, interest is logically money holders' theft of the product created by active agents of production; it is a genuine social and economic privilege. Agents with lucrative employment opportunities and with no disposable funds can find agents with disposable funds who are unable or unwilling to use them directly but are willing to offer their use in exchange for compensation. This compensation is the interest on the loan. Therefore, a loan in itself is not the cause of interest. An additional condition is necessary: the profit orientation of the loan of disposable funds. Therefore, an entrepreneur borrows to invest in real capital because—in normal times—the investment will provide him additional profit on which he or she may debit the interest payable to the lender.

If profit is insufficient or non-existent, the entrepreneur still has the choice—rightly or wrongly—to borrow. From this point of view, Bernácer is not completely against the productivist thesis, provided we think in real terms (in constant monetary value units and not in physical terms) about both capital and product and we make no petition about the appropriation of investment overproduction. Still, if we reason by contradiction, we observe that the entrepreneur, knowing (or anticipating the result of the decision will be the same) that the planned investment is not likely to generate a surplus value at least equal to the interest of the loan, does not commit to either an investment or a loan. Bernácer's position is not ambiguous: there is, once again, a sequential approach, as the relations between the determinants of interest are unequivocal and irreversible:

- Requirement 1: we need a market free from unearned income-yielding assets,
- Requirement 2: we need disposable funds: savings or money creation,
- Requirement 3: we need the production market to provide compensation for the invested disposable funds.

If these three conditions are met, there will be a loan market for businesses, with possible interest. However, without the first condition, it is not clear why disposable fund holders would oppose the use of loans in industry, without interest. It would suffice that loan risk (impairment of the value of the monetary capital or insolvency of the borrower) is then provided according to techniques that currently exist (indexing and credit insurance).

Interest: Exogenous to the Production Circuit

The production market-financial market complex is a hierarchical structure in which the second dominates the first. At the moment, the financial market commands production and employment and, ultimately, investment programmes, production growth, and therefore economic and social progress. The instrument of this domination is the interest rate. "Interest is therefore a phenomenon that goes from outside to inside the company; it is not an 'indigenous' fact. Current interest indicates the profit level of capital that should not be exceeded, as a lock indicates a canal's maximum level. Without interest, we would allocate all capital that would offer savings compared to the maintenance and depreciation cost. Interest delays savings capitalization, even if it is high. Anyone who believes that interest causes savings valued in monetary terms and produced by capital in real terms has inverted the terms" (Bernácer 1955, p. 162).

This long quotation from the author summarizes his theory of interest, a theory with three components:

(a) Theory of voluntary abstinence,
(b) Theory of cash, or "disposable funds" in Bernácer's language, and
(c) Theory of real capital productivity.

Determination of the Interest Rate

The determination of the rate of interest is based on its formation in the financial market and its duality. The formation of interest rates on the financial market

At a given time, the financial market receives demands for disposable funds (money) from different origins:

(a) (Pre-existing) securities providers,
(b) Sales of real assets (unearned income-yielding assets, like securities (a),
(c) Borrowers (regardless of loan allocation, even if it is for consumption),
(d) Real capital direct industrial investors, against the issuance of new debt securities. These securities, moreover, will be part of (a) during the next period, when the current buyers will be sellers.

Money suppliers compete, and ceteris paribus, the interest rate for each asset tends towards equilibrium under the marginalist theory of prices.

To obtain disposable funds required for investments, the entrepreneur must offer the financial market the same interest as his or her competitors seeking disposable funds, after which he or she may acquire real capital assets in the production market and, on the labour market, hire the labour necessary for their implementation.

The Duality of the Interest Rate

In fact, in the two markets, there are two complex long-term interest rates: the interest of the actual financial market and the industrial investment profitability rate. The first is clearly defined by the supply and demand interaction for unearned income-yielding assets due to the unification trend of different investments yields resulting from general arbitration. A concrete form of these yields is represented by the fixed interest bonds, for example. The second depends on many factors and is essentially based on the ratio $\frac{\text{Sales Price}}{\text{Factor and intermediate consumption costs}}$.

It is measured only at the production unit level and may be substantially different because of the low mobility of real factors. This rate fluctuates with changes in effective demand, productivity, and wage levels. Furthermore, the business cycle phase depends on the relative position of interest rates on the financial market. In contrast, the mobility of money capital in the financial market is the cause of greater market volatility and a greater uniformity of concrete interest rates on the financial market.

This duality of interest rates is at the origin of the explanation for cycle mechanisms. The role of the interest rate in fluctuations and economic growth will be discussed first in the analysis of the disequilibrium of the capitalist system and then in the comparative study of the second section. It is therefore too early to talk about it here because, from Bernácer's point of view, interest must be considered a disturbing element of equilibrium and not a necessary element of it. This reason also encourages us not to further investigate the effects of the interest rate on the production market beyond what has been seen previously.

We start by defining and analysing disequilibria.

Disequilibria

Various theories explain the economic disequilibrium and link it with unemployment

Virtuality of General Equilibrium or Failures of Automatic Regulators

Some other variables are considered in Bernácer's equilibrium theory: the effect of international trade, gold price movements, and second-hand goods transactions

The Effects of International Trade

Bernácer (1955, p. 67) stated, "The fact, perhaps surprising, is that trade imbalance affects supply and potential demand in the same way. By itself, it does not imbalance the internal market, if not indirectly, to the extent that it can simultaneously increase or decrease effective demand and supply". Bernácer's position is explained by the fact that he implicitly considers the balance of payments to be, by definition, in a state of equilibrium, and, thus, there is automatic compensation between surplus or current transaction deficit and capital deficit or surplus (in the monetary sense, of course). In this light, the current transaction surplus creates its own monetary compensation. Therefore, for example, an excess of imports over exports, in real terms, has compensation in potential demand financed by credit from abroad, or gold dishoarding used in one way or another to resolve the current transaction deficit.

Due to a lack of serious debate on this international economic issue, we are content to accept the author's view, stressing the hypothesis ceteris paribus that *commercial* imbalance may not extend indefinitely. Nonetheless, this hypothesis remains relevant to Bernácer's general approach to self-adjustment mechanisms. In conclusion, international trade has a neutral impact on immediate overall equilibrium.

Gold Price Movements

When gold is considered as a good, when the payment for a balance of trade is made in gold, the effects are similar for both trader countries:

(a) In a country with surplus imports, the surplus of "real" goods is exchanged for "gold-goods", which does not alter the effective supply;
(b) In a country with surplus exports, the surplus of exported goods is replaced by "gold-goods", which has the same effect as in (a).

Bernácer (1955, p. 70) said, "Gold is substituted with exported goods in the commercial stocks. The exporters' 'surplus' of goods is paid by gold importers, like when exporting oranges and importing coal, the orange exporters are paid with the money of coal importers, while in the country where gold comes from, gold exporters are paid by importers with the surplus of common goods".

The particularity of gold therefore resides in the potential monetary effects on supply and demand of these movements, that is, when banks' gold deposits give rise to common issuance.

Disposable funds increase as in the case of money creation in a closed economy: it follows an increase in potential demand.

The stocks of goods that compose potential supply decrease due to gold's disappearance from the real goods market. Therefore, variation occurs in the opposite direction of the potential supply and demand, which explains the inflationary effect of gold imports, followed by issuance and the deflationary effect of gold exports accompanied by *gold demonetization*. Due to their internal subsidiary effects, gold movements are a disruptive element of equilibrium. Even so, they are not in themselves a priori inflationary or deflationary; therefore, we need an additional condition for this: money issuance as compensation. We are inclined to say that issuance must be incriminated, that gold movements do not allow judgements of the attitude of the central bank, for example, that cash gold is among many reasons to issue paper money. By generalizing Bernácer's position, every monetization of real goods is a source of imbalance. Bernácer also notes that these effects involve non-virtual movements of gold. Moreover, when the deficit payment is not really made in gold, we return to the previously considered case (see above) of a neutral compensation effect of real property movements by "monetary capital" movements.

Second-Hand Goods Transactions

Some goods that are produced in prior periods reappear on the market during a current period, with their old buyers feeling the need, according to the current language, to *resell* them or *achieve* them. Bernácer distinguishes two cases:

(a) Traders' purchase from individuals to resell to individuals.

In this case, supply and potential demand simultaneously increase because the price paid by the trader increases the demand, while goods transferred by individual increase supply. It follows an a priori increase in supply and the concomitant effective demand, or a concomitant increase in business stocks and individual disposable funds (cash). When they relate to consumer goods, these transactions have no direct effect on overall equilibrium.

(b) Nevertheless, some of these goods are sought not as competitors of contemporary production goods but rather because their ownership provides unearned income (either in the strict sense of interest or in the broad sense of value-added on speculation). These goods are jewellery, collections of antiques, rare books, precious metals, real estate, property rights in general, and debt securities. Such transactions constitute a considerable volume of national financial transactions. It is sufficient to consider the sum of stock transactions, sales, and mortgages on real estate. An opinion poll in Spain shows that such transactions are equivalent to one-third of the national income. This issue will later be subject to special attention and considered from another point of view.

Nevertheless, this second type of transaction has direct and indirect effects, as previously analysed. These effects are the subject of a specific study in the analysis of imbalances. When Bernácer incorporates second-hand transactions in his general equilibrium model, he refers to the first type of goods.

Bernácer's Equilibrium Model

At the risk of repeating ourselves, we recall that Bernácer never uses the term "model", and he never claims to provide an overall equilibrium model. Even so, it seemed interesting to present what he modestly called the "market equation" as a general equilibrium model for the convenience of later comparison with other authors.

Particularities of Economic Equilibrium

"The economic equilibrium is a dynamic equilibrium; there can be balances of this kind when the antagonist's internal forces cancel each other out" (Bernácer 1916, p. 83). There are three basic conditions for equilibrium:

(a) The notification condition of equilibrium

Demand and supply for each good, and thus the overall demand and supply must be equal.

(b) The environmental homogeneity requirements

Incomes from different industries must be proportionate to the effort and risk; otherwise, less attractive activities will be abandoned. This is a condition for the equilibrium of the set of goods' and factor's prices.

(c) The interest rate in various markets proportionate to yields and investors' forecasts

With these principles in mind, imbalances will occur immediately. Nevertheless, their normal development must be reduction rather than amplification so the overall stability of the set is not in jeopardy. The regulation of equilibrium is the role of automatic mechanisms.

Indeed, in choosing a type of economic system,

- Either we concede the existence and effectiveness of self-regulatory mechanisms,
- Or we resort to economic planning.

The historical observation of regulator failure must lead to an analysis of the causes of this failure and not to an outright rejection a priori. The question is twofold:

- Is their effectiveness questioned?
- Are there exogenous phenomena to these mechanisms that prevent their proper functioning?

The following analysis of disequilibria will provide answers to these two questions. The analysis of economic equilibrium in dynamic terms shows that the regulation of production and consumption is a major problem. While it is true that equilibrium occurs in markets where supply and demand instantly react to one another, we must observe the activities that lead to these markets and that feed its two main components: production and consumption. However, these two activities, unlike supply and demand, have a delayed reaction to one another.

Therefore, we can observe delays in the functioning of reciprocal self-regulating mechanisms that adjust production to consumption.

These differences distort the observer's appreciation of the disequilibrium phenomenon, sometimes showing relative overproduction and sometimes showing relative under-consumption. By the way, Bernácer would prefer the second interpretation and considers that the adjustment mechanism works in this case. Nevertheless, this adjustment usually leads to a restriction of production and unemployment.

General Equilibrium Model Constitution

This presentation is inspired from the mathematical appendix in 1955 Bernácer's book, p. 229 (Figs. 3.6 and 3.7).

	BEGINNING OF THE PERIOD	END OF THE PERIOD	VARIATIONS DURING THE PERIOD
Money supply: monetary aggregates	M	M′	ΔM = M′ − M
Customers' cash	A	A′	ΔA = A′ − A
Companies' cash	Ca	Ca′	ΔCa = Ca′ − Ca
Stock of companies' goods	St	St′	ΔSt = St′ − St
Companies' working capital	K	K′	ΔK = K′ − K
Companies' fixed capital	X	X′	ΔX = X′ − X
Loans and allocations/endowments/grants to companies	Z	Z′	ΔZ = Z′ − Z
Loans for companies' working capital	H	H′	ΔH = H′ − H

Fig. 3.6 Table of variables of general equilibrium model

Total national income	R
Total value of production	P
Potential demand	Dp
Real demand	D
Potential supply	Sp
Real supply	S
Positive operating result of companies	B

Fig. 3.7 Table of aggregates for the period

Decreased Form of the Market Equations

We have, by definition,

$$R = P$$
$$M = A + Ca$$
$$K = E + Ca$$
$$H = Z - X$$

Potential demand and supply are expressed by:

$$Dp = R + A + \Delta M$$
$$Sp = P + E$$

Effective demand:

$$D = Dp - A' - \Delta H$$
$$D = R - \Delta A + \left(\Delta M - \Delta H\right)$$

And therefore includes the income in the period minus the increased household cash and plus the money creation (ΔM) not assigned to companies' working capital (ΔH), that is, (ΔM−ΔH). This creation of money is therefore allocated either to household consumption or to companies' creation of fixed capital.

The effective supply is $S = Sp - St'$

$$S = P - \Delta St$$

It is equal to the production in the period minus stock formation.

Balance assumption:

$$D = S$$

$$R - \Delta A + \Delta M - \Delta H = P - \Delta St$$

Terms of equilibrium:

Given	R = P
It is necessary and sufficient that	ΔA − ΔM + ΔH = ΔSt
Now, we have	ΔA = ΔSt
When	ΔM = ΔH
And since	ΔK = ΔSt + ΔC
We have	ΔA = ΔSt → ΔK = ΔA + ΔCa
And under the definition of ΔM:	ΔK = ΔM
And since	ΔM = ΔH
So	ΔM = ΔK = ΔH

That is, in equilibrium, the demanders' (consumers' and investors') cash exchanges during the period will be equal to the change in suppliers' stocks when exclusively financed by money creation. Otherwise, in the words of Bernácer (1955), "*In equilibrium, a working capital increase is equal to that of loans for working capital and to the amount of created money*".

If there is disequilibrium (e.g., D > S):

$$D - S = R - \Delta A + \Delta M - \Delta H - (P - \Delta St)$$

$$D - S = \Delta St - \Delta A = \Delta M - \Delta H$$

Even so, $\Delta M = \Delta A + \Delta Ca$
So $D - S = \Delta St + \Delta Ca - \Delta H$
And since $\Delta St + \Delta Ca = \Delta K$
So $D - S = \Delta K - \Delta H$
$|\Delta K - \Delta H|$, therefore, measures the deviation from equilibrium

$$(D > S \text{ or } S > D)$$

The basic condition of equilibrium is that any increase in working capital is financed by money issuance, which involves two sub-conditions:

(a) There is money creation.
(b) Money really finances companies' working capital.

Complete Market Equations

They have the same morphology as the decreased-form equations. They include:

(a) Changes in the cash gold: ΔCg
(b) Current transaction equilibrium (goods, services, and monetary gold): W
(c) Transactions in used goods (goods produced in previous periods and already sold for the first time by producers): L

The equation for effective supply becomes:

$$S = P - \Delta St - \Delta Cg + W + L$$

That of effective demand will be:

$$D = R - \Delta A + \Delta M - \Delta H + W + L$$

The deviation from equilibrium will be expressed as:

$$D - S = \Delta K - \Delta H + \Delta Cg$$

ΔCg is a complementary factor of the equilibrium, while W and L are neutral elements.

The new equilibrium condition is expressed in relation to the first. In addition, money creation should not only be equal to the increase in companies' working capital but also help finance cash gold increase.

Like Bernácer, we have envisaged increases or disequilibrium formulas where D > S. It is obvious that the reciprocal is true, and we should reason about variance in both directions.

The Notion of Change in Companies' Working Capital

This concept is key to Bernácer's equilibrium model. Its importance is based on the fact that Bernácer considers the formation of stocks and that investment is a very precise and concrete concept: it is the company's acquisition of capital goods for their implementation in production. In this respect, the economic act is not a production good but a purchase. The equilibrium on the market is assessed after the completion of transactions but not before.

The change in companies' working capital is the expression of a non-transaction (or non-demand). The two terms in this variation include changes in companies' cash (ΔCa) and stocks (ΔSt). The first represents additional payment methods from these companies that are not converted into demand on the market. The second represents the period surplus, which was not requested by the same company's customers (consumers or other businesses). Therefore, both aggregates represent a potential of demand unexpressed as such on the market.

It therefore appears that the basic condition of equilibrium expressed in terms of the funding modality of such non-demand seems perfectly consistent. The accumulation of idle cash (ΔCa) or unsold stocks (ΔSt) disturbs the equilibrium if its funding source is in the income for the period because the basic equality P = R is neglected. Nevertheless, there is a way to fund this accumulation without jeopardizing equilibrium: money creation.

Explanation for Overall Disequilibrium

Disequilibrium Emergence

Price fluctuations and unemployment are the signals of the emergence of economic disequilibrium.

Price Fluctuations

Price fluctuations express an imbalance between supply and demand either on the market for goods or at the overall level. When the price change is limited to one industry, it expresses mutations in consumer habits and results in demand transfer from one product to another.

Such misalignment limited to certain markets does not instantly affect the overall market a priori. When such misalignments increase, a generalized price change occurs, and disequilibrium, after its spread between industries, reaches the entire market. The effects of a generalized change will be discussed later.

From the index of imbalance between supply and demand to the price index:

(a) Dynamic analysis

At the beginning period, buyers (consumers and investors) have only income from prior periods for their initial expenses. During the period, these expenses will allow companies to pay new income and so on. Therefore, at any time, the situation is the result of the conjunction of past and on-going transaction effects, within a short-term framework with either an upward or a downward trend.

The price movement is complex and such that, at a given time, the ratio of the current price to the price for any reference time is the sum of successive price changes.

(b) The total disequilibrium coefficient

Let D_i mean the effective demand for period i, expressed in units of income for the period (i−1) and S_i mean effective supply for period i expressed in units of income for the period (i−1).

With the same unit, it is possible to compare D_i and S_i, claiming that a priori, these two values are different. The ratio $\frac{D_i}{S_i}$ expresses the disequilibrium coefficient between demand and supply for the period (i). In fact, the ratio expresses the average equilibrium for the period and not the difference between the beginning and end of the period. The total disequilibrium coefficient of the period compared to period 0 will be expressed as

$$\frac{D_0}{S_0} \times \frac{D_1}{S_1} \times \ldots\ldots \times \frac{D_i}{S_i} \times \ldots\ldots \times \frac{D_n}{S_n}$$

Let

π D/S ratio

π−1: the difference in effective demand in relation to the effective supply

N_i: the price level observed at the beginning period (i)

ΔI_i: the index of observed prices, as $\Delta \text{Ii} = \frac{N_i}{N_{i-1}}$

I therefore represents the price change in two successive periods, while π is the average disequilibrium coefficient for the same period.

We demonstrate that:

$$\text{I} \rightarrow \pi \text{ when } \Delta t = t_i - t_{i-1} \rightarrow 0$$

When the period is very short,

$$\pi = \frac{I_i}{I_{(i-1)}}$$

$$\pi - 1 = \frac{I_i - I_{(i-1)}}{I_{(i-1)}} = \frac{\Delta I}{I}$$

The deviation of demand relative to supply is equal to the relative variation in prices.

When $\Delta I \rightarrow 0$; $\frac{\Delta I}{I}$ is the derivative of the function I (price level) at the point considered.

Taking $\Delta I \rightarrow 0$; $\frac{\Delta I}{I}$, I can be considered linear, and its variations are then proportional to the time.

I is obtained by differentiating:

$$\frac{dI}{I} = (\pi - 1)\,dt$$

And integrating:

$$\ln I = \int (\pi - 1)\,dt + k$$

$$I = e^{\int(\pi-1)dt+k}.$$

The price index for period t_n compared to period t_0 is equal to

$$I_n = e^{\int_{t_0}^{t_n}(\pi-1)dt+k}.$$

Where the law is as follows:

The total price index for a period is the sum of the partial disequilibria of each sub-period that compose it (disequilibria between effective demand and supply).

Bernácer, thus, succeeds in formulating a law of price movement based on independent variables other than prices, which implies no determination of the base price.

This law leads to:

- A synthetic formulation of price fluctuations including, without separating, real factors and monetary factors;
- A rejection of the unequivocal quantitativist determination $\Delta M \Rightarrow \Delta P$

We will comment only on the second part of this result because the hypotheses involved are quite varied.

Unemployment

Unemployment is figuratively an emergence of market disequilibrium: it is a subsidiary effect of price fluctuations.

(a) Technological unemployment

Disequilibrium restricted to a market and sustainable between supply and demand produces unemployment due to consumption or investment mutations. The overall equilibrium and the original employment level can be restored to the extent that the demand transfer (or eventually supply) of one product to another is achieved without considerable delay. In this case, technological unemployment is not serious. Nevertheless, it tends to worsen the situation when added to an "effective or latent organic unemployment".

(b) Full employment level

In the case of a generalized increase in prices, real wages decline, while real profits increase. The effects of such an increase depend on entrepreneurs' attitudes. If companies use increasing profits to create fixed investment, demand for investment goods, which generates income, will dominate consumption, which is weakened by employees' declining purchasing power. In that case, the increase is neutral in regard to the equilibrium and the employment level. If companies hoard (investments in the capital market) or allocate excess profit to fund their working capital, it will result in a decline in aggregate demand and an employment level lower than the original level.

Still, a generalized price increase does not necessarily lead to unemployment. Bernácer also considers the case of a generalized price decline that leads to more or less the same effects. Nevertheless, we will find the analysis of these two situations in the cycle analysis.

The Causes of Disequilibrium

The disequilibrium is due to both structural and cyclical causes; although the two aspects are often intertwined, some types of structure have a direct influence on certain types of situations.

Structural Causes

(a) The market for production and employment: monopoly and unionism

The structures that sometimes cause disequilibrium are the markets and the central political power. Most modern macroeconomic analyses are implicitly based on the existence or lack of virtual iso-units, usually called a pure and perfect competitive market. Second, theorists introduce different market structures in terms of overall explanations for disequilibrium. Bernácer proceeds in the same way.

Settling a monopoly on consumer goods has two effects that are paradoxical only in appearance: depression and inflation. Monopoly has the immediate effect—or the goal—to set a more profitable price than the perfect competition price. The immediate effects are declines in production, in real income, and in the employment level. The depression of economic activity—or if we prefer to avoid the ambiguity of the word *depression*—the restraint of the entire production system below its actual capacity causes the underuse of production factors and insufficient production.

Nevertheless, on the labour market, a certain viscosity is introduced due to the organization of employees. Indeed, trade unions generally manage to keep nominal wages at their previous level (where the economy was in equilibrium) even if employment falls, such that the decline in overall real income that is not accompanied by a correlative decrease in nominal income reflects an inflationary environment. Bernácer does not consider that this trade union action prevents an excessive decline in effective demand. He aims to show that the two structures that distort the self-regulatory mechanism of production and employment produce cumulative unbalancing effects: to the depressive effect of monopoly is added the inflationary effect of trade union claims. The combination of both effects exacerbates disequilibrium.

The monopoly generalization can have multiple origins, such as mergers and agreements between micro-units, legal monopoly, and nationalization. They generate two social problems—inflation and permanent unemployment—and an aberrant effect that is irrelevant compared to the logical purpose of monopoly: a continuous cumulative process of a decline in monopoly profit because of the effect of the real decrease in overall income on demand. Bernácer said, "… but if monopolies multiplied on a large scale, following the current nationalization trend or rather the government's establishment of industrial companies, this effect would trigger serious inflation and, at the same time, unemployment".

(b) A congenitally disequilibrating institution: the financial market

This institution has improved under the capitalist regime through stock exchanges and, to some extent, through banks. It is itself the cause of many evils. We have already developed this point in our study of hoarding, unearned income, and interest—the three perverse aspects of the financial market—so there is no need to repeat it here.

(c) The central political authority or tax office

We will not discuss here all the causes of disequilibrium from the government's economic and social policy. We will focus on only one institution, taxes, which figure prominently in Bernácer's analysis of disequilibrium.

If we accept the general appearance of an effective demand curve, we observe that indirect taxes (and, to a great extent, direct tax) produces an effect similar to a monopoly. The price increase resulting from a direct tax for the buyer causes a decrease in demand and, thus, in the production of goods affected by this tax. Indeed, taxes are later charged on the taxable person, in general, the final consumer, who bears the effective charge from the direct tax. Of course, the rigidity of these agent behaviours depends on their dominant position in the economic and social hierarchies, and there can be repercussions for both indirect tax and direct tax.

Cyclical Causes

These causes depend on the agent behaviour in accordance with current data, such as the internal financial situation, the phase of the cycle (upward or downward), anticipation, and the professional, economic, and social environments. Among these agents, company decisions, through their production, investment, employment—and therefore income distribution—play a key role. If we take the accounting approach to equilibrium, we can highlight how companies' behaviour, such as their trade policy, can change a general equilibrium to a general disequilibrium (Fig. 3.8).

We recall that, in the income approach, the overall equilibrium is achieved when the stock variation is equal to the change in consumer and investor cash (disposable funds). Nevertheless, this accounting equilibrium is destroyed every time company tactics, especially its sales policy, cause an acceleration (positive or negative) of the flow of goods compared to the flow of cash expenses. Indeed, at some point, companies can adopt a policy of commercial aggression in terms of prices in order to force their sales: a voluntary price decrease will increase the speed of goods flow and will thereby involve a difference between this flow and that of consumer and investor cash expenses. It can also voluntarily make supply scarce and cause artificial disequilibrium that will increase prices. At this time, the same difference between the two flows will occur in the opposite direction.

We can summarize the disturbing factors of equilibrium in the following composite diagram (Fig. 3.9):

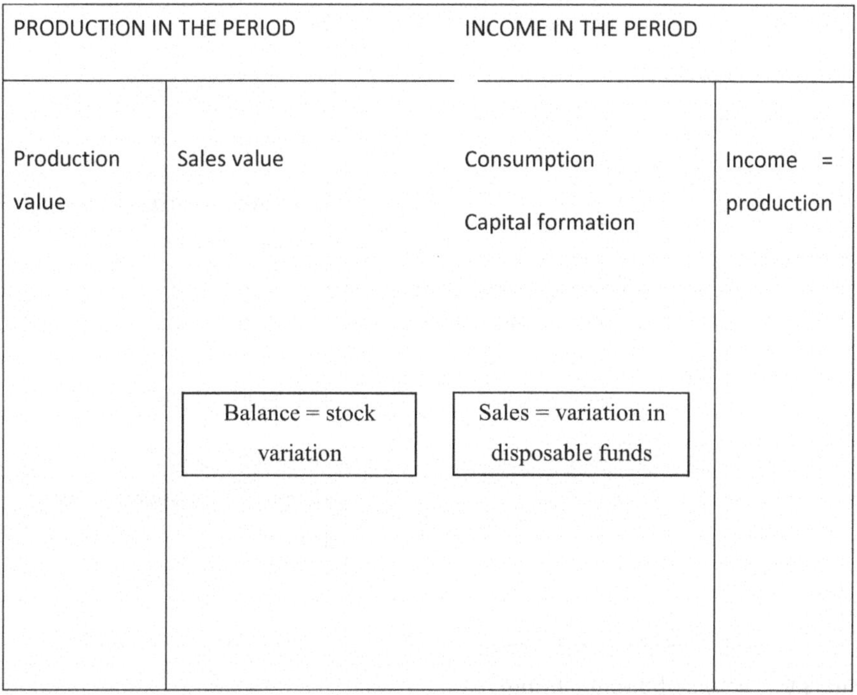

Fig. 3.8 Balanced production/income in the period

Most theories are describing economic disequilibria rather than explaining their basic factors, unlike Bernácer does.

Theories of Major Disequilibria

The next sections are focusing on the theory of employment and the theory of cycle.

Elements of the Theory of Employment

Human labour is a factor of production, and as such it has a specific definition and market. Bernácer was the first to reject the notion of labour cost. Human work is not of a materialistic nature nor is it a commodity

NATURE	FACTORS	CAUSES
Real elements	Stock variation	Company policy (incentives for consumption and investment)
Monetary elements	Hoarding	Productivity perspectives on the financial market
	Loan for companies	Interest rate
	Money creation	- Deliberate monetary policy - Monetary policy caused by hoarding variations: extra element

Fig. 3.9 Factors of disequilibrium

with a production cost; rather, it is a means to produce what people need, regardless of the form of the production organization and regardless of the historical regime. Labour is more than just paid work for a salary: entrepreneurs also work, and work is not the only factor that has a price, a sale, and a market. Economic activity has no other purpose than the satisfaction of human needs, so man and producer and man and labour must not be separated, as these concepts are closely related.

Without production, there is no life and thus no needs to satisfy, and there is no production without labour. Therefore, labour is the only legitimate means to own a product. From a more technical point of view, labour does not need to claim any mythical "cost of reproduction" to participate in distribution.

Although labour has no cost, it has a price. In a pragmatic way, this price can be considered to be the price fixed by the labour market, given the organization of production in which work is implemented in specific structures—production units—which therefore call for a labour market. The price may also be considered the basis of the product distribution, taking into account the type of production organization to the extent that production and consumption are dissociated actions in advanced societies.

Labour Market

On the labour market, the worker is in an unfavourable negotiating position: this is a basic principle that explains the palliatives that this situation has generated. Given this weakness, governments have been historically led to impose by law, by collective agreements or by favouring trade union intervention, a wage-fixing procedure that responds to social issues. According to Bernácer, this process is only an expedient from an economic point of view.

Neoliberals are sceptical of the possibility of finding an automatic regulator of the labour market, revealing a certain powerlessness to propose current coherent solutions: Keynes (1936) maintains that he invented the unemployment equilibrium concept, which is a pure aberration to Bernácer. It seems that the notions of unemployment and of general equilibrium are incompatible because at least one market is unbalanced: that of employment, unless it is only unbalanced because of the ambiguity of Keynes' equilibrium concept. Nevertheless, it is certain that this reference to Keynes's equilibrium reveals either a whiff of classicism in its approach to economic problems or an intellectual subjection to his neo-classically inspired teachers. Bernácer, taking the semantic opposite of the Keynesian expression, refers to "the unemployment disequilibrium", which, according to him, is the greatest scandal: the tangible proof of the total aberration of the human race in economic organization, given his collective ethics.

Bernácer notes that palliative employees have so far failed to solve the overall problem of employment, and he believes that the cause of this problem lies somewhere other than the market, somewhere deeper. Is Malthus's unemployment theory relevant? Is technical progress a permanent cause of unemployment? Bernácer refutes these questions before giving his own explanation.

Rejection of the Classical Theory of Unemployment

Why is there always or almost always a surplus labour supply? Unemployed people need to work in order to survive, but they do not deliberately choose not to work: they are prevented from it. Will general equilibrium disappear if unemployed people work? If we accept the equivalence between product and income, we can see that if the surplus workforce were employed, goods would be produced in an amount equivalent to that they would then request on the market.

Malthus (1820) argued that natural resources were insufficient to sustain the entire world population, that there was no humanitarian solution to this problem and that the surplus population must be exterminated. History contradicted this pessimistic author, as human genius has been able to discover resources in sufficient quantities: land to be cleared is not lacking, only the labour to clear the land is lacking.

This analysis suggests that Bernácer considers that the only obstacle to growth is the amount of disposable labour, all other things being equal. The natural factor is therefore not behind unemployment or inadequate production levels because needs and labour are abundant. The scarcity of monetary means constitutes an artificial barrier. The cause of unemployment is not natural but institutional. Therefore, if Bernácer were to advocate money issuance as a means to increase employment level, it would address the symptoms instead of the root of the problem: unearned income and hoarding.

Technical Progress

Technical progress is not itself the cause of sustained decline in employment levels.

(a) *Case of a localized introduction of technical progress*

If we take the production function of an industry in which sensitive technical progress derived from work occurs, it is clear that labour productivity increases in this industry and that, following the market absorption capacity and increased productivity, the industry employment level either remains steady, decreases, or even increases.

If we retain only the worst theory on employment levels in that industry, examining its implications for the overall employment level remains.

Case where progress is achieved through fixed capital investment

We can assume that there is compensation between unemployment in the industry with progress and overemployment in areas upstream of the goods producers of fixed capital and, eventually, of intermediate goods producers. To do so, we must admit that all industries were initially in an equilibrium of full employment, that progress does not simultaneously touch other industries than the one considered, and therefore demand growth for capital goods from the industry with progress causes an employment increase in upstream industries. If the technical coefficients of inter-industrial relations and the investment acceleration principle are considered, the model becomes complex and compensation at the employment level can be equal to, lower than, or higher than the underemployment in the first industry.

What should especially be remembered for its inability to quantitatively demonstrate the existence of equilibrium is the qualitative tendency towards equilibrium represented by compensation, at least to some extent. Therefore, if automatic regulators work properly, disequilibrium is not a priori unavoidable.

Case where progress is achieved without fixed capital investment

This rare case can result from rationalization, simplification, or reorganization. Nevertheless, we must recognize that these actions are often associated with a fixed capital investment. This case is rather an isolated one and an additional cause of technical progress that should not be underestimated, especially in light of the statistical verification of the production function—as in Malinvaud in France—using the Cobb-Douglas function (INSEE 1965): this famous residual factor would explain half of: (1) the growth of the French economy. See the critical commentary by Stoleru (1973) and François Perroux (1973) and the relevant book by

Carré, Dubois, and Malinvaud (1972). In this case, technical progress creates unemployment in the considered industry but generates production growth if the market capacity allows it.

(b) Case of a generalized incorporation of technical progress

The generalization of technological progress can result in two cases: where the localized technical progress, considered in (a), eventually propagates to other industries, and/or where the "natural" and on-going flow of technical progress eventually affects all industries in economic activity. In these cases, technological progress decreases the employment level measured in the amount of working hours to a constant production level. Then, the solution in a stationary economy is to find a new dosage between work and leisure activities at the individual and community levels. Almost always adopted to date, the solution to reducing employment levels in terms of labour units—instead of just reducing labour duration—is an absurdity in many respects, whether economic or not.

The alternative to a stationary economy with unemployment caused by technical progress is that of full employment maintained with production growth and, thus, social well-being. This growing movement is generally observed in industrial economies over the long term but at what degree of price fluctuations and unemployment? Thus, we see that salvation is, in all cases, found mainly in production growth and secondarily in a generalized reduction in working hours.

Let us consider the different cases produced by the general incorporation of technical progress:

Employment levels are maintained with production growth and with the following types of market reactions:

- Demand absorbs surplus production.
- Market fails to absorb surplus production: stocks increase and then production is slowed and employment decreased.
- Production levels are maintained and employment levels reduced (because entrepreneurs think the market will react as in s_{12}).
- Working time decreases: payroll decreases without lowering wages (since there are no unemployed people), momentarily promoting increased profits and fixed capital formation. Effective demand can

thus be maintained and even increased since overall demand for investment goods dominates demand for consumer goods. Overall productivity is expected to increase again due to fixed capital increases, which should favour real wage increases. We are then led to the s_{11} case.

- Number of workers decreases: the effect on payroll may be identical to the s_{21} case. Nevertheless, competition among the unemployed (labour market disequilibrium) lowers wages such that the level reached by payroll in s_{22} is lower than that in s_{21}. In turn, final demand will be even lower if we assume that employed workers continue to save as they would in equilibrium. Thus, the demand decrease is amplified. Momentarily, profits and fixed investment grow, increasing production that can be either absorbed or rejected by the market.
- Demand follows production: we return to cases s_{11} and s_{21}: growth is simply postponed.
- Demand does not follow production: we return to case s_{12}, where reducing employment and crisis have been delayed but amplified and increased. In the debate on solutions, Bernácer particularly protests against the solution often adopted by entrepreneurs in the history of industrialization, which consists of reducing the number of workers instead of reducing work duration. Even if we relativize the conclusions in the model above and even if such a reduction in working time has no absolute benefits, as it appears in case s_{21}, we can at least assert that this solution is better than s_{22}.

We have much to say about this model, which appears in *Society and Happiness* in 1916, and then in Bernácer's 1922 article. Nonetheless, we reserve our analysis for the chapter "*Rate of Interest, Economic Activity and Politics*" (see below).

Thus, having shown that technical progress is a neutral element with regard to equilibrium, Bernácer nevertheless notes that it produces perverse effects by interposing agents' behaviours.

Indeed, consumers (employees and other income collectors) have the monetary income needed to purchase all products (if we assume that P = R).

Why do consumers fail to grow to be demanders in terms of their total purchasing power? If this situation is sustainable, why don't they work as much as they did previously (before the incorporation of technical progress)—that is, when their purchasing power was lower—given that their needs have not changed? Why do workers fail to spontaneously reduce the duration of their working day, which would lead them to consistent behaviour in regard to their initial choice to not consume or invest more? These questions illustrate the entirety of the issue. Hoarding and the financial market should be included in the explanation of these behaviours, which are incoherent only on the surface.

Bernácer's Theory of Unemployment

For Bernácer, unemployment is basically caused by hoarding and follows a specific process.

The Genesis of Unemployment

The following quote from Bernácer (1955, p. 111) sets the tone: "The existence of permanent value-added, the difference between prices and wages, is unfounded in the free market and in the context of the value theory that the classical school and Marx himself support".

Indeed, Bernácer focuses his discussion on unemployment genesis on comparing the final product prices and costs or profit and wages. He introduces the issue using the example of effective demand decline. In this case, prices fall, generating a profit decrease and, consequently, a decrease in production and employment. Nevertheless, this decline in employment should lead to wage decreases and could therefore increase profits and thus boost production, employment, and business in general. As a result, we return to the equilibrium at the starting point, provided that the ratio $\frac{\text{profit}}{\text{wages}}$ remains constant.

We must therefore examine the various hypotheses for the misalignment between prices and product costs (finished products include consumer goods and production goods).

H_1 Ratio between prices and costs remains the same: we could say that the sliding scale works flawlessly and without time intervals.

In this case, money is neutral, and the quantitative theory of money applies perfectly, without changing the level of activity and employment, all other things being equal. The only effect is the increase in the value of money units when prices fall and money depreciation when prices increase.

H_2 Prices increase more or decrease less than costs:

The ratio $\frac{\text{price}}{\text{cost}}$ grows.

Production activity is more profitable after a price change than before it: production levels tend to increase even as the purchasing power of workers decreases and that of the "boss class" increases. This situation cannot linger for long.

(a) If production increases, workers will earn higher salaries, and the ratio $\frac{\text{price}}{\text{cost}}$ will tend towards the equilibrium level before a price increase.

In this case, the increase in aggregate demand is caused by expenditures by consumers and beneficiaries' additional investment in the misalignment caused by rising prices; followed later by workers' additional consumption expenditures when, as a result of increased production, their salaries increase.

(b) If production increases do not occur, it is because super-incomes from the "employer class" are not spent on the production market. In this case, hoarding (uninvested savings) generates aggregate demand decreases, then production decreases, and, finally, declines in the employment levels.

H_3 Prices increase less or decline more than costs:

$$\text{The ratio} \frac{\text{price}}{\text{cost}} \text{decreases.}$$

Production activity is less profitable and is likely to fall, thereby increasing unemployment. If free competition between workers is perfect, lower employment levels should generate lower wages and thus lower costs, as well as a tendency of the ratio $\frac{\text{price}}{\text{cost}}$ to return to its equilibrium level before the increase.

Fixed income collectors—the beneficiaries of the price decrease—see their purchasing power increase. Purchasing power surplus will stimulate aggregate demand increases, provided it is not hoarded. We therefore return to hypotheses H_{2a} and H_{2b}.

The three hypotheses envisaged by Bernácer do not occupy the same place in his mind.

According to Bernácer, hypothesis H_1 is a particularly impractical case; therefore, Bernácer is anticlassical because he admits neither money neutrality nor a quantitative theory of money a priori. Hypotheses H_2 and H_3 have a real experience value and reach the same conclusion: unemployment is created and maintained by hoarding. An imbalance in the production market, whether upward or downward, may cause, depending on the hoarder's attitude, a new equilibrium with either product growth or unemployment.

Hoarding, a Major Cause of Unemployment

We have seen that hoarding controls the return to equilibrium in the previous hypothesis and also therefore controls the employment level. Starting from a given equilibrium at the end of period 1, the period 2 hoarding (Ho) of a portion of period 1 savings causes aggregate demand contractions, triggering a cumulative process of production depression, of overall income, and of employment:

Suppose there is no hoarding at the end of period 0:

$$Sa_0 = I_1$$

And equilibrium in monetary terms at the end of period 1:

$$P_1 = R_1 = C_1 + Sa_1$$

We have, under the accounting convention of income expenditure:

$$Sa_1 = I_2 + Ho_2$$

Suppose:

$$C_2 = C_1$$

Given:

$$I_2 < Sa_1$$

Production will be lower during period 2:

$$P_2 = C_2 + I_2 < P_1$$

We observe that a decrease in aggregate demand (C_2 + I_2) generated by hoarding—that is, non-demand—on the production market in period 2 of the portion of savings (Ho_2) in period 1 triggers the depressive process:

$$\text{Production} \Rightarrow \text{Employment} \Rightarrow \text{Wages} \Rightarrow \text{Cost} \Rightarrow \text{Aggregate demand} \Rightarrow \text{Production}\ldots$$

Indeed, $P_2 < P_1$ => unemployment => $C_3 < C_2$, and possibly => $I_3 < I_2$ so that $P_3 = C_3 + I_3 < P_2$ and so on.

At the end of this process, unemployment becomes chronic when salaries reach a level that no longer sustains workers: "It is the true origin of the iron law, which is not the result of boss or workers will, but the fate of the economic system" (Bernácer 1916, p. 241). In this analysis, the debated point is not the boss's alienation of value-added. Here, what the worker does not earn benefits no one; "it is a deadweight loss for the community" (Bernácer 1916, p. 236). This process leads to collective impoverishment and to the gradual extension of proletarianization to all levels of society, including small entrepreneurs. Expedients, rather than solutions, have been tried. Thus, we might believe that, in such conditions, trade union action to prevent falling wages stops the depressive process. This is not the case because this action introduces rigidity in the system, distorting the regulator mechanism of the market, and leading, when the crisis continues, to rapid unemployment increases. This action protects the individual interests only of those workers who are fortunate not to lose their jobs in this economic and social storm.

Illustrating this principle, Bernácer asserts that the worsening of crises since the mid-nineteenth century was due to the introduction of social laws during the First World War and the 1920s. It goes without saying that such legislation was profoundly respectable. Nevertheless, it has led to public works of questionable usefulness on the pretext of creating jobs: only the effect-income was considered, not the effect-utility.

A Theory of Cycle

Our deductions in the previous chapters allow us to present a consistent explanation. According to it, the cause of such a phenomenon (i.e., crisis) is not an evil inherent to the liberal regime, in which it is developed with such virulence. It would rather obey an internal contradiction of the institutional system in which incompatible elements were left with a functioning free economy.

"Once these elements separate, the regime of economic freedom, which has proved most effective in stimulating production and well-being, will act similarly in establishing stability, and with it, distributing justice" (Bernácer 1916, p. 241).

Cycle Process

The various aggregate characteristics of the volume of economic activity do not move in a monotonous, chronological fashion. They follow upward or downward movements identified in the four phases of the cycle: the downward phase, which includes the transition from a stable state of full employment to a depression; the depression, which is a more or less permanent state in which economic activity reaches its minimum; the upward phase, which can even be called recovery; and finally, prosperity (full employment equilibrium). Is it also essential to show the reason why this movement is not monotonous and why prosperity is inevitably followed by a downward phase: in other words, we must demonstrate the instability of the economic equilibrium.

Upward Phase: Recession

In times of relative prosperity and equilibrium, there are four causes of spontaneous disequilibrium in the current economic and financial system. Their sole source is the use of savings. Savings may be allocated to:

(a) Increase household disposable funds (cash holdings),
(b) Increase trading volume or previously created assets,
(c) Increase companies' working capital, and
(d) Reduce debt and reduce the money supply to increase financial intermediary cash.

Hypotheses (a), (b), and (d) result in a decrease in effective aggregate demand and an increase in potential demand and stocks (potential supply). Hypothesis (c) results in increased stocks without increasing potential demand. Nevertheless, the increase in stocks leads to lower prices. Furthermore, as the situation usually progresses, it leads to a decrease in production provoked first by increased stocks and second by a decline in effective demand. This production decrease heralds the next phase.

Depression

Decreases in prices, industry profits, and fixed capital formation are all foils for placing savings in the production circuit. Hoarding in cash form or in the form of transactions of unearned income-yielding assets is consolidated, justified, and encouraged. In this environment, comparing income from transactions of unearned income-yielding assets and income from fixed capital formation in production is more favourable to the first use and thus hastens investment decline. At constant prices, the total income decline should result in a decline of savings capacity. Nevertheless, falling prices allow fixed nominal income collectors to increase their real savings (current employees, civil servants, unearned income perceivers, and pensioners), while unemployment leads to lower consumption. Therefore, the decrease in production does not generate a significant decline in savings; it only causes a shift in savings.

The influx of disposable funds on stock exchange and property markets increases prices and lowers interest rates. Nevertheless, price increases far compensate for declines in interest rates. At times when the securities experienced fluctuations of approximately 10% (or more) between two stock exchange sessions, the speculative rate of interest reached 10% per day. Therefore, that rate could compensate for a current investment interest rate of 10% per year.

For this reason, an increase in demand for such assets is not discouraged by interest rate decreases. This financial market paradox, which has been denounced above, explains the basic instability of the capitalist system: that the automatic regulator—the interest rate—no longer plays its intended role.

Is readjustment between prices and costs on the production market inconceivable, allowing equilibrium to be restored?

(a) The *wage rate*: unemployment tends to decrease and partially restore the $\frac{\text{price}}{\text{cost}}$ equilibrium. Nevertheless, the overall volume of labour costs decreases and helps to further reduce the demand for consumer goods.
(b) The *interest rate*: the influx of cash savings lowers the interest rate, and non-speculators may be tempted to invest their savings in the production market. Unfortunately, capital formation, encouraged by low interest rates, is not realized because its main incentive comes from the consumer goods market, which is under depression.

At an overall effective demand level, we cannot see how investment can take over from consumption in such an unfavourable situation. "The only thing that can generate production is demand, and while needs that could promote this demand exist, some feel that they have lost the means to effectively nurture demand. That is why this market regulation system, perfect in theory, is inappropriate to adjust production based on needs" (Bernácer 1916, p. 241).

What is the cause of this gridlock? "The means of production are no less abundant, but they are in stagnation, and humanity is miserable just because of the paralysis of the circulatory mechanism." Would it be enough to find a way to infuse money into the system? Bernácer answers this question by invoking, without naming it, a "money trap": "there is no need to provide funds at low prices to the market. We succeed by inflating the price of securities but not the productive economy".

Upward Phase: Recovery

Bernácer does not believe that spontaneous recovery can occur in depression, unlike prosperity—if we use the expression—which carries the recession "foetus". He believes that the causes of recovery are accidental and that there is no control mechanism that automatically generates the trend reversal.

Cost decreases (in wages and interest) are powerless in spurring recovery since the basic element that instigates a crisis is that investment is lower than savings. However, investment can increase—subject to favourable costs—only if entrepreneurs have an optimistic judgement of the future and the future evolution of prices and profits. These anticipations will play a key role in resolving the crisis, but nevertheless they are the devil in the economic structure: we do not know how to seize them or how to generate them, and they are related to psychology—we know that Bernácer excludes it from the actual economic field—and events. It is therefore logical that Bernácer ultimately considers that recovery is random; we could say that the cause of recovery is an exogenous element of the economic system sensu stricto.

Two conditions, alternative and cumulative, must exist to cause a return to prosperity: raising prices or substantially reducing costs.

(a) Price increase

Price increases are the result of a significant increase in demand, which depends on favourable events, including government budget deficits, wars, revolutions, and natural disasters (disasters and crop failures). History provides examples of good correlations between price movements and wars. Regarding budget deficits, the author expresses reluctance: it is not panacea, as the provoked price increase is almost certain, while the decrease in unemployment that should follow is less sure.

(b) Cost reduction

Cost reduction can result from a series of unexpected events that promote recovery: discoveries and inventions. We can also include innovation because Bernácer's point of view on this point is very close to that of Schumpeter. Indeed, the possibility of sustainable cost reduction is a powerful incentive for entrepreneurs and stimulates large investments.

These investments then spur the significant increase in demand that causes recovery. We could add that depression is often suitable for reconsidering production organization and then for the application of innovations. The accidental nature of these events or the discontinuity in flows of technical progress explains the varying length of depression periods. In the two recovery modalities examined, (a) and (b), a restoration of a certain ratio $\frac{\text{price}}{\text{cost}}$ seems necessary but not sufficient to spawn recovery. Exogenous variables that can be grouped under the name "optimistic prospects" must be added.

Prosperity

The relative increase in demand compared to the previous production phase leads to stock reduction and, with greater or lower variation, to increases in production, employment, and capital formation. Therefore, all things being equal, any increase in demand generated by a production increase generates, in turn, a further increase in production that lasts for a while.

Why does prosperity fail to persist indefinitely? Under what enigma does a crisis—and without exception, prosperity—always follow?

The Inevitability of Crisis

If we assume that an exogenous event in economic activity is necessary to cause recovery, we observe that the economic system hosts the crisis virus. Therefore, the cycle in Bernácer's theory is asymmetrical. Must we therefore rank Bernácer among the stagnationists? We think not: the economy is a subset of all human activity. Bernácer is confident of all the elements that cause recovery other than economic elements, so he is not pessimistic; he believes that economic structures can improve.

Consider what would happen if prosperity lasted indefinitely. One of its consequences—and, simultaneously, one of its conditions—would be that all disposable funds are spent on the production market. Therefore, a "disposable funds vacuum" would occur in the financial market, causing price decreases for income-yielding assets and thus a strong interest rate increase. For example, a 50% decrease would double the interest rate. A sharp interest rate increase would attract disposable funds on the financial market, encourage hoarding, and make investment doubly difficult due to a lack of capital and a high price of money, which distort the calculation of profitability investment.

A crisis occurs, then, generated more by *double* failure in effective demand than by an increase in the interest rate. *Doubly* insufficient effective demand is attributable to a fall in investment or consumption because of hoarding or an increase in supply due to the increased productivity of new investments. Indeed, during a period of prosperity, strong demand and high profits favoured investment in working capital and fixed capital. Even so, the fixed capital formation effects occur with a delay, so when hoarding occurs, signalling the end of the prosperity period, supply is too strong to face effective demand at the moment. Stocks (working capital), already constituted at their normal levels, accumulate; this is the prelude to recession.

Cycle Mechanism

The General Model: Hydrodynamic Analysis

In the stable equilibrium diagram of an economy, considered with only the production circuit, income expenditure has only two possible routes: consumption and investment. The introduction of the financial market adds a third possible choice: demand for unearned income-yielding assets.

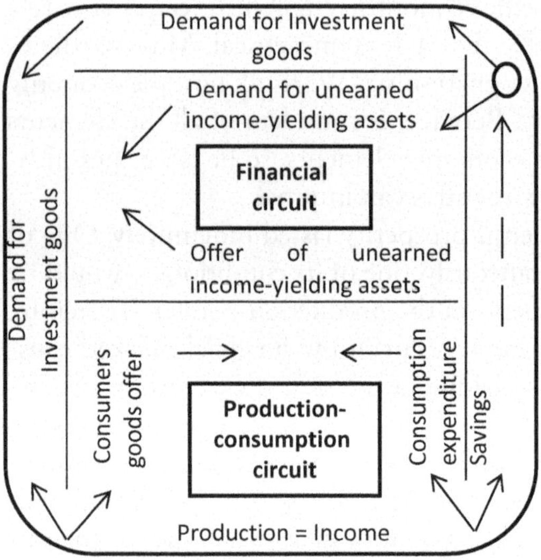

O Hot spot where savings must be allocated to either investment or hoarding.

Inspired by Bernácer, we have introduced into our figure several additions, including the nerve centre, which seems to correspond well to this author's ideas.

Disequilibrium occurs in this circuit when the cash flow of demand for investment goods is different from the actual flow of the supply of these goods.

(a) The cash flow of demand for investment goods is relatively insufficient compared to the real supply flow. These goods cannot be sold at a "fair price".

(a_1) Growth in demand for capital goods is relatively poor compared to the real supply flow. These goods cannot be sold at a "fair price".
(a_2) Decrease in demand for investment goods is not accompanied by an increase in demand for consumer goods: the market disequilibrium for the first set of goods extends to market for the second ones and depresses the overall effective demand: this is the crisis.

(b) The cash flow of demand for investment goods is relatively higher than the actual supply flow due to the demand for technical innovations application, for example. Rising prices for goods increases profits, resulting in increases in production and total income.
(c) Since the production circuit has attracted relatively more money in (b), it creates a certain scarcity of money in financial markets and increases the interest rate. This interest rate increase attracts new disposable funds on the financial market. Meanwhile, production potential increases. Therefore, production and supply rise, and when disposable funds flow back from the productive circuit towards the financial circuit, (increased) supply is excessive compared to (decreased) demand. This marks the period of depression, which lasts until an accidental event causes a significant increase in demand.

The distribution of savings between the two demands—investment and hoarding—at the focal point of the model is therefore of utmost importance. There is also a secondary distribution at the choice level: hoarding or consumption. This secondary choice, which is not explained well by Bernácer, may nevertheless be an outcome at the beginning of a crisis, as we saw in (a_1). For simplicity, we shall confine ourselves to the analysis of what happens at the hot spot.

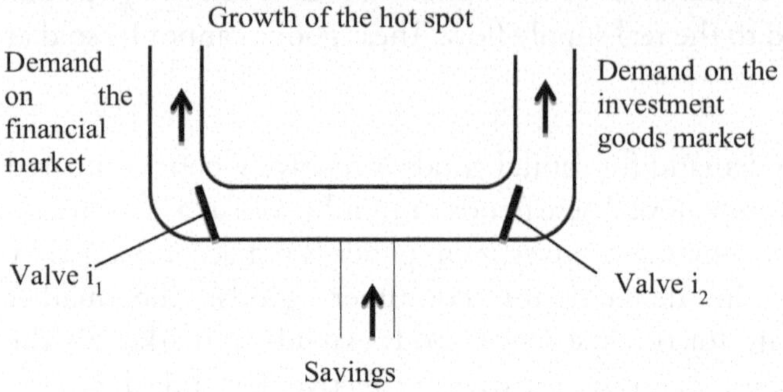

Let a flow of savings that leads to the bifurcation be a hot spot, where both doors are slightly open to the two possible outcomes. Let i_1 be the interest rate offered by entrepreneurs willing to invest in savers and i_2 be the financial market interest rate (average yield rate from different investments "as unearned income"). i_1 and i_2 are the relatively large openings of the two access doors for two competing markets. Bernácer illustrates this mechanism by describing the following scenario: replace savings with liquid and the slightly opened doors with two valves in a simple hydraulic device. "This mechanism offers a certain analogy with an elemental device of Physics, called a *hydraulic ram*.

In this device, a high flow stream of water gains increasing speed until its vital spark is sufficient to close the outlet valve, watcr flows back strongly, raising the level of water at such a height that the received pulse becomes zero; then, the drain valve opens again quite naturally, water comes out and assumes sufficient speed to reactivate the *water hammer*."

In the case of economic cycles, the financial market represents the valve function. When a spontaneous movement of increased demand occurs and absorbs the money savings flow, the current races itself, and when the monetary gap on the financial market acquires a certain intensity, the access opening emerges, attracting the savings flow or return flow of funds coming to the market for capital goods. The latter undergoes depression until the eradication of the financial market provokes the water hammer once again. This mechanism can be put into perspective by taking the differentiated intensity flows heading to the two markets, considering that intensity is a function of the interest rates of i_1 and i_2, which represents the valves.

The Asynchronous Movements and Asymmetry of the Cycle

We saw that growth and crisis are intermediate states of prosperity and depression, respectively, but they are also somehow epiphenomena of these two extreme states.

(a) Time lags

Therefore, growth and crisis can occur with depression and prosperity, respectively, with setbacks attributable to delays in the implementation of previous commitments. Prosperity and depression do not always exist in a pure state, as there is usually a period of contradictory movement. Indeed, each period is *loaded* (in an obstetrical meaning) with future conjuncture "seeds" and produces fruit from past circumstances.

Booms and crises are the result of asynchronous movements. These misalignments cause increasingly strong tensions that explode in the form of crisis or expansion, as "fire occurs due to fuel accumulation" (Bernácer 1955, p. 143).

(b) Elasticities

Cyclical accidents occur when the power of an event is greater than a structure elasticity. Indeed, we observe that in the periods that precede a crisis, speculation is strong on the financial market for two reasons:

- Prosperity induces favourable income expectations: prices rise because demand is strong and holders have little reason to divest their unearned income-yielding assets;
- Relatively high income from prosperity (especially profits) allows high savings to remain disposable in the event of efficient investments.

These two combined causes (hoarding in non-production investments and hoarding in cash form) are able to trigger the crisis on their own. Currently, credit allows the lack of money on the production market to be overcome for some time, but generally, it results only in delays and worsened crisis.

(c) Asymmetry in trend reversal

We have seen that the fate of a crisis at the end of a boom period is not the same as that at the end of a depression period. Crisis is an endogenous element of the economic system, while a boom is caused by outside factors, as shown in Bernácer's cycle theory and explains the various actions that the government or agents take to cause recovery. According to Bernácer, this reasoning is insufficient to explain the need to involve the government. The sometimes-parallel paths of Keynes's and Bernácer's analyses diverge because of different philosophical options.

To explain the cycle, the idea of asymmetry is based on the concept of dominant structure: the financial market, through its instability and because the market, by nature, provides income without work, holds a privileged position in the economic system compared to the production market. So-called financial capitalism and the current role of the bank are well-known elements of domination that support Bernácer's conceptual analysis.

Catalysing the Rigid Structures of the Cycle

Crises have been precipitated and exacerbated by the rigidities of the monetary and financial system, including credit control and the gold standard. Among the rigid structures mentioned above, gold, as a monetary standard, has historically played an important role. Indeed, gold is ideal for hoarding.

We might believe that hoarding gold has fewer disadvantages than hoarding common money because the acquisition of gold implies exchange against common money. Nevertheless, compensation in common money does not generally go towards the production market; it remains in the financial circuit, at least in times of depression, when gold appears to the investor as the ideal refuge for value. The demand for gold—one asset among many—increases sharply, and the gold price rises, thus monopolizing the precious money supply, which is essential to the operation of the market. In this highly unstable landscape, product prices still fall and crisis intensifies, while gold increasingly appears like a safe asset.

In boom times, the opposite effect occurs. Money demand on the financial market, to increase consumption and investment, causes gold dishoarding and a decline in its exchange rate, and therefore increases the money supply on the production market, intensifying inflation.

To illustrate the role of gold in the case of depression, Bernácer cites the example of the great crisis of 1929 and the economic and monetary disorder that followed the First World War: countries were forced to abandon the gold standard or to devalue. According to Bernácer, France had more difficulties than Britain in climbing out of the Great Depression because it devalued later than Britain did.

Rigid Structures of Cycle Propagation

Like an earthquake, a crisis has an epicentre and theoretical concentric regular waves of propagation. In fact, the spread is quite irregular because it depends on the differential permeability of the propagation medium.

The economic environment has its challenges and its diversity: internationally, the key obstacle is the customs barrier, and diversity lies in institutional differences. Exchange is the vehicle of cycle propagation. In this respect, "fixed exchange rates, such as those established by a common monetary standard system—for example, the gold standard—are the most suitable device for the rapid spread of cyclical waves" (Bernácer 1916, p. 10). Historically, this propagation led to multiform protectionism—including tariffs and quotas—to "help defending against evil foreign competition".

There is an effective means of "defence": a variable exchange rate that works inversely to the price movement. Nevertheless, on behalf of a dominant mythology about maintaining parity, we prefer to suffer serious crises or to incur heavy borrowing over devaluing or letting the foreign exchange fluctuate. Even so, these expedients have proven mostly ineffective, and therefore we invited the government to intervene in the foreign exchange market: "We appealed for government intervention in foreign exchange, the most damaging arbitration o trade and economy". We must note here that many economists—and many of the most serious—tried to demonstrate the application of pure economics principles through statistical verification. These essays are commendable. Nevertheless, these authors should be cautious and should temper the legitimate satisfaction they gain from their essays since the researcher is in the social sciences arena.

Sometimes, the hypotheses or variables in the real model do not match the hypotheses and variables in the theoretical model. Then, can we apply one set to the other? Now, suppose that the choice of hypotheses and variables is relevant in reality compared to the theoretical diagram. Does this validate the theoretical principle? Is the choice among all hypotheses and real variables guided by an intellectual bias, without which there is no direction and, thus, no scientific research?

Further, suppose that, without any damage—assuming that we can find choice criteria free from any prejudice—we enact this choice of hypothesis and variables. Therefore, we agree to ignore certain hypothesis and certain variables, and we agree to represent a complex reality of hypotheses and variables used on one hand and hypotheses and variables neglected on the other hand with the simplest subset of hypotheses and variables used. To say that this subset is representative of the set or that the sample is representative of the population is, strictly speaking, begging the question.

Do not interpret our remark as an absolute position. In contrast, we are asking for economic research from a place of modesty and scientific relativism. Our field has a specificity that we should not hide: its almost non-experimental characteristic makes the separation of independent variables more often imaginary than experience based.

Bernácer therefore illustrates that the gold standard does not insulate the exchanging country from instability, choosing three episodes of prices in the United States, Great Britain, and Spain in 1904–1914 and 1922–1932. He notes that in the first two countries, prices had fluctuations of high amplitude while, in contrast, prices remained stable in Spain. The maximum deviations for the two respective periods were 6 and 12 points in Spain, 22 and 64 points in Britain, and 18 and 40 points in the United States (100 in each country in the beginning periods: 1904 and 1922). Even so, in both periods, Spain had a system of flexible exchange rates, while the other countries implemented the gold standard. The author, therefore, concludes that his postulation that the gold standard promotes the propagation of the cycle is verified by historical experience. We do not reject the results of this examination, and we believe that the method followed in this essay is at least as satisfactory as those in other essays by other economists. We simply aim to highlight, in regard to the general principle of these statistical verifications of macroeconomic models, the remark we made previously.

A Main Effect of the Cycle: Universal Waste

Depression can grow to infinity, and prosperity has a limit: the economy therefore works below its capacity. The fluctuations in the self-regulating mechanism only work unilaterally in the sense of depression. Therefore, the cycle results in an action and a reaction:

- The tendency, inscribed in human nature, towards progress,
- The resistance force developed, in the opposite direction, by the system.

As a result, humanity has tried in vain to discover and invent forms of progress, as most efforts do not materialize. These living forces are fully utilized for only one purpose: evil (war). As soon as peace returns, the braking forces begin to work again, leading to the paradox that peace is a condition associated with poverty and unemployment. How can we reconcile the idea that progress is useless with the reality that there are so many ills to cure, so many gaps to fill, so many needs to be met, so many things to improve, and so much human and material energies to use? "Humanity lived and still lives subject to the torture of Tantalus: it sees ways to improve its fate without succeeding in achieving them; the assurance of being able to live by the sweat of its brow, following the divine sentence, is not even given to him to let his spirit rest" (Bernácer 1916, p. 149).

Bernácer protests against certain paradoxes that distort the system:

– The idea that work is the noblest way for humans to earn a living, while in reality, work is debased, depreciated, and despised in the current economic organization.
– The idea that trade is the most obvious expression of cooperation among societies, while in reality, these societies have sometimes striven to create obstacles to trade development.
– The idea that work is a necessary but costly effort, while in reality, work is a right, and it is, therefore, sometimes used for unnecessary production.

Bernácer's view, similar to that of economists and biologists, is that there is a natural order that is disturbed by artefacts, that is, by human creations. By institutionalizing political and social struggles after a misguided analysis, humans progressively move away from the natural order; if this continues, Bernácer ultimately sees for our civilization a state of "very advanced and destructive barbarism".

This first part of the book introduced in depth Bernácer's work and life. Growing in a particular economic and political environment that has impacted his work, his unique concepts and ideas were not in the mainstream. They contributed to nurture new economics in the twentieth century. Bernácer's analysis of capitalism highlights recurring disequilibria that generate constant unemployment and cyclical economic crises.

The next chapter completes and makes the analysis deeper by focusing on the monetary factors of economic crises and their role in the overall economic theory.

References

Bernácer, G. (1916). *Sociedad y felicidad – Ensayo de Mecánica Social* (Society and happiness – Essay on social mechanics). Madrid: Ed. Beltrán.

Bernácer, G. (1922). La teoría de las disponibilidades como interpretación de las crisis y del problema social (The theory of disposable funds as interpretation of crisis and social issues). *Revistanacional de economía*, (40).

Bernácer, G. (1945). *La teoríafuncional del dinero* (The functional theory of money) (2nd ed., 1956). Madrid: Consejo Superior de Investigaciones Científicas.

Bernácer, G. (1955). *Una economíalibre sin crisis y sin paro* (Free economy without crisis nor unemployment). Madrid: Aguilar.

Carré, J.-J., Dubois, P., & Malinvaud, E. (1972). *La croissance française. Unessaid' analyse économique causale de l'après-guerre* (French growth. Essay of postwar causal economic analysis). Paris: Seuil.

De Brunhoff, S. (1967). *La monnaie chez Marx* (Money with Marx). Paris: Editions sociales.

Denis, H. (1950). Trois théories de l'intérêt du capital (Three theories of capital interest). *Revue Économique*.

George, H. (1879). *Progress and poverty*. Boston: EP Dutton & Company.

Hansen, A. H. (1953). *A guide to Keynes*, New York; French translation: *Introduction à la Pensée keynésienne* (Introduction to Keynes' thought). Paris: Dunod, 1967.

Keynes, J. M. (1936). *Thé oriegénérale de l'emploi, de l'intérêt, de la monnaie* (General theory of employment, interest and money). French translation Paris: Payot, 1959.

Kolm, S.C. (1973). *Justice etéquité* (Justice and equity). Paris: C.N.R.S.

Machlup, F. (1944). Period analysis and multiplieer theory. In *Readings in business cycle theory*.

Machlup, F. (1971). *Essais de sémantique économique* (Essays of economic semantics). Paris: Calmann-Lévy.

Malthus, R. (1820). *Principles of political economy*. London: John Murray.

Marx, K. (1963) *Œuvres de K. Marx*: « Économie I » (Marx's works by: "Economics I"), Bibliothèque de la Pléiade, Paris: Gallimard, especially: « Introduction générale à la Critique de l'économie politique » (Including: "General introduction to the criticism on political economy").

Perroux, F. (1973). Les phénomènes de propagation et l'inflation (Propagation phenomena and inflation). *L'actualité chimique, 2*, pp. 79–92.

Robinson, J. (1953). *The rate of interest and other essays*. London: Macmillan Company.

Savall, H. (1973, September). Germán Bernácer, économiste espagnol (1883–1965). Une thé oriegénérale de l'emploi, de la renteet de la thésaurisation (General theory of employment, unearned income and hoarding). PhD dissertation at the University of Paris II, 602p. Mimeographed.

Savall, H. (1975). *G. Bernácer:L'hétérodoxie en science économique* (G. Bernácer: The heterodoxy in Economics). Paris: Dalloz, Collection Les Grands Économistes.

Savall, H. (2012). *Origine radicale des crises économiques: Germán Bernácer, précurseur visionnaire* (Radical origin of economic crises: Germán Bernácer, a visionary precursor). Charlotte: IAP.

Schmitt, B. (1966). *Monnaie, salaireset profits* (Money, wages and profits). Paris: PUF.
Smith, A. (1961). *La richesse des nations (The wealth of nations)*. Spanish translation, preface by Bernácer. Madrid: Aguilar.
Spinoza, B. (2013, 1st ed 1677). *L'Éthique* (The ethics). Paris: Material.
Stoléru, L. (1973). L'équilibre et la croissance économique. In *Principes de macro-économie* (1 édition 1967). Paris: Dunod.

4

Monetary Factors of Crisis: Hoarding Versus Investment, Inflation, and Deflation

4.1 The Place of Money in Overall Economic Theory

Thanks to advances in economic theory and, particularly, the richness of the twentieth century's experiences with fluctuations in general and those of money, it seems natural to consider the economics field a monetary world in which prices, incomes, and savings are expressed in money and make sense of that condition.

Our educational programmes currently address "real" phenomena in the first year of college and monetary issues in the second year. Kaldor argues that the vast majority of the world's bankers and a bewildering number of economists still accept the dichotomous hypothesis. We also believe that, subconsciously, we still differentiate real and monetary issues, and we fear that this distinction is not always related to a didactic preoccupation. (Savall 1973, 1975, 2012)

Bernácer was lucky to be self-taught, as he began his analysis with monetary issues. Thus, he focused on the heart of the problem all his life. It is convenient to categorize theorists based on the two conceptions of economic phenomena: dichotomous or integrationist. Classical,

H. Savall, *Radical Origins to Economic Crises*,
https://doi.org/10.1007/978-3-319-93366-5_4

neoclassical, and neoliberal economists would thus be ranked among dichotomists such as Hawtrey (1937), Robertson, Allais, Marx, and perhaps Wicksell. The latter is the hinge between the two defined classes: with Wicksell, the dichotomous approach has left its mark.

In addition to the interest rate, the monetary rate is the normal rate, presented as a natural or real rate established in an economy where money plays no role. Myrdal later highlighted this anomaly (Marchal and Lecaillon 1967, p. 284). The integrationists—the founders of modern monetary analysis—include, in chronological order, Bernácer (1922), the Frenchmen Nogaro (1924) and Aftalion (1927, 1935), the Englishman Keynes (1930), the Austrian Hayek (1931), and the Swede Myrdal (1931).

We could also refine the typology since there is a world between Walras, Marx, and the classical school and Robertson, Allais, and other proponents from the liberal school. Indeed, all integrationists seem more homogeneous than dichotomists, which is logical since the latter category spans a period of almost a century and a half. We still cannot confuse, without nuance, Ricardo and Robertson or Friedmann, and we cannot deny the progress made by the Cambridge and Chicago schools over the classicals.

We therefore propose four generations of economists in the approach to monetary theory:

(a) The classical economists, for whom "money is nothing" (Piettre 1965, p. 32) if not a veil or a varnish (Marchal 1966, p. 3);
(b) The authors (neoclassical or not) who sensed that money is a specific good, such as Walras and his theory of desired cash or Marx and hoarding;
(c) The post-classical economists who integrate money in actual models and thus have a didactic dichotomous approach: Wicksell, Robertson, and Allais, according to Nême (1956);
(d) The modern monetarists, for whom the analysis of economic phenomena is immediately monetary and who build their analyses on the inherently direct collection of the money element: Bernácer, Nogaro, Aftalion, Keynes, Hayek, and Myrdal.

Functions of Money

Money has three functions: value measurement, circulation, and value conservation. This classic distinction does not seem appropriate to separately analyse the description of the mechanisms on one hand and the issue of money on the other. We suggest defining two areas of analysis: money has a passive function in which it suffers the effects of phenomena and has instrumental active functions. The passive function is related to its value, and we will examine its problems in the next chapter on value and money. Active functions can be defined as the circulation of money in an immediate and a spatial time space. We thus define a kinetic and spatial function—money as an instrument of contemporary distribution—and a dynamic-temporal function—money as a temporal link between accumulation, income, and expenditure. The kinetic and spatial functions will not be considered because neither Bernácer nor other monetarists did so. First, we must first define the concept of money.

General Definition of Money

We define money as compensation for real property in full discharge and immediacy. The compensation characteristic appears in the Marxian expression of a general equivalent or in Bernácer's "individual debt obligation of the holder on the social wealth" (1945, p. 38). Money as a particular good has no intrinsic value.

Marx speaks of "abstract wealth" (de Brunhoff 1967, p. 55), while Bernácer says that money, in its essence, is independent from any material condition. Compared to Schumpeterian definitions of money, "any object that has or does not have own value" (de Brunhoff 1967, p. 39), Bernácer has a decidedly non-metallist conception of money. Keynes demonstrates a very similar attitude from in "A *Treatise on Money*" (1930). The general discharging power of money also characterizes the definitions of the above-mentioned authors and those of Hawtrey and Robertson, who define money as "anything generally accepted in payment for goods or debts" (Cordebas-Nême 1956, p. 82). This attribute of money is generally recognized by authors and thus calls for no additional comment.

Nevertheless, Bernácer, in contrast to all these quoted theorists, emphasizes the immediacy of the discharging effect, which suggests a stricter definition of money in regard to credit.

Money and Credit

Where is the boundary between money and credit? Does the quasi-money concept belong to the micro-economy? Is it appropriate to speak of quasi-money at the macroeconomic level? These are questions suggested by Bernácer's monetary theory. Money should have a general and immediate discharging power in order to fully perform its functions. Any obstacle to these functions is the boundary between money and other assets, whether financial or real. These obstacles are, for example, the need to borrow, to obtain an advance, to sell or to mortgage an asset in exchange for true money, which everyone will accept as payment in its current form and without transformation. Therefore, at the overall level, financing is provided by money existing in the economy and being newly created by the issuing institution. Credit is therefore either an issuance of money at the overall level or an inter-agent transfer of money transfer. It is the means to acquire assets, among other goods: it is money supply and demand for assets, and it cannot be both at once. Illiquid financial asset is not money at the social level.

We support Bernácer's rigorous point of view because it avoids some confusion for which Keynes has been criticized in his concept of money. To avoid semantic ambiguity, Bernácer creates the concept of disposable funds and avoids using the word "money" in the strict sense. For both the individual and the community, assets can be sorted by decreasing order of liquidity. Ahead, we can find the amounts of money for which agents have the greatest latitude for use: they can either hoard or allocate them for exceptional expenses for consumption or investment or place them in financial or real form, etc. This amount of money represents perfectly free purchasing power; it is the "maximum disposable funds" (Bernácer 1922, p. 18). In addition to these disposable funds is cash with the same apparent nature as the previous funds but is pre-spent, intended for expenses either incurred or required for debt repayments.

The organization of modern life demonstrates that every agent has a budget in which certain expenses are mandatory: incompressible and current needs, indebtedness, contractual savings, and taxes. Materially, this money is not different from maximum disposable funds, but functionally, it has a character of minimum disposable funds. Both liquid assets form the bulk of the money supply. Other assets, financial or real, are arranged in order of increasing capital, from deposits of less than three months to real estate, and constitute a portion of potential demand for money.

We chose to bring into opposition Bernácer's strict definition and Keynes's more blurred definition. The latter seems to lead to misunderstandings, particularly in the definition of income. At a macroeconomic level, can we spend future income? The budget deficit or advances from the central bank to the economy occur in money form, but short-term loans do not: they cannot be spent by both borrowers and by lenders. In our view, Keynes's vague definition of money has an air of classicism, applying a microeconomic concept to overall analysis. We believe that the concept of money becomes clearer if strictly defined. Nevertheless, we currently observe usual definitions a trend of assimilating credit to money, which seems to proceed from confusion between microscopic and macroscopic monetary problems.

Materiality of Money

The history of various physical forms of money is not directly a component of monetary theory. It must be admitted that this history offers a lesson on the evolution of the materiality of money. Briefly, we could say that money has dematerialized in history, as driven by three factors: the inelasticity of metal production, the strengthening of the central political structure (government), and the development of production and trade. Some contemporary authors' affection for gold can be seen as a dedication to its role as international money, especially since World War II. When we note the place of gold in the international monetary system during the 1960s and the speculation that it is still undergoing, we wonder whether we can completely ignore the question of materiality. Is it entirely a story of the past? Is it a mere fleeting resurgence?

To understand monetary theory, we believe it is useful to clarify the positions of theorists faced with this problem. Among the supporters of the money sign, the most advanced position is Knapp's nominalist theory, which bases the value of money solely on its legal definition. Without a doubt, this theory is extreme or perhaps precedes historical events. In contrast, the position of Ricardo and of the money school is resolutely metallist. It lays the foundation of monetary orthodoxy that most nineteenth-century and some contemporary authors support. Did Pareto not assert that paper money was counterfeit money? To what extent did Jacques Rueff depart from the myth of gold (Rueff 1963)—are his ties with gold due to a concern for realism (descriptive analysis) or a scientific belief (normative analysis)? On this point, Bernácer, whose thoughts often aligned with those of Jacques Rueff, was in complete disagreement with Rueff.

Between these two entrenched positions, many authors find it difficult to integrate paper money and scriptural money to the scheme of metallic money. Writing at a time when the use of paper money was spreading, Marx, among others, could not consider paper money as money in the same way he considered gold. Nevertheless, he struggles to enforce his anti-quantitativist reasoning on paper money. Charles Rist still discriminates between these two forms of money.

Twentieth-century economists have less trouble adopting a non-metallist attitude because the severance of domestic money and gold began in the First World War and the expansion of scriptural money is the result of factual observation. Thus, Wicksell in the late nineteenth century, followed by Bernácer and Keynes, build their analysis on non-metallic money. We found a copy of an *undated* three-page letter written by Bernácer in French, entitled "Lettre à Monsieur Richard, un partisan acharné de l'étalon-or ["Letter to Mr Richard, a Staunch Supporter of the Gold Standard"], where the author derides the generally felt need to fix money's value to precious metal. This polemic is interesting, a kind of dialogue in which the author writes the questions (arguments supporting the gold standard) and responses (arguments against the metal standard). Regarding England's prosperity in the nineteenth century—the era of the gold standard—Bernácer says, "the truth is that it was done through its very effective work, when other countries were not mechanized, helped by its trade policy". If we still had to show that the author's monetary conception was not metallist and was based on work and market demand, we could not find a more meaningful quote.

We believe that Bernácer goes even further, as in his general model, he considers gold as a commodity—an object of speculation and, therefore, an unearned income-yielding asset—that takes a major place in his theory. This idea fits perfectly with the generalization of hoarding and unearned income. Supporters of non-metallic money, therefore, adopt an intermediate position between the metallist and nominalist theses, with money being detached from its metal definition but keeping an eminently real foundation: the quantity of goods and services for which money is the counterpart. The main consequence of this position is in the order of economic praxis, with monetary policy as a clear incentive for economic activity.

Dynamical and Temporal Functions of Money, Link Between Accumulation, Perception, and Income Expenditure

Accumulation and Collection of Income

Corporate Working Capital

We previously reported that working capital plays a key role in Bernácer's analysis of money and equilibrium. Working capital is the host structure for income accumulation, whether fixed, certain (wages and unearned income), or random (profit). It can accumulate in accordance with the product stocks, cash, or generally both. Money held by production units—true crucibles of income creation—represents, at any time, temporarily undisposable incomes for final holders (households). This income retention may have disequilibrium effects on overall economic activity by depressing effective demand. Nevertheless, it may have no harmful effect to the extent that this held income flow corresponds to held goods flow. The cybernetic synchronization of delays in production, product payment, income payment, and all payments in general is expected to balance all cash and goods flows.

The working capital of production units is equal to the amount of their stocks increased by the amount of their disposable funds:

$$K = St + c$$

It can also be nurtured by household transfers (direct loans or bank loans) that are unprocessed into fixed capital creation (H):

$$K' = St + c + H$$

This new element of working capital has the same depressive properties for demand as the accumulation of non-distributed earnings, regardless of its allocation within working capital.

$$K' = St' + c' = St + c + H$$
$$H = (St' - St) + (c' - c)$$

Money gathered in the hands of final non-demanders, regardless of its origin, has a regulating effect on demand over time. It helps contain current income expenditures while the expenditure of previous income occurs. This analysis through successive periods, already implicit in Bernácer's first book, was completed in the 1922 article. By his own admission in *Banking Policy and Price Level* (1926), Robertson had to correct it and draw his concept of "day", an ill-defined unit of the time fraction.

Bernácer did not stop there because in genuine macroeconomic analysis, it is necessary to consider inter-agents' diachronies, such as macroscopic time as a whole, which is not likely to be divided. Thus, in his final version of functional theory of money, Bernácer, after dividing time for the purpose of observing cash behaviour, reconstructs the continuous movement. After inspiring Robertson, he somehow surpassed him, thereby escaping the criticism that splitting time into days arouses.

The Status of Profit

"Profit is ... the difference between cost and price... Profit is, therefore, between two prices: elements of production and produced products" (Bernácer 1945, p. 330). While cost arises with production, profit occurs at the time of sales. According to Bernácer, profit is residual, random, functional, and dynamic.

Profit, Balancing Market Residue

As a motor and impetus of the implementation of productive combinations, profit is unique since it is not predetermined at production: it is a residual calculated *ex post*, opposing the Marxist constancy of the profit rate. The fact remains that Bernácer always accuses Keynes of not having the same design as him. In *Treatise on Money*, Keynes uses a concept of double profit: the normal and the exceptional. Bernácer condemns this position, which was inherited from Marshall (1890), and therefore cannot agree with marginalists and especially with Wicksell (1900), who says that there is no residual: "That goes without saying for me, he said, and even I have always considered as such, although I did not make a satisfactory analysis of the subject" (Wicksell 1958, p. 93).

Profit as a Random Income

This quality is the outcome of residuals. The difference between an *ex ante* fixed price—that of cost elements—and only an *ex post* known price—those of goods and of sold services—profit is linked to the selling price level and, therefore, has an uncertain existence and volume. Nevertheless, relativizing all revenues is better. In a sequential analysis, Bernácer seems to suggest implicitly, in each period, that the relations between different incomes—certain or random—experience adjustments such that the predetermination of the factor price is relative. It is more apparent than real, and profit depends as much on products' selling price as on their cost and, therefore, the randomness of profit should not lead to slight or total instability or a disappearance of the profit rate.

Ullmo discovered another of Keynes's contradictions about profit: he thought that his theory on employment (the Keynesian demonstration of the existence of involuntary unemployment from the rejection of the law of markets) is inconsistent with Keynesian theory; he contests the "differential profit similar to that of classical theory. We cannot see, indeed, a reason", says Ullmo (1969, p. 165), "that wages should be equal to income provided by marginal productivity… The situation where the employee receives less income from marginal productivity becomes steady; there is no longer any economic automatism that opposes this situation. The theory of fair wage therefore vanishes into an outcome of Keynesian analysis".

Bernácer admits that he sometimes succumbed to the temptation to argue that market stability implies that products are sold with "normal" or "expected" profit. In this regard, Bernácer admits two meanings of market stability, protecting himself from criticism of certain aspects of his analysis that suggest stagnationism, criticism that could reduce, in our view, the generality of his theory:

- Strictly speaking, stability implies that prices, costs, and profits are invariable.
- In every sense, stability is the situation in which incomes tend to maintain a certain relation between them, with the $\frac{\text{profit}}{\text{cost}}$ relation being a specific example.

While the requirements for strict market stability are not essential, the $\frac{\text{profit}}{\text{cost.}}$ constant is necessary and sufficient because, ultimately, a change in the $\frac{\text{profit}}{\text{cost}}$ ratio would change supply and therefore the market cost equilibrium. Based on the strict definition of stability, Bernácer assumes:

Stability in every sense requires that

$$\frac{P'}{P} = \frac{\Delta St'}{\Delta A} = \frac{P' - \Delta St'}{P - \Delta A} = \frac{P' - \Delta St'}{D}$$

P' = fixed income for the period

$\Delta St'$ = cost of stock variation

$\frac{P'}{P}$ = average cost of the product unit

$\frac{\Delta St'}{\Delta St}$ = average cost of the stock unit

$P' - \Delta St'$ = cost of sold products

D = price paid for sold products

$\frac{P' - \Delta St'}{D}$ = relative selling price

When $\Delta St = 0$, there is stability in strict sense, if $\Delta A = 0$; it is also true when

$$\Delta St = \Delta A \neq 0, \text{so we can write}$$

$$\frac{\Delta St'}{\Delta A} = \text{relative cost of stocks}$$

Stability in every sense requires that

$$\frac{P'}{P} = \frac{\Delta St'}{\Delta A} = \frac{P' - \Delta St'}{P - \Delta A} = \frac{P' - \Delta St'}{D}$$

To be precise, the relative producing cost = relative cost of stocks = relative selling cost.

We believe that Bernácer wants to demonstrate the need to evaluate production, stocks, and sales through the same calculation method. This alternative is the problem of accounting profit and the principle that in equilibrium, purchasing power from production is divided between stocks and sales, according to a same unit relative price.

Bernácer shows the opposite case, that is, that stability, in every sense, may linger even if prices are not maintained. Let the relation of relative production costs unlike those of sales be:

$$\frac{P'-St'}{D}:\frac{P'}{P}-\frac{P'-\Delta St'}{D}\times\frac{P}{P'}=\frac{P-\Delta St'\frac{P}{P'}}{D}$$

$$\Delta St'\times\frac{P}{P'}=\Delta St \text{ because } \frac{\Delta St}{\Delta St'}=\frac{P}{P'}$$

From which comes

$$\frac{P-\Delta St}{D}=\frac{P-\Delta St}{P-\Delta A}=\frac{S}{D}=\frac{1}{\pi}$$

Thus, we find Bernácer's basic equation of money value, from which it appears that stability, in the speaking sense, is only a special case of stability in every sense, as:

$$\Delta St=\Delta A\Rightarrow\pi=1.$$

Profit as a Functional Income

According to Lebraty (1967, p. 20), "Profit, in the neoclassical model, is considered as functional income. It compensates for entrepreneur activity. If competition terms are met, there is nothing beyond that compensation. Residual profit does not exist. Neoclassical resumes here the old idea of functional benefit. This conception was already present with some scholastics… For St-Bernard of Siena (1404–1444), Profit appeared indeed as the compensation for a social service… These ideas were developed by Spanish Jesuits in the sixteenth and seventeenth centuries, especially Molina (1535–1600) and Juan de Lugo (1593–1666). The functional concept of profit was also developed by the classics. In *Treatise on Political Economy* (1803), J.B. Say says that profit is an element of production cost that pays the entrepreneur for managing work; therefore, it has the nature of a price. Smith's idea is less clear: profit still contains a part that can be considered as a salary, which ignores one of the necessary conditions of the neoclassical operating model, and residual profit is normally likely to appear alongside functional benefits".

Bernácer takes no position on the issue of functional benefit, as defined. Even so, we believe we have to talk about it first because of Bernácer's fondness of the term functional and second because we have located alongside this ambiguous concept. Lebraty's definition of functional profit is very close to—and perhaps confused with—the concept of normal profit condemned by Bernácer. Even so, this idea of functional is not without interest. Indeed, in Bernácer's view, profit can be described as functional since it is compensation for an entrepreneurial function and has itself one function: to incentivize progress. We believe that this semantic accuracy is helpful because it illuminates Bernácer's thoughts on the issue and leads to the problem of profit, income, or uncertainty income.

Profit, Risk, or Uncertainty Income? Link Between the Present and the Future?

Kolm's (1967) question, which criticizes Knight's (1921) distinction between risk and uncertainty, also falls within an alternative working hypothesis on the debate between static analysis and dynamic analysis. According to J. Lebraty (1967, p. 74), "J.B. Clark (1899) had the merit to emphasize the distinction between static and dynamic states, analyzing the components of change". Nevertheless, for Knight (1948, p. 137), it is essential that the basic consequences of change do not come from the change itself but rather from the uncertainty it implies: "If any of these changes or all at once occur regularly, gradually or periodically or according to a known law, their impact on the price system and economic organization could be clarified quickly".

Lebraty summarizes these ideas in modern terminology whose spirit—if nothing else—seems to correspond to Bernácer's thinking: Can we not, in fact, analyse economic reality as the field of perpetual confrontation between entropy and negentropy... could market forms not be analysed as a reaction to the system entropy, such as production units' desire to protect themselves from uncertainty in a random universe? According to the Robert Dictionary, entropy means a "mathematical function expressing the principle of energy degradation. This degradation results in a growing state of disorder of nature". Negentropy, an undefined word, means the principle of the reaction to entropy.

In the first part of his book, Lebraty (1967, p .142) connects "the emergence of the uncertainty concept in the theory of profit" to the existence of true profits. We believe that Bernácer would have agreed with this analysis because his demonstration of the constancy of the $\frac{\text{profit}}{\text{cost}}$ ratio seems to be the transposition of this idea in a macroeconomic order.

In Bernácer's approach to profit as a necessary element of *ex post* equilibrium and the intertemporal link from the perspective of progress, we highlight Austruy's (1960, p. 19) idea as follows: "benefit is not only the reward of past successes; it is also collected from today's society to ensure to upcoming society a better future".

Role and Disposability of Profit

According to Bernácer, certain authors attribute the cause of market disequilibrium to profit existence. Does the author refer to followers of Walrasian analysis? Speaking of a balanced situation, Walras (1877, p. 216) said, "we will assume our entrepreneurs do neither profit nor loss…". However, Marshall, at about the same time, conducted a careful analysis of the "element fricassee" of entrepreneur gains, as Schumpeter (1961, p. 1049) describes. Does he therefore also assert opposition even within the marginalist neoclassical school? Schumpeter does not believe so; he attributes this action to the difference in the approach between Walras's eminently static model and Marshall's resolute direction towards the analysis of a changing and growing world. Bernácer is obviously more similar to the Cambridge School.

Bernácer noted elsewhere—not without irony—that among those who criminalize profit, there are both supporters of deflation theory and supporters of inflation theory. The author considers that profit is an integral component of value, generated at the time of product sale, and that, in view of demand analysis, it is not necessary to discriminate a priori between different kinds of income. Profit is also purchasing power; its randomness has no effect in this regard, and we have seen that Bernácer ultimately considers that all income involves some uncertainty. We established that profit is not, *sui generis*, a type of income that is functionally different from other types. Bernácer goes further: he argues that to pretend to find an equilibrium position in the market's monetary economy, it is at least necessary for a type of income to be potentially variable and random in the short term. The fact that the company retains temporary profit-income does not mean that this income may become disposable either for reinvestment (virtual circuit: companies—households—companies + real circuit: companies—capital goods market) or for consumption expenditures (real circuit: companies—households—consumer goods market) at some point. We agree with the previous analysis on working capital.

We simply recall Bernácer's dynamic temporal approach. First, at any time in a given economic space, there is profit distribution (and other income), and second, during a given period, there is staggering profit (and other income) distribution. Therefore, real time is never split due to the a priori non-coincidence of different types of income periodicities and different types of agents. At any time, disposable income for expenditures consists of income from different *vintages* (remember that this expression is ours. Samuelson's (1964, 1971) model of the oscillator in which incomes are dated and Solow's production function where capital is dated, i.e., "vintage", apply this idea): the previous year's profits, salaries for the previous month, wages for the previous fortnight, and savings accumulated over years. Thus, current events are conditioned by past events: theories based on an analysis of simultaneous effects and alternative solutions considered outside a concrete time dimension and a sequential approach seem very weak.

We have already mentioned two specific problems raised by profit: its quantum determination requires waiting to the end of the accounting period. Furthermore, profit disposability, as income to spend, also requires waiting for a generally longer period than other kinds of income require. As the distribution of profit to households is not realized, profit earned by the company, pending allocation, should be treated as a household savings transfer (Z). When distribution occurs at the end of the period, some of the profits—dividends—will increase households' disposable funds (A). In the hands of companies or households, profit is income like any other and does not affect aggregate demand as long as no decision is made on acquiring capital goods from a company or household consumption.

A remark about the counter-cyclical nature of undistributed profit should also be added. Bernácer shows that in the case of production growth, additional production cannot find on the market all income needed to acquire it because a fraction—profit—is not yet disposable for demand (either for investment or for consumption). The reverse occurs in cases of lower production. Thus, from an analytical perspective of fluctuations, upward or downward trends of production and employment levels are hindered (Ullmo 1969).

Income Perception and Expenditure

At a time agreed upon in advance, a part of the company disposable fund changes hands to pay wages or unearned income or to reimburse household loans. The largest fraction of these transfers is the provision of current income and results in an expense in a relatively short time. Nevertheless, from the time perspective, the question raised by the gap between income perception and expenditure is ultimately resolved to all the problems involved by non-consumption and savings use in an arbitrarily defined period of time.

Non-consumption or the Ambiguity of the Savings Concept

We introduce this concept to align with Bernácer's spirit of analysis (1941). Any other approach would use the concept of savings, but Bernácer's theory is based on cash breakdown, while mainstream classical, neoclassical, or Keynesian theories rely on equality or even on confusion between savings and investment. Thus, it seems essential to define a non-consumed product as simple non-consumption without prejudice regarding the various uses and forms of this non-consumption.

In the logic of a welfare and need economy and provided that it is possible to distinguish between sustainable consumer and capital goods (Nême-Cordebas 1960), final consumption is naturally households' first choice. Therefore, unconsumed income is generally a residual. Bernácer does not truly comment on the dual nature of this residual: is it just financial or a residual in the sense that a decision focuses first and primarily on an alternative use for income: consumption?

Nevertheless, taking into account both the role of the financial market as attractive for savers' cash investment and the evidence of cash use behaviour differences, we believe that Bernácer's position, which is not as sophisticated as the consumer choice theory or as Friedmann's permanent income theory (1956), is quite different from them due to its refusal to excessively simplify the point of view of Keynesian and post-Keynesian theories (Duesenberry 1949). Following Keynes, contemporary economists generally acknowledge the superiority of a breakdown analysis for aggregate demand for consumption goods on one hand and demand for investment goods on the other. Bernácer not only preceded Keynes in this direction, but more importantly, he did not follow him, as if he had deemed it important, Bernácer would have had time to ponder this question for twenty-six years after the publication of the *General Theory*. It seems that the problem did not occur to him because, in nearly 200 pages of *Functional Theory of Money*, he justifies his analysis by comparing it systematically to his Anglo-Saxon contemporary on many points, but he does not feel the need to talk about it.

According to Keynes's *General Theory*, income is either consumed or saved, while according to Bernácer, income is either spent in the production circuit as demand for consumption and investment or invested outside production to acquire unearned income-yielding goods.

$$\text{According to Keynes, } R = C + Sa$$

$$\text{According to Bernácer, } R = (C + I) + Ho$$

$$= \text{aggregate demand} + \text{hoarding}$$

Allow us to note that the Keynesian approach is, in this respect, dichotomous, while Bernácer's approach is forthrightly integrationist. Keynes, who breaks down production on one hand and income on the other, takes a classic approach.

Schmitt (1966) argues:

$$P = C + I \quad \text{real point of view}$$
$$R = C + Sa \quad \text{monetary point of view}$$
$$\text{But} \quad P = R$$
$$\text{So} \quad I = Sa$$

According to this reasoning, the market is absent, unless we include only:

$$I = \text{investment property supply}$$

And

$$Sa = \text{demand for investment goods}$$

Nevertheless, how can we reconcile this analysis for the Keynesian breakdown of money supply?

$$M_1 = M(Y) + M_2(i)$$

Or how can we recognize the residual conception of savings as demand for investment goods?

We do not aim or attempt to show the internal contradictions of the Keynesian analysis. Instead, for the issue at hand, we will adopt the generally accepted point of view that the choice in expenditure alternative focuses on C, whereby S is a residual, an amorphous use of income, according to Keynes. We will not seek to determine why Keynes, in his desire to differentiate his analysis from that of his neoclassical masters, emphasizes—too much, perhaps, in our view—the fact that saving is not an income conservation reflex that is generally susceptible to the interest rate and a basic component of the classical money market on which interest is created. Agreeing on both points, Bernácer anticipated Keynesian analysis.

Nevertheless, Bernácer fundamentally disagrees with Keynes's analysis. Less attached than the latter to the demonstration of unemployment equilibrium, a stone thrown by the ardent English economist in the neo-classical pond, Bernácer, the self-taught academic, resolutely adopts a dis-equilibrium hypothesis in which equilibrium appears as a particular and almost fortuitous case. Keynes, perhaps influenced by Bernácer, tried to position his analysis in this direction in the *Treatise on Money* in 1930 (Harrod 1971).

His equation:

$$\pi S = +(I - S_a)$$

Where

S	is the volume of production
π	general price level
E	income
I	investment
Sa	savings

Bears a resemblance to Bernácer's (1922):

$$D = R + (A - A')$$

Where

D	is the demand value
R	income
(A–A′)	dishoarding

Bernácer shows that the second component of each equation is the same:

Let Sa and Sb be savings at the beginning and end of the period, respectively

Ia and Ib be investment at the beginning and end of the period, respectively
Sa–Ia = A cash hoard at the beginning of the period
Sb–Ib = A′ cash hoard at the end of the period
Sb–Sa = S savings in the period
Ib–Ia = I investment in the period

It comes as:

$$\begin{aligned} A - A' &= (S_a - I_a) - (S_b - I_b) = S_a - I_a - S_b + I_b \\ &= (I_b - I_a) - (S_b - S_a) \\ &= I - S \end{aligned}$$

Keynes Bernácer

$$E + (I - S) = R + (A - A')$$

The difference between the two economists' equations lies in the first component, as Keynes takes πS, the production value, while according to Bernácer, D represents the actual demand. The origin of this difference is Bernácer's inclusion of stocks. Keynes' neglect of stocks is renewed in the *General Theory*, in which stocks appear in the text without being integrated into general equilibrium equations, which would destroy, in our view, the entire Keynesian edifice based on the eq. I = Sa.

Bernácer is, therefore, correct to say that Keynes's *General Theory* is a withdrawal in regard to his most advanced position in the *Treatise*. We believe that Keynes understood Hawtrey's analysis of stocks, including hoarding (I–Sa) in *Treatise* and M_2 (i) in *General Theory*—he also understood Wicksellian analysis in terms of cumulative processes and imbalances, as he quotes in *Treatise*. What happened, then, between 1930 and 1936—that is, between *Treatise* and *Theory?* Why does Keynes no longer refer to Wicksell in *General Theory*? Why does he fail to incorporate hoarding in the general equilibrium model in 1930, instead of relegating it to the interest rate market? Why does he fail to integrate stocks, instead merely quoting them outside the general model?

Because his target is not economic theory but rather economic policy, we believe that Keynes, for the sake of didactic simplification, builds in *General Theory* an explanatory or demonstratively simple model of his privileged themes: under-employment, interest rates, and public expenditures, in defiance of more subtle analysis that could minimize his major conclusions by nuancing them. His book is rather a doctrine than a general theory. Our comments are not inconsistent with our positive general assessment of the Keynesian contribution to economics: our judgement is similar to A. Barrère's (1952, p. 1):

> J.M. Keynes's topicality is likely no longer *General Theory*; it is certainly not that of his texts on excess savings, major works, fiscal deficit or monetary expansion. Only a superficial interpretation may suggest that these particular aspects constitute the bulk of his work, while they are only the application to the Depression, which no longer corresponds to the present situation. Keynes's topicality is in the spirit of his message. It is a standing invitation to transcendence, to synthesis and to conciliation that give impetus to his economic analysis. It is also an example proposed to the researcher, who must strive to identify objectives likely to be proposed in economic activity to better meet human needs of his time. (Barrère 1967, p. 7)

Even if not integrated into the general equilibrium model, hoarding has, in Keynesian analysis, an important place and plays a prominent role in Marshall's works. In contrast, Wicksell has virtually ignored this phenomenon, which weakens his monetary theory, while Hawtrey takes a position that is more advanced than Keynes's and similar to Bernácer's. He gives great importance to changes in working capital and the close relation between changes in stocks of goods and in cash, thus highlighting company budget constraints.

On this point, Hawtrey (1937) echoed Bernácer, showing that decline in demand may not result in production decline if there is an increase in stocks. Nevertheless, this solution implies that companies can dispose of new cash. From this perspective, Bernácer's, Keynes's, and Hawtrey's theoretical solutions are the same: to avoid drops in production and therefore employment, we must resort to fiduciary issuance (which is necessary but not sufficient, according to Bernácer).

Allocation of Unconsumed Income: Savings and Hoarding

If we agree with Bernácer that unconsumed income cannot be mistaken for savings because savings is invested in production, we assume that non-consumption in one period consists of two components: savings and hoarding. Savings is the unconsumed income allocated to productive employment, while hoardsumed income is assigned to employment outside the production circuit.

Such a broad definition allows a comparison between different theories. The definition of hoarding, for example, can also illustrate the interruption of the production process observed by Marx, Keynesian cash, and Bernácer's double hoarding. Authors who give importance to the hoarding concept commonly see it as a leak from the production circuit. Nevertheless, if we deepen the two concepts, especially taking into account their integration into the overall analysis, we realize how fragile our definition is due to various points of view on it.

The criterion for defining savings is these funds' productive use. Nevertheless, Bernácer identifies two possible uses of savings in production: fixed capital creation and stock building. Indeed, both uses have fundamentally different effects since the first is a market demand for finished goods, while stock building is mostly non-demand. Robertson adopts a definition similar to Bernácer's, while Hawtrey and Keynes use a broader one.

For Keynes, investment is somehow an investment of savings, while Robertson (1940, p. 140) defines the same word as "capital formation (sometimes currently called, rather confusingly, by the name investment)". This distinction is so basic in Bernácer's theory that, despite our preconceived thoughts about the word "investment", we tried to avoid its use in our research in order to clarify our analysis.

In our view, the ambiguity of the Keynesian concept of investment is serious, as it destroys its analysis in the propensity to invest and the marginal efficiency of capital, as not all investment is functionally homogeneous. Therefore, the motivations for and effects of different parts of the set (fixed capital and stocks) cannot meet the same criteria for analysis. The origin of confusion is a misunderstanding of the dates of the classicals: consumer goods in stocks are considered as capital. Like Bernácer, Joan Robinson (1951) denounced the ambiguity of the word "*capital*" in former and current theories.

We will not dwell on the weakness of the classical point of view, with a few exceptions. First, this weakness results from an absence of elementary observations of reality. Second, it leads to the negation of growth possibility. From this confusion arises that about the savings function: how could it have been written at the end of the last century and in the 1930s that savings were the cause of crisis? In this regard, weren't so-called savings in fact non-demand on the market for contemporary production goods? Are these savings not precisely hoarding? In his first book, *Society and Happiness* (1916), Bernácer condemns certain effects of savings. Nevertheless, he incriminates only a fraction of savings; in *Theory of Disposable Funds* (1922), he qualifies these as hoarding.

Still, hoarding is not absent from nineteenth-century theories; various writers, including Marx and Marshall, give it some place in their analysis. It seems that the Marxian concept of hoarding is similar to that of Keynes and Marshall. Hoarding is a psychological phenomenon apprehended at the individual level. On this point, and with regard to Marx, S. de Brunhoff's interpretation coincides with H. Denis. The latter goes even further; in his article op. cit., p. 440, without naming it—but using the same numerical example as Keynes (2%)—he mentions the liquidity trap, assuming that when the interest is very low, confrontation between lenders and borrowers is disrupted because hoarding becomes less risky and less expensive.

Walras (1889) also touches on the concept. Nevertheless, it is surprising that Wicksell, the father of the cumulative process, ignored the issue. Bernácer, who ignored Wicksell's work until the publication of Keynes's *Treatise*, built his theory of employment and fluctuations on hoarding and consolidated the Wicksellian theory based on the interest rate, establishing close relationships between the interest rate and hoarding.

According to Bernácer, hoarding is savings—an abstention of purchasing power—that does not achieve its economic purpose: sustainable goods demand. It is part of a larger phenomenon in which disposable funds impact not only capital goods but also consumer goods. Therefore, a priori, the shift observed between income collection and expenditure as demand for goods also exists in consumption.

Nevertheless, Bernácer notes that disposable funds that aspire to be consumed in the short term are less volatile than those intended for savings because there are compelling needs for consumption that regulate consumption expenditures. We are not far from Keynesian constancy on the propensity to consume in the short term. The difference between the two authors comes from Bernácer's more rigorous and bolder analysis of savings.

The latter detects very well that, as soon as the money supply consists of unevenly unstable fractions, we must focus our analysis effort on the most unstable portion (for Bernácer: savers' disposable funds) in order to highlight the instability factors of the entire economic system and disequilibrium mechanics. While we do not reproach Keynes for ignoring hoarding—since it is present in his theory of interest—we regret that he did not more directly integrate it into the equilibrium model. It calls the latter into question because the point of view then clearly changes even if, in many respects, Bernácer's and Keynes's analyses are often very similar in their overall philosophy.

Comparing classical and Keynesian analysis, Bernácer shows that Keynes's position appears as an abortive attempt at heterodoxy. Classicals, concerned with demonstrating equilibrium, write that $P = R \Rightarrow I = S$. Logically, Keynes' methodological position seems difficult to keep legitimate because Keynes's concern for heterodoxy begins with the observation of facts, especially after the Great Depression of 1929. Therefore, logically, his theory should aim to demonstrate disequilibria, and he should have had, according to Bernácer (and we agree) extended his essay in *Treatise* to a systematic analysis of the difference between income that is not consumed and income that is invested: hoarding.

The Change Factors of Hoarding

Bernácer does not give the same power to the banking system as Wicksell, Hawtrey, Robertson, Keynes, or, more generally, Swedish and English economists do. According to Bernácer, there is no privileged decision-maker in this area: monetary authorities, financial intermediaries, companies, and households all have their role to play. If there had to be one, maybe Bernácer would give major importance to companies and households and savings and disposable funds managers. Indeed, he criticizes Hawtrey—and Keynes in particular—for not seeing that change in equilibrium is not necessarily due to overall change in the money supply.

Implicitly, these authors did not consider that change in money supply can be neutralized by agent behaviours (companies or households) either by hoarding or by dishoarding, we believe, by the extension or reduction of usual payment deadlines. Nevertheless, in an article entitled "Zum problem des neutralengeldes" included in *Beitrâgezur Geldhere* of Hayek, 1933, Koopmans (1933) takes two of Bernácer's ideas without knowing it, according to Piettre's praise op. cit., pp. 420–421: the link between supply and demand for money and the rest of the economy and the occurrence of hoarding and dishoarding. We believe, for our part, that Koopmans brings to economic theory more than an "enhanced expression of quantity theory of money": he puts the pattern of monetary equilibrium into perspective. Below, we summarize the presentation of Piettre: $C + S + \Delta M = C + I + \Delta L$

With ΔM: change in money supply et and ΔL: change in hoarding. Two cases follow:

$$\text{If } \Delta M \uparrow \Rightarrow \text{let } \Delta L \nearrow (\text{no inflation})$$
$$\text{let } (\text{C}+\text{I}) \nearrow (\text{inflation})$$

$$\text{If } \Delta L \uparrow \Rightarrow \text{let } (\text{C}+\text{I}) \searrow (\text{deflation})$$
$$\text{let } \Delta M \searrow (\text{equilibrium without deflation})$$

We could not establish whether Koopmans was impacted by Bernácer's 1922 article, which was sent to 150 world-renowned economists. Nevertheless, the proximity of the two authors' analyses (since we cannot speak of borrowing) is great.

Explicitly, English economists do not resolutely adopt the income theory, applying it to different functions of money, as they have defined them. Hawtrey, for example, searched in the banking system for the cause of demand changes. Bernácer considers that, regarding expenditure analysis, Americans have a more realistic position. Nevertheless, he does not agree with Catchings's overproduction theory (1925) or with Moulton's under-consumption theory because, as already seen, Bernácer, who is optimistic in this respect, considers that the unmet need reserve is huge.

However, Bernácer gives these American writers credit for having acknowledged—after him but before Keynes—that purchasing power embodied in money has depressive effects on prices, production, and employment, as long as it is not turned into demand. Moulton therefore shows that savings without investment opportunity seeks and finds lucrative investment opportunities outside the production circuit. According to Moulton (1936),

- There is a shared identity between market price and distributed income amount;
- A lack of consumer demand is therefore not because prices and distributed incomes are different;
- Statistical studies (in the US between 1900 and 1930) show that there are incomes that are spent neither in consumption nor in production;
- The cause of this discrepancy is that the production is a profitable business only if there is sufficient demand, but savings is aggregate non-demand.

On this point, Moulton's analysis is similar to Bernácer's. Nevertheless, it lacks a more detailed analysis of invested savings use (Bernácer's analysis on working capital seems higher) and the determination of price fluctuation causes. Like most of his contemporaries, Catchings (1925) confuses total savings and invested savings.

However, we believe that analysis of aggregate demand ventilated into consumption on one hand and investment on the other hand, as it appears with Catchings and Moulton and then for Keynes, highlights other disequilibrium factors in the short term from the analysis of the ratio $\frac{C}{I}$. The absence of such analysis in Bernácer's works, of course, limits its generality. Nevertheless, we believe that his theory can be improved from the analysis (C + I).

According to Bernácer, there are several causes of changes in hoarding, but the main one lies in a structural complex that yields unearned income: financial market. This market, whose structure offers the possibility to serve interests and whose cycles allow speculative value-added, is a constant temptation for investors to invest their disposable funds rather than engage in the production process, in which potential productivity is generally lower at an equal risk.

We recall that the hoarding concept is often understood in a very limited sense of metallic money or paper money, like the image of wool socks. In his handbook, Guitton (1969) speaks about hoarding only for gold, emphasizing the importance of gold hoarding volume. Bernácer would certainly agree with this last point. Nevertheless, he describes a much broader content to hoard, as summarized in our "double hoarding" denomination. According to Bernácer, hoarding is keeping the purchasing power embodied by money out of productive activity. It therefore comprises:

(a) hoarding in the ordinary sense—fixed money;
(b) moving money into the financial system under non-productive transactions, which, for the most part, are speculative.

We do not know other economists who adopted such a definition. The wide field given by Bernácer to the definition of hoarding naturally results from its functional approach. For production activity, the employment level, and cash money waiting for blissful speculation—the Keynesian concept of hoarding—plays the same role as money currently used in financial market transactions.

Investment, Fixed Capital Formation, and Stocks

Bernácer considers that fixed capital formation should not be confused with stock formation. His analysis at the overall level is obviously not very refined. It would be necessary to deepen it with the table of inter-industry trade on one hand and in view of growth on the other hand. Without this, Bernácer's theory seems summarily established. We believe he must not be criticized for not extending his analysis in both directions, as in the 90 years that have now passed, economics has accelerated progress in this direction.

In contrast, we believe that his analysis raises—but does not announce—these directions, which naturally led to detailed analysis of national accounts and to production growth. Without seeking to establish Bernácer's merit in this historical perspective on the dynamics of ideas, we will focus especially on his writings to show that his analysis is superior to that of most of his contemporaries on this point, an upheaval of classical ideas and a contribution to the reality of economic analysis.

Bernácer's ideas seem to be "adopted by Koopmans in his theory on pure demand: demand in which there is no equality between the set of goods in demand and in supply. There is no Walrasian equality" (Guitton 1969, p. 343). To explain this disparity, Koopmans raises the overall equilibrium equation:

$$\mathrm{C}^* + \mathrm{I}^* + \Delta L = \mathrm{C} + \mathrm{S} + \Delta M$$

Where

C* and C represent consumption, anticipated and achieved, respectively.
I* and I anticipated and realized investment, respectively;
ΔL change in demand for cash; and
ΔM change in money supply.

Therefore, he uses the *ex ante/ex post* opposition to represent this shift, while Bernácer stigmatizes this shift in the ratio $\pi = \frac{\mathrm{D}}{\mathrm{O}}$, where D and O are different, a priori, from income and production due to changes in stocks.

Koopmans's theory on pure demand defined precisely thus reflects Bernácer's basic premise, described earlier in time, that a priori and in general, all goods in demand do not perfectly coincide with all goods in supply, regardless of the approach—static or dynamic—and regardless of the organizational system—market economy or planned economy—that there is no natural order that resolves the conflict of supply and demand in a confusion of two sets: real (supply) and virtual (demand).

We insist on this idea because it explains Bernácer's entire system of economic reasoning. In our view, it constitutes Bernácer's real revolution in economic thought, a revolution that is primarily a rejection of any classical analysis or philosophy but especially the beginning of a contemporary trend on economic research based on the concepts of indeterminacy, dynamics, and relativity of rationality.

Bernácer's essential criterion for discerning stocks and capital formation is demand: it is the voluntary decision by the one who will implement the good in question.

- *Case of capital goods*: productive capital goods are, in the hands of their producers, part of supply, which is a weight decrease in the market for goods: it is demand for disposable funds (cash). On one hand, once acquired by the person who will implement it, it can achieve its purpose, which is to increase production, all things being equal. On the other hand, payment for its price injects an amount of disposable funds upstream. It results in decisions to produce, through income distributions; it is the lifeblood of the production unit.
- *Case of consumer goods*: confusing consumption goods stock formation with investment, as Keynes implicitly did, following the classicals, seems absurd and inconsistent with his analysis on entrepreneur behaviour.

Keynes writes in real terms:

$$P = C + I$$

Where C represents the volume of produced consumer goods. He also writes in monetary terms:

$$R = C + Sa$$

Where C represents the volume value C; therefore, on one hand, equilibrium between supply and demand is achieved, and on the other, prices have remained constant in the meantime.

What company would, from a general situation considered to be in equilibrium and seeing an increase in its stocks of finished goods during the period, consider that its unsold goods are a positive element of the previous period's activity, all things being equal? It is common sense to differently consider the case in which the comparison of two consecutive equilibrium sheets of the national economy highlights that:

- In the first case, the productive capital goods item increases, reflecting net fixed capital formation and thus announcing future production growth, with its impact at the level of employment and well-being.
- In the second case, the consumer goods stocks item increases, potentially reflecting a relative saturation of consumption and announcing, all things being equal, rather less favourable prospects for production programmes and employment for the following period.

Obviously, the effects that are reasonably expected cause or maintain prosperity and growth in the first case and lead to a certain slowdown in activity or even to a reversal of the trend in the second case. We can discuss the perhaps too-entrenched principle of discrimination between demand for capital goods and stocks formation that Bernácer argues because it implies neglecting the technical and economic importance of minimum stocks, whose renewal after a boom time may represent real investment demand. The author does not completely ignore this problem when he says that stock formation can result in income distribution. Nevertheless, we believe that the difficulty of generally apprehending voluntary stock build-up by companies prevented him from refining his analysis in this sense, as opposed to subject stock formation, which expresses non-demand.

Disparity between savings and capital formation also has a temporal basis. Dynamic analysis aims to show that when income arises together with products from producers, we must wait to earn it back in the form of expenditures, and this return ultimately depends the current product's fate and future production plans. Money is a demand fee that comes from production and leaves with demand (Bernácer 1945, p. 277).

The spatial lag between decisions to invest and save (generally, investors are not savers) and the time interval between the accumulation of savings and the realization of investment are two factors that accumulation should, in perfect logic, produce an automatic non-coincidence, a priori, of savings (= non-consumption) and of investment. Even so, the time lag, in particular, can theoretically be as large as we want, and history has shown that this theoretical case often becomes reality. The analysis of this lag is essential for understanding the general movement of the economy and market mechanisms; it is also a key element of the system's instability (Fig. 4.1).

Thus, money from the shifts it introduces in income creation and in the implementation of expenditures contains within it—by its nature and by function—the seeds of all its value problems. Its analysis is not a matter of pure intellectual speculation; it is actually at the heart of economics as the synthesis of many essential elements of economic activity.

4.2 Value of Money

The concept of value is inseparable from the structure of product distribution. Moreover, it is only meaningful to the extent that there is a relative scarcity of product, as well as freedom in the choice of products. This system exists in most countries, but we can imagine other systems in which value does not have the same meaning or even has no meaning, as in the French utopian socialism regime of distribution according to each one's needs or on strict rationing, as is sometimes practiced in times of war.

If we assume that value distribution is a superior system, we will assume that the theoretical basis of value concept is doubly related, on one hand, to the distribution structure, and on the other hand, to the circulatory mean, which is its instrument: "value is not an immanent concept that appears in any conditions. It comes from social need and meets a certain distribution system that is not the only one imaginable". It is therefore logical that the value has as standard the money unit. Dissociating value and money is therefore absurd.

COMPARED ELEMENTS	BERNÁCER 1916–1922	KEYNES 1930	HAWTREY 1932	KEYNES 1936
P = R Automatism	Yes	No	No	Yes
I = S Automatism	No	No	No	Yes
Definition of equilibrium	When saving is equal to fixed capital formation		"If all costs include income and if all income is spent or invested and if investment is equal to installed capital, equilibrium is assured."	
Cause of equilibrium	P = R or I ≠ S Hoarding (S–I)	P ≠ R => I ≠ S	P ≠ R => I ≠ S Costs = income ≠ price (difference = profits)	

Fig. 4.1 Comparative table of equilibrium elements

The distribution into value is not without its drawbacks. Two major problems will be solved: preservation in time of the unit value and double determination of the value of goods and income. The solution to these problems is the effectiveness of structures and particularly of the market, which is the ultimate exchange structure.

According to Bernácer, value is not an abstract concept; it is a certain amount of money units that allows assessing both income and expenditure and efforts of production and product. It is therefore in favour of the concept of exchange value and not of use value. Money value is therefore strictly defined in relation to goods value, as the opposite of the general price level. On this point, Bernácer agreed with the unanimous opinion of his colleagues.

Nonetheless, he is different from certain writers when he says that there is no positive expression of value out of the price. Any income distribution in the production process results in property value increases. The cost is all the factor prices and the difference between cost and price. With cost, profit forms all of income. At a macroscopic level, this reasoning seems relevant, especially because Bernácer says that it does not harm the fairness of distribution between different stakeholders in production.

The Quantity Theory of Money

The only theory of money developed until Bernácer's *functional theory* was the quantitative theory of money (QTM). We can consider that the most recent theories on money demand, for example, are QTM sub-theories.

The starting point of this family of theories is an equation in which the first component expresses trade in monetary terms and the second expresses it in real terms, with the dependent variable linking the two being the general price level. This equation is implicitly based on the market equilibrium hypothesis and, of course, on money neutrality.

Commented Presentation on Quantitative Theories

QTM is, somehow, a degenerate theory. Occurring first in classical and then in neoclassical hypotheses and endeavouring to show the existence of a simple relation of proportionality between money supply changes and general price level changes, quantity theory formed a coherent whole based on the deductive method. We believe criticisms based on observations of facts led theorists sometimes either to reject QTM—in a minority movement—or to maintain it by reformulating and denaturing it. We will punctuate the history of this theory by the neoclassical formulations of Irving Fisher, the Cambridge School, Keynes, the Chicago School, and Maurice Allais.

In his seminal book of 1911, Irving Fisher (1911) establishes an obvious and simple accounting truth that in a given period, cash flow is equal to the volume of incoming payments.

$$MV + M'V' = PT$$

> From this accounting relation, quantitativists will draw causal relations, i.e., normative significance. By stating that M ' is proportional to M, that V and V' are structural constants, and that only M is likely of autonomous variations, if T is inelastic, we will conclude an unequivocal connection between M in P, refusing by postulation the one-to-one connection of P in M. (Bourcier de Carbon 1970, p. 92)

Bernácer considers that the quantity theory structure was elevated to the glory of money neutrality, a principle on which prices can change only under action to change the money supply. Nevertheless, the introduction of V as an independent variable is a logical contradiction to the principle of money neutrality.

Fisher reduces the scope of this variable, considering that *normally*, money velocity is constant. In this regard, Bernácer considers that all modern writers, repudiating the principle of money neutrality, should *logically* refute the quantity theory in the name of thought consistency.

This causal and mechanical action of M on P has an attenuated role in the formulation of the Cambridge School. In our opinion, the latter leads quite naturally to the Keynesian formulation that we shall observe below.

In these English authors' point of view, money supply is a fraction of income, with the relation between the two being the proportion considered as a constant of the income saved as cash. This point concurs with Allais's demonstration; see below.

$$M = k\,R$$

If we exclude the Walrasian intuition of *desired cash*, Marshall is the first neoclassical to formulate theory on the demand for cash, which is the expression of the structural preference of fortune and income of everyone. This analysis was assumed by Pigou, Hawtrey, and Robertson.

Hawtrey (1932) dealt specifically with an analysis of cash structure, as Keynes adopts in *Treatise on Money*. Robertson focuses on the differential effects of monetary expansion on different social groups, thus preceding the theory of Aujac's sociological analysis (Aujac and Mainguy 1950). Nonetheless, his most original contribution is the integration of time into expenditure and income analysis. Even so, this integration is less sophisticated than Bernácer's. Pigou, in *Realistic, Psychological and Institutionalist Theory on Money*, negatively reacts to the mechanistic conception of traditional quantity theory and attempts to develop quantity theory in which the observation of reality (relation between quantity of money and production level, technical progress, and real wealth), the agent psychology (the will and temperament of the cash demander), and the money issuance operating system (bank action on cash volume, dear to Wicksell and all English writers after him) will be integrated.

In fact, in our opinion, the Cambridge School announces the theory of income developed by Bernácer and then by the French Nogaro and Aftalion. Keynes is precisely at this crossroads and will synthesize all these elements first in the *Treatise on Money* and then in *General Theory*. In the first book, Keynes borrows the distinction between different types of cash that constitute the money supply from Hawtrey: income from deposits, business deposits, and savings deposits. However, in contrast to Bernácer, who first expressed this idea, Keynes does not truly integrate this analysis into his theoretical model on money.

In *General Theory*, Keynes particularly tries to show the influence of M on production volume and employment. In this regard, note that in this book, Keynes adopts a very intellectual prejudice oriented toward an analysis of unemployment. It therefore makes sense that he adopts a quantity theory on money relativized in regard to the employment level and tries to show how, according to him, money supply expansion increases demand, then production, and finally the employment level. He therefore considers that quantity theory on money is not applied to the unemployment situation. His followers will deduce, a contrario, that quantity theory will be applied to full employment.

In this context, we should emphasize the scientific abuse we commit in social sciences each time we invoke the doctrine of this or that particular author with the subconscious confusion between the master's works and those of his successors. From this point of view, quarrels between orthodox Keynesian and mongrel Keynesian doctrine, as raised by Joan Robinson, and those between the various theorists of Marxist doctrine are significant.

It is almost certain that if we neglect the successive enhancements made to Keynesian theory, *General Theory* would appear as far more contingent, more cyclical and with less universal ambition, as some enthusiastic authors acknowledged. The importance of this book seems to be more historical than theoretical and it seems greater due to aroused thoughts and by conducted experiments than by absolute value from its analysis or recommended solutions.

If we accept this interpretation of Keynes's position on QTM, the general employment level is not a significant hypothesis, while the implicit hypothesis of perfect competition and the absence of completion time for the achievement of economic phenomena that govern Keynesian analysis constitute very important limitations for the purposes of generality and reality of the Keynesian model.

Indeed, differentiated income elasticities, according to the categories of agents and business industries, means that the overall unemployment does not conflict with sectoral or categorical bottlenecks. Thus, monetary injection can cause localized inflation that then spreads throughout the economic space before beneficial effects on the overall level of employment ensure the expected full employment.

The non-substitutability and non-fluidity of disposable factors in all economic spaces that we observe in reality destroy the implicit hypothesis of perfect competition in which the compensation effect of localized misalignment at the macroscopic level is based so that their propagation outweighs their compensation.

Finally, time is strangely absent from this analysis because the implementation of factors and the additional production achievement require time that technical progress is far from reducing. In this regard, we must emphasize Robertson's superiority among Cambridge theorists. Less ambitious, less revolutionary, and less imaginative than Keynes, after Bernácer, he opened a fruitful path for economic research.

The homogeneity of the economic macrocosm and the timeless framework of economic analysis are the two flaws of the Keynesian model. Therefore, in our view, as an analyst and not as an instigator of economic policy, Keynes is more similar to his neoclassical contemporaries at Cambridge than to the economic analysts of the past 60 years. He helps us leave the nineteenth century, but does he really prepare us to live the twentieth? We argue the ambiguity of Keynes' position on QTM without giving him the benefit of doubt. Our view seems quite similar to that of Jean Marchal (1959).

With the neoliberal school, Milton Friedman (1956) offers a new formulation of QTM: a theory on money demand. However, it seems unconvincing in terms of both its arguments and its method. This theory can be roughly summarized in the following proposition: with the money supply being independently fixed by monetary authorities, under complex socio-psychological mechanisms, functions of capital demand, real or expected prices, income, interest, and securities yield, demand varies and tends to adjust to supply

In this theory, we find two neoclassical invariants: autonomy of the money supply and the dichotomous analysis it implies. How can we still say that money supply is autonomous and that actual events have no direct control over monetary phenomena? The sophisticated presentation of the second term in the Chicago equation could illustrate the theory's modernity. Nevertheless, a summary analysis of this theory emphasizes the foundations that the flamboyant neoclassical school did not disown.

We could make similar criticism as Hicks (1957) regarding the mathematical formulation of Don Patinkin (1956a, b). Marchal (1967, p. 916) criticizes not only the conclusion of Patinkin's quantity theory—that "changes in monetary circulation determine changes in the same direction and proportional of the price general level"—but also and especially the approach he said to be "very ancient and determines well the essence of quantity theory". This criticism is based on neutrality. Marchal emphasizes that, with his method, Patinkin explicitly denies the dichotomous approach alleged to be old. Nevertheless, he falls into the trap of money neutrality when neglecting the expectations and effects on income distribution. Piettre, op. cit. Summarizes Patinkin's theory using the formula on the real equilibrium effect according to which agents maintain a constant proportion between cash and intended purchases such that any increase in cash would lead to increased expenditures and therefore to price increases. Like Marchal, Piettre criticized the lack of reality of the fixity hypothesis and the lack of structural analysis but insists, rightly in our view, on neglecting time in the analysis, which is an additional criterion of classicism.

The last major attempt to reformulate QTM is Maurice Allais's econometric theory that he calls "hereditary formulation, relativistic and logistics of demand for money". From an operational perspective, Allais (1965, p. 346), relying on disconcerting statistical studies, shows that the ratio of expenditure in money supply $\frac{\text{Expenditure} = \text{Income} = \text{PQ}}{\text{M}} = \text{k}$ is substantially constant. Introducing through his analysis several elements that were missing in earlier theories, such as time and changes in income (heredity and relativism), and integrating a time of collective memory factor and a coefficient of psychological expansion, which seem to be interesting concepts, the author also shows that speed is invariant.

The general object of our analysis is a sufficient departure from the only quantity theory. We therefore do not propose an exhaustive critical analysis on Allais's theory. Nevertheless, we would like to note that, in our opinion, univocal action of the money supply on prices has not been demonstrated, and we return to this point according to Bernácer's general criticism because this formulation seems to perfectly illustrate the ambiguity of quantity theory.

Bernácer's Criticism of Quantity Theory of Money

Bernácer arises the problem of QTM in terms of logic. A theory has to propose a scientific explanation of reality. Fisher's equation of exchange should satisfy this requirement. The question is not whether Fisher's equation is correct but whether it expresses a true functional relation with independent and dependent variables. Therefore, Bernácer formulates an econometric criticism that can be summarized in the following proposition.

Let P: the unknown price level (dependent variable); T: transactions; and V: the circulation velocity of money supply M.

- According to price theory: P = f (T)
- And in the same manner: T = f (P)
- Or it seems logical to write: V = f (T, M)

So, it cannot be only a univocal action of M on P.

In fact, this logical criticism extends economic theory. It appears that Bernácer integrates the real in the monetary more than any other contemporary, beginning from the observation of facts and the need for intertheoretical consistency: he integrates price theory into monetary theory through the market, which will lead him far beyond his antiquantitativist contemporaries. He formulates his functional theory on money based on the two components of the market.

Bernácer accuses Marshall and Pigou of giving an absolute value to price and not an index value, starting from price at the basis period. The author considers that it is a classicism sequence in which analysis is devoid of any reference to time. He reproaches Hawtrey to neglect any concept of speed and highlights his difficulty in integrating his analysis on stocks—which Bernácer considers interesting—to the quantity theory to which Hawtrey is attached: his approach still seems too traditional.

Bernácer considers Robertson's quantitativism displayed in *Banking Policy and Price Level* with less severity. He is interested in the transformation of the Fisherian V into $\frac{1}{k'}$ with k representing the period of money circulation. Of course, Bernácer does not fail to note the difficulty of measuring k, but he considers that this intuition is conceptually important and that Robertson focuses on the transformation of money into income, the *only monetary transmission that had an effect on transaction volume and on production.*

Similarly, for Robertson, T is no longer the real volume of transactions, which can be greater or less for the same product depending on whether transactions on financial assets are more or less numerous. T becomes the real volume of production and P the price index of current products. According to Bernácer, this perspective, an extension of Marshall and Pigou's theory, is similar to income theory.

Regarding Keynes, Bernácer distinguishes two quite different hypotheses: that of *A Tract on Monetary Theory* included in *General Theory*, and one more similar to his own view, *Treatise on Monetary Theory*, which Keynes denied six years later. Bernácer accuses Keynes of dismissing time in his formula n = Ikp, by which he departs from Fisher and Robertson and nears his neoclassical masters, Marshall and Pigou. He even blames his ambitions to escape from current prices by the artifice of the production cost (cost + normal profit).

This exclusion of exceptional profit, which specifically reflects price movements by nature, sterilizes the analysis. Bernácer's interpretation of quantity theory seen by Keynes can be summarized as the general price level is based on liquid cash; in *Théorie générale,* this principle is called preference for cash. If the monetary and banking system does not meet changes in preference for cash, the interest rate will vary. If the supply from the marginal efficiency of capital on the interest rate reaches a certain value, it will follow a variation of I, which will result in aggregate demand and employment level changes. Should full employment prevent a production increase, product and labour prices would increase.

Therefore, it seems that Bernácer agrees with the almost unanimous view among Keynes commentators. Implicitly, he admits that Keynes has an income perspective, which represents progress in our science, and, explicitly, he admits that Keynes plans the strict application of quantity theory in his traditional version of unequivocal action of M on P in the sole case of full employment. Nevertheless, Bernácer's criticism seems sharper, as it establishes the principle of time relativity on the money value concept. Bernácer implies that within temporal analysis, the monetary equation has no meaning.

We could summarize the general and basic criticism of Bernácer's quantity theory as follows. If we assume that the monetary equation on exchange expresses a truism, it must be admitted that all variables can actually vary and are independent since any of the elements (M, M′, V, V′, P, T) can, by varying, cause an adjustment process. Bernácer, alongside the psychosocial criticism he ignores or wants to ignore, attempts to show the importance of changes in V (and/or V′).

He considers that even if M and T are constant, speed is a possible cause of variation in P. What is the significance of the change in V? Is it an acceleration of one flow in relation to the other (money flow of expenditures or a real flow of goods)? Bernácer considers that the cause of such a *differential acceleration* is the change in the "exchange ratio" between the two flows. Thus, the price change would cause misalignment, and he concludes that there is an inter-relation between all variables and an irreversible non-causality of M on P, leading to the very negation of quantity theory.

Bernácer admits that the concept of the speed of income generation could be successful if it were possible to quantify the breakdown of the money supply into its various functional fractions. Nevertheless, he is not fooled by the limits of an analysis that he proposed in 1922, as Hawtrey, Robertson, and Keynes seem to follow him in this respect, even though it is impossible to define objective criteria on the subdivision of the money supply.

We believe we can summarize Bernácer's position on the theory of money in the following three points:

(a) Monetary equation of the form P = f (M) is a *truism* that has no explanatory property and is less operational.
(b) An instantaneous monetary equation has no meaning, and it is important to know the evolution of the M/P relation.
(c) All variables involved in the monetary equation are *interdependent* and do not give preference to any theory on the analysis of causes of change: it may be the propensity to consume and/or invest, the creation of money, hoarding and dishoarding, without any hypothesis about their psychosocial causes.

Summary of Criticisms of Quantity Theory

Without returning to mercantilism, Law, Tooke, and Carey acknowledged that monetary affluence could stimulate activity, which should decrease the prices of manufactured goods. Several authors associate John Stuart Mill with these antiquantitativist precursors. Nevertheless, we believe that, on this point, the thought of this modern formulator on the law of supply and demand is not perfectly consistent. We believe that because of his dogmatic position, Stuart Mill (1848) does not include in his analysis several relevant observations that are neglected because they are inconsistent with the general pattern to the point that they seem inconsistent compared to the whole.

Such examples—like several in economics—explain his delay in the late nineteenth and early twentieth centuries. Walras (1883) and the concept of desired cash, Marshall's concept of hoarding, and Keynes's concept of inflation offer some notorious examples of theorists' inability to logically integrate all those views in a general model that is consistent because of its internal logic and resistance to statistical analysis.

We will give special place to a theoretical stream that is most developed in France, where scientific hegemony from Anglo-Saxons has always found—rightly, we believe—some intellectual resistance, which has been beneficial to scientific progress. Menger, the precursor of the theory on money demand, Von Wieser, the precursor of income theory and Wicksell, the instigator, in various ways, of the Keynesian theory, entirely refuted the quantity theory. Nevertheless, we owe a great deal to Aftalion and Nogaro for the qualitative or psychological theory of money, otherwise suggested by the terminology or by the Walrasian analysis of desired cash. This analysis from the behaviours and expectations of two French economists inspired Keynes and then experienced a renewal with a sociologically dominant base in France and later in the United States.

Nogaro's criticism of quantity theory is primarily methodological. It is based on statistical observation that shows, first, that there is no proportionality between movements in money stock and those of prices and the limited changes in flow velocity are not enough, in this case, to quantitatively explain price changes. Therefore, the quantity theory is incomplete and insufficient, and the coincidences sometimes found between money movements and prices movements do not ascertain, strictly speaking, a causal link. Nogaro (1924, p. 156) charges the dichotomous approach on which it is based the essential vice of quantity theory; it is the premise on which the French economist based his criticism. Early on, (Nogaro) captures the phenomena expressed in monetary form. He considers cash incomes, and he reproaches traditional authors and Keynes in *Monetary Reform* for "not considering the integration of the money theory and the production theory". This is exactly the position Bernácer took a decade earlier in his first book, and he maintained it afterwards.

We noted in the positive aspects of Nogaro's theory many points of resemblance with Bernácer's theory. To determine prices, Nogaro takes elasticities into account, and he considers decreasing costs and taking progress into account, which places him against the tide of the mainstream marginalist thinking and makes him more similar to the Spanish economist. Even so, it is especially in the content of the income theory of money that Nogaro's theory resembles those of Bernácer: "It is thus from an increase in personal income that an increase in money stock can increase price" (Nogaro 1924, p. 164). Like Bernácer—but without undertaking an exhaustive analysis—Nogaro gives the company a privileged role in the transformation of money into income, a necessary condition for money stock movements to affect prices. This importance of the company, considered through an analysis of working capital, is further enhanced by the inclusion of supply in price movement patterns. This idea is basic, according to Bernácer. Both authors described it during the same period (1924–1925) and put their theories of money at a level of unquestionable superiority over contemporary theorists.

Nogaro (1945, p. 241) asserted that "the corollary of production normal development is a corresponding increase in money stock". Bernácer preceded him by a dozen years, setting the conditions for money issuance, which is necessary for full employment and business growth. However, Nogaro had an original idea different from Bernácer's theory. He differentiates products, showing that a general rise in prices is often, in fact, an average increase because some goods are relatively scarce compared to others on the market at some point, such that the relative inelasticity of production and, consequently, supply may cause a rise in prices on a general (average) level.

We conclude our discussion of Nogaro's theory with this quotation from the report to the Congress of French-speaking economists, in 1947, on the theory of inflation: "In short, if we consider the quantity theory as expressing an action as it were mechanical, that changes in the quantity of money would exert on prices irrespective of factors affecting *supply and demand* on various markets, it should be recognized that it does not correspond to any reality".

Aftalion's (1927, p. 87) statistical observations between 1922 and 1924 find variations structured as follows: foreign exchanges, prices, speed of money circulation, and, finally, money supply. He sets out the theory of income in these words: "The theory of income only considers as direct and safe factors of money value changes those that modify national income and income into money without a corresponding increase in production. The result is a lack of proportionality between the movements of circulation and prices… and the theory of income not only refutes the proportional action of circulation on prices; moreover, it admits the possibility of price action on circulation". This monetary theory is a psychological theory that incorporates the volume of the budget deficit, the credit facilities that may explain increasingly speculative demand, the speed and efficiency of economic information, and social trends, such as union pressures and bottlenecks in production. According to Bourcier de Carbon, monetary theory becomes dynamic, explains acceleration and deceleration, and integrates phenomena of memory and anticipation. According to Marchal and Lecaillon, Aftalion brings, after Wicksell, whom he did not know, before Keynes's *Treatise on Money* and *General Theory*, and before Myrdal's monetary equilibrium, a revolutionary view that is profoundly evocative on monetary issues.

More similar to this analysis, Gurley and Shaw (1962, p. 18)) emphasize the adjustment process between supply and demand for money as they define it and use the concept of disposable funds that is dear to Bernácer, following a methodology and concepts that he would not have disowned: "Let's call money supply the new money creation by the banking authority… during a given period. Let's call demand for money the money supply disposable at the beginning of the period…". Bienaymé (1964) argues for a predominance of real trends in the growth process and thus the dependence of the money supply, from Gurley and Shaw's model, and the notion of financial detours. He introduces substitutes for money supply (the creation of financial assets).

This bracket of recent history on theories shows that the instruments and the analysis model initiated by Bernácer over a century ago remain topical. If we take, in order of importance, the catalogue of L. Bourcier de Carbon's assumptions on which the quantity theory would be based, we can admit that when the first two of these conditions are met, the quantity theory is likely to apply:

- Cash rigidity,
- T rigidity,
- Nonexistence of time reactions,
- Nonexistence of stocks,
- Nonexistence of quasi-money supply,
- Nonexistence of specific financing techniques.

We will endeavour to reformulate criticisms of QTM by grouping.

- Reversing the action of M on P

This principle formulated by Bernácer, Nogaro, Aftalion, Gurley, and Shaw, among others, implies admitting the predominance of real factors or the market over price movements: it emphasizes the inter-relation of variables and leads, according to Bernácer, to the negation of the essential conclusion of quantity theory.

- Relativization of QTM and cycle theory

This principle leads us to admit the possibility of varying goods supply following the demands caused by money supply variation. This adjustment can be achieved through stocks (Bernácer and Hawtrey) or through production and employment levels (Bernácer, Nogaro, and Keynes). The formulation, which is too broad in the case of Keynes, is more nuanced in the case of Bernácer. Cautious not to use the ambiguous concept of full employment, Bernácer uses the expression "reciprocal market adjustments".

– Hoarding

In line with J. Stuart Mill and Walras and overlooked by Wicksell, the concept of hoarding became more vigorous with Menger, von Wiesell, Marshall, Robertson, Aftalion, and Keynes. However, Bernácer used the concept only to pivot from his monetary equilibrium theory. Nevertheless, the concept is not fully integrated in all the analyses since, for all these authors, excluding Aftalion and Bernácer, considering hoarding does not lead to questioning the quantity theory.

Marx seems to give more significance to hoarding than anyone else in his time. According to Marx and Bernácer, value reserve, regulators of goods circulation, and hoarding do not have the same status.

– Dynamization of monetary theory

Implicit in Wicksell and Simiand and then brought to a full-fledged variable state by Bernácer, Robertson, Samuelson, M. Friedmann, and M. Allais, time integration sometimes leads these authors either to justify or to reject the quantity theory.

– The logics of the analysis

The dichotomous approach is the first criticism of Bernácer and Nogaro. Bernácer nonetheless goes further by stating that quantity theory is a tautology and, as such, does not deserve so much discussion: we can both accept and reject it according to what we want it to say.

This notion represents the ambiguity of the current terminology: we believe that the quantity theory is a semantic corpse. We cling to that expression to represent the only formalized theoretical edifice of monetary theory. Nevertheless, we doubt that Allais aimed to show that increasing M proportionally increases P. We are convinced that Allais's relativistic and logistical hereditary theory establishes only that an almost constant relation exists between M and PQ without defining the source of variations. If our interpretation is correct, then Bernácer would have supported Allais's theory, just as he never rejected the formula MV = PT, that is, that exchanges in one period (PT) are realized by a monetary instrument (M) that circulates V times during the period. In our opinion, this ambiguity explains the contradictions of Stuart Mill, Keynes, and the renewed interest in "theory" by resolutely modern authors. Against this quantity theory, several authors have tried to build income theory, including von Wieser, Bernácer, Aftalion, Nogaro, and Keynes. Their theories, approaches, methods, and variables are different. We will analyse Bernácer's contribution in the following section.

The Functional Theory of Money

Bernácer (1945, p. 217) described his own theory as functional, as he "found it on the different function of different portions that must be differentiated in the money supply". Another denomination would be possible in reference to dominant theory: "the basis of the theory of money should not be the quantity of money in circulation, as postulated the quantity theory of money, but the income of the economic subjects. Perhaps, because of this, the income theory would be a more characteristic and understandable denomination".

Functional Partition of Money Supply

Money supply is not perfectly homogeneous: the various units that compose it are not absolutely interchangeable. It is possible to identify several kinds of money supply, provided that this differentiation is punctual, static, and temporary because the stock that money supply represents leads to a flow that constantly transforms the quality of those monetary units.

The idea is intuitive but, in our view, it greatly enriches the analysis: a euro that we are about to spend on consumption has an economic potential for production that a hoarded euro does not.

All the supporters of the income theory of money implicitly make this reasoning. A monetary unit is valuable only according to the decision attached to it. In this respect, any monetary unit contains three "cases" at the macroeconomic level, where transfers balance. It can be used to demand a consumption good, to demand an investment good, or to demand nothing on the product market (hoarding in every sense).

In the article "Theory of disposable funds as an interpretation of crisis and social issues", which was published by Bernácer in 1922 with a French summary and distributed to 150 renowned European and American economists, the author returns to—and deepens—the ideas presented in his first book, *Society and Happiness*.

Bernácer's concept of disposable funds is similar to Keynes's concept of liquidity, subject to our comments on the definition of money. Nevertheless, disposable funds, as immediately disposable monetary cash, has varying degrees reflecting the agent's degree of decision freedom. Bernácer's underlying idea, which he does not clarify, is a true theory of distribution. The monetary unit, as additional purchasing power distributed by the production, does not have the same effects on production, on employment, or on growth and progress, depending on whether the beneficiary is an agent whose low income will be fully consumed or if it is an agent whose income is such that the money unit comes to enlarge the savers' stock of disposable funds. In the second case, savers' stock of disposable funds will increase.

Bernácer see two differences between his concept of disposable funds and Keynesian liquidity. According to him, as the price of abandoning cash, interest has an explanatory virtue only through a microscopic approach. Nevertheless, the main difference between the two concepts arises from their very essence: Keynes's liquidity is not compatible with the assumption I = S. Indeed, we believe that there is confusion in Keynesian analysis. I = S is a *flow* of savings and investment, and its equality is perfectly compatible with the existence of liquidity *stock* as long as this stock remains unchanged. Even so, the stock liquidity preference, according to Keynes, depends on the interest rate and is thus eminently variable. Our opinion is that there is inconsistency between the (I = S) assumption and the liquidity function. We share Bernácer's conclusion that the liquidity concept as established by Keynes is, by definition, irrelevant compared to the equality assumption for investment and savings. The Keynesian model's neglect of stocks seems to be responsible for many inconsistencies in Keynes's analysis. From this point of view, after Bernácer, Hawtrey, and Koopmans conduct more a robust analysis, but they were unable to make their different intuitions perfectly consistent between them because of these authors' lack of a fair functional analysis of money, as noted by Bernácer.

This analysis begins from the idea that the overall volume of the money supply is constant, while there are internal movements of money from one "fund" (category) to another, reflecting a change in function. Even so, these internal movements motivate significant changes in overall equilibrium. Bernácer (1955) does not emphasize that this analysis includes or implies behaviours and decisions among agents responsible for these internal movements, and, finally, his analysis certainly has a positive, objective approach that analyses real facts and not agents' intentions. Nevertheless, this analysis does not seem incompatible with Nogaro's psychological (1924, 1947) or Aujac's sociological analyses (Aujac and Mainguy 1950), which complete and enrich it, as significant misalignments can arise without altering overall money supply. In our view, Bernácer is the most antiquantitativist among monetarists because he does not merely show that the quantity theory is wrong, as there are many inter-relations between variables and non-causality of M to P, but he especially shows that there are causalities beginning from a disruption in the internal structure of the money supply. This contribution by Bernácer seems modern, given its structural analysis, and original, given the monetary theory it contains. In terms of idea coherence, although Bernácer never uses the term *structure*, we assert that all of Bernácer's analysis is structuralist, evolutionary, and institutionalist.

We must emphasize that a change in money's function does not always coincide with a change in the money's holder: the determining factor is not the change of hands. Aware of the difficulty of statistically apprehending this moving money supply, Bernácer advocates that banks open separate accounts for current expenses and for savings. This way, we can observe changes of hands without changing function, and vice versa. Thus, when disposable funds pass from the hands of the saver to those of the investor through a loan, there is no effect on goods market equilibrium, as these amounts will not reach the producer of capital goods, which is the object of the investment. In contrast, when the consumer debits from their savings to make a purchase for consumption, a functional change occurs without immediate inter-agent transfer, an act that will affect the production market equilibrium.

	BERNÁCER (1916–1922)	HAWTREY (1919–1937)	KEYNES (1930)	KEYNES (1936)	
Productive capital	Disposable funds for consumption	Consumers' cash balances	Income balances	Income motivation	Transaction motivation
	Disposable funds for company	Traders' cash balances	Business balances	Business motivation	
					Precautionary motivation
Speculative capital	Disposable funds for savings	Investment market cash balances	Saving balances	Speculative motivation	Speculative motivation

Fig. 4.2 Comparative table about fractional analysis of money supply

We summarize Bernácer's, Hawtrey's, and Keynes's fractional analyses of the money supply in the following table (Fig. 4.2).

For simplicity, we call savers' disposable funds speculative capital, although this expression is not as clear in Bernácer's writings. Bernácer considers that the precautionary motive is difficult to differentiate from the transaction motive and that it is of little analytical interest. We want to emphasize that the parallelism of the fractional analysis from the three authors is more apparent than real. Hawtrey (1919) does not draw strong conclusions from the fractioning money supply. Keynes bases one of the terms of liquidity preference on the interest rate and speculation motive. Meanwhile, Bernácer takes the greatest advantage of this partition by refining money supply analyses and the agent behaviour that underpins them and by focusing his analysis of and conclusions on equilibrium theory on savers' disposable funds. Robertson, without conducting a systematic analysis of the money supply structure, uses the concept of differentiated cash.

The Structure of the Money Supply According to Bernácer

After describing transactions that have no influence on money value (unrequited payments or payments with deferred compensation, payments for asset transactions, payments for consumptive services or income transfers, and payments for intermediate consumption), Bernácer describes the money supply structure in a diagram we reproduce.

In this structure, total disposable funds (C)—especially the stock (a) of savers' disposable funds—are especially unstable. Indeed, if the natural function of saved disposable funds is investment, that is, the fixed capital formation of production units, there is, unfortunately, a possibility for savings to be diverted from their natural function: the acquisition of unearned income-yielding assets.

Therefore, Bernácer saw before Keynes that agents could be incited not to consume or invest to the extent that there are lucrative investment opportunities outside production. Then, Keynes partitioned the money supply into two masses, M1 and M2, with the first being based on income and the second on the interest rate. Bernácer, meanwhile, considers that element (a), savers' disposable funds, and, to a lesser extent, element (c), companies' disposable funds, are functions of the attractiveness of what he calls the "financial market", which materialised not only through the existence of an interest rate provided by the market but also through the prospects—often more attractive—of value-added. In this regard, Bernácer's analysis is more complete than Keynes's analysis and including value-added in the dynamic analysis confirms Bernácer's implicit hypothesis, which forbids assumptions on price stability and immediately takes place in a system in perpetual motion (Fig. 4.3).

$$M = \text{Money supply} = a + b + c$$

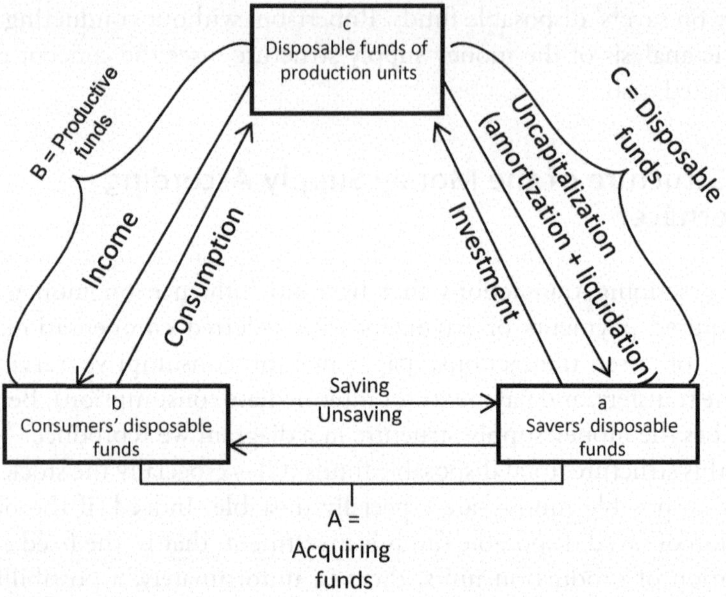

Fig. 4.3 Circuit of disposable funds

A = (a + b): Funds likely needed to acquire all production and stocks: it is, at any given moment, the maximum capacity of potential demand for products.
B = (b + c) circulation of final goods between producers and consumers: market for final consumption products.
C = (a + c) disposable funds: overall amount of savings disposable for any use (consumption, investment, investment in an outside production circuit).

The arrows represent flows, and the rectangles represent monetary stocks.

It should also be recalled that the Keynesian concept of liquidity is—in a sense—narrower than Bernácer's. For the latter, hoarding may consist of moving money. This money is said to be hoarded not because it is tied up but rather because it is outside the production circuit, whether pending the completion of an investment or a speculative transaction or in progress for such an operation. According to Bernácer, hoarding is not only cash savings, it is mostly non-expenditure in the production circuit, which can result in either cash holding or investment in unearned income-yielding assets. Bernácer's foundation of hoarding is concrete, while that of Keynes and Marx is psychological.

Dynamic Theory of Money Value

Bernácer's monetary theory includes a time dynamics perspective, assumes the necessity of market to create the social value of money and founds the monetary equilibrium on a positivist approach.

Bernácer's monetary theory is immediately placed from the time dynamics perspective. Recall that Henri Guitton (*The Economic Fluctuations*, 1950, p. 386) cites Bernácer in "Chapter II: The Birth of the Dynamics and as Precursor of Successive Periods Analysis, First Formal Framework of Econometric Models".

One of pernicious errors of economic research has been "the research of invariable measures of a thing's value. Many economists allow themselves to be dragged by the vain illusion of a common measure of goods and services independent from money… Absolute value units are as unrealizable as circle squaring or perpetual motion… The economist has no recourse but to rely on money unstable value itself, as the geographer takes as a reference point the variable level of sea areas. Our kingdom is that of relativity".

Necessity of Market as Basic Structure for the Social Value of Money

> Individuals are unable to quantify their needs, their satisfaction, and their preferences. It is only in the virtue of a large number of individuals' participation and through monetary instruments and market mechanics that it is possible to reach the numerical expression of value. For this reason, Robinson's economy, which we abuse so much in economic reasonings, teaches nothing useful about the theory on value. (Bernácer 1945, p. 17)

We can ask two very different questions: why is the point equilibrium between supply and demand (*ex ante* concept of the *mathematical-psychological speculation*) or the analysis of the *ex-post* realized equilibrium, which is a *mathematical-statistical* problem, fixed at a certain level? Bernácer solves only the second question, as it is the only way that allows" satisfactory expression of effective demand and supply for money evaluated in terms of goods for statistical analysis on these quantities" (*Ibid*, p. 22).

In 1929, Bernácer gives the first explicit formulation of the money value V:

$$V = \frac{1}{I} = \frac{P + \Delta St + \text{Trade balance}}{R + \Delta A + \text{Balance of payments}}$$

I represents the price index, P production, R income, ΔSt changes in product stocks and ΔA changes in cash.

Determination of a Dynamic Formula for Money Value

The effective demand flows for a given period are equal to the income flow of the period minus the formation of disposable funds A (acquisition fund).

$$D = R - \Delta A \tag{4.1}$$

Supply flow for the period is equal to the production flow decreased by stock formation E.

$$S = P - \Delta St \tag{4.2}$$

Even so, production is to income what the object is to its image:

$$P = R$$

The condition for equilibrium is:

$$\Delta A = \Delta St$$

The increase in money supply is ΔM = ΔA + ΔC; this increase involves money creation in the same amount and results in an increase in working capital, which becomes:

$$\Delta K = \Delta St + \Delta c$$

Given,

$$\mathrm{A} = \mathrm{M} - \mathrm{c}$$

The supply is unchanged, but the demand changes by replacing R by P in (4.1).

$$\mathrm{D} = \mathrm{P} - \Delta A$$
$$\mathrm{D} = \mathrm{P} - \Delta(\mathrm{M} - \mathrm{c})$$
$$\mathrm{D} = \mathrm{P} + \Delta c - \Delta M \qquad (4.3)$$

Hypothesis of the Absence of Paper Money Issuance

When there is no money creation,

$$\Delta M = 0 \text{ and } \mathrm{D} = \mathrm{P} + \Delta c \qquad (4.4)$$

In this case, Δc represents incomes that will be distributed by companies only during a subsequent period, due to their periodicity (profits, interests, and certain royalties and compensations, etc.)

If D and S are different,

$$\mathrm{D} - \mathrm{S} = \Delta St + \Delta c - \Delta M$$
$$\mathrm{D} - \mathrm{S} = \Delta K - \Delta M$$

And in the absence of money creation, there is deviation from equilibrium:

$$D - S = \Delta K = \Delta St - \Delta A \qquad (4.5)$$

The following equality is expressed: when there is disequilibrium on the product market, the deviation is equal to the change in working capital (ΔK), that is, to the difference between stock variation and variation in household disposable funds.

If $\Delta St > \Delta A (\Delta K > 0)$, it is because, for the acquisition of a quantity of goods during the period, an amount of income greater than the final production of the same amount of goods distributed has been spent. This results in a price increase.

If $\Delta St < \Delta A (\Delta K < 0)$, the opposite occurs and prices fall.

The Investment of Savings in Production

What are the effects of the transfer of households' disposable funds to companies?

1st time: savings are accumulated by households, at the cost of, all other things being equal, effective demand.

2nd time: households transfer to companies disposable funds, for ΔZ amount.

The demand becomes, by transformation of (4.4):

$$D = P + \Delta c - \Delta Z \qquad (4.6)$$

3rd time: companies' use of ΔZ may be allocated partly to fixed capital formation z and partly to working capital ΔH:

$$\Delta Z = \Delta H + z$$

This investment results in the distribution of a fraction (r) of ΔZ into households' income. The new disposable funds become:

Time	Demand expression	Supply expression	Conditions for equilibrium and effects
t_0	$D_o = P - \Delta A$	$S_o = P - \Delta St$	$D_o = S_o$ when $\Delta A = \Delta St$ Yet $\Delta M = 0 \rightarrow \Delta A = \Delta M - \Delta c$ $= -\Delta c = \Delta St$ A company's disposable funds are allocated to stock financing $D_0 \neq S_0$ $D_o - S_o = \Delta St - \Delta A = \Delta St + \Delta c = \Delta K$ The disequilibrium is equal to an increase in companies' working capital
t_1 = savings transfer from households to companies ΔZ			
	$D_1 = P - (\Delta A + \Delta Z)$ $D_o - \Delta Z$	$S_1 = S_o$	$D_1 < S_1$ = trend towards recession
$(t_2)'$ = Company use of savings transfer $\Delta Z = \Delta H + z$ (general case)			
	$D_2 = D_1 + z$	$S_2 = S_1 + z$ $= P_o - \Delta(St_o - z)$	$D_1 < D_2 < D_o$: recession compared to (t_o) equilibrium $D_o = S_o$ and reconsidered in relation to (t_1) disequilibrium
$(t_2)''$ = use of saving transfer by companies to exclusive working capital financing $\Delta Z = \Delta H$ (this particular case is unrealistic because stock formation indirectly leads to new income formation)			
	$D_2 = D_1$	$S_2 = S_1 = S_o$	$D_2 = D_1 < D_o$: recession compared to equilibrium in t_o and compared to $(t_2)'$ planned imbalance
$(t_2)'''$ = saving transfer use by companies to exclusive financing for fixed capital formation $\Delta Z = z$			
	$D_2 = D_1 + \Delta Z = D_o$	$S_2 = S_1 = S_o$	$D_2 = D_o = S_o = S_2$: we return to the equilibrium reached in t_0. The investment takes over consumption in aggregate demand

Fig. 4.4 Demand and supply equilibrium conditions

$$\text{Companies} \quad : c' = c + (\Delta H + z - r)$$

$$\text{Households} \quad : A' = A + r$$

And demand becomes:

$$D = P + \Delta c - \Delta Z + z$$

$$D = P + \Delta c - \Delta H \tag{4.7}$$

ΔH = transfers of savings from households to companies intended for stock formation or, more generally, for working capital increases (stocks and disposable funds pending assignment).

The table we propose below summarizes the various cases to consider.

General hypothesis: ΔM = 0 (absence of money creation) (Fig. 4.4)

The main lesson to be drawn from this model is twofold:

- Even integrated into monetary theory, supply has a less active role than demand in the production process. It seems that Bernácer implicitly considers that demand is the driving force for activity; the author thus breaks with classic tradition and heralds a modern Keynesian analysis.
- In the absence of money creation, additional stock formation by companies generates recession, other things being equal.

In terms of monetary theory, sensu stricto, this model tends to show that in the absence of the so-called autonomous money supply variation—the quantitativist hypothesis—disposable funds variation and therefore the money supply change in the *internal structure* are enough to cause variation at the production and employment levels.

Bernácer's analysis favours the income and expenditure approach instead of the purely monetary approach, which involves analysing agents' behaviour, as later explained by Nogaro and Aftalion and deepened by Keynes, Perroux, and Aujac, among others. His refusal to combine economics with other disciplines in an attempt to base his analysis on observable facts at a macroscopic level—which was understandable at the time—is part of a current of modern economic thought that could be described as econometric, etymologically speaking. He attempts to ascertain economic laws on an aggregate measure and thus announces, following physiocrats, the establishment of national accounting.

Nevertheless, from the monetary point of view quoted by Hayek, Koopmans's quantity theory has some similarities to certain aspects of Bernácer's theory, which, remember, came first.

Thus, the terms $\frac{\Delta M}{\Delta t}$ and $\frac{\Delta L}{\Delta t}$ from the Dutch economist monetary equation highlight the importance of adjustment between *money creation velocity* $\frac{\Delta M}{\Delta t}$. and hoarding velocity $\frac{\Delta L}{\Delta t}$. According to Bourcier de Carbon, monetary perspectives and expenses compete without excluding each other, as rooted in Wicksell. We believe that Bernácer's theory, more than that of Wicksell, who remains, in our view, too attached to quantity theory, deserves this synthesis role between these two perspectives that we believe to be inseparable. Thus, Bernácer can be freed from most of the criticisms of monetarists and expenditure school supporters, as Pen summarizes. As for us, we will make some of these remarks to Bernácer's name: he neglects M for being too soft, according to Pen's expression, he integrates the interest rate in the analysis (*infra*), and his economic expectations are related to expenditure analysis. Finally, Bernácer escapes the main criticism of the expenditure school because he does not minimize the importance of money creation or destruction for the system.

Bernácer is antiquantitativist, given the functional aspect of his analysis and his attempt to define a dynamic money value theory: the second aspect of his so-called functional theory. The expression Bernácer gave to the monetary value in 1929 resulted from an insufficiently dynamic approach in which time was integrated only through stock variations (real and monetary) and in his opinion, the concept of money value, expressed in terms of total income at a given time, was too classical. During the 1930s, Bernácer gradually placed the concept of money value into the perspective of the time variable: basically, for him, writing an equation on money value at a given time has little meaning. We must resolutely go one step further in terms of economic science by saying that money value exists only as a function of the time variable.

Therefore, he tries with great effort to integrate three parameters of his economic thought on monetary analysis: the structural method, where money involves the value creation structure of the market; functional analysis, where money is not a homogeneous entity; and finally, temporal analysis, which is actually the hallmark of our time, as it analyses evolutions. There are no immutable criteria for size appreciations, especially economic ones. It is less important, for example, to define distribution criteria for the current period than to strive to improve the future or to analyse the past evolution of the distribution structure. It remains to determine how Bernácer tries to integrate time in monetary theory.

Definition of the Disequilibrium Coefficient

Let $\pi = \frac{D}{S}$ be the demand-supply ratio for a given period; when this coefficient is equal to 1, it means that, on average, across the market, products have been sold at a price such that one value unit of production was exchanged for one income unit. When $\pi \neq 1$ (general case, a priori), π represents the price of one unit of goods value expressed in income units. Compared to 1, the numerical value of π indicates a price's general trend above or below the average price at equilibrium. According to the author, π should not be confused with current price indexes. π represents the entire population of real prices weighted by the real quantity of goods and not the sample of price indexes, which can be more or less representative. Conceptually, π is more similar to the retail price index than the wholesale price index because intermediate operations on non-final goods are excluded from the π calculation. Finally, this coefficient is different from the retail price index since it includes the prices of final production goods while excluding what Bernácer calls consumptive services.

π therefore appears as an ideal price index whose weighting would be perfect, involving no hypothesis on the determination of weight coefficients. The commonly used statistical indexes could be, in our opinion and despite what Bernácer believes, a useful approximation of π, being to π what the sample is to the population or what a poll is to an exhaustive census.

Formula According to the Split Time Method

In the following section, we use "index I" to refer to Bernácer's ideal index.

Let V_0 be the value of a set of goods at time t_0 and V_i and V_n, the value of the same set at respective times t_i and t_n. We can define the indexes for the successive prices:

$$I_1 = \frac{V_i}{V_0} \ldots I_i = \frac{V_i}{V_0} \ldots I_n = \frac{V_n}{V_0}$$

Or the indexes:

$\frac{V_1}{V_0}, \frac{V_i}{V_{i-1}}, \frac{V_n}{V_{n-1}}$; the product of which is equal to $In = \frac{V_n}{V_0}$.

The considered goods set includes all the goods that are really exchanged in nature and in quantity at different periods $(t_1 - t_0)$, $(t_i - t_{i-1})$, $(t_n - t_{n-1})$.

We emphasize the period and time (or epoch) duality. Let t_0, t_1, t_{i-1}, t_i, t_{n-1}, t_n be times or epochs, while periods are defined as the time that elapses between two successive times $(t_1 - t_0)$ $(t_i - t_{i-1})$ $(t_n - t_{n-1})$. This distinction is implicit in Bernácer's analysis. We make it explicit because it is essential for understanding what follows. The πi are defined with respect to periods and V_i (and therefore I_i) in relation to epochs; hence, there is a need to demonstrate that the passage of I_i to π_i is strictly acceptable, provided we take infinitesimal periods; this was mentioned but not detailed by Bernácer.

$$\frac{V_1}{V_0} = \pi_1 \frac{V_i}{V_{i-1}} = \pi_i \frac{V_n}{V_{n-1}} = \pi_n$$

$$I_n = \frac{V_n}{V_0} = \pi_1 \ldots \times \pi_i \ldots \times \pi_n$$

Thus,

$$\log_e I_n = \log_e \pi_1 + \ldots + \log_e \pi_i + \ldots + \log_e \pi_n$$

When $(t_i - t_{i-1})$ is very small, we can write

$$\log_e I_{n=} (\pi_1 - 1) + \ldots + (\pi_i - 1) + \ldots + (\pi_n - 1)$$

$$= \left[\sum_{i=1}^{i=n} \pi_i \right] - n$$

$$\boxed{\begin{array}{l} \sum_{i=1}^{i=n} (\pi_i - 1) \\ I_n = e \end{array}}$$

This equation expresses that the relation between money and prices occurs through the market and that the change in money value $\frac{1}{I_n}$ at a given *moment* (t_n) is a function of disequilibria (π_i) between supply and demand flows in previous periods. In this sense, Bernácer's theory announces Allais's "hereditary" theory.

To move from the discrete method, where time is split, to a continuous method in which the period is infinitesimal, we must overcome a calculation difficulty. By taking π_i instead of V_i, we make the mistake of taking the differences between the average values of *the periods* (π_i = average of $\frac{D_i}{S_i}$) rather than the extreme differences between the beginning and end of the periods (*moments*). Nevertheless, splitting periods moderates the mistake of taking π_i as an approximation for I_i.

On the other hand, we consider that at a macroscopic level, income and expenditure flows appear more continuous for each agent because of non-concomitance of decisions. This claim reduces the value of Robertson's hypothesis on the difference between income and expenditures. We believe his analysis applies only at a microscopic level, and Bernácer identified this difficulty. Indeed, after being the first to formulate this diachrony between income and expenditure, the starting point of his temporal analysis, he attempted to return to continuous macroeconomic movement by overcoming the internal contradiction implied by successive period splits. By splitting the period, Bernácer succeeds in taking into account the continuous movement through successive πi, true indicators of the demand-supply flow ratio that really occur on the market.

Bernácer's approach seems very rich in that it overcomes analytical dualities, such as stocks and flows, time and period, instants and time intervals. Most authors' shortfalls are due to their inability to overcome or even perceive these essential dualities.

Formula According to the Continuous-Time Method

Second, Bernácer establishes a formula for the ideal price index—the inverse of money value—depending on income, demand and supply, and continuous time.

The three functions share an independent variable: time, defined between the instants a and b:

Product function=Income	$P_{ab} = \int_a^b P(t)dt$
Aggregate demand function	$D_{ab} = \int_a^b D(t)dt$
Aggregate supply function	$S_{ab} = \int_a^b S(t)dt$

The product-income and demand functions can be illustrated as follows (Fig. 4.5):

The segment D_4 P_4 represents the accumulation intensity of unspent income at the instant t_4, corrected by the term $(\Delta M - \Delta H)$.

The area under the curve [t_0 d_0 d_4 t_4] is the volume of demand flow; we distinguish between the instants t_0 and t_4.

The area under the curve [t_0 P_0 P_4 t_4] represents the volume of income flow between the instants t_0 and t_4.

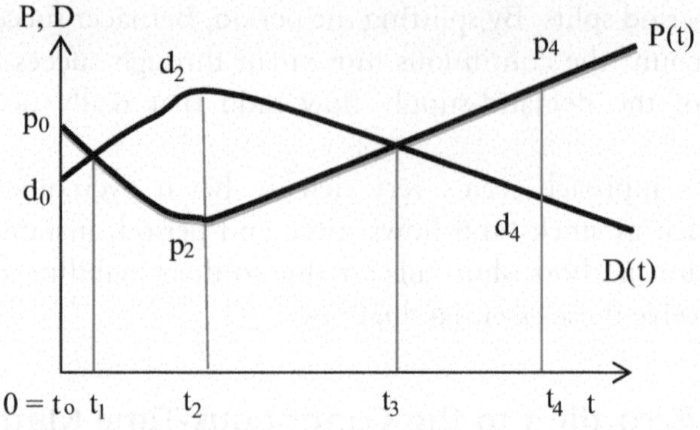

Fig. 4.5 Production and demand functions

The area $[(t_0\ P_0\ P_4\ t_4)-(t_0\ d_0\ d_4\ t_4)]$ represents the cash accumulation between t_0 and t_4.

Between the instants t_0 and t_i, the gap between income and demand is expressed as

$$\Delta A-(\Delta M-\Delta H)=\int_{t_0}^{t_i}P(t)\,dt-\int_{t_0}^{t_i}D(t)\,dt$$

Expression in terms of stocks = expression in terms of flows.
The demand equation is:

$$\int_{t_0}^{t_i}D(t)\,dt=\int_{t_0}^{t_i}P(t)\,dt-\Delta A+\Delta M-\Delta H$$

Yet $\Delta M = \Delta A + \Delta c$; Δ related to the period (t_i-t_0)

$$\int_{t_0}^{t_i}D(t)\,dt=\int_{t_0}^{t_i}P(t)\,dt+\Delta c(t_i-t_0)-\Delta H(t_i-t_0)$$

Consider the supply: (Fig. 4.6)

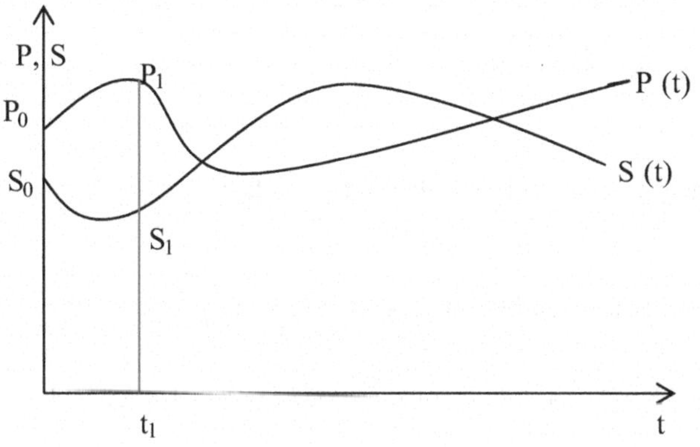

Fig. 4.6 Supply and production functions

We have seen that S differs from P by the term (ΔSt + ΔCg).

So, (St_1 P_1) represents "stock accumulation intensity" and bullion cash at instant t_1.

Stock variations and gold cash between t_0 and t_1 are equal to the difference in areas under the curves P(t) and S(t).

$$\int_{t_0}^{t_i} P(t)\,dt - \int_{t_0}^{t_i} S(t)\,dt = \Delta St + \Delta Cg$$

Δ related to the period ($t_i - t_0$)

The supply equation is:

$$\int_{t_0}^{t_i} S(t)\,dt = \int_{t_0}^{t_i} P(t)\,dt - \Delta St(t_i - t_0) - \Delta Cg(t_i - t_0)$$

So we can define the area between demand and supply curves as:

$$\int_{t_0}^{t_i} D(t)\,dt - \int_{t_0}^{t_i} S(t)\,dt$$

$$= \int_{t_0}^{t_i} P(t)\,dt + \Delta c(t_i - t_0) - \Delta H(t_i - t_0)$$

$$- \int_{t_0}^{t_i} P(t)\,dt - \Delta St(t_i - t_0) - \Delta Cg(t_i - t_0)$$

$$= \Delta c(t_i - t_0) + \Delta St(t_i - t_0) - \Delta H(t_i - t_0) + \Delta Cg(t_i - t_0)$$

Working capital (K) being equal to the stocks (St) increased by company disposable funds (c) is:

$$= \Delta K(t_i - t_0) - \Delta H(t_i - t_0) + \Delta Cg(t_i - t_0)$$

Consider the graph of D(t), S(t) and their difference [D(t)–S(t)]: (Fig. 4.7)

For each point on the curve D(t)–S(t), we can define the gradient of the tangent by taking as an approximate value the gradient of the secant cutting the curve at two points as close as we want on either side of the considered abscissa on the curve. With this function in derivative form and area difference ∫D(t) and ∫S(t) being itself an area, we can write:

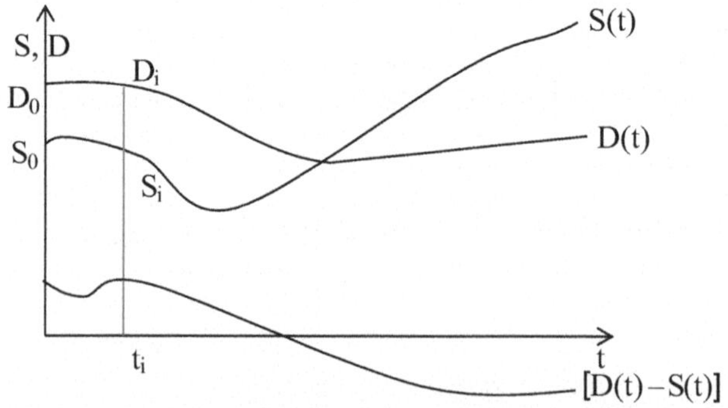

Fig. 4.7 Supply and demand functions

$$D(t)\,dt - S(t)\,dt = (K - H + Cg)\,dt$$

Dividing both sides by S(t) dt, and integrating from t_o to t_i, we obtain:

$$\int_{t_0}^{t_i}\left[\frac{D(t)}{S(t)} - 1\right]dt = \int_{t_0}^{t_i}\frac{K - H + Cg}{S}\,dt$$

Since $\frac{D}{S} = \pi$, $\int_{t_0}^{t_i}(\pi - 1)\,dt = \int_{t_0}^{t_i}\frac{K - H + S}{S}\,dt$.

From what we saw, π is an approximate value of I:

$$\pi - 1 = \frac{I_i - I_{i-1}}{I_{i-1}}$$

$$(\pi - 1)\,dt = \frac{dI_i}{I_i} = d(\log_e I_i)$$

$$\log_e I_i = \int_{t_0}^{t_i}(\pi - 1)\,dt$$

$$I_i = e^{\int_{t_0}^{t_i}(\pi - 1)dt}$$

$$\boxed{I_i = e^{\int_{t_0}^{t_i}\frac{K - H + Cg}{S}dt}}$$

Compared to the previously established formula $In = e^{\sum_1^n(\pi_i - 1)}$, the formula I_i very appears as a transposition of I_n according to the continuous-time method.

Thus, Bernácer establishes a dynamic functional relation between the money supply, represented by one of his fractions (K–M + Cg), and prices, represented by an index (I_i). This formulation seems to integrate, among other things, psychological and sociological behaviours of agents—households and companies—by transfer, expenditure, and production decisions involved together in the variables K, H, and S. In contrast to authors such as Nogaro, Aftalion, and Keynes, Bernácer refuses to analyse motivations, the *ex ante* psychological elements. He takes into account only the tangible appearances of those decisions completed *ex-post*.

Temporary Conclusion on the General Theory of Money

Although it is difficult to describe Bernácer's original and autonomous thought, we could situate his essay in a path parallel to the general trend of thought on monetary equilibrium, whose representatives are mainly Swedish and English—Lindahl, Myrdal, Hawtrey, and Robertson—but not exclusively, such as Koopmans. Bernácer appears as a straightforward theorist caught between these two schools on one hand and Wicksell and Keynes on the other.

Like all these authors, and in reaction to the neoclassical current, Bernácer undertakes an analysis of the integrated general equilibrium. Dissociating equilibrium from money analyses seems more difficult for him than for his contemporaries. Money may not hold, in his work, the same scientific status as for most of economists of his time. In many ways, he seems to have a more modern perspective in both writing and method.

We could, in a few lines, try to summarize the innovations contained in Bernácer's monetary theory:

- Relativization of the concept of monetary value in relation to space and time,
- Total detachment from money materiality,
- Discovery of a perverse function of money: double hoarding,
- Link between variations in savings and money value, and
- Role of the gap between savings and investment in business fluctuations.

In an attempt to qualify Bernácer's theory, we emphasize that this monetary theory is

- Synthetic: integrating the two components of the market in a monistic real-monetary view,
- Dynamic: integrating time as an independent variable in itself,
- Structuralist: highlighting internal movements of the money supply,
- Additionally, it is an income theory, focusing on the income creation function through money.

Finally, this theory contains a theory of interest that will be the subject of the next chapter. Only after this analysis can we establish monetary policy comparisons.

References

Aftalion, A. (1935). *Monnaie, prix et changes* (Money, prices and exchanges) (1st ed 1927).

Allais, M. (1965). « Une reformulation de la théorie quantitative de la monnaie » ("Reformulation of the quantity theory of money"). Paris: Sedeis.

Aujac, H., & Mainguy, Y. (1950, April–June). L'influence du comportement des groupes sociaux sur le développement d'une inflation (The influence of social groups behavior on inflation development). *Économie Appliquée*.

Austruy, J. (1960). *Structure économique et civilisation* (Economic structure an civilisation). Paris: Sté d'édition d'enseignement supérieur.

Barrère, A. (1952). *Théories économiques et impulsion keynésienne* (Economic theories and Keynes' impulsion). Paris: Dalloz.

Barrère, A. (1967). *Preface to the French translation of Hansen: Introduction to Keynes' thought*. Paris: Dunod.

Bernácer, G. (1916). *Sociedad y felicidad – Ensayo de Mecánica Social* (Society and happiness – Essay on social mechanics). Madrid: Ed. Beltrán.

Bernácer, G. (1922). La teoría de las disponibilidades como interpretación de las crisis y del problema social (The theory of disposable funds as interpretation of crisis and social issues). *Revista nacional de economía*, (40).

Bernácer, G. (1945). *La teoría funcional del dinero* (The functional theory of money) (2nd ed., 1956). Madrid: Consejo Superior de Investigaciones Científicas.

Bernácer, G. (1955). *Una economía libre sin crisis y sin paro* (Free economy without crisis nor unemployment). Madrid: Aguilar.

Bienaymé, A. (1964). *Croissance et monnaie en plein emploi* (Growth and money in full use). Paris: Cujas.

Bourcier de Carbon, L. (1970). *Analyse économique (Economic analysis)*: t. 1, «La répartition » « The distribution); t. 2, « La monnaie et le crédit » (Money and loan). Paris: Montchrestien.

Catchings, W., & Trufant Foster, W. (1925). *Profits*. Boston: Houghton Mifflin Company.

Clark, J.-B. (1899). *Distribution of wealth. Essentials of economic theory*. Boston, 1907.

Cordebas-Nême, C. (1956). La théorie monétaire de Sir Dennis Robertson (Monetary theory of Sir Dennis Robertson), PhD dissertation, University of Paris.

Cordebas-Nême, C. (1960). Essai sur les fonctions de consommation et d'épargne (Essay on the functions of consumption and saving). Alger: Librairie Ferraris, Extrait des *Annales de la Faculté de Droit d'Alger.*

de Brunhoff, S. (1967). *La monnaie chez Marx* (Money with Marx). Paris: Editions sociales.

Duesenberry, J. S. (1949). *Income, saving and the theory of consumer behavior*. New York: Oxford University Press.

Fisher, I. (1911). *Purchasing power of money*. New York: Cosimo.

Friedmann, M. (1956). *Théorie quantitative de la monnaie, nouvelle formulation* (Quantity theory of money, new formulation).

Guitton, H. (1950). La valeur de.la monnaie dans l'économie contemporaine (Money value in contemporary economy). *Revue Économique*, V.

Guitton, H. (1969). *La monnaie* (Money). Paris: Dalloz.

Gurley, J. G., & Shaw, E. S. (1962). *Money in a theory of finance*. Washington, DC: The Brookings Institution.

Harrod, R. (1971). *La monnaie* (Money), French translation. Paris: Dunod.

Hawtrey, R. G. (1919). *Money and credit*. London: Longmans Green and Company.

Hawtrey, R. G. (1932). *The art of central banking*. London: Longmans Green and Company.

Hawtrey, R. G. (1937). *Capital and employment*. London: Longmans Green and Company.

Hayek, F. A. (1931). Preise und production; translated in English: *Price and production*. London: Routledge; 2nd ed 1935, Beitrage zur Geldtheorie, Vienna, 1933.

Hicks, J. R. (1957, June). A rehabilitation of classical economics? *Economic Journal*.

Keynes, J. M. (1930). *A treatise on money*. New York: Harcourt, Brace and Company.

Knight, F. H. (1921). *Risk, uncertainty and profit* (7th ed., 1948). Boston: Hougton Miffin Co.

Kolm, S. Ch. (1967). *Les choix financiers et monétaires, théorie et techniques modernes* (Financial and monetary choices, theory and modern approaches). Paris: Dunod.

Koopmans (1933). « Zum problem des neutralen geldes », in Beiträge zur Geldhere, de Hayek.

Lebraty, J. (1967). *Profit, décision et incertitude*, (Profit, decision and uncertainty). Paris: Cujas.

Marchal, J. (1959). La restauration de la théorie quantitative de la monnaie par Don Patinkin et ses limites (The restoration of the quantity theory of money by Don Patinkin and its limits). *Revue d'Économie Politique*.

Marchal, J. (1967). *Monnaie et crédit* (Money and credit). Paris: Cujas.

Marchal, J., & Lecaillon, J. (1966). *Les flux monétaires* (Monetary flows). Paris: Cujas.

Marshall, A. (1890). Principles of political economy, Londres: Macmillan Company.

Menger, K. (1950) Grundsatze der Volkswirtschaftleehre, Translated in English: *Principles of Economics*.

Mill, J.-S. (1848). *Principes d'économie politique* (Principles of political economy). French translation (1873).

Moulton, H. G. (1936). *Income and economic progress*. Washington, DC: Brookings Institution.

Myrdal, G. (1950). *On penningteoretisk jamvikt*, 1931, French translation: *L'équilibre monétaire*. Paris: Librairie Médicis.

Nogaro, B. (1924). *La monnaie et les phénomènes monétaires contemporains* (Money and contemporary monetary phenomenon). Paris: Giard.

Nogaro, B. (1945, 1948). *La monnaie et les systèmes monétaires* (Money and monetary systems). Paris: LGDJ.

Nogaro, B. (1947). Théorie de l'inflation (Theory of inflation), Rapport au congrès des économistes de langue française.

Patinkin, D. (1956a). *Money, interest and prices: An integration of monetary and value theory*. Evanston: Row, Peterson and Company. (New York: Harper and Row, 1965).

Patinkin, D. (1956b, june). La théorie quantitative de la monnaie: une analyse par l'équilibre général (The quantity theory of money: an analysis through general equilibrium), Économie Appliquée.

Piettre, A. (1965). *Histoire de la pensée économique* (History of economic thought). Paris: Dalloz.

Robinson, J. (1951). *Economics of imperfect competition*. London: Macmillan Company.

Rueff, J. (1963). *L'âge de l'inflation* (the age of inflation). Paris: Payot.

Samuelson, P. (1964). *L'économique (Economics),* French translation. Paris: Colin.

Samuelson, P. (1971). *Les fondements de l'analyse économique* (The Foundations of Economic Analysis): V. 2, Stabilité des systèmes et théorie dynamique (Stability of the systems and dynamic theory). Paris: Gauthier-Villars.

Savall, H. (1973, September). Germán Bernácer, économiste espagnol (1883–1965). Une théorie générale de l'emploi, de la rente et de la thésaurisation (General theory of employment, unearned income and hoarding), PhD dissertation at the University of Paris II, 602 p. mimeographed.

Savall, H. (1975). *G. Bernácer: L'hétérodoxie en science économique* (G. Bernácer: The heterodoxy in economics). Paris: Dalloz, Collection Les Grands Économistes.

Savall, H. (2012). *Origine radicale des crises économiques: Germán Bernácer, précurseur visionnaire*, Radical origin of economic crises: Germán Bernácer, a visionary precursor). Charlotte: IAP.

Schumpeter, J. (1954, 1961) *History of economic analysis*. New York: Oxford University Press.

Ullmo, J. (1969) *Le profit* (profit). Dunod. (Preface to L. STOLÉRU: *L'équilibre et la croissance...* (Equilibrium and growth ...), *op. cit.*).

Walras, L. (1877). *Éléments d'économie pure* (Elements of pure Economics). Paris: Guillaumin.

Walras, L. (1883). *Théorie de la monnaie* (Theory of money).

Walras, L. (1889). *Éléments d'économie politique pure* (Elements of pure political economics). Lausanne.

Wicksell, K. (1958). Marginal productivity as the basis of distribution in economics. In *Selected papers on economic theory*. London: Allen and Unwin.

5

The Interest Rate as a Factor of Instability and Crises

> A theory is as much valued because of what it provokes as that it contains truth. (Perroux 1935, p. 216)

> The interest phenomenon raises one of the most difficult issues in economic theory. (Klein 1949, p. 117)

The interest rate deserves specific analysis detached from the *General Theory* of money as a strategic variable of equilibrium and fluctuations models. As such, anything previously analysed about money functions and the partition of money mass, as well as the brief presentation about Bernácer's theory on interest, is an essential prerequisite for understanding this chapter that explores the birth and the essence of the interest rate according to Bernácer. (Savall 1973, 1975, 2012)

5.1 Overview of Bernácer's Theory

Possessing disposable money (actual disposable funds) allows assets to be owned. This ownership is unique since it gives rights to a portion of products in the form of various types of unearned income (unearned incomes,

H. Savall, *Radical Origins to Economic Crises*,
https://doi.org/10.1007/978-3-319-93366-5_5

land rents, interests from government funds or industrial securities). According to agents, it is therefore profitable to affect the use of money to something other than the acquisition of goods from contemporary production, and the unearned income produced by a money unit invested as such is the interest rate. As a result, production will find new financial support only to the extent that it can compensate for the money that is to be invested, "this bonus to be given to wealth to attract it into industry is the only thing that may basically constitute interest" (Bernácer 1916, p. 139).

Historic and Positive Theory of Interest: Genesis of Interest

The following quotation immediately locates the interest rate problem in Bernácer's works: "There is an economic cause that forces to interest to be paid regardless of its fairness or not, and only this force matters from a scientific point of view" (Bernácer 1925, p. 18).

Furthermore, the author builds his positive conception, far from any metaphysical conception, in noting that those who borrow capital pay interest because if they do not do so, they could not obtain capital. He also notes that interest exists, which needs no explanation, and that it is necessary to analyse why the borrower agrees to pay.

Existence of Interest in the Precapitalistic Universe

Interest has always existed throughout various times, types of social organizations and labour, and production ratios and techniques in living memory. Powerful individuals often had to pay interest on loans, although they could collect, through taxes or through monetary mutations, necessary money for their expenses. Especially in his 1916 book, Bernácer shows how the plutocracy of money in the nineteenth century succeeded through its control over the government, gaining perpetual unearned income in exchange for money shovelled into unproductive expenditures (such as colonial wars). Scholastics should have rejected the concept of interest in the name of morality. Nevertheless, Bernácer observes that interest resisted, survived, and overcame religious and political prohibitions.

That pre-existence of the capitalist system itself and especially of the development of the industrial economy, in which physical capital holds an unprecedented place in economic history, puts us on the path of Bernácer's analysis on interest rates. Interest is certainly related to money, but it is not an intrinsic and exclusive institution of industrial capitalism.

Existence of Interest, Regardless of Non-capitalist Economic Regime Structures

We note that the interest rate has not disappeared in countries whose economic systems are generally different from the capitalist system and partly due to the presence of nationalized business industries. In the early 1920s, where the rate reached its peak in the U.S.S.R., in French nationalized companies and in the subsequent reform of the management of Soviet production units, interest did not disappear, and it has yet to do so.

Whatever the nuanced interpretation of the role of interest in various types of structures and systems, interest—in its existence if not in its essence—remains a common phenomenon in all economic areas, regardless of their mode of production, of their economic or para-economic structures, or of their systems. Therefore, there should be a general theory of interest rates in the sense that Marx establishes a *General Theory* of money, which should not be confused with the critical analysis of a capitalist political economy. Bernácer has no such ambition, but he does raise the issue.

Failure of the Process of Interest Legitimacy

Some theories on interest have no scientific object; they aim to demonstrate that interest is sometimes an immoral institution and sometimes the opposite. The legal theory is from this last point of view, founding interest on the distinction between bare ownership, usufruct, and the gratification of capital. Justifying the institutionalization of interest is tendentious, and we believe that the legal argument, which relies on the legal institution of property rights, is limited to show that interest is consistent with the dual structure of capital, claiming legitimating interest. In all this, it seems that economic observations are distorted: the normative merges with the descriptive and nature merges with artefact.

Bernácer, in making this objection to interest partisans, refuses to demonstrate his theory. He therefore does not use moral, ethical, or alienation concepts. Even so, this refusal is not absolute, his theory is not colourless, and his insistence on seeking the origin of interest and drawing economic policy conclusions represents an admittance of a preconceived idea. In our opinion, it does not detract from the scientific nature of his theory: could there be scientific research without a preconceived idea? We should not criticize Bernácer for his prior intuitions; we must watch how he then handles them in his methods, theoretical verification, and experimentation.

It is obvious that by basing the first origin of interest on the theory on unearned income, Bernácer (1945) reveals where his observations of economic activity lead him: to criticism of an unstable and unfair social order. This hard criticism is nevertheless the logical result of his theoretical construction of interest—not the starting point. We have seen that Bernácer notes that interest is a widespread phenomenon, and therefore he does not choose a priori between good economic regimes in which interest would be non-existent and bad regimes in which it would toil on.

To his credit, Bernácer does not justify an existing ideology: he conducts a very comprehensive analysis of reality by reasoning from hypotheses and observes that the disappearance of individual unearned income should logically lead to the extinction of interest.

Convergence of Historical Method and Positive Approach

In a descriptive order, history corroborates simple factual observation, tending to instil belief in a natural order of interest, whether legitimate or not. Stopping at this stage of the analysis would imply accepting the natural order, resigning before any obstacle, and renouncing to convert the natural framework or to defend against a sometimes-hostile environment. Current insight could promote the progressive depletion of raw materials and a lack of overall nutrition, and we may, as a starting point for research and action, accept these omens as a potential warning to encourage progress if not as a prophecy of what will be. Given this observation of facts and in the name of history, should we adopt Malthus's pessimistic attitude (1846) about wars or people's misery, which he naturally considers inevitable? The scientist must be careful to be, in a sense, optimistic or pessimistic: he must particularly reject the exact idea of fate. In this way, Marx and Engels oppose Malthus.

Nevertheless, we discuss the normative order here. However, in this area, every hope is allowed, despite the enormous difficulty in choosing a collective procedure to define economic purposes. Still, we must establish that the abolition of interest is possible if we can show that it is useful, even necessary. Appealing to the current or historical order to demonstrate an alleged failure to realize this reform is somewhat unscientific. We must, in the theoretical field, accept the idea of an economy without interest: the leap of imagination for the economist likely to be greater only when we refer to the isotropic universe of perfect competition, which is used by classical, neoclassical, and Keynesian thought.

The Interest Rate and the Extension of the Theory of Unearned Income

According to Bernácer, the interest rate should be considered as the consequence of his theory of unearned income.

The authorship of theories invented by Malthus (1820) is often attributed to Ricardo. Villey writes (1958, p. 130), "Two years before Ricardo's *Principles* (1817), it is Malthus who invented the law on land rent". Perhaps Malthus was a victim of a divine curse or of historical Darwinism. Prophetic of Ricardo and Marx, according to Villey, Malthus seeks to justify the high cost of English wheat, according to H. Denis (1966).

Nevertheless, it appears that Malthus's theory on unearned income is wider than Ricardo's. Gide and Rist (1920, p. 177) agree: "Ricardo's theory (on unearned income)... admits the only existence of differential unearned incomes and only retains the latter case from those considered by Malthus. It seems that Malthus got it right compared to Ricardo… It is clear that in a society reaching a certain level of population density, the mere fact that the land is in limited quantity is sufficient to give all the lands and their products a scarcity value independent of their productivity difference. And even though they would all be of equal fertility, it would change nothing. There is none that cannot find a buyer with money". Gide and Rist explain Ricardo's position through the contradiction between a broad sense of unearned income and the theory of labour value. Bernácer overcomes this apparent contradiction because he adopts both concepts but nuances the second. According to him, the principle of labour value is reflected by asserting that only work is a legitimate means for individual ownership of a product. Even so, work—despite being a main source—is not the only source of value. There are other sources of value—such as land—that will be subject to collective ownership in his reform of economic structures. Bernácer's analysis resembles Smith's since, according to Denis (1966, p. 291), Malthus justifies "Smith's theory for which land rent is a debit from the fruit of labor, due to the monopoly situation in which the landowner is".

The Extension of the Theory of Unearned Income

Gide and Rist (1920, p. 647) concluded at the end of their chapter on unearned income that, given its great role throughout the nineteenth century, the theory of unearned income may become a mere historic curiosity in a few years. Bernácer's writings between 1916 and 1956 (without interruption), Robinson's work in 1951, legislations on urban land and capital gains to properties, and the idea of land socialization—which periodically survived and was sometimes practiced—refute Gide and Rist's scepticism.

Far from filing the theory of unearned income away in economic history, we will consider the extensions proposed by economists, such as the two English authors already mentioned. Evaluating these essays until 1920, Gide and Rist (p. 848) note, "The great mass of economists either stayed true to Ricardo's conception or endeavoured to deepen and develop it, but without denying own income from land.

From there emerged a double and curious evolution in the theory of unearned income":

- Authors who, similar to Ricardo, consider unearned income "as an economic anomaly due to special circumstances (unequal fertility of land and law of diminishing productivity)";
- Modern theorists who "no longer see but a normal consequence of the regular game of the laws of value".

In the first theory, the differentiated yields of the land, as a reservoir of resources and as a location, and the differentiated skills of man and machine are discussed. For example, rent appears as unearned income. Nevertheless, profit most attracted unearned income theorists, to the point that Marshall defines profit as composite unearned income. For these authors, this extension of the theory is a kind of outlet for which the general theory of unearned income is the master key that explains all individual differences in income. Piettre agrees that since the concept of unearned income was diluted to that of supply and demand disequilibrium, unearned income producers, and unearned income consumers; unearned income appears as a result of a de facto situation.

The second type of extension is based on the concept of non-differential or absolute unearned income. J. Stuart Mill is an illustrious representative of this thought, as he says, "If all the land in a country were necessary to culture, it could fully provide unearned income" (Piettre 1965, p. 151). According to these authors, where does unearned income come from?

Some argue that it comes from the relative scarcity of product; it requires only a sufficiently large demand and a sufficiently limited product. We could rank among these theories those of Adam Smith, Robinson, and Bernácer, since they define unearned income as monopoly income, a privilege enjoyed by, among others, landowners, producers on an imperfect competition market, and sellers who take advantage of information or locations. We find this idea in Pigou and Robinson's theory of exploitation in which the market structure is held directly responsible for compensation below marginal productivity.

Nevertheless, Piettre (1965, pp. 69–72) notes that "even extended in this way, this doctrine on unearned income is still insufficient". Speaking of "what Liberals have not seen", he adds, "They assigned to unearned income a de facto cause; but they do not see the deeper reason, due to technical and legal structures of the capitalist system". Further, he adds, "No more than they saw the origin of these unearned income, Liberals could not find the remedy within their system… unearned income arising from structural causes demanded also structural remedies, and that is why some authors… recommended either the nationalization of the unearned income by a single tax (George, Stuart Mill) or the land nationalization (Gossen, Walras)".

In this sense, these authors were neoliberal precursors (especially Allais), as they expected through such reforms (with compensation to former owners) only to abolish a monopoly and to better enable the game of liberal mechanisms. Despite the superiority of these authors' analysis regarding Liberals, A. Piettre shows the failure of their theories: even those who denounced these facts disregarded the value-added from floating capital. An element of reality failed to enter the liberal analysis, making it a victim of an abstraction of outside reality.

Bernácer's theory seems to meet Piettre's call. According to Bernácer:

- Unearned income is an eminently structural phenomenon.
- Unearned income is not only a phenomenon of real estate but increasingly also one of *floating capital.* When calculating the real interest for a price movement system, Bernácer, integrates the value-added of *unearned income-yielding assets*.
- *Reform* must address the *structures* and allow compensation for former owners.

According to the criteria borrowed from Piettre, Bernácer presented the most complete and current theory on unearned income. Bernácer goes beyond Robinson in his basis on the theory of unearned income. Beyond market structures (symptomatic aspect) are incriminated some legal, political, and social institutions that can be roughly encompassed in the generalized right to private property.

After situating Bernácer's theory among Gide's modern theories—since unearned income, according to Bernácer, is a general phenomenon and not just a differential—we must furthermore distinguish Bernácer—and probably Robinson as well—from those who consider unearned income to be a normal consequence of the regular game of the laws of value. Bernácer considers that the normality of the phenomenon—in view of legal institutions in a descriptive order—should not hide the anomalies from this situation in a normative order.

From Unearned Income to the Interest Rate

Among these various or nuanced conceptions of unearned income, we can retain as a common denominator the idea of unearned increments, which seems to match Bernácer's broad concept that we defined as *non-work income.*

Non-surprisingly, many authors have advocated the confiscation of unearned income through taxation. On this point, Proudhon (1953, p. 74) made this famous remark, "Who made the land?—God. In this case, owner, go away!" In 1851, the English philosopher Herbert Spencer (1893, chapter IX, p. 107) said that the repossession of land by the state was "in accordance with the highest state of civilization" and in harmony with moral law. Later, he made a restriction that seems relevant in regard to the labour theory of value: "all that the community is entitled to claim is the area of uncultivated and original land". Bernácer, in his reform project, evoking the change from the current regime to the rational system he advocates, also seems anxious to indemnify work accumulated from savings and crystallized in property.

Bernácer rejects the collective appropriation of unearned income through taxation as an archaic and timorous solution: only unearned income-yielding assets themselves must be taken by the community, with the former causing the latter, of course. However, his idea remains less extreme Fabian's collectivism, which advocates both confiscation of interest and unearned income due to skillfulness. Indeed, according to Bernácer, a Christian economist, personal skillfullness is in the domain of intimacy; it is inherently out of trade. From this point of view, economic egalitarianism has limits and, we believe, degenerative properties. Despite agreeing to the confiscation of interest, Bernácer would probably refuse to touch the skillfulness of gaining unearned income, as called for by some authors.

Land nationalization, as advocated by Stuart Mill (1848), Henry George, and Walras (1896), is similar to what Bernácer advocates. Nevertheless, Gide and Rist note that these authors are all individualist: they do not blame the property itself, and capital interest does not find enemies among them. Bernácer's position therefore seems more advanced: he admits possession for personal use of goods legitimately owned through work. We cannot dissociate capital interest from unearned income, and Bernácer had to focus throughout his life to show its harmful nature and to advocate its outright abolition.

Physiocratic Component

In his 1940 article devoted to Bernácer, Robertson described Bernácer's theory as a piece of neo-physiocracy. In turn, in the same article, he describes Keynes's theory of interest as mercantilist. The elements of the pseudo-physiocracy of Bernácer's theory are detailed below.

Both statements are absurd. We do not defend Keynes's theory here because it seems too monistic. Nevertheless, we would like to pinpoint the error in Robertson's interpretation when he says that Bernácer—unlike Keynes—admits that there is a productivity but only the productivity of nature. This inaccuracy is twofold:

(a) The productivity of nature does not exclude the fact that work is of paramount importance in the human kingdom. Nature is a passive factor of production. Bernácer is more similar to Smith, Malthus, and Ricardo than to physiocrats.
(b) If Bernácer establishes his principle of interest on land, it is because, originally and ultimately, land is exemplary of *non-reproducible wealth*, and its ownership or perpetual use by individuals is therefore an aberration for the economic organization. Even so, Robertson did not want to recognize that the interesting parts of Bernácer's theory lie in the extension of the land rent concept. Bernácer's theoretical contribution is the way he integrates floating unearned income and value-added in a truly dynamic theory of unearned income.

Robertson observed that compared to Keynes, Bernácer's theory has a productivist aspect. Nevertheless, he confused productivity. First, land does not have productivity in itself and, thus, real or physical productivity does not have the same status for Bernácer as it does for the proponents of the productivist theory of interest. For them, theoretical considerations of productivity can justify the existence and the ownership of interest by individuals who provide capital goods. According to Bernácer, productivity is, in fact, the technical progress *objectively* incorporated into production assets.

However, value has two components: nature—a collective property in Bernácer's reformist perspective—and work in every sense. Therefore, there is no reason for some individuals to have a monopoly over this capital interest. As a result, the man-machine couple allows overall productivity to be generated because, in some cases, the entrepreneur can maintain enough difference between the net value-added and wages so that he can generate a surplus on which he can debit capital interest. When circumstances permit (wages, price, demand, and technical progress levels), production is a lucrative business that encourages the entrepreneur to borrow for investment by paying interest. The interest rate does not originate from the physical productivity of capital or from land.

Physiocratic History and Contemporary Theories

Turgot's fructification theory is a pre-classical theory with a real component. Bernácer discovered this theory after the publication of *Society and Happiness* (1916) while seeking documentation to support his writings. For *The Capital Interest* (1925), he directly read Turgot's text first in Böhm-Bawerk's (1902) book and then found echoes in his own theory. He most appreciated the similarity of their method for equivalence and capital exchange: in general, any capital is the equivalent of land with income equal to some fraction of this capital.

Strongly criticized by Böhm-Bawerk, Turgot's essay is better understood, in our opinion, by Schumpeter (1954, p. 214), who believes "that the equivalence land-capital is not a simple data because there is a kind of determination of the exchange ratio between land and floating wealth". This is exactly Bernácer's original position. Llau (1961, p. 17), following Böhm-Bawerk, has a more nuanced but still too severe judgement: "the fructification theory is only a vicious circle: interest is explained by land-capital equivalence due to supply and demand conditions, which are explained by land rent-interest equivalence".

Therefore, the explanation of interest genesis presupposes the existence of interest (since land rent-interest equivalence implies that interest exists). We believe that Böhm-Bawerk misunderstands and underestimates Turgot's economic works. Fortunately, our contemporaries, such as Faure and Vigreux (1947), have undertaken a scientific rehabilitation of his works. We find the argument that criticizes the assumption of interest existence particularly weak; this assumption seems to be the starting point of any positive approach. Böhm-Bawerk (1884) reconsiders this argument against Henry George's theory, which founds interest on time-related unearned income.

The most troubling similarity we observe is between Bernácer's theory (only at its starting point) and Montagne (1919, p. 28). This latter presents a "theory of biological interest" from natural factors, making three proposals:

(a) Any living wealth grows and multiplies automatically and
(b) Any non-living wealth can be exchanged against living wealth,
(c) So any non-living wealth provides income from the fund established by the automatic increase of living wealth.

Drawing from this author, we could reformulate the starting point of Bernácer's theory in its physiocratic aspects:

(a′) Any living wealth provides, through work, a certain product; but it is acquired by owner individuals who therefore demand a part of the product, and
(b′) Any non-living wealth can be exchanged against living wealth,
(c′) So any non-living wealth (such as money) can provide income from the product.

Physiocratic Elements of Bernácer's Theory

As part of basic economic law, that is, seeking maximization of well-being—maximum product for minimum personal effort—the human is naturally likely to look for privileged economic situations. In this regard, the existence of individuals, even many, who depart from that principle does not contradict that effect in the overall plan (Bernácer 1916).

What is the relation between interest and land?—Wealth (assets) loaned to others yields interest or benefit to its owner, equivalent to what this owner would obtain by using it to acquire land. Why is land, among all wealth, the origin of the capital interest phenomenon? - Bernácer provides an answer to this question in four points:

(a) Laws of product distribution do not imply that capital should be given anything other than what is necessary for its preservation and renewal.
(b) Interest is not a phenomenon inherent to capital but rather a general quality attached to wealth. Capital is one type of wealth among many and, as such, it produces interest even if it is not productive.
(c) This quality of wealth implies that it has employment-compensated use without work or it provides value-added.
(d) There is no production without more or less incorporation of work.

All these conditions are satisfied in unearned income from land because land is subject to private ownership.

Finally, the final switch from unearned income to interest results from loan definition, thus announcing a monetary component of interest. Loans, as a transfer of the use of the benefits of asset ownership to others, is another possible use, which is not lucrative in itself; if there were no other uses, the lucre of capital would tend towards zero. Nevertheless, because the borrower can obtain a great advantage from or has the desire to use a loan and the lender agrees to lend at the only condition of obtaining benefit equivalent to what land purchase provides to him, the borrower will promise him equivalent compensation, derived from his/her product or income, to receive the loan.

History and Present Observation of the Physiocratic Component

Given Bernácer's abstract logical argument that land is the origin of interest, it should be noted that Bernácer lived in a predominantly agrarian country, Spain, in the early twentieth century. If we add to that the archaic structures of land ownership—*minifundia*—*latifundia* dualism coupled with the socio-political phenomenon of caciquism rule—it is understandable that this man of progress—in all meanings of the word—was sensitized to the question of unearned income from land. Recall that one of the stumbling blocks of the Spanish Republic was the failure of land reform, and the Franco regime, despite its promises, did little in this direction.

If we look at the issue of land—arable land, energy storage or living space, urban or not—from our current perspective, we observe that the solution to land value-added problems, the socialization of land, the expropriation of land, and spatial planning involve resolving the issue of unearned income ownership. We will limit ourselves to merely mentioning this issue even though it needs further thorough analysis.

5.2 The Monetary Component in Bernácer's Theory of Interest Rate

After defining the genesis of interest, Bernácer analyses the phenomenon in its present historical context. His approach is therefore resolutely monetary, and interest was analysed as a monetary phenomenon in a complex reality. In this way, Bernácer precedes Keynes and differs from Robertson and Ohlin, whose measured conception of the interest rate, a fragment of orthodoxy in the matter, still falls within a very classical approach in which monetary phenomena are gradually and later introduced in the real universe. Wicksell (1964) takes a more monetary approach than Robertson and Ohlin. Nevertheless, we believe he was unable to totally disconnect from the classical approach, as he located the natural interest rate alongside the monetary rate of interest, confounding his disciples.

We briefly recall the three elements of the monetary component in Bernácer's theory:

(a) There is a *parallel* market to the production market in which supply is represented by unearned income-yielding assets.
(b) This market is supplied on the demand side by savings of disposable funds, which form the potential demand for assets or the potential money supply.
(c) This market is very unstable because of speculation and absorbs or rejects disposable funds (hoarding or dishoarding) that flow from or back to the production circuit.

Determination of the Interest Rate

The average profitability is the following ratio:

$$\text{Income assets} = \frac{(\text{Periodical income} + \text{Value added})\,\text{Noted at time}\,(\text{i})}{\text{Asset price at time}\,(\text{i}-1)}$$

$$= \frac{R_i + V_i}{P_{i-1}}$$

Unlike most classical, neoclassical, and Keynesian theories, Bernácer takes value-added into account. Taking account of this term completely changes the results of the analysis.

$$\rho_i = \frac{R_i}{P_{i-1}} + \frac{V_i}{P_{i-1}}$$

$$= \frac{R_i}{P_{i-1}} + \frac{P_i - P_{i-1}}{P_{i-1}} = \rho i_1 + \rho i_2$$

Hypothesize that R_i is given

(a) when $P_i = P_{i-1}$: stability of asset prices

$$\Rightarrow \frac{R_i}{P_{i-1}} = \frac{R_i}{P_i}, \text{ and the second term } \frac{P_i - P_{i-1}}{P_{i-1}} = \text{value-added is zero.}$$

(b) when $P_i > P_{i-1}$: rise in asset prices

The interest rate is stable because the prices are stable.

$$\Rightarrow \frac{R_i}{P_i} < \frac{R_i}{P_{i-1}} \Rightarrow \rho_{i_1} \searrow$$

$$\rho_{i_2} = \frac{P_i - P_{i-1}}{P_{i-1}} > 0$$

ρ_{i_1}	ρ_{i_2}	ρ_i
↓	↑	= cte
↓	↑	↓
↓	↑	↓

(b_1) $\rho_{i_2} = \rho_{i_1}$: particular case
(b_2) $\rho_{i_2} < \rho_{i_1}$
(b_3) $\rho_{i_2} > \rho_{i_1}$

Even so, $\frac{R_i}{P_{i-1}}$ is of the order of 2 to 10% per year, depending on the type of security, while $\frac{P_i - P_{i-1}}{P_{i-1}}$ may be around 10% per day in fluctuation periods.

Given that in a short-term analysis, the term ρ_{i_2} can be superior to the term ρ_{i_1}, the case (b_2) would be relatively common. This case is very important because it destroys all of Keynes's analysis on the fluctuation of the interest rate in the short term. Indeed, this hypothesis is that value-added outweighs the interest calculated at constant prices. If prices are constant, the interest rate is also (*a*); however, if prices fluctuate, interest (defined by Bernácer = ρ_i), except in a fortuitous event (b_1), may fluctuate either in the same direction (b_2) as (ρ_{i_1}), interest defined by Keynes, or in the opposite direction (b_3). For the fluctuations of ρ_{i_1} and ρ_i to be in opposite directions, it is necessary and sufficient that:

$$\frac{P_i - P_{i-1}}{P_{i-1}} > \frac{R_i}{P_{i-1}}$$

Taking a high rate of 10% per year for $\frac{R_i}{P_{i-1}}$, it is necessary and sufficient to have—such as for the stock exchange, a constant increase in each session of approximately $\frac{1}{2600}$ (on the basis of 260 sessions per year)—approximately 0.04%—is a very plausible hypothesis for all securities and is often exceeded for some categories.

This result is very important because it shows that there is no real short-term regulating mechanism for price explosion or collapse. Indeed, when Keynes defines interest as equal to (ρ_{i_1}), the decrease of (ρ_{i_1}) provokes a demand restraint for securities, and the fixation of a relatively stable equilibrium price (rate of interests) seems possible. Thus, the extension of Bernácer's analysis indicates that the interest rate is very unstable and leads to Wicksell's analysis of the cumulative process: he detected the problem but did not fully highlight it because he reasoned in terms of constant prices.

Again, the superiority of Bernácer's analysis is shown through his temporal dynamics: without knowing Wicksell's theory, he underpins it and then goes beyond it. The cycle is thus perfectly described because logic and experience show that while the $P_i > P_{i-1}$ movement may last longer, the speculator's psychological reflexes ultimately and inevitably cause a trend reversal through downward speculation or that in the absence of other causes, player expectations are enough to cause the anticipated phenomenon. Symmetrical reasoning can be triggered when the movement is: $P_i < P_{i-1}$.

Hoarding, Circuit Production, Loss of Power

The entrepreneur will retain disposable funds attracted by the financial system only by paying them at a rate at least equal to the rate in effect on the market. Wicksell, Bernácer, and Keynes agree on this point: therefore, the decision to invest seems subject to the interest rate, whether extrinsic or exogenous.

Nevertheless, it seems that Bernácer's theory is, more than others, focused on the rarefaction of disposable funds on the production market due to permanent attraction, sometimes increasing and sometimes mitigated according to the context, from the unearned income-yielding asset market. For Bernácer, capital is not rare, saving is not rare, but *disposable funds on the production market* are rare because of double hoarding. The interest rate the investor has to pay is the price of dishoarding—as shown in Keynes' general theory—but it is not necessarily unique and equal to the average profitability rate on the financial market (ρ_i).

Nothing stops us from thinking that the investor's borrowing rate may be a priori equal, inferior, or superior to (ρ_i), according to the situation and specifically to the proximity of the cycle trend reversal.

Interest as the Equilibrium Price of a Money Supply and Demand Fraction

According to Bernácer, interest appears as an instantaneous equilibrium price: the economist deduced from the compromise between these two opposing trends (buyer and seller) his theory of value. Why would we proceed differently for interest, which is also a price? It is not inconsistent with our argument about equilibrium price instability. We basically emphasize that according to Bernácer, supply and demand for unearned income—not interest—is the driving force that controls the market. In other words, what operators desire and exchange on the financial market is unearned income (income + value-added), while interest is only the result of an *ex post* calculation and is used mainly as an indicator of transactions on the production market.

Nevertheless, in the whole economy (with both circuits being taken into account), there is a supply and demand aggregate for money. Supply is fuelled by incomes in the period, dishoarding, and money issuance. Demand is composed of expenditures on the production market and investment in the financial market. Interest is not the result of a conflict between overall supply and demand for money but rather of only a fraction: savings of disposable funds on one hand and unearned income-yielding assets on the other. According to Bernácer, only financial demand determines interest. We return to one of Bernácer's fundamental ideas—that of the money supply split—on which Keynes bases the preference for liquidity concept and the interest rate.

Money Information Insufficiency

In addition to describing observations of the financial market, Bernácer's theory addresses two causal questions.

Why and how can investors generally assume to serve interest to capitalist savers? Bernácer argues that it is because they can make capital grow in the industry since, with equal work, an increase in the productive fixed capital stock increases the productivity of the productive labour-capital pair.

Why and how is investment in the capital market profitable while not really productive? Bernácer argues that if there is no productivity in a physical sense and that some agents debit from the product, this is a thievery of workers. Next, we will analyse these two issues more thoroughly.

The Real Component in Bernácer's Theory of Interest Rate

Investors borrow when, with the prospects for demand growth being favourable, interest demanded in return is less than the surplus that the new investment would produce. This law of cost-benefit calculations, which is generally accepted in principle and rarely contested, is adopted by classicals, neoclassicals, Bernácer, Keynes, and our contemporaries. Wicksell's natural interest concept, Keynes's marginal efficiency of capital concept, and Bernácer's productivity of physical capital concept proceed from the same idea.

Physical Capital Productivity

Bernácer rejects the classical theory of capital productivity because classicals', neoclassicals', and Marx's idea of capital is too vague in content and too broad in sentiment. It results from confusion between fixed capital—a tool and productive equipment—first and the money needed to operate the production unit second. Therefore, Bernácer admits, of course, that the capitalization of the production process results in an increase in productivity and that the entrepreneur is stimulated to invest as a result of this expected surplus.

We believe Keynes's position has been exaggerated since he does not integrate the real factor of capital productivity in his theory of interest. When he confronts the rate of interest with the marginal efficiency of capital in an analysis very similar to Wicksell's, he admits that capital productivity and the interest rate are vaguely related. Perhaps in his desire to stand out from neoclassicals, he insists too much on the fact that interest is fixed from production. Undoubtedly, does this formulation exceed his thought?

From this point of view, Bernácer's formulation, which highlights the dominant role of exogenous production factors in the process of determining the interest rate, also allows the real factor to integrate. Interest is a perennial institution in the production system because physical capital—all things being equal—has real productivity.

Bernácer rejects the classical theories that give a real, monistic explanation of interest. He fervently opposes Senior's (1836) and Carver's (1893) theories of abstinence, which explain the lender's point of view. He also condemns Say, Malthus, and Leroy-Beaulieu's productivist theories, which reflect the borrower's point of view, but he admits that some elements of these theories should be acknowledged.

Some classical theories that Böhm-Bawerk considers naive describe interest as a surplus in physical quantity that releases capital utilization. We will not dwell on this aspect, and we will be content to refer to the famous Robinsonade of the fisherman, netting, and fishes.

Other, more sophisticated classical theories—the motivated theories of productivity—involve the notion of surplus in value. Nevertheless, does physical net productivity imply net productivity in value? Physical surplus can sometimes generate a value decrease. Moreover, pursuing reasoning instead of productivity theory, we can say that a surplus value will never correspond to this physical surplus.

We assume that Llau's logical argument positions him, like the authors he incriminates, as a proponent of the deductive method. Nevertheless, experience has shown that, from a time-dynamic perspective, investment generates a wave effect on all activity and, given the stock of constantly renewed potential needs, a distribution structure similar to that of industrialized countries since the Second World War. Investment may generate, in each period, surplus value through demand development. We must emerge from the classical optics of the stationary economy. Bernácer never adopted it, even in his early writings, and in a very Schumpeterian way, he trusts the entrepreneur to choose investments that will generate surplus value.

Real Non-productivity of Money Capital

Distinguishing between productive physical capital and money capital, Bernácer demonstrates in his basic analysis of working capital that three components—stocks of finished or semi-manufactured products, debts, and monetary cash—have no productivity in the way that production factors should be productive. It would be better to refine the analysis by differentiating stock tools from suffered stocks or seasonal surpluses. The first could be equated to real assets (productive fixed capital), and we believe that the serious and operational use of private company and national accounts may be achieved only through this partitioning. In contrast, given the analysis of productivity value, the second type of stocks should be equated with debts and monetary cash.

Where does the confusion between fixed capital and circulating capital—which often occurs in microeconomic and macroeconomic analyses—come from? Is it not because their common denominator is the application of interest to the full use of capital? Even so, accepting this confusion while trying to identify the exact nature and origin of interest implies doing so without the necessary tool for this analysis; thus, we fall into circular reasoning.

Renewal of Fixed Capital and Net Investment

Is it logical to consider net investment and the simple renewal of amortized fixed capital equal? Most macroeconomic theories of equilibrium confuse these two concepts either implicitly when they lack precision or deliberately by equating these two concepts as a homogeneous whole. Is this confusion acceptable?

The debate is really about the analytical contents of the investment function. Is there a single function of investment, such as the Keynesian function:

$$I = f(Y, i)$$

Where investment, appearing as a function of income and the interest rate, appears to meet the definition of new or net investment.

Should we not, again, make a distinction such as:

$I_t = It_1 + It_2$ is total investment,
$I_{t1} = f(Y_t)$ is capital renewal,
And $I_{t2} = f(Y_{t+1}, i_t)$ is new investment.

It does not appear that Bernácer raised this issue. Nevertheless, it is important to address it since this analysis is not inconsistent with his general equilibrium model, and he destroys the Keynesian equilibrium insofar as the rate of interest occurs only in the investment function and in only one of the two terms of the function.

Is the Interest Rate the Privileged Independent Variable for the Decision to Invest?

We question the whole modern strategy of production units. We will not develop this controversy here because the role of the interest rate will be analysed further; from this point of view, Bernácer's analysis seems to be questioned just as those of all other authors, including Keynes. We only raise issues here without trying to address them:

- In respect to interest, is the strategy of production units the same when investment financing is internal (self-financing) and when it is external? Does not the development of self-financing in the industrialized world (private and public industries) change the ratio of power between investor and lender?
- To what extent are entrepreneurs generally or individually free to choose to invest at a given rate of interest, driven as they are by the imperatives of growth and competition and encouraged by advantageous tax measures, thereby caught in a development psychosis at all levels? Just as these phenomena are located at strategic, industrial, or spatial points, propagation effects, rightly precious to Perroux, are felt, expanding first to one-time phenomena and then generating a cumulative growth process. In this regard, note that competition, even if oligopolistic, is a favourable structure for the spread of investment incentives.
- What role does the interest rate play in the decision to invest, compared to the importance of market structure, firms growth prospects, and innovations in products and services? These factors limit the influence of the interest rate—compared to the place it occupies in traditional economic theory—to the extent that for the entrepreneur, through his/her more or less optimistic expectations and opportunity to pass the interest rate, whatever its current level, onto his/her costs, the decision to invest is a real gamble for the future of his/her business.
- From an overall point of view, does the investor-borrower, thanks to an upward trend in the general price level in recent decades, have a more automatic reflex to index his/her prices and a reflex to consider that the net interest rate is infinitesimal when monetary erosion effects on loan repayments' real value is deducted from the nominal rate?

5.3 Sociological Component

In his first two books, *Society and Happiness* (1916) and *Interest of Capital* (1925) (and especially in the first), Bernácer insists on the sociological component of his theory of interest. Subsequently, he advocated the suppression of interest until the end of his days. Nevertheless, he focused on developing the economic argument sensu stricto. On this point, despite his anti-Marxist statements—and we are still confident that Bernácer and his contemporaries knew little about Marx's works—and a few references that he quoted in his works, Bernácer's analysis is similar to that of Marx. The basic point of divergence lies primarily in Marx's (and the classicals') narrow and in some respects out-dated definition of work, while Bernácer, writing half a century after Marx, gives work a more contemporary and diverse meaning. The entrepreneur, in the dynamic perspective of Schumpeterian functionality and in the reality of production unit structure and current legislation, is a worker entitled to compensation. This difference between the two authors may seem essential to orthodox Marxists. Nevertheless, we believe Bernácer has a sociological approach that recalls Marx.

Interest, a Thievery of Producers' Value Creation

Bernácer's functional cleavage between producers and non-producers does not coincide with the class cleavage formulated by Marx. It is conducted in two stages: a first division occurs between exploiters and exploited in the industry; a second division occurs within the exploiter class. The common denominator between the two authors is the status of unearned income perceivers, who participate in sharing the product without contributing to the production effort. The parasitic characteristic of unearned income perceivers joins Bernácer's and Marx's points of view. In *The Capital*, Marx calls them parasites and honourable bandits (Fig. 5.1).

Why does Bernácer reject the first cleavage mentioned above? We believe that his motivation is more positive than his reluctance to think in terms of classes. How can Denis, true to Marxian theory, currently evade the problem raised by the perfect non-coincidence between capitalists and savers or between entrepreneurs and savers? According to

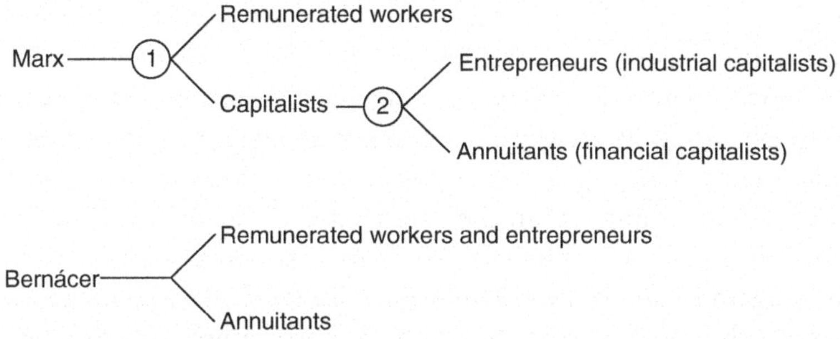

Fig. 5.1 Comparative classification of annuitants, capitalists, entrepreneurs, and workers: Bernácer vs. Marx

Bernácer, saving is not only a reality of the capitalist class, and entrepreneurs may not be capitalists in terms of Marx's definition. Bernácer's definitions of savings and of a company are essentially functional. In condemning loans with interest from savers to companies, Bernácer does not condemn a class of *intuitu personae* agents; he condemns harmful function or institution, even achieved by small employees, as is the case in existing pension funds.

Interest and Profit: Interest, Ownership of a Surplus by Unearned Income Perceivers

Is there any relation between these two phenomena? Marxists seem to hold out (Denis 1950, p. 7): "our analysis shows quite clearly the unity of Marxist explanation, the basis of which is the labour-value theory and the theory of workforce exploitation that results. This is because if we could not, thanks to the theory of exploitation, explain the profit rate *before*, the interest rate and independent of it, we would lose any chance to complete our research and would be left to dwell on the uncertain ties and contradictions of non-Marxist theory". How can we reconcile this point of view with that of Marx, who said, "The interest-yielding capital … is part … of antediluvian forms of capital that precede by far the capitalist mode of production..." Similarly, de Brunhoff (1967, p. 113), quoting Marx, said, "usury (interest) survives in capitalist production pores…".

Denis (1950, p. 11) appears to accept the theory of capital productivity and stigmatizes the unearned income perceiver's behaviour—not that of the entrepreneur—in refusing to support the business risk. "What we know to explain is, in no way, the existence of a positive interest rate that includes itself as long as *there are opportunities to exploit the work force*; but the interest rate is lower than the profit rate. We explain this mainly by the possibility given to capitalists to exchange *gain* in a *random* amount—profit –, against gain in a fixed amount—interest." Bernácer, supporting a synthetic theory of interest, may accept this position. Nevertheless, the psychological approach of an unearned income perceiver would bring nothing to the analysis of interest genesis. Whatever he says about the reason why the disposable fund holder prefers the entrepreneur's behaviour to that of the unearned income perceiver; it would still be necessary to ensure that the saver really had that choice. Bernácer believes that there are structural barriers (psycho-sociological, technical, etc.) that prevent the saver from freely determining his or her behaviour by allowing him or her direct access to industrial production. Marxists, by assimilating savers and capitalists, briefly say that the saver is free from choice.

To summarize these two views, we describe them in parallel (Fig. 5.2):

Marx, Bernácer, and Keynes's ideas seem to converge on the bases of sharing: "It would be excessive to infer after Fan Hung (1939) that Marx, as Keynes will do later, considers rate of interest as a monetary rate, the determination of which is then specifically a monetary problem". The fact remains that the interest rate category in *Capital* is based mainly on the analysis of supply and demand for disposable funds, with the latter being distinct from real capital because money is separate from goods, capital from productive capital, and financial capitalists from industrial capitalists. In this sense, like Fan Hung, we can talk about the existence of monetary theory on the interest rate in *Capital*. Denis (1966, p. 442), we have seen, has a different interpretation: "Thus, we see that the rate of interest is neither the price of money nor the price of savings; it is essentially the expression of capitalist choices between capital direct investment and capital indirect use via loan". However, Marx (1962, p. 24) says, "There is no general law of profit sharing between interest and company profit other than that dictated by competition".

MARX	BERNÁCER
Capitalists have the opportunity to exploit the workforce by investing their disposable funds in production. They can make profit from that	Disposable funds holders can earn income without working through the acquisition of some non-produced assets (interest)
Some capitalists (financial) prefer certain amounts of profit through loans. They receive interest Other capitalists (industrialists) prefer random income directly collected from production. They collect company profit	Some savers earn interest by lending to entrepreneurs Entrepreneurs receive only a random part of the profit, which is shared among unearned income perceivers

Fig. 5.2 Comparative table of Marx/Bernácer: capitalists' and entrepreneurs' roles

If we accept S. de Brunhoff's theory, we discover another common point between the German, Spanish, and English economists: the monetary component of interest, which, through a conflict between supply and demand for money, helps explain not the origin but the determination of the interest rate. Even so, like Denis, we assume that the shape of the curves is questionable, as Bernácer foresaw when taking into account changes in asset prices. We also see that Marx's theory analysis is capable of decisively illuminating discussions initiated by non-Marxist economists on the form of demand and supply curves of capital or on the liquidity preference, integrating each partial analysis in the only valid framework.

Both commentators on Marx agree on the order between profit and interest, highlighting the basic difference between Bernácer and Marx: "One of the consequences" of a unitary conception of credit "is precisely that financial capital participates in sharing a given annual average profit, and not the formation of average profit rate" (de Brunhoff 1967, p. 108). This unitary conception is based on capital market unity, the single rate of interest, and the complementarity of financial systems.

According to Marx, the supply of disposable funds comes mainly from financial capitalists, including banks, which agree on a certain interest rate, the money demand of industrial capitalists: "this financing mechanism involves dividing the capitalist class" (Ibid, p. 125).

Internal Conflict of the Capitalist Class: Unearned Income Perceivers Against Entrepreneurs

Bernácer analyses the nature and the effects of the internal conflict of the capitalist class, according to Marx's concept.

Nature of the Conflict

This internal conflict has, according to Bernácer, the status of a conflict of interest between unearned income perceivers and entrepreneurs and between lenders and borrowers. For Marx, this conflict takes a decidedly violent form: We must now insist that any attempt to explain the interest rate level at a given time should take utmost account of the ongoing struggle between two categories of capitalists. It should even take into account the particular situation of some social groups within the two considered classes: big financial capitalists who dominate the banks and small financial capitalists who are dominated. The clash between these various social groups leads to the complexity of these phenomena.

A second difference between the two authors lies in their definitions of the capitalist class. According to Bernácer, this class is not a homogeneous socioeconomic class in which a capitalist can sometimes take a lender-unearned income perceiver position and other times that of a borrower-entrepreneur. Bernácer takes into account the singular function of an unearned income perceiver to brand the capitalist class. For Marx, the common denominator for different kinds of capitalists, which allows them to be considered as a whole, is economic power, social domination, and labour alienation power.

What most divides the two authors is the time of surplus share, which is important because it explains the most discriminating of Bernácer's attitudes against unearned income perceivers. According to Marx, capitalists collectively and previously collect profit: "It is impossible to explain interest if we do not *first* explain the profit". We can admit with Denis (1966, p. 437) the denunciation of the attitude—as a reaction to a Ricardian tradition—of the marginalists whose error "is that it (marginalism) wants to account for all capitalist incomes through the interest rate, reducing the 'profits' themselves to a negligible fraction of these incomes or explaining these 'profits' through the amazing Anglo-Saxon theory on entrepreneurship supply and demand". If marginalism is moving in this direction, it is because its primary purpose is to justify capitalist income. Unfortunately, by claiming everything is a result of interest, it actually loses the opportunity to give a coherent explanation of interest. Bernácer would approximately agree with this criticism of marginalism. Nevertheless, he does not subscribe to the Marxist theory of a prior and overall collection of profit before profit sharing between the company's profit and interest. In this regard, Bernácer denounces the Orthodox pseudo-theories that are most often intended to justify an established social order, that is, collect on a surplus by unearned income perceivers. He refuses, in fact, the idea of a mythical service achieved by money-capital in the production process and therefore refutes the fact that it should be paid as compensation from lenders to producers.

Marx agrees on this point: "it is indicated by the existence of the interest rate collected by lenders for the benefit of the active capitalists" (de Brunhoff 1967, p. 127). The following quotation by de Brunhoff is even more explicitly elaborates the difference between making physical capital and making money capital: "what appears as an antagonism of profit distribution is related to the functional difference in productive capital and money capital, although the latter itself, even if unproductive, is an indispensable link in capital circulation … The Saint-Simonian facet of Marx, violently treating financials as parasites, is due to his whole theory of money and of the role of money capital".

Nevertheless, it must be emphasized that according to both Bernácer and Marx, money capital non-productivity is appreciated in a normative order. Indeed, in a descriptive order—where the analysis of the capitalist system is historically realized—both admit that money capital, which is functionally required, receives a part of the product; we thus agree with the monetary component of the theory of interest analysed previously. Thus, Marx considers that "industrial capitalists therefore need a credit system, and they benefit from its existence, provided financial capitalists are paid with a part of the profit. The average profit sharing (given elsewhere) into interest and company profit depends only on the conditions of supply and demand for disposable money on the market… Thus, the only data on sharing are that the interest rate can neither be zero nor be superior or equal to the general rate of profit".

The idea of a parallel market that communicates with the production market, as analysed in Bernácer's works and leading to a synthetic theory of interest, is also present in Marx's analysis. Denis's interpretation (1966, p. 443) bring it closer to Bernácer's analysis since it condemns the monetarist monism of the Keynesian theory of interest and concludes with the need to consider social factors: "what we said should be sufficient to demonstrate the basic mistake committed by Keynes when he uses facts specific to the 'money market' to explain the phenomenon of interest as a whole". Further, "social factors… would summarize the capitalist division between the two classes that form within them, a financial capitalist class and an industrial capitalist class". Finally, "we imagined that the interest rate is controlled by movements from one class to another (larger or smaller number of lenders and borrowers) and by their transaction volume on the capital market".

The Effects of Conflict

Nevertheless, Marx's analysis seems too monolithic, as it is centred on *ex post* profit sharing: "Marx goes so far in reducing interest to a simple diversion of profit that he does not even take into consideration risk, calculations and lender and borrower expectations" (de Brunhoff 1967, p. 131). This author seems to condemn the *predetermining* of profit to share between interest and company profit that Marx advocates. This is exactly Bernácer's position, as we have already analysed in the inherent theory of profit. This is the great point of divergence between the two economists, and conflict effects between unearned income perceivers and therefore entrepreneurs cannot have the same nature.

Marx's view seems to be that of the stationary economy in which profit is predetermined because of the principle of profit rate stability and then shared a posteriori between the two classes of capitalists. We can criticize Marx for his neglect of reality, and since the interest is contractually predetermined to the production period, we can particularly deplore his lack of a dynamic perspective.

In contrast, this perspective is present, in Bernácer's very dialectical analysis of the role of conflict. For him, indeed, the predetermination of interest and, instead, the *ex ante* indetermination of profit is a factor of instability and therefore of system movement. Fixed a priori, the rate of interest determines the level of production and employment for the period in the short term and the growth rhythm in the long term. Conversely, the profit rate assessed a posteriori determines the interest rate offered by entrepreneurs for the following period, thereby specifying the degree of attraction of productive activity for disposable funds pending investment. Additionally, the conflict of interest between lenders and borrowers becomes important in this second stage. Regarding the economic effects of the conflict, Bernácer therefore appears more similar to Keynesian analysis of entrepreneurs' expectations or to Wicksellian explanations of the situation than to Marx's more static approach.

Interest, Unearned Income from Production on Private Property Means Monopoly

Though he rejects it for other reasons, Bernácer admits that the socialist theory is a positive theory of capital interest. It seems that Bernácer alludes to the theories that Böhm-Bawerk (1884) calls socialists of the chair—such as Schaffle—or to the theories of exploitation similar to Proudhon's theory. In other writings, including *The Theory of Disposable Funds* and *Free Economy, Without Crisis and Without Unemployment*, Bernácer develops the theme of the social organization's impediment of workers' ability to implement their work by themselves and to create their own businesses. This theme is not far from the socialist idea of monopoly through private ownership of means of production.

In his reform, Bernácer supports the socialization of this ownership and does not believe it is the origin of interest. This institution certainly strengthens the sustainability of the interest phenomenon, but according to him, we must particularly search among non-reproducible goods the original cause of the interest rate; it is precisely this monopoly or, if preferred, the private ownership of land. Thus, the physiocratic and sociological components of Bernácer's theory of interest can be reconciled.

Bernácer's Definition of Interest: A Synthetic and Functional Theory

Currently, the theory of interest cannot have a monistic characteristic. Interest cannot be explained with only a real component or with only a money component. It is necessary to integrate the many elements that explain the interest phenomenon. Should the preference for time, as Llau suggests, be used to explain the interest rate? If so, are we not likely to fall into the circular reasoning that this author exactly wanted to avoid? The question is whether to know if we can consider the time preference a real, primary phenomenon that—alongside other factors—helps to generate interest in the economic universe. This debate is likely to resemble the debate about whether the chicken or the egg came first.

In this respect, Bernácer's position is clear-cut: he rejects all theories similar to Böhm-Bawerk's agio: for him, the underlying assumption of all these theories is the *natural* (and therefore inevitable) existence of the interest rate. By saying that these theories do not prove the origin of interest but only aim to justify it, Bernácer resolutely takes a further step. If we assume, in fact, that interest exists and that we should not try to eliminate it, the need to update all future values comes naturally, but we did not show that the update is in the nature of things. Bernácer's position on this issue is very original and firm, we will further analyse the role of interest. Once this exclusion of the time preference from the causal analysis of interest is complete, Bernácer offers a synthetic definition of the interest rate.

Double Requirement for Interest Existence

The common denominator of goods-producing assets is that their supply is relatively rigid. This rigidity has varying degrees. Thus, in the short and medium terms and even in the long term, land seems to be the archetype of these assets, featuring a rigid supply, non-reproducibility, and a land-owner monopoly.

Existence of a Market for These Assets

Reasoning by contradiction, Bernácer says that if these assets are not transmitted, it would be a necessary evil in the sense that the unearned income market would not exist, that there would not always be such an attraction for unearned income for disposable funds holders. Bernácer seems to lament that access to this market is too easy and too well organized, such that the fluidity of disposable fund movements increases. In support of this observation, it should be noted that through information, communication development, and provided ease of access, the current stock exchange constitutes the most volatile market despite certain regulations limiting daily price increases (measures that appear to be quite ineffective). It is the best-organized market in which potential—and sometimes real—fluidity in supply and demand is such that massive value transactions can be achieved in minutes. It remains a mystery as to why not as much thought is put into organizing certain other markets that are far more useful to the community.

In this regard, Bernácer has a very anti-liberal and anti-capitalist perspective, and the solution he recommends is the elimination of the financial market as a means to abolish interest and, through it, unearned income.

Ravages of the Unearned Income-Yielding Assets Market

The consequence of the existence of unearned income-yielding assets and the organization of transactions for these assets is the backflow of the disposable money supply, most often from the production market to the financial market and sometimes vice versa. The chronic ill plaguing production is the money leakage that results from double hoarding and abstention of demand in the production system. This potential reduction has a dual effect on employment: a direct effect through non-demand and an indirect effect through the artificial scarcity of disposable funds in the production system and the subsequent existence of the interest rate.

Interest: Payment from Production to Return Disposable Funds to Production

Disposable funds (money supply) are placed in productive activities, which is relatively risky because total compensation includes the interest rate offered by producers and the risk bonus added to the compensation they would have earned from due diligence investments on the financial market. Thus, there is sufficient productivity in real capital investment to enable monetary capital to be paid.

The Double Functionality of the Interest Rate

Bernácer's theory of interest is functional for two reasons. In existing economic systems, interest has a real function at the production and distribution levels and a monetary function as a result of the conflict between supply of and demand for money.

The interest rate has a real functionality. It occurs in the calculation of investment cost and, consequently, determines the production and employment levels in the following period, thus deflecting the course of production activities during the other successive periods. It also requires entrepreneurs to anticipate profit sharing and therefore to fix their prices according to the interest rate and their investment programmes on the expected profit rate. This profit will be, all other things equal, at a higher level than it would be if the interest did not exist. Therefore, there is a dialectical relation between the interest rate and real productivity *in value.*

In Bernácer's theory, the interest rate also has a purely monetary function: that of the instantaneous equilibrium price—despite being extremely unstable—between supply of and demand for money. The issue is knowing the content of this supply and demand. According to classicals, supply and demand, that is, savings and investments, respectively, are mainly real data. According to Keynes, money supply is given: it is a fraction of savings that is independent of the interest rate (liquidity preference), while demand is investment. For him, interest is the price of liquidity withdrawal. Bernácer, meanwhile, sees the money supply, independent of the interest rate and savings fraction, which he calls disposable funds that face the two markets. For him, money demand is twofold and ordered according to the following hierarchy: money demand appears first on the financial market and then on the production market. The disposable funds holder arbitrates following his anticipation of the economic situation.

Robertson was correct to find some similarities between Bernácer's (1916–1922) innovative theory and Keynes's one (1936). Nevertheless, Bernácer's theory is more complete and more original.

Qualification of Bernácer's Theory

Llau (1961) quotes Bernácer in the bibliography of his Book II *Contemporary Theories of Interest: Synthetic Theories*, Title I "*The Development of Synthetic Theories from Neo-Classical Inspiration*". He quotes only two of Bernácer's articles: "*Sparen, Kapital und Zins*", *Kyklos*, 1953, p. 135, and "*Osservazione sulle teoria dell interested*", *Moneta e Credito*, 1953, p. 265.

Therefore, it seems that Llau did not deepen the analysis of Bernácer's theory of interest, which is a shame; otherwise, he would have granted it a special place among traditional classifications in his Subtitle II "*The Dynamic Synthesis*", next to the generalization of the theory of interest: Perroux's theory. Indeed, like Bernácer did previously, Perroux (1950a, b) criticized Keynesian theory, investment's sensitivity to the interest rate, and especially the inadequacy of the hoarding concept and the need to clarify the temporal approach. In contrast to Bernácer, Perroux emphasizes the preference for time as an essential factor of interest. It is not because of the potential similarity between Perroux and Bernácer's theories that they should have been compared at the end of Llau's book but rather because of the importance Bernácer gives to synthesis and to temporal dynamics.

Nevertheless, we should reproach Llau for believing that Bernácer's theory was inspired by neoclassicals. We summarize the elements of the neoclassical view, as defined by Llau:

- Existence of basic equilibrium,
- We place ourselves in equilibrium to analyse the phenomena,
- We think in terms of real prices (MQT and money neutrality),
- Analysis at the micro-unit level and generalization at the macroscopic level,
- Any lender is an abstainer whose motivations are introspective,
- Static analysis: abstract, empty, and time,
- Economic unit behaviour: profit maximization and equality between producers.

None of these elements is present in Bernácer's general theory and in interest particularly.

In conclusion, we assert that among all theories, Bernácer's is one of the most synthetic and dynamic.

The Interest Rate, Economic Activity, and Policy

The Interest Rate and the Level of General Activity

Bernácer's theory is part of this group of theories that attribute a dominant role of the interest rate in determining overall activity: its level, its equilibrium, its fluctuations, and growth. On this point, our comparative analysis will encompass two theories that historically frame those of Bernácer: Wicksell's and Keynes's theories.

The Interest Rate, Equilibrium, and Employment Level

Time and employment are key factors of economic equilibrium in Bernácer's theory.

Equilibrium and Time

Between the two concepts of equilibrium as either an abstract standard that serves as theoretical reference or as an observed tendency resulting from economic cybernetics, Bernácer seems to take a position similar to the second conception. To operate well, the economic system must have a natural propensity toward equilibrium. Nevertheless, certain structures are opposed to achieving equilibrium. In this regard, unearned income is, according to Bernácer, the foremost obstacle. The regime advocated by Bernácer must allow the precise achievement of cybernetic conditions for equilibrium, the natural tendency of the economic system.

Nevertheless, we may wonder whether it is appropriate to analyse equilibrium. How can the mind reconcile equilibrium, which is so often present in theories, and disequilibrium, which is more often observed in reality? Does equilibrium fall under a normative analysis, while disequilibrium falls under a descriptive analysis?

Guitton (1951, p. 41) suggests an interesting answer to our many questions that illuminates Bernácer's position in this regard. Like Bernácer, Guitton has a relativistic view of economic phenomena: It is the scale of observation that creates the phenomenon. Whenever we change the observation scale, we encounter new phenomena. It seems that both authors give a discreet place to equilibrium in theoretical construction: the concept of equilibrium "is like an invisible bedrock of the whole cycle theory, of all theories of the cycle". Both give neoclassicals grief for ignoring or even despising any research that explains disequilibria, "The truth here is to say that Say's theory is a static theory that ignores time, i.e., inherently eliminating the problem to solve. It is not the moment of pure reason where the market may operate; it is not the variably long duration, which always allows adaptation delays to fade and equilibrium to form, which are most interesting for economic life. It is the in between. It is in transition. All classicals are authors who are not interested in transient phenomena. To them, transition is accidental, which, in their eyes, is an imperfection. Even so, it is precisely in this accident, in this imperfection, in this transition that most human actions take place". These lines might well be written by Bernácer between 1922 and 1942, that is, between the publication of *Theory of Disposable Funds* and of his review article entitled, *Basic expression of the value of money*. In analysing the concrete economic system, the analysis of disequilibria attracts most of his attention.

Does this mean that equilibrium is a concept that must be absent from the economist's concerns? Bernácer, no more than Guitton, believes so: the essence of the economy is invisible, it is never entered, and it is still beyond tangible. For this reason, it is true that over time, products are likely to be exchanged for products: equilibrium is presented as a limit.

What should be the economist's instrument to approach disequilibria? Guitton (1951, p. 180) could support Bernácer's theory: "There remains the last consideration, that of intermediate adjustments over a shorter period, between the instant and the duration. Here, it is no longer possible to ignore prices. The market situation is dominating; that is, the price level that sets supply and demand levels to historic prices, we want to say to actual prices that, from moment to moment, follow each other on the market; to these prices inflated with the past and already impregnated with the future, there is never a concrete equilibrium of supply and demand".

Far from excluding each other, equilibrium and disequilibrium are two dynamics that "happily complete each other according to the time we build the theory". Guitton (p. 181) thus uses Allais's method to distinguish two areas of analysis: dynamic equilibrium and dynamic disequilibrium. This author, like Bernácer, has a conception of equilibrium that is totally relativized to time: equilibrium is not a static state that is opposed to dynamic disequilibrium; equilibrium is itself a dynamic element dominated by the principle of the interdependence of phenomena resulting from the observation of secondary or lasting effects, while dynamic disequilibrium is controlled by the principle of causality and dedicated to the observation of primary or momentary effects on visible and experienced factors.

Additionally, between these two dynamics, there are dialectical relations such that each acts on the other. Therefore, what is the result of this dialectical process? "The equilibrium is a model that is approached; the actual situation is a line of disequilibria. From this gap between the model and the facts results a process of expansion or of contraction that generates economic movement" (Ibid, p. 180). Stoléru (1967, p. 87) makes an undoubtedly didactic and more classic distinction between "static economic equilibrium" on one hand and, on the other, a dynamic vision of economic activity that he calls "economic growth". We wonder whether in this dynamic approach, equilibrium, and disequilibria coexist or mutually exclude each other.

Bernácer adds an additional dimension to the equilibrium concept. Indeed, it seems that Bernácer particularly considers the instantaneous market equilibrium, while when he addresses the overall level and reasons on the aggregate, the word "equilibrium" disappears from his vernacular. We could try to interpret his thoughts in stressing that in the macroeconomic approach, only movement matters and only implicitly, in contrast to an ideal trend: growth. In the course of this dynamic, the component disequilibrium occurs obviously and the equilibrium component implicitly. Concrete history attempts to reveal which of the two prevails at a given time.

Bernácer's economic universe is extremely dynamic, as Guitton (*Ibid*, p. 181) illustrates: "equilibrium reminds us of the perfection of beings who no longer live. Disequilibrium, based on new variations, is related to the imperfection of beings who act, who move, who change, who, in a word, live".

Equilibrium and Employment

Is economic equilibrium, even decreased to the state of a limit, an end in itself? Should we not leave room for a quantity concept of equilibrium involving either endogenous criteria or exogenous criteria from the economic universe? Is there any incompatibility between them, whether more justice in the organization of the business and in the distribution of the product, economic efficiency, and growth momentum?

If we had to choose only one of the innovations of Keynesian analysis to justify the Keynesian revolution sometimes attributed to *General Theory*, we would not hesitate to choose the concept of full employment. Bernácer, in 1916 and again in 1922, to name only writings before *General Theory*, defined his main economic purpose as the elimination of what he then called a social problem, or unemployment. Keynes waited to do so until the great crisis and convinced himself, four years after its start that it would not resorb; then, he recommended a full-employment policy. We do not quarrel with Keynes on his ideas' anteriority; we allow him the advantage he had over Bernácer in making himself heard. We return to Bernácer and Keynes the merit of reversing the sequence of traditional priorities (money and finance—economy—social) and setting a new order of priorities (social—economy—money and finance) in which the endogenous and exogenous criteria to which we alluded earlier are made compatible. This positive point ignores some shadows of Keynes's works: why does he remain marginalist and retain, for example, the real wage rate, which would be equal to marginal productivity? Why does he feel obliged to demonstrate an equilibrium of unemployment if not to raise controversy against classicals with the same analytical instruments?

In this respect, Bernacér's achievements are brighter: no marginalism and chronic unemployment are branded by Bernácer in the name of unemployment *disequilibrium*. However, this quarrel over words, even if it once again reveals the static aspect of Keynes's analysis, should be ignore because of the importance that both economists attach to the concept of the employment level in terms of both scientific analysis—with the concept of equilibrium thus relativized to employment—and economic policy, and many countries with very different socio-political structures incorporate this primordial objective into their laws and practices.

Bernácer and Keynes determine the employment level by the same broad factor: expenditure (or income). For both authors, effective demand depends on hoarding (according to Keynes, the liquidity preference, and according to Bernácer, a preference for unearned income-yielding assets), capital productivity (for Keynes, the marginal efficiency of capital, and perhaps average productivity according to Bernácer) and on the interest rate fixed by the financial market. Meanwhile, Robertson refutes the role of the interest rate in building effective demand.

Bernácer and Keynes explain unemployment differently. Like Rueff (1931), Bernácer admits that union action promotes wage rigidity, but unlike Keynes and Rueff, he does not believe that wages are determined by the marginal productivity of labour. The classical theory cannot explain unemployment only "by invoking a wage rigidity that would stabilize wages at a higher level than those of equilibrium. We sense that things are not so simple: unemployment depends, of course, on labour market characteristics and on what happens on the manufactured goods demand side: little demand, little production, and little recruitment. This aspect is completely ignored by classical theory" (Stoléru 1967, p. 60). Bernácer preceded Keynes by twenty years in this explanation of unemployment through aggregate demand, and it seems to be this gap that separates him radically from Bernácer and Rueff. The latter has the nostalgia of self-adjustment: like most economists before World War II, he believes that the solution is a wage decline. Bernácer is strictly against this because, beginning with his first book published in 1916, he takes the demand effect into account.

Bernácer likely did not adopt wage decline as a solution because of his temporal approach. Indeed, from a certain given equilibrium point, a decline in prices triggers a cumulative depressive process because there is no necessary concomitance between declines in prices and planned declines in wages. Therefore, at the end of the dynamic process, Bernácer comes to the same conclusion as Keynes: declines in wages are not an effective automatic adjuster.

Bernácer explains unemployment sustainability with double-hoarding, and his explanation is more thorough than Keynes's pragmatic observation of a strong probability of unemployment, because investment opportunities decrease and a portion of savings will remain unused. This final cause could be equated with Bernacér's explanation. Unfortunately, the Keynesian concept of hoarding is too narrow, which seriously limits the general scope of this analysis. Additionally, Bernácer finds it illogical that an employment decrease is achieved by reducing the number of employees but not the number of worked hours. Marxian theory might suggest that this results from an entrepreneur's dual strategy based on the constancy of the profit rate per labour unit used and on the desire to maintain competition between employees through an unemployment reserve.

Wicksell, Bernácer, Keynes, and the Concept of Equilibrium

Thus, Keynes and Bernácer stand out from most of their contemporaries, including Pigou and Rueff, and from Wicksell, a predecessor of some of their theories and temporal analysis. Nevertheless, Wicksell remains very close to marginalists and to his teacher, Böhm-Bawerk. Llau (1961, p. 87) says, "The analysis on determining this real rate borrows all its elements from Böhm-Bawerk and from the first neoclassicals".

Wicksell, in fact, retains the marginalists' lessons on capital efficiency and labour productivity. His equilibrium level is completely independent of the employment level; his theory of employment is, like his theory of the natural rate of interest, the most obvious remnant of his classicism. For him, unemployment has the same ephemeral and accidental nature as it does in classical theory. His main contribution is in the nature of the equilibrium, which is fortuitous according to him and is due to accident and to the disparity of the cyclical movement of natural and current interest rates.

Despite his previously denounced sequels to marginalism, Keynes innovates in the reference he makes to the employment level. Unlike Wicksell, Keynes introduces a purpose of the economic system: full employment. However, his equilibrium seems very static and, thus, his analysis remains inferior to that of Wicksell. In his theory, Bernácer includes Wicksell's temporal analysis qualities—after him but without knowing him—and those of Keynes's employment level analysis well before Keynes. Unlike these two authors, Bernácer adopts no marginalist reasoning.

We briefly compare theories from these three authors in the following table. According to them, the interest rate plays its main role as an essential component of the theory of equilibrium and even serves as the only balancing factor. These authors disagree about the origin of interest, not about its function in the economic system.

Bernácer cannot agree with Wicksell's monetarism (1898, p. 108)—according to which "the rate of interest depends primarily on money excess or scarcity"—or with the too-psychological basis of Keynes's interest

Elements of the equilibrium concept approach	WICKSELL (1893–1898)	BERNÁCER (1916–1922)	KEYNES (1936)
Statistic analysis	No	No	Yes
Dynamic analysis	Yes	Yes	No
Reference at the employment level	No	Yes	Yes
Marginalist analysis	Yes	No	Yes
Importance of the interest rate	Yes	Yes	Yes

Fig. 5.3 Comparative table of Wicksell/Bernácer/Keynes: equilibrium

rate. We believe that Bernácer might agree with Keynes if he called the liquidity preference a preference for non-expenditure in production and based it on a more concrete structure than mere psychology, namely, profitable investment opportunities offered by the financial market outside production. Perhaps Keynes, a happy speculator in the stock market, like his illustrious compatriot Ricardo, had no personal reason to condemn this institution (Fig. 5.3).

The Interest Rate and Business Climate

Despite Tsuru's difficulty in building a Marxist-inspired model of cycles and de Brunhoff's statement qualifying the generally accepted view that Marx was not interested in fluctuations, we chose to follow the orthodox way to interpret Marx's thought, as Bartoli suggests (1950, p. 221): "Theory of general equilibrium, Marx's theory is used to analyse why the equilibrium is disturbed but seems ineffective when it comes to determining why the cycle is the form of capitalism development". We therefore limit our comparative analysis to Wicksell's thought flow, which, through Bernácer, leads to Keynes.

Explanations for the Two Interest Rates and Fluctuations

For these three authors, the interest rate is a key element of the theory of general equilibrium and thus of fluctuations. "The role played by the interest rate in equilibrium has, for Swedish authors, much greater importance than those of the various factors behind building this rate" (Llau, *Ibid,* p. 83). We can compare this attitude to Bernácer's perspective when he writes that changes in hoarding (non-demand) explain the phases of the cycle. Nevertheless, as he says, this would be like making a symptomatic analysis because the difficulty lies in determining the root causes of hoarding and its variations. The interest theory and the mechanics of the financial market explain this root cause.

"According to Wicksell, who originated the thought, the interest rate is essentially dichotomous. In fact, according to him, there are two interest rates. One is determined in a real economy without money. The other is determined in a monetary economy, but in a very different manner from which it appears in a real economy" (Ibid., p. 88). We cannot better illustrate how Wicksell remains a nineteenth century economist, although many economists of the twentieth century, it is true, remain dichotomists. His disciples, beginning with Myrdal, strive to mitigate this trace of classicism in the Swedish teacher.

Keynes did not succeed in resisting the attraction of neoclassical theory. To quote Harrod (1971, p. 164), "We must now ask the main question: what determines the level of this neutral rate compatible with full employment equilibrium? The answer is this: propensities to invest and propensities to save, i.e., exactly the same forces, determine the natural rate of interest in classical diagram. Many passages from the *General theory* fairly reflect his misapprehension about it".

What is Bernácer's position on these two theories, which are very similar and well known? First, he rejects the concept of the natural interest rate; according to him, there are really two interest rates, but they are two current rates, to use Wicksellian terminology. Both rates obey relatively independent variables.

Bernácer's Model

Let us attempt to interpret Bernácer's analysis.

(a) The production market fixes a *virtual rate of interest* depending on:

- Aggregate demand and price levels,
- Employment and wage levels, and
- Incorporated technical progress levels. This rate of interest is expressed in terms of value, and t is also as abnormal or unnatural, as it is potentially unstable because it incorporates a cyclical factor linked to the movements of all these variables (and especially the first four, which can be particularly mobile in the short term).

This interest rate is connected to the expected profit level and represents the maximum that entrepreneurs can pay to borrow and invest.

(b) The financial market sets an *effective* rate of interest: the average rate of return on unearned income-yielding assets, that is, the average unearned income that a disposable funds holder can withdraw from outside production investment.

The interest rate depends on:

- Demand for unearned income-yielding assets, whose variations are linked to that of double hoarding, and
- Income from these assets, including unearned incomes, stipulated interest, and capital gains.

Among these variables, demand and therefore capital gains are very unstable elements, which means that the effective interest rate is potentially unstable.

(c) The relations between the two rates.

When there is no money issuance, income is either spent on production or hoarded, as defined by Bernácer. Therefore, as a result of complementarity, there is conflict between the respective levels of aggregate demand for goods and the demand for unearned income-yielding assets. Therefore, because the observed wage rigidity is in decline and there is a regularity of progress and of fixed income assets in the short term, even with all things being equal, we observe that there is a contradiction a priori between the virtual interest rate and the effective interest rate. The respective instability of both rates and their dialectical relation seem to be the basis of the explanation of fluctuations, according to Bernácer. In addition to this analysis of disequilibria, see the above chapter, *Disequilibria*, for a detailed presentation of Bernácer's theory.

Comparative Analysis of the Three Theories

Bernácer's theory quotes Wicksell and Keynes. However, a detailed analysis should conclude about the predominance of many disparities in the analysis. We choose four points for comparison: the dynamics of rates, the determination of capital productivity, the hypothesis on prices and the importance of money factor.

(a) *The dynamics of rates*

Let us call i_n Wicksell's natural rate of interest and, to some extent, Keynes's neutral rate.

i_m Wicksell and Keynes's monetary rate of interest

i_v Bernácer's virtual rate

i_e Bernácer's effective rate

i_n and i_v play the same role as in our previous discussion, although they are very different in nature. i_m and i_e play the same role and have quite similar natures.

Wicksell explicitly considers (and Keynes seems to implicitly admit) that:

i_n is stable and $i_m$unstable.

Bernácer admits that:

i_v and i_e are both unstable.

The three authors assert, a priori and in general, that the two rates never coincide spontaneously ($i_n \neq i_m$ for some of them and $i_v \neq i_e$ for others).

(b) *Determination of capital productivity*

Wicksell and Keynes determine the marginal productivity of capital, while Bernácer rejects the marginal analysis and believes that the average productivity is taken into account in the macroeconomic assessment of new investment opportunities. Keynes and Bernácer consider the levels of prices, profits, and factors in assessing what Keynes qualifies as capital efficiency. Wicksell, a classical, defines marginal productivity in real or physical terms. "Note also that the productivity to which Wicksell refers is physical productivity and not in terms of trade, for which he stands back in relation to some of his teachers. The natural rate conceived in a hypothetical situation—where exchanges are made in nature—can therefore vary under the effect of changes in capital-intensive production processes" (Llau, p. 89).

(c) *Hypothesis on prices*

Ohlin (1937, p. 178) criticized several shortcomings of Swedish analysis: "We need an analysis that is not based on a monetary stability hypothesis". Whatever the merits of the Swedish school with Wicksell—who introduced dynamics to our discipline—at its head, we also note a lack of dynamic data processing and a certain incoherence that prices remain particularly stable for the duration of the cumulative process. Keynes must receive the same reproach, and Robertson even more because he introduced an analysis of successive periods in 1926, after Bernácer preceded

	PRICE	CONSISTENCY WITH RESPECT TO A DYNAMIC ANALYSIS	OBSERVATIONS
WICKSELL	Stable	Incoherent	Price changes observed between the beginning and the end of cumulative processes are not involved in the same explanation of disequilibrium
BERNÁCER	Unstable	Coherent	Prices–like all other variables –are in perpetual motion in continuous time
ROBERTSON	Unstable	Coherent	Even so, he rejects the role of interest rates in determining the effective expenses
KEYNES	Stable	Coherent	Even so, the analysis is static or metastatic

Fig. 5.4 Comparative table about Dynamic analysis: Wicksell/Bernácer/Keynes

him by four years and (1940, p. 51) "subconsciously" inspired him, by his own admission (Fig. 5.4).

(d) *Importance of the money factor*

Bernácer emphasizes the difference between the path he followed in the development of his theory and that followed by Keynes, who was interested almost exclusively in monetary problems during the first—and the longest—part of his career, starting from the *Monetary Reform* to his voluminous *Treatise on Money*. It is only in the brief part of his career before the publication of the *General Theory* in 1936 that he opened his research to other, more critical issues, such as full employment, the production level, and an outline of cycle theory.

Bernácer proceeds in reverse. From his mainly generalist book *Society and Happiness* in 1916, he gradually extends his specialization to monetary problems and interest because he suggested the key to these problems in his first book. We should add that Bernácer preceded Keynes by nearly two decades and was able to complete his theoretical works through his synthetic book, published in 1955: *Free Economy, Without Crisis and Without Unemployment*, a sort of homecoming or reformulation of *Society and Happiness* but with a conviction that was no longer intuitive but supported, strengthened by 40 years of shocking events and fruitful analysis as Director of the Studies Department at the Bank of Spain.

What is the significance of this comparison, which seems—like any similar comparison—quite artificial? Bernácer criticizes Keynes for not persevering in seeking a solution to the unemployment issue and money crisis. Therefore, failing a dynamic analysis test, Keynes tries, in his *Treatise* (1930), to suggest solutions based on a single hypothesis of economic conditions: depression and unemployment. He encourages deviationism among his disciples and governments by suggesting that his recommendations are—*sui generis*—adaptable to all market conditions and, for example, to the situation of permanent inflation that the world has known since 1945.

Nevertheless, does Bernácer recommend what has been qualified as monetary policy, as conceived by the Chicago neoclassical school, and does he suggest, in opposition to his analysis of money value, that the quantity theory is the theoretical framework in which all stabilization policy should be found? Our next title on monetary policy offers negative answers to these questions. Let us simply note that Bernácer falls between the quantitativist Wicksell and Keynes, the defender of public expenditure who encourages the fable of *all-out* government intervention in the economy and the impulsive theorist who partially denies his scientific past to lead all his disciples to believe monetary policy operations are no longer necessary.

We can speak of a misunderstanding between Keynes and Bernácer based on the Keynesian equality Savings (S) = Investment (I), which Bernácer takes as a main element of controversy to the point where Bernácer considers Hawtrey to be closer to the truth, as he assumes that (S – I) represents disposable funds absorption. This point echoes the fluctuation approach through hoarding that Bernácer supports. Nevertheless, Bernácer seems to us, against his will, more similar to Keynes. Indeed, he reproaches Hawtrey for the privileged role he gives to banks in money creation: he shows that *loaned* money (our emphasis) does not have the same function as real expenditures in the production system.

Similarly, he criticizes Hawtrey for his fundamentally monetary theory, according to which anti-cyclical public expenditures have the main effect of injecting money that the banking system should have generated. Bernácer noted that if it were really a simple injection a priori, there would be no reason why liquidity absorption—the original cause of demand contraction—will not reoccur. Through these two criticisms of Hawtrey, Bernácer shows, without emphasis, that his view is similar to Keynes's. For them, cash equilibrium excess does not become spent income in itself; for this transformation to occur, agents must make expenditure decisions. Otherwise, issuance has no effect on activity levels.

Perhaps Bernácer's criticism of the insufficient space Keynes gives to money in the solutions he advocated in *General Theory* and the fact that Bernácer took a position that neither excludes the Keynesian perspective nor a priori the monetarist perspective mislead his readers. Thus, Wallich wrongly understands Bernácer's thought as he wrote in a letter (September 3, 1958), referring to the inflation after the war: "Nonetheless, I do not think that these inflationary pressures have a monetary origin", which would imply that Bernácer were quantitativist.

Other Components of the Cycle Theory

Interest is not only a basic element of the explanation of the cycle in the reviewed theories; it is also necessary to analyse three other components:

- Demand is a key element of the fluctuation process;
- The cycle is characterized by cyclical downturns, and it is important to provide a coherent explanation;
- Finally, the question arises as to why the cycle is a form of business movement: is stability impossible?

The Preponderance of Demand in an Activity Level Setting and in the Course of the Cycle

Walras had intuitions that he should have exploited: he sensed the role of hoarding in his concept of desired cash and that demand plays a more active role in the economy than supply. Unfortunately, these concepts are not included in his diagram of overall equilibrium and, somehow, even contradict it.

Wicksell did not give great importance to the role of the demand for products, and it does not appear in his equilibrium and fluctuations theory, unlike those of Bernácer and Keynes or even of Schumpeter, indirectly through innovations. Bernácer's categorical assertion is that the most elementary observations of our economy show that the market and, by reflection, production, and employment are governed by demand; supply only yields to the impact of demand.

Compared to the Keynesian argument, which is essentially based on agents' psychology and particularly demand expectations from entrepreneurs, Bernácer's demonstration seems more solid. Indeed, it explains why agents hoard or dishoard, thus fluctuating the amount of aggregate demand and thereby causing the cycle. Somehow, Bernácer's explanation, which came before Keynes's, implicitly encompasses agents' behaviour, but it does not settle for noting agents' psychology. Furthermore, it tries to determine the structural foundations of this psychology, namely, the existence of financial market institutions on one hand and the human psychological reflex to search for maximum satisfaction with minimal effort on the other.

Why does aggregate demand differ from aggregate supply: because certain causes on the supply side are excluded, such as delays due to economic conditions or changes in production curves, or because some agents use a portion of their incomes either to spend out of contemporary production or to hoard sensu stricto? Where does this use come from if not from historical practice, which shows that we can gain income without work or that we can increase our wealth through capital gains, two aspects of the same institution that was strongly denounced by Bernácer: *unearned income*.

As a more complete theory of demand than Keynes's theory, Bernácer's theory does not discriminate between consumption and investment. However, most authors admit that, by partitioning demand into consumption and investment, Keynes—following Wicksell—made an important innovation. Does this mean that Bernácer would be retrograde by refusing to follow them in this way? We could describe at length that autonomous investment and multipliers are essential to the Keynesian demonstration of the government's need to substitute public expenditures for ineffective private expenditures. Bernácer's criticism is implicit. Nevertheless, this first response is only partially satisfactory.

According to Bernácer and Keynes—with nuance from the former on the scope of his expectations—the most important argument is that the private investment demand is a function of demand for consumption. Based on this observation, these two authors have diametrically opposed political attitudes. Keynes, who is pessimistic, relies on the government to substitute for ineffective private buyers, as he does not foresee the psychological disruption that World War II would cause in consumer habits and in the acceleration of technological change, which naturally calls for consumption and product growth. Bernácer, who is optimistic, knows that humans' natural tendency is to consume and that the solution is not in the miraculous intervention of the government but rather in structural reform, beginning with certain legal and social institutions.

Cycle Process

Two main factors explain the cycle process: the relation between fluctuations in the interest rate and fluctuations in business on one hand, and the trend reversal on the other hand.

Relation Between Fluctuations in the Interest Rate and Fluctuations in Business

Wicksell argues that the expansion due to price inflation driven by the current interest rate, which is inferior to the natural rate, generates an increase in the current rate from banks. If the new current rate is set above the natural rate, price deflation and depression follow. Additionally, Wicksell suggests that if there is under-employment, relatively low interest does not lead to price inflation. Nevertheless, he believes that there is normally full employment, so he has the same position as Keynes in regard to the quantity theory. Robertson also matches periods of rising or falling rates of interest with expansion and recession periods, respectively; the origin of this position from Wicksell and Robertson seems to be their quantitativism.

Instead, Keynes and Bernácer seem to adopt similar positions because the two opposite phases of the cycle—expansion and depression—can both cause interest rate inflation. Inflation is considered harmful, regardless of the phase that caused it.

Trend Reversal

By granting banks the power to set the rate of interest i_m either below or above i_n, Wicksell explicitly accepts that the economy's fate is in the hands of banks and that they generally tend to fix i_m below i_n as they attempt to increase their loan volume. Deducing that prosperity phases are longer than crisis phases seems to be a logical consequence of his position. While we are not sure that he reached this conclusion, he assigns the banking system a power it does not seem to have nor could assume: that of stabilizing the cycle and controlling economic movement. Wicksell's optimism about the symmetry of the cycle—in contrast to the conclusions that we expected from his cumulative process—and the possibility of adjusting activity simply by manipulating the interest rate not only is contradicted by the observed facts but also represents an intellectual attitude more similar to that of neoclassicals.

In contrast, Bernácer and Keynes admit that there is a trend reversal; nevertheless, they note the following:

- *The cycle is asymmetric* in the process of triggering its phases: crisis is fatal. No automatism could reverse the trend when the liquidity preference is high (as Keynes argues) or when the financial market yield is large (as Bernácer argues). Even so, these two conditions are one and the same: an increase in *double hoarding* presupposes that we are in a depression situation. Hence, we invent the "Bernácer-Keynes's theorem" for this purpose: in a weak economic situation, no endogenous automatic mechanism can cause business recovery or trend reversal.

Bernácer (1934, p. 26) expresses this phenomenon as follows: "Depression crisis is fatal. The exact game of the financial market commands it through the demand restriction that it inevitably causes. The change whereby we pass from depression to prosperity is more contingent… There is no spring that acts automatically when moving from depression to prosperity, while there is one in reverse. Development always depends on the fortuitous concomitance of various favourable stimulants that can be decreased to the three we have already discussed: increase in government and private expenditure, intensification of industrial investment, and increase in the new money supply".

These three conditions exposed by Bernácer must be fulfilled simultaneously. Indeed, if the expenditures in consumption grow without investment increases, inflation of consumer goods prices should result in stagflation and not recovery; the third condition represents the introduction of money necessary for additional funding in the production system, the *new effective money supply* means either dishoarding or issuance not followed by hoarding or both concurrently.

Bernácer (1934, p. 27) does not ignore the feedback effect of inward capital flow on the financial market, namely, interest rate deflation; he says, of course, that "the depression process spontaneously creates favourable but not determinative circumstances to recovery" (our emphasis). Bernácer, two years before the publication of the *General Theory*, includes psychological factors to explain that because the crisis awakens mistrust in industrial activity, dishoarding is granted only at the cost of a high risk bonus, which is therefore a condition incompatible with a cyclical hypothesis at first based on the prices of unprofitable products. We must add to it the system inertia caused by low prices and large stocks.

The analogy between Bernácer's and Keynes's analyses is troubling and may be explained through observations of events. Nevertheless, we draw attention once again to the fact that Bernácer did not wait for the end of the Great Depression to adopt this attitude. Keynes struggled to discard his neoclassical heritage: he was somehow a victim of the rigidity of a whole system of thought. Wicksell believes that the solution lies in the attitudes of certain special agents, even in the midst of the economic system—banks—while Bernácer and Keynes believe it lies outside the economic system. We will have the opportunity to clarify this point.

Bernácer and Keynes ultimately find:

- *That there is disparity* in the duration of different phases. Keynes demonstrates the existence of unemployment equilibrium and shows *a contrario* that unemployment is the rule observed in reality and that prosperity is the exception. Bernácer takes exactly the same position, arguing that this rule is why depression periods drag on and almost always persist much longer than expansion periods.

Compared with classicals and neoclassicals, who are optimistic and confident about the dogma of equilibrium among adjusting mechanisms, Bernácer and Keynes are pessimistic, and their nature must be clarified. Far from Malthusian prophecies, both authors' pessimism is the result of an observation that nevertheless immediately opens on a voluntarist vision of the economy. Beyond descriptive analysis, most of their contribution comes under the economic praxis field. The solutions they advocate do not have the subsidiary nature—sometimes unknown or limited—of some neoclassical suggestions (nationalization of land for Walras or the elimination of interest for Allais). Unlike them, Bernácer's and Keynes's solutions are integrated at the heart of their analysis.

Impossibly Spontaneous Stability of the System

Wicksell, Bernácer, and Keynes agree that the system contains no effective stabilizers. Nevertheless, these authors' goals seem different.

Wicksell seems anxious to stabilize the value of money and therefore the general price level. He believes that banks can succeed, provided that they agree to set the going interest rate at the natural (or normal) interest rate. Even so, why should banks stabilize the system? Would this not exaggerate their role, and is it logical to ignore the government's role in this regard? The absence of a reference at the activity level—and, through it, employment—seems even more serious. Still, without intervention, within the entire system defined in terms of profit and unearned income rationalities, there are no stabilization solutions.

Bernácer's and Keynes's main objective is to ensure full employment. Both seem anxious to negate the economic entropy of the cycle because it usually results in unemployment. Keynes, placing himself along a historical opportunity trend, appeals to the government and asks it to play a particular role in the economic macrocosm: the role of a *producer* agent, detached from the traditional economic imperatives on profit and careful investment choices. Although Keynes undoubtedly goes too far in this direction, he was followed in theory and in practice. Bernácer, placing himself against the tide of experienced history proposes to Liberals to scuttle the previously untouchable rights to absolute private property and unearned income. He also proposes to Socialists to refuse economic centralization and state-controlled economic systems and to accept a system in which there is freedom, profit, and self-management. We believe he would be more demanding of the government than Keynes: he asks for a reform of basic structures and of discriminatory regulation.

The Interest Rate, Product Growth, and Social Progress: Bernácer's Ethical Dialectics

In this point in our analysis, Wicksell's theories are noticeably absent. We indeed deplore the absence of references to the employment level in his works, so it is normal that the theories of monetary equilibrium and of cumulative processes based on the interest-profit relation did not address ethical issues.

The Purpose of Economic Activity: Social Progress

Bernácer's and Keynes's appealing approaches identify the man behind their economic analysis. Piettre (1965, p. 319), evoking "the triple Keynesian revolution", highlights that at the principle level, Keynes replaces the physical concept of mechanisms by those of psycho-sociological functions, and thus, "we go back to the human mechanisms". The subtitle of Bernácer's first book bears the mark of a physicist, *Society and Happiness. Essay on Social Mechanics.* The author undoubtedly wanted to associate the idea of a rigorous analysis of mechanisms, giving the latter term every sense, to the idea of the purpose (Happiness) and of the environment (Society).

It is heartening to find these humanist options among economists, whether physicists, polytechnicians, or not. Stoléru (1967, p. 585) ends his book with a chapter entitled, "Economic progress and social progress" and with the following sentences, "Beginning with the analysis of the very general equilibria of the economy, this book ends with the analysis of individual income, and this return to the human is a symbol of what should be the real economic purpose 'or more'. There is nothing more to fear than to see the supremacy of human values over other values fade".

By 1932, Paul Valéry, as quoted by Stoléru (1967, p. 586), strongly asserted this supremacy: "We live under the surprise regime. Even so, we must not doubt that arts and techniques may change, speeds, powers, the usable precision, relay use may grow beyond any current conjecture, the individual value will always ultimately be the essential support of values of all material creations or organizations".

Whatever the differences between Bernácer and Keynes, the fact remains that the economic system has only relative rationality compared to a certain purpose. From this point of view, Bernácer's rationality seems more rigorously established. There is perfect coherence between his concept of labour, a "unique" factor of production, of full employment, and of the market, and its condemnation of unearned income.

We could characterize economic and social progress through the individual maximization of the $\frac{\text{purchase power in real terms}}{\text{worked time}}$ ratio or through re-creating, as Bernácer does, the $\frac{\text{total accommodation of needs}}{\text{worked time}}$ ratio. Alternatively, we could consider Bernácer's positivist approach and take as an approximation the more concrete ratio $\frac{\text{nominal wages}}{\text{nominal prices}}$. Finally, in Bernacér's view, we should ensure the increasing trend of this ratio over time.

Prospect of Growth in the Analysis

Achieving the social and individual objectives of progress generally pass through product growth. From this point of view, is Keynes's analysis sufficiently general? Does it sufficiently take into account the enormous opportunities offered by the full use of factors? In terms of the purpose of Keynesian analysis and despite the blunders in the choice or presentation of instruments such as the multiplier or the role of autonomous investment, the answer must be resolutely affirmative. Nevertheless, Keynes's metastatic analysis, his hypothesis on decreasing returns, and his neglect of constant returns to scale, of structural evolution, and of incorporated technical progress, are all weaknesses that show Keynes's discomfort in strongly considering the hypothesis for a quick-growing product in the 1930s.

The physicist Bernácer is aware of the disruptions that techniques can introduce into production in the medium term. He therefore conducts an analysis that, without being a growth theory because it is boosted in the short term, which is a favourable framework for a fluctuation analysis, constantly has that goal in the background. Bernácer is thus not stagnationist. His analysis contains a growth dynamic mechanism to which he often refers, namely, that in light of spare production capacity, there is an unsuspected reserve of backlog needs of a theoretically infinite quantity if we include potential and temporarily insolvent needs.

This attitude is crystallized through his refusal to qualify the "overproduction crisis". Any crisis revealing product excess contains underconsumption that surrounds a social body due to double hoarding. Additionally, we must of course identify the problem of social product distribution. Bernácer's growth approach is very clear when he says that in a situation of unemployment, it is less important to demand a better distribution of profit—which would increase income slightly—than to stimulate its growth by involving all potential workers in domestic production. Nevertheless, Bernácer does not neglect the issue of distribution because in the rational system he advocates, workers would conduct their own work in self-managed production units and thus escape alienation through participation in the full sharing of company profit for their own benefit.

The Rate of Interest, Growth, and Progress Disincentive

Bernácer and Keynes apply the same negative role to the interest rate in determining employment and product levels and in growth and economic progress movements. In the short term, the interest rate determines the new investment, given the marginal efficiency of capital (according to Keynes) or the average level of net profit, that is, prices of products, of factors, and of technical productivity (according to Bernácer). Future additional income depends on current new investment. Keynes seems to consider it only for a given technical situation, but it seems in certain passages that Bernácer, in a perspective very similar to that of Schumpeter, sees in investment embodied technological progress. We believe that Bernácer's perspective is wider, and in the history of ideas, it is more current than that of Keynes.

It seems that Bernácer does not consider technical progress as an ex post accounted residual that we can understand only in the relatively long term. Technological progress has a more concrete status; it is a technique incorporated in the short term and that has effects in the short term and in the long term. Recent studies show that the reality since World War II should also be interpreted.

First Effect: Investment Increase

According to Keynes, product growth depends on investment growth. Even so, demand for investment is an increasing function of income and a decreasing function of the interest rate.

$$\Delta Y = \mathrm{f}(\Delta I)$$
$$\Delta I = \mathrm{f}'(\mathrm{i}, \mathrm{Y})$$

According to Bernácer, these equations summarize only one aspect of the phenomenon, with interest being only part of the investment cost. It is also better to "boost" these equations by dating them:

$$(\Delta Y)_1 = \mathrm{f}\left[(\Delta I)_1\right]$$
$$(\Delta \mathrm{I})_1 = \mathrm{f}'(\mathrm{i}_1, \mathrm{Y}_0)$$

Second Fact: Increasing Scarcity of Disposable Funds

On this point, Bernácer's analysis is richer than Keynes's analysis. Being dynamic, it also integrates the negative effects of the financial market. Indeed, if with the interest being i_1, investment could reach $(\Delta \mathrm{I})_1$ during the period, during period 2, the financial market contracts as $\mathrm{i}_2 > \mathrm{i}_1$ and i_2 attracts new disposable funds from unearned income-yielding assets. Disposable funds become scarce on the production market, which prevents the recovery of working capital. The production market is very depressed, which can cause a crisis, except in the case of money creation and in the use of new money in the production system.

Bernácer's Ethical Dialectics

In this theoretical approach, there is dialectical movement between the interest rate on one hand and growth and progress on the other.

One acts on the other and vice versa, thus causing wasted social energy. Bernácer (1934) notes that the system is obliged to decrease the rate of progress to avoid aggravating certain problems (crises, unemployment, and inflation), while war is a circumstance that promotes technical progress and economic activity, while all work has a role in production.

We qualify this dialectic as ethical because it shows that if we do not intervene from outside the system, the economic system generates constant antagonism between its different objectives. Therefore, Bernácer and Keynes admit that the system requires intervention on the interest rate to reduce or eliminate economic entropy.

The Interest Rate and Monetary Policy

The interest rate is linked with the monetary policy through the general price level, the objectives of the economic policy, and through its cyclical and structural actions.

The Interest Rate and General Price Level

Based on the interest rate, Wicksell and Bernácer built two theories on the general price level. These two theories are radically different from the mode of analysis, especially given their extensions to economic policy. They are mentioned in *Selected Writings on Monetary Problems*, published under the supervision of Baudin (1964), but it seems that they were not compared because they are found in different parts of the book: Wicksell's article is in Chapter V *Interest* and Bernácer's in Chapter VI *Inflation*.

Wicksell's Theory (1907): "Influence of the Interest Rate on Prices"

"If, all things being equal, large banks around the world decreased their interest rate, for example, to a point below the normal level, and if they kept it there for a few years, all prices of goods would begin to increase progressively, never reaching a limit to their increase. Conversely, if large banks raised their interest rates… then all prices would begin to fall continuously without reaching any limit at the exception of zero" (Wicksell, p. 241). Therefore, what are the causes of mismatch between i_m (interest rate set by banks) and i_n (normal or natural rate)?

(a) To increase the volume of their loans, banks can lower i_m. This result, all things being equal, will increase the money supply, decrease savings, and therefore increase consumption and the general price level. Wicksell's quantitativism and his classic conception of the savings function emerge. We must blame Wicksell for the contradiction between his savings function f(i) and the logic of cumulative processes. Indeed, the proposed sequence by Wicksell,

$$\Delta i_m \Rightarrow \Delta P \Rightarrow \Delta S, \qquad (S = \text{savings})$$

Should continue in the following sequence:
As $S = f(i_m)$

$$i_m = g(S)$$

And $\Delta S \Rightarrow \Delta\, i_m$
For example $\uparrow S \Rightarrow \downarrow i_m$
Thus, the cumulative process, which is a very interesting element of Wicksell's contribution and, in accordance with Bernácer, is incompatible with Wicksell's definition of savings.

(b) Spontaneous changes of i_n (marginal productivity of capital) cause *potential* adjustments of i_m from banks only belatedly. Wicksell implies that i_n tends to increase when i_m follows at a delay, which results in price inflation. Banks, for the reasons given in (a), usually set i_m below i_n, and when a crisis is announced, they set it above i_n, therefore causing deflation.

Davidson's criticism also shows that the cumulative processes observed by Wicksell has no coherent explanation and that, from the same perspective as a spontaneous increase in i_n (technical progress and therefore an increased return on capital), the logical sequence is as follows:

Progress ⇒ ↑ i_n ⇒ exceptional profit ⇒ ↑ production ⇒ ↓ prices ⇒ ↓ i_n; therefore, the progress does not a priori change i_n's initial position in relation to i_m, and variation in i_n does not cause the cumulative process itself. Wicksell then appeals to time lags to support this process and is right in doing so. Nevertheless, he does not fully demonstrate that disparities between i_n and i_m cause or maintain the process.

We do not reproach Wicksell for emphasizing cumulative processes; in contrast, following Myrdal (1950), we criticize him for not constructing a perfectly consistent theory about them. His monetarism is excessive because in the real world, money is far from being fully integrated. Production, wages, and unmet needs are potentially absent from his equilibrium model. His view seems to be one of aggregate product stagnation. In all these respects, the superiority of Bernácer's analysis is clear.

Interestingly, Wicksell (1934, p. 168) had the intuition of describing money action reversibility on price: "price inflation, when it begins to be viewed by the public as a common phenomenon, becomes itself the cause of interest rate increase". Nevertheless, the monetary equilibrium model does not allow for spontaneous fluctuations in price due to real phenomena, for example.

Because of this classical inverse excess—monetary monism—due to the lack of structures and their influence on behaviours, the (surprising) absence of a role of public power and the failure to incorporate a temporal approach, Wicksell and the Swedish school deserve some criticism. Marchal's and Lecaillon's praises (1966, p. 238) are excessive when they speak of the "revolutionary character of Wicksell's thought" or welcome his "immediately monetary" analysis, with money "with all its attributes including its reserve function" and his dynamic analysis or (obvious) explanation of the variation of M by banks' action.

In summary, Wicksell condemns any interest rate deflation below the natural rate, prophesying an unlimited increase in the general price level.

However,

- If i_n is defined in real terms, technical progress is made in such a way that, to ensure stability, i_m must grow at the same rate as i_n. Will it grow to infinity?
- If i_n is defined in value, according to the correction made by Myrdal, i_n will also grow to infinity over the long term but at a rate lower than that in the previous case: i_m must also grow to infinity.

This calls for two observations:

- Experience shows that i_m varies within fairly strict limits: approximately 2–20%;
- Would Wicksell deem healthy from a strictly economic perspective and fair from a social perspective that i_m growth, considered as the logical result of technical progress, results in a growing stranglehold of unearned income perceivers when they share the fruits of labour?

Let us summarize the theory of Wicksell's general price level as follows:

$i_m < i_n \Rightarrow \downarrow i_m$ with respect to the equilibrium position
$(i_m = i_n) \Rightarrow \uparrow$ Price
$i_m > i_n \Rightarrow \uparrow i_m$ with respect to the equilibrium position
$(i_m = i_n) \Rightarrow \downarrow$ Price

Bernácer conducts a radically different analysis.

Bernácer's Theory: Monetary Stability Against Full Employment: Theory of Secular Inflation

As his research developed, Bernácer strengthened a theory on the state of intuition in his early writings—that of "incompatibility of interest with money value stability", as he described in his letter to Baudin (February 27, 1959). He devoted an article in the Italian review *Rivista bancaria* to present this theory based on several new arguments. Baudin, noting this, translated and included it in the aforementioned collection of selected texts on monetary problems.

Bernácer (1957, p. 261) tackles one of the most difficult classic postulates: the natural essence of the interest rate: "this optimistic premise that what must be is to be was the great mistake of classical economics. Instead, we must consider what is and what should be without confusing the two terms. We must draw the necessary reforms from their comparison. To do otherwise would be tantamount to falling into the false assumption that everything is complete and that there is nothing to change".

Thus, the author establishes the principle that to analyse the interest rate and its effects, we must first assume that its disparity is theoretically possible; otherwise, the researcher will preclude any explanatory outcome. One of the essential foundations of Bernacér premise is that savings are not a function of the interest rate. This principle, which Bernácer stated before Keynes and before one of the most authoritative commentators on Keynes, Kurihara (1955, p. 271), ruled in its favour, implies that "savings motivations in addition to rewards in the form of interest are too numerous to allow us to fear that savings would fall to zero in a situation of full employment before capital becomes sufficiently abundant to lose its scarcity value".

A Classic Relic: Preference for Time

Bernácer says the preference for time is not a factor of the existence of interest; rather, the latter causes this. Some authors—including contemporary ones—almost unanimously recognize the importance of time preference as a component of the interest rate. According to Bernácer, it simply reveals how the origin and nature of interest were unclear up to his time and especially how current economists are unable to imagine an economy without interest. In addition to criticizing their lack of logic, Bernácer reproaches them for their lack of imagination, without which any progress seems illusionary.

(a) *Two prices of money*

Under capitalism, money has two prices:

– A static price stipulated in goods

$$V = \frac{1}{P}$$

– The price of credit, or the dynamic price of money

$$V_t = V_{t-1}(1+i)$$

Observation of the facts shows that over time, i, the interest rate, is relatively stable; on the contrary, P, the general price level, is particularly unstable.

(b) *Logical or mathematical statement*

In a system where the interest rate reigns, current nominal income is worth more than future nominal income of the same amount; this is the logical corollary of the time preference postulate.

At time t_o, let nominal price be P_o.

This nominal price, all other things being equal, becomes at time t_n: $P_n = P_o (1 + i)^n$

When i> 0 and n> 0, which is the case in practice,

$$P_n > P_0$$

$$V_n = \frac{1}{P_n} < \frac{1}{P_o} = V_o$$

Thus, in a system where any amount bears interest—such as the present capitalist system—any current value (V_o) is greater than its future value (V_n), which contradicts the phenomenon of savings because saving implies preferring future expenditure to current expenditure.

In such a system, there is, other things being equal, a means to stabilize only V_o over time:

So that $V_o = V_n$, it is necessary and sufficient (n being positive ≠ 0) that $(i = 0) \Rightarrow (1 + i)^n = 1$

Therefore,

$$V_o = \frac{1}{P_o} = V_n = \frac{1}{P_0 (1+i)^n}$$

If we observe, as is the case in reality, a positive interest rate, as small as it is, we must admit that the system has an intrinsic property to depreciate the future value of money.

Bernácer proposes another solution to stabilize the money value besides the interest rate: contraction, all things being equal, of the useful money mass, or if we prefer, the volume in trading value. This scenario implies that we perfectly control the volume and the uses of the money supply. Such a relative scarcity of money should logically lead to an appreciation of the monetary unit, but we observe that, at best, it would lead to stabilization. This paradox is explained by the opposite and depreciating action of the interest rate. Thus, there is a downward trend in money and fluctuation values that correspond to various circumstances, whether spontaneous or generated by economic policy (Fig. 5.5).

The line xy represents the secular decline in money value, and the curve AE represents the effective movement of value; each segment of this curve is a type of cycle.

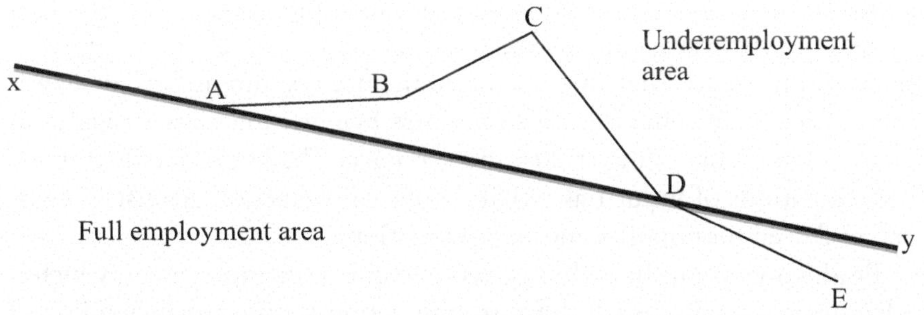

Fig. 5.5 Money value and employment evolution

AB = price stability, start of recession
BC = depression
CD = inflation
DE = hyperinflation

Therefore, the theory is contradicted by several authors, according to whom it would be possible to find an area where full employment is consistent with an absence of depreciation.

In the figure, we must choose between following the horizontal line where money value remains constant at the cost of subsequent unemployment and the vertical line where the market is in equilibrium with full employment but where money depreciates. Bernácer estimates that, in contrast to some post-Keynesian beliefs, there is no evidence that there is a compensation solution for inflationary and deflationary trends because they are divergent. The simultaneous elimination of the two trends would therefore be possible only if we eliminate interest, but most economists do not even consider this option.

The Economic Statement

Having demonstrated the process of monetary unit depreciation using the internal logic of the system, Bernácer returns to tools of economic analysis to show the convergence of the two methods. History has shown that when the monetary unit value was to be set, it was followed by a contraction in activity accompanied by unemployment. This situation incited production agents, workers, and entrepreneurs to ask the government to intervene. They first organized themselves into unions, demanding collective agreements and sometimes heightening class struggles in various forms, including strikes and sabotage. The latter obtained internal regulations of industrial activity, external protection against foreigners, and even monopolies and nationalization.

Production agents have thus agreed to combat unemployment, which is a legitimate action in itself. Even so, this action is unfortunately followed by negative effects: the reduction or elimination of economic freedom, the increase in product prices due to customs duties, a weakening of competition, and a production decline due to social struggles and to the operating cost of the government's political machinery.

Inflation is documented in historical facts and in system logic. Of course, the secular inflation rate is not the same as the interest rate. Nevertheless, the two rates are similar in absolute value over the long term. In his letter to Bernácer (May 9, 1958), Wallich notes, "what commonly happens in practice is that the depreciation rate approximates the market interest rate. It shows that the depreciation phenomenon is a schedule phenomenon of interest and not independent; it is adjusted according to the circumstances… Experience shows us that price stability is not enough to eliminate interest, not even to reduce it. On the contrary, the traditional means successfully used to maintain money stability is the increase in the discount rate at the cost of, naturally, worsening the abovementioned contraction phenomena".

Summary Assessment of Bernácer's Theory

Statistically, we could ignore our demonstration of the convergence of the economic statement and logical statement of theory, showing that in a particular period of history and in a particular country or group of countries, the average price movement did not follow the average interest rate. Nevertheless, we find a positive correlation at other times. Should we conclude that the proposed theory is groundless? If we maintain this reasoning, on one hand, we would need to apply this conclusion to all statistical and economic studies, and on the other hand, by pure logic, we would only support that this demonstration is neither favourable nor unfavourable.

We will not defend Bernácer's theory on these grounds. The logical presentation does not exclude, first, the possibility of strong fluctuations in the observed rate on both sides of the trend rate and, second, the logical possibility of a combination of factors with the same trends or opposing trends. These additional factors may create disturbances for the logical effects presented in the theory without contradicting it.

Bernácer's approach to the development of his theory may seem overly deductive. All of Bernácer's economic thoughts lie instead on a synthetic method shown by the following logical sequence:

Inductive Method Based on Empirical Observation of Facts

(There is ongoing inflation and relatively stable interest rates over the long term.)

Theoretical hypothesis ⇩

(There is a correlation between secular inflation and interest rates.)

Deductive method based on the logical processing of the theoretical hypothesis

⇩

(The interest rate explains the preference for time and involves the depreciation of future values.)

Confrontation of results ⇩

(In history, no attempt has been made to reduce or eliminate the interest rate; we sometimes tried to stabilize the money supply, which caused unemployment, and most commonly, we allowed downward price movements to occur.)

Rejection or confirmation of the hypothesis

⇩

(The hypothesis is confirmed: the future interest rate depreciates in the absence of money supply stabilization; when it is undertaken, it causes unemployment.)

Statement of the theory

(Money value stability is incompatible with full employment because of the interest rate; it represents the inflation rate trend.)

We have not subjected Bernácer's theory to a comprehensive econometric analysis, so we hold back from supporting him outright.

Nevertheless, we emphasize that, in our view, Bernácer's theory seems relevant when interpreted as follows:

(a) There may be causes of inflation other than the existence of the interest rate;
(b) The interest rate is a cause of secular inflation because agents have an incentive to anticipate their spending through borrowing;
(c) If the interest rate exists, any true political stabilization of money value seems doomed to fail;
(d) The corollary of (a), after elimination of the interest rate, will remain a secondary cause of secular inflation;
(e) When choosing between money stability and full employment, the second objective should be preferred *in all respects*.

Thus, we believe we have explained a theory that can challenge attitudes without denaturing them. Nevertheless, let us note that interest is an institution so deeply rooted in the capitalist system that Wallich (1958, *Ibid*), a North American economist and sympathizer of Bernácer, wrote the following to him after reading his article published in the Italian magazine: "Nevertheless, I do not believe that we should see in downward trend of money value the result of the rate of interest, which is only a part of the national product and is not a burden accumulated on the backs of producers".

We believe that Bernácer's implicit idea that interest—by its very existence and whatever its level—is a factor of money value instability would be perfectly defensible if the author failed to address the issue from a statistical point of view and especially if he abandoned coupling the interest rate and secular inflation. In other words, the weakness of his argument is not in his conclusion but rather in his attempt to measure the phenomena. Indeed, we recognize, of course, that there are numerous causes of inflation.

Therefore, the existence of the interest rate is only one cause of inflation among many. Hence, the inflation rate measures the repercussion of multiple variables, with one of them being the interest rate. Therefore, it is questionable in terms of simple logic that the correlation between the inflation rate and the interest rate is good regardless of the circumstances. This illogism in Bernácer's theory is explained by the fact that he developed this theory later in life—when he was 76 years old—and as he said in his letter to Baudin, he did not have time to subject this idea to sufficiently rigorous logical processing.

Nevertheless, presented in terms of a structural analysis, the theory seems well founded. We would analyse it from strictly logical point of view:

- The structure of monetary value can easily yield interest, as is actually the case in practice, especially currently;
- The first corollary is that any use of this money value, such as an investment in capital goods, will yield interest, maintaining the same current value and money value;
- The second corollary is that any future nominal value is less than the current nominal value from which it was deduced that it was necessary to apply a discount rate on future values to convert them to current values. The applied rate is generally but not necessarily the current interest rate. According to Bernácer, this principle, called the time preference, has no real content, and we agree: it is the only logical result of the existence of a socio-legal institution: the interest rate;
- The principle of discounting—as an application of the interest rate– indicates that all other things being equal, money value has an institutional propensity to depreciate.

In conclusion, the existence of the interest implies the anticipation of future expenditure and thus causes inflation. Other factors can counteract or amplify inflation, which does not destroy the value of the logical proposition of Bernácer's theory.

Economic Policy Objectives

We consider economic policy in a restricted sense, using the interest rate and/or money as means.

Wicksell's Forgotten Objectives: Full Employment

Bernácer and Keynes are precursors of modern economic analysis: they aim for dignified labour and high levels of employment. No theorist would currently dare to build theories in which this goal is absent, at least conceptually. In terms of quantitative estimates of full employment and of the establishment of priorities, there are certainly some economists without the courage to have faith in the possibility of full employment a priori and against all obstacles. These economists sometimes offer arguments that are strangely out-dated today. One of the most fallacious arguments is that of protecting private savings made through money. Even so, there is a fair way to protect small savers: indexing the nominal value of the price level instead of allowing them to believe in the effectiveness of stabilization and of a positive nominal interest policy that, indeed, does not compensate for capital depreciation. It is no wonder that the security of savings is thus hedged outside the production market.

Keynes's Forgotten Objective: The Stability of Money

It has often been said that the *General Theory* was written under the pressure of events, which explains the specificity of some of Keynes's analysis. We understand that for Keynes in the 1930s, and even more for the English population disappointed with the post-WWI policy of returning to the parity of the pound, stability might seem a worthless concern in comparison to the need to revive prosperity and full employment. Keynes's omission of the stability objective can be explained by the dialectical position that dominated the history of doctrines until his time and that opposed the traditional sequence of priorities mentioned above. This oversight is less serious than that of Wicksell because Keynes basically sought full employment, and it later became possible to solve the issues raised by the *new situation of the political economy*.

Relatively absolved by history, Keynes nevertheless had to admit that the analysis of the *General Theory* must be conducted according to the topicality of the ideas it contains. In this regard, it is also unfair to praise Keynes for the adaptations made after him or to blame him for post-Keynesian extensions or weaknesses introduced by his opponents. Still, while Keynes says that full employment equilibrium is possible and desirable, the policy he advocates to combat under-employment is not necessarily appropriate at high levels of employment policy, as demonstrated by the facts. In this respect, Heller and Friedmann's "dialogue" (1969, p. 7) is a dialogue among the deaf, as they have anti-cyclical perspectives corresponding to very different situations and the reader may thus fail to fully grasp the absurdity of their debate; therefore, it is better to analyse these economists in opposition.

If Keynes's position is explainable, it may not be excusable. His 1936 book would have more strongly merited its title if it had included a second part devoted to the economy of full employment and the conditions for its smooth operation: the first part could be entitled, *In Search of Full Employment*, and the second, *Beyond Full Employment*.

Summary of the Two Goals or the Incompatibility Between Full Employment and Monetary Stability in the Current Capitalist System

Before Keynes advocated full employment, Bernácer established the double goal of full employment and stability in his earliest writings *Society and Happiness*, 1916, *Theory of Disposable Funds*, 1922, and *The Interest on Capital*, 1925. According to him, these two objectives form only one: *full employment in stability*. This concept is not a vain speculation of vocabulary; rather, full employment requires a stable foundation in order to be sustainable. Bernácer's cycle theory shows that inflation and deflation are detrimental to high levels of employment.

The corollary of this analysis is the demonstration of incompatibility between the two objectives within the current capitalist system, and in his chapter on this reform in *Society and Happiness*, Bernácer asserts the need to be creative to invent an intermediate system between Marxism and capitalism, and he proposes measures to fulfil the conditions required for the new regime.

In theory, Bernácer's objectives were the best among similar economists, given the anteriority and prominence of his discussion of the *paradox: leave the interest rate, and therefore the unearned income, unchanged; we condemn the man either to unemployment or inflation.*

Cyclical Action and Its Limits

The main levers of the Government cyclical action are the manipulation of the interest rate and money issuance

Manipulation of the Interest Rate

Naturally, Wicksell promotes interest rate manipulation by banks themselves in order for it to coincide with marginal productivity of capital. Therefore, we believe Wicksell inspired modern neoclassical policies based on quantity theory and the manipulation of the interest rate and money supply. Thus, Bienaymé (1964) claims that Wicksell's classicism aims to use the interest rate to illuminate quantity theory, showing the autonomous action of i on P. We can make two observations on this policy postulation.

In Terms of Realism

As Wicksell describes the possibility of an agreement between all banks throughout the world, we wonder if it is healthy to attribute such economic power to private agents and if it is reasonable to believe that banks have an interest in setting i_m at the level of i_n, assuming that it is indeed the real condition for equilibrium. Keynes would suggest that central banks, which are usually nationalized, can play this role under the government's initiative. This may be true, but what would induce different nations to agree? Is any transnational economic area sufficiently homogeneous and integrated to establish a precise concept of the global general interest? In this regard, monetary events in history and, more recently, the current problems of global governance in the crisis of 2007–2012 should dishearten us.

In Terms of Efficiency

History shows that the manipulation of the interest rate and, to a lesser extent, of the money supply have proven powerless to reduce the cycle and particularly to sustainably prevent inflation. Can Bernácer address this situation?

Keynes's suggested interest rate deflation actually seems effective in increasing overall private expenditures. In addition, it approaches Bernácer's desire to eliminate the interest rate entirely. Even so, how does Keynes suggest we achieve this? As a logical extension of his mercantilist theory on interest, he suggests that decreasing money scarcity on the production market will allow inter alia the decline in the interest rate and therefore investment recovery. Even so, it is not certain that "new-born" money is used in production and that increases in activity precede price inflation. Indeed, localized tensions due to supply rigidities can cause inflation to spread without an immediate increase in production. However, interest rate deflation certainly encourages loans but is limited because it will not last long, and the rate will inevitably increase. The theoretical way to keep the interest rate low is the permanence of its issuance and therefore of monetary inflation.

According to Bernácer, the upward manipulation of the interest rate is inflationary and causes unemployment, in contrast to Wicksell's view of interest rate decreases, which is not necessarily a guarantee of full employment but is certainly a cause of inflation, unlike in Keynes's view. To Bernácer, Wicksell's theory would be absurd, and Keynes's theory first contains an internal contradiction and second is too apprehensive because it does not cause an interest rate decrease through the mechanism of supply and demand for money; Bernácer believes it is necessary to institutionally remove interest.

Balancing Issuance: Complementarity of Monetary Policy

According to Bernácer, the theoretical means to stabilize prices while ensuring full employment is to make money neutral, which should not show a tendency to depreciation nor to revaluation. The conditions for monetary neutrality are threefold:

(a) Uniformity

All market industries should be in a perfect competition regime, but this condition has never been historically realized.

(b) Access to credit by all producers.

There should be freedom of "economically healthy" credits to encourage production expansion to the extent allowed by production factors and by demand for products.

(c) Lack of income from production

Removing Unearned Income and Therefore Interest.

These three conditions are listed in increasing order of importance. Condition (c) will be analysed in the action on structures. Condition (a) shows that monetary policy is inseparable from a *real* policy to rationally organize production; it was mentioned in Chap. *Bernácer's Rational System* and will be reviewed in the section *Doctrinal Options*.

Here, it is important to clarify condition (b), that is, what the author meant by the freedom of "economically healthy" credits. This condition implies two types of monetary policy:

- *Money issuance*, which is an essential complement to the disposable funds necessary for trade and production development. This complement to money creation will be facilitated by agents' cash deposits in banks; therefore, the author seems to evoke the credit multiplier resource. Deposits would be encouraged by what is sometimes called melting currency or stamped money. Without the discounts and penalties recommended by Bernácer, banks in most industrialized countries achieved the same result by diversifying their services and by strong regulations coupled with well-designed information; therefore, they possess more persuasive, less repressive, and thus more sustainably effective means. This concern was shared by several authors in the interwar period, including Bernácer and Keynes.

As a corollary to this complementary function of money issuance, Bernácer emphasizes the need to monitor hoarding and dishoarding movements, which his regime would not completely remove. His experience in the Studies

Department at the Bank of Spain emerges in this recommendation; it is also reminiscent of a cybernetic or self-monitoring system that we mentioned elsewhere. To ensure stability, it is essential that information about money use is well developed and maintained. Bernácer's thinking leads to the establishment of an economic information and statistical system: national accounting. No regulation activity seems to be effective without a constant strong knowledge of hoarding, money creation, credits, general price levels, and stocks to determine the necessary amount of any complementary money.

Suggested by Keynes and Beveridge (1948) and formulated by Lerner (1953), this additional financial policy is sometimes described as *functional finance*, a term that Bernácer—the first promoter of the idea—did not disavow. This policy should be countercyclical; Samuelson (1964, 1971) also used the term compensatory finances to define it.

- *Allocation of the issuance to working capital* in a high-employment economy appears to be the product of Bernácer's thought. We found no greater categorical statement than his, namely, that in full employment, stability requires money creation at the same proportion as growth in the working capital of production units. We discussed this idea enough in terms of money value, market equilibrium, and the rational system to be content to recall the primordial condition of stability in Bernácer's theory.

The Debate on Funding Sources: Public Expenditures or Credit?

Beginning in 1934, Bernácer emphasizes the exceptional nature that public expenditures should have. He admits that public expenditures are a remedy to emerge from depression. Can this remedy always be effective? The author's answer is negative, and there are three possible financing modes for public investment:

- Taxes: Bernácer is hostile to its existence and to its development;
- Loans: the author admits that loans are a theoretically acceptable solution. Nevertheless, their development would heavily worsen the provision of interest, which would burden the government budget

unless the government prefers the third option, which is convenient but contrary to its objective;
- Inflation: this solution avoids loan shortcomings but maintains instability and leads to a paradoxical situation: reduction or elimination of loans' *real* interest.

Bernácer thus supports public expenditures, provided they are episodic. He therefore accepts that this method is only a palliative and is also often—though not necessarily—inflationary. In any case, it is not an ultimate solution to the almost permanent situation of unemployment. The only viable solution would be interest-free loans to finance community facilities in an almost stabilized economy. To understand Bernácer's view, which may seem regressive in comparison to the dominant Keynesian theory, it must be stressed that in his regime, where the market would operate more effectively than in the current system of self-managed production units, the government should replace private initiative only for community facilities through more rational institutions. The government has, for this purpose, funds provided by the recovery of unearned income and eliminated from the private field. Moreover, the government has a buffer function for the economic activity we analyse currently.

Bernácer is therefore opposed to the panacea of the public investment advocated by Keynes. Keynes's idea was nevertheless attractive. Thanks to deficit spending, the government kills two birds with one stone: it decreases interest and finances government investment. Currently, retrospectively and with disruption in industrialized countries' economy, Keynes's proposed policy takes a historic character that does not mask its weaknesses and its inability to solve topical problems. Once again, Bernácer's thought, attentive to the combination between real and monetary, does not fall into the excesses of the monetarist monism of Keynesian thought.

The Need for Structural Action

The perverse effects of continuous issuance in Keynes's theory, which we have denounced, require us to consider other options for the stability of a full-employment system because we cannot give up either of the components of this economic policy objective. The cyclical action of compensatory and functional issuance contemplated by Bernácer may appear at first glance as a development issue, like Keynes recommended. Nevertheless, Bernácer finds that the presence of unearned income-yielding assets on the market—in competition with the production market—maintains a chronic risk of instability, and therefore the previously planned monetary control can have efficacy only in a structurally stable system.

The objectives of the structural action are to:

(a) Make disposable to the production circuit all money required to trade from contemporary production, so we must discourage double hoarding.
(b) Distribute between the producers of the product only, so income is spent entirely on investment and consumption and growth in the product results from worker's active and perfectionist participation in the production effort.

Realizing this dual objective implies:

(c) Removing non-labour income, that is, unearned income,
(d) And to do so, eliminating unearned income-yielding assets from the market by regulating the transferability of these assets.

The results of propositions (c) and (d) converge with the results implied by proposition (b), with the cost of the expense freed from one of its elements: interest. The outcome of proposition (a) is stabilization or, even better, harmonised growth. We will not dwell either on the ethical nature of those measures or on the concrete provisions to implement them—they will be the subject of our chapter on reform. Bernácer goes well beyond neoclassical or Keynesian policies and, without accepting Marxist proposals, he calls for structural reform, of which the characteristics and the spirit that animates it are singularly topical.

References

Bartoli, H. (1950). *La doctrine économique et sociale de Marx* (Marx's economic and social doctrine).

Baudin, L. (Ed.). (1964). Textes choisis: problèmes monétaires (Selected writings: Monetary problems). Paris: Dalloz et Sirey.

Bernácer, G. (1916). *Sociedad y felicidad – Ensayo de Mecánica Social* (Society and happiness – Essay on social mechanics). Madrid: Ed. Beltrán.

Bernácer, G. (1922). La teoría de las disponibilidades como interpretación de las crisis y del problema social (The theory of disposable funds as interpretation of crisis and social issues). *Revista nacional de economía*, (40).

Bernácer, G. (1945). *La teoría funcional del dinero* (The functional theory of money). Madrid: Consejo Superior de Investigaciones Científicas, 2nd ed., 1956.

Bernácer, G. (1955). *Una economía libre sin crisis y sin paro* (Free economy without crisis nor unemployment). Madrid: Aguilar.

Beveridge, W. H. (1948). *Full employment in a free society*. London.

Bienaymé, A. (1964). *Croissance et monnaie en plein emploi* (Growth and money in full use). Paris: Cujas.

Böhm-Bawerk. (1902). *Histoire critique des théories de l'intérêt du capital* (Critical history of capital interest theory), 2nd ed in French (1st ed Innsbruck, 1884).

Carver, T. (1893). The place of abstinence in the theory of interest. *Journal of Economics*.

De Brunhoff, S. (1967). *La monnaie chez Marx* (Money with Marx). Paris: Editions sociales.

Denis, H. (1950). Trois théories de l'intérêt du capital (Three theories of capital interest). *Revue Économique*.

Denis, H. (1966). *Histoire de la pensée économique* (History of economic thought). Paris: PUF.

Friedmann, M., & Heller, W. (1969). *Politique monétaire ou politique fiscale* (Monetary policy or taxation policy), French translation. Paris: Marne.

Gide, Ch., & Rist, Ch. (1920). *Histoire des doctrines économiques* (Economic doctrines history), 2 vol., Paris: Sirey (7th ed. 1947).

Guitton, H. (1951). *Les fluctuations économiques* (Economic fluctuations). Paris: Sirey.

Harrod, R. (1971). *La monnaie* (Money), French translation. Paris: Dunod.

Klein, L. R. (1949). *The Keynesian revolution*. New York.

Kurihara, K. K. (1955). *Post Keynesian economics*. New Brunswick: Rutgers University Press.

Lerner, A. P. (1953). *Economics of employment*, French translation: « Économie de l'emploi ». Paris: Sirey, 1972.
Llau, P. (1961). *La détermination des taux d'intérêts* (Rate of interest determining). Paris: Cujas.
Malthus, R. (1820). *Principles of political economy*. Londres: John Murray.
Marchal, J., & Lecaillon, J. (1966). *Les flux monétaires* (Monetary flows). Paris: Cujas.
Marx, K. (1962). *Le capital (The capital)*. Paris: Éditions sociales.
Mill, J.-S.(1848). *Principes d'économie politique* (Principles of political economy), French translation (1873).
Montagne, J. (1919). *Le Capital: Théorie de l'intérêt des capitaux proprement dits*. (Capital, theory of the actual capital interest).
Myrdal, G. (1950). *On penningteoretisk jamvikt*, 1931, French translation: *L'équilibre monétaire*. Paris: Librairie Médicis.
Ohlin, B. (1937). Some notes on the Stockholm theory. *Economic Journal*.
Perroux, F. (1935). *Introduction à la théorie de l'évolution économique de Schumpeter* (Introduction to Schumpeter's theory of economic change) (J.). Paris: Dalloz.
Perroux, F. (1950a). Revenu national et politique quantitative (National Income and quantity policy), *Banque*.
Perroux, F. (1950b). *La généralisation de la théorie de l'intérêt* (Theory of interest generalisation), *Banque*.
Piettre, A. (1965). *Histoire de la pensée économique* (History of economic thought). Paris: Dalloz.
Proudhon. (1953). Qu'est-ce que la propriété? (What is property?), *Textes choisis*. Paris: Dalloz.
Ricardo, D. (1817, 1970). *Principes de l'économie politique et de l'impôt* (Préface de Ch. Schmidt). Paris: Calmann-Lévy.
Samuelson, P. (1964). *L'économique (Economics)*, French translation. Paris: Colin.
Samuelson, P. (1971). *Les fondements de l'analyse économique* (The foundations of economic analysis): V. 2, Stabilité des systèmes et théorie dynamique (Stability of the systems and dynamic theory). Paris: Gauthier-Villars.
Savall, H. (1973, September). Germán Bernácer, économiste espagnol (1883–1965). Une théorie générale de l'emploi, de la rente et de la thésaurisation (General theory of employment, unearned income and hoarding), PhD dissertation at the University of Paris II, 602 p. mimeographed.

Savall, H. (1975). *G. Bernácer: L'hétérodoxie en science économique* (G. Bernácer: The heterodoxy in economics). Paris: Dalloz, Collection Les Grands Économistes.
Savall, H. (2012). *Origine radicale des crises économiques: Germán Bernácer, précurseur visionnaire* (Radical origin of economic crises: Germán Bernácer, a visionary precursor). Charlotte: IAP.
Schumpeter, J. (1954, 1961). *History of economic analysis.* New York: Oxford University Press.
Senior N. W. (1836). *Outline of the science of political economy.*
Spencer, H. (1893). Social statics. Justice, French translation.
Stoléru L. (1967). L'équilibre et la croissance économique. Principes de macroéconomie (Equilibrium and economic growth. Macroeconomics principles). Paris: Dunod.
Vigreux, P. (1947). Turgot, textes choisis (Turgot, selected texts). Paris.
Villey, D. (1958). Petite histoire des grandes doctrines économiques (Short history of major economic doctrines). Paris: Génin.
Walras, L. (1896). *Études d'économies ociale* (Studies on social economy).
Wicksell, K. (1934). *Lectures on political economy.* London: Routledge and Kegan (English translation of his book published in 1913).
Wicksell, K. (1964). L'influence du taux d'intérêt sur les prix (Influence of rate of interest on prices), in *Textes Choisis*; vol. 1 : « Problèmes monétaires » (Monetary concerns). Paris: Dalloz & Sirey. Translation of an article of Wicksell published in *The Economic Journal*, 1907; vol. XVII: « The influence of interest on prices ».

For Further Reading

Savall, H., Péron, M., Zardet, V., & Bonnet, M. (2015, 2017). *Socially responsible capitalism and management.* New York: Routledge.

6

Improving Capitalism Through Freedom, Ethics, and Efficiency

This chapter introduces Bernácer's approach to improve capitalism. His recommendations are based on a philosophy, some principles, and specific methods to propose a new economic system.

6.1 General Philosophy of the Economic System Recommended by Bernácer

To highlight Bernácer's thought, the three principles of a rational economic system will be presented then illustrated, i.e., the production, circulation, and distribution processes.

The Three Principles of a Rational Economic System

The rational economic system advocated by Bernácer is founded on three principles: freedom, justice, and efficiency. (Savall 1973, 1975)

Freedom is the natural framework of human development. History is written through the struggle between oppressors and the oppressed, with individual and collective freedom at stake. This struggle is a legitimate

H. Savall, *Radical Origins to Economic Crises*,
https://doi.org/10.1007/978-3-319-93366-5_6

condition of any system in which humans are involved, and it is a basic criterion with which to evaluate it.

Justice is a similar condition and must be considered, along with freedom, as an exogenous condition for the existence of a stable social system. It is, in a sense, another aspect of freedom in the full sense of the word.

Efficiency is a synthesis component: it is both an endogenous, specific condition of an economic system that must be subject to the conditions of freedom and justice and a corollary of the relevance of these two exogenous conditions compared to that of the system. In other words, efficiency is not only compatible with freedom and justice but also enhanced by them. Thus, there is a logical solution that enhances these three variables simultaneously.

Petitio Principii: The Solution Lies in the Development of Capitalism

We will use two examples to explain Bernácer's position on the principle of reform.

After his criticism of political economics, Marx advocated a system that is paradoxical to capitalism: he believed that since the latter is a poor system, another system with the opposite view had to be designed. This position would be rational if the whole capitalist system was actually ineffective. For Marx, the solution is to change the economic structures completely.

Keynes, after criticizing classical economics, advocated superficial and provisional Government action that replaces private initiative whenever it fails. This solution is a symptomatic remedy, without addressing the root of the problem. It is, paradoxically, both the opposite of the Marxist solution and, because of the evolving nature of disease and therapy, a solution that gradually but certainly leads to the nationalization of an economy to a certain extent.

Bernácer's position lies between these two views: we can obtain a freer rational system that is fairer and more effective through developing a system that has proven growth and capacity to implement technical progress: capitalism. Bernácer does not totally reject existing structures, as Marx did, and he advocates deeper action than Keynes proposed: offering a greater guarantee of freedom, justice, and efficiency.

Therefore, can we design an economic system without unemployment and without fluctuations that allows all in society to arrange their lives according to their needs and to find income security from their work and purchasing power? "What our research tells us is that deviations of our economic organization, far from being due to the nature of things, are motivated by the breach of natural economic laws" (Bernácer 1945, p. 181).

Among all problems to avoid, money is at the forefront because it is used in transactions outside production when income arising from production allows only buying what is currently produced. This situation is the cause of the collapse of capitalism and does not ensure economic freedom. Therefore, private initiative should not be substituted with a plan that prescribes individual actions; we must instead strive to find ways to guarantee individual freedoms.

Additionally, the normal functioning of any system is the result of a more or less conscious cybernetic process. Any intervention in the system must aim to restore—not destroy—the normal functioning of the system.

Summary Model of the Rational System

The rational system is decentralized and guarantees the full employment of productive forces.

Structural Constraint: Decentralization

This economic system, which features competing production, consumption, and self-determined investment units, is guaranteed by the existence of markets that are free from any Government intervention.

Through their production and investment initiatives, entrepreneurs play a vital role. These initiatives seem to be more effective than a centralized plan and are better able to implement technical progress than a centralized making structure.

Decentralization is also found within monetary organizations: savings collection and expenditure financing are decentralized in micro-units of financial intermediation.

Individual and Overall Objective: Full Employment

For given techniques and work schedules, full employment is a condition of the overall maximization of a product, and therefore of economic well-being, at the overall and individual levels. It is a condition for progress. Work, the only legitimate source of income, is a right and a duty, a means and an ethic.

Social peace and prosperity can be achieved with full employment, and any individual or group activity must meet the criteria of social utility.

One of the benefits of this organization is the overall stability of general equilibrium: product supply adequately meets product, employment, and money market demands, and the waste of economic energy that fluctuations entail is likely to be avoided.

Production

Production includes production units, market, and capital formation.

Structure of Production Units

There are several specifications that we call structure: private property status, self-managed functioning of enterprise, and profit.

Private Property Status

Private property is essential to freedom. The only way to obtain property in the new regime is work because savings, as shown above, are accumulated through work. The only form of capital property is a real good that is produced through labour. Among real properties, land belongs, as a bare property, to public authorities, individuals, or private communities (production units or others) who own the usufruct only as an accessory right. In contrast, consumer goods are the full and complete property of individuals.

Between these two extremes, the means of production ownership belong to private communities of workers. Therefore, three property regimes coexist:

- Individual private property (consumption goods),
- Collective private property (reproducible goods),
- Shared property with a bare public collective property and private usufruct (nature in general, especially land; non-reproducible goods).

Thus, in the new regime, there is a significant attenuation of private property, affecting mostly capital goods and public goods. This ownership regime reform is related to Bernácer's fight against monopoly and unearned income in the current capitalist system.

Transmission of individual property assets due to death should be a fully recognized right, with a total exemption of duties. Inheritance tax has no reason to exist in a regime in which private property is essential to the full product of labour: it legitimizes tax-exempt transfers. Moreover, the opportunity for an individual to leave property to loved ones is a great stimulus of production and especially of savings and a perfectly logical corollary to the right to private property. In the current practice of inheritance tax, Bernácer sees proof that property is considered a privilege in the current system.

Morphology and Self-Managed Functioning of Production Units

In every business, the community of workers owns the means of production: "laws should promote the acquisition of the capital securities of each company by its workers, officers and employees. Naturally, the staff is renewed by cooptation, and the corporate changes and retirement of workers to benefit from their accumulated savings would result in the transfer of securities to new active workers at a nominal value, i.e., without possibility of bonus" (Bernácer 1916, p. 188).

In Bernácer's rational economic system, private ownership of the means of production would remain, but on one hand, it would be emptied of its speculative contents and, on the other hand, the exercise of its political rights would be subject to effective participation in the company's collective work. Then, capital vs. labour dichotomy would be abolished.

Collective Profit of Production Units

This terminology is ours. The author gives little information. Nevertheless, we believe we can say that, in his mind, all workers in the production unit must be truly active and not passive, as indicated by employee ownership or profit-sharing. Long before it existed, Bernácer (1916) basically described the post-Yugoslav type of production system.

> Interest disappearance does not imply the same for industrial profit. These are two different things that the productivist theory used to confuse. Interest is the non-labour reward; profit is the result of more significant or more efficient work than others. (Bernácer 1945, p. 187)

Therefore, in Bernácer's rational economic system, the production unit profit would be maintained for two reasons. First, it would be the deserved fruit of micro-unit collective work and shared among the stakeholders of the production effort. Then, this profit would be a necessary stimulus to increase collective efficiency and labour productivity within the company. This stimulus will be more powerful if profit rewards the success of real architects in economic competition, and if profit benefits workers rather than being shared between workers and sponsors. Everyone knows that compensation is more stimulating if it represents a large fraction of personal income.

As an institution, profit guarantees a permanent state of development in production units. Would profit risk become an issue of speculation, and would it return to becoming unearned income? Bernácer thinks not because securities will be transmitted only by workers-owners in the case of corporate change and through transfer at cost (= nominal value). Sometimes, the fraction of profit comes from causes external to the company, from community progress in general, or even from privileged operation conditions: if the fraction of profit were not left at the disposal of the company, it would be debited as a special tax for the benefit of public authorities.

The Structure and Market Extent

Market is a concept that is always evolving; the competitive market and its extension to the international market are discussed in this section.

Competitive Market: Ideal Structure Reference

Like most theorists, Bernácer believes that the concept of a competitive market is ambivalent: it is both an underlying hypothesis of implicit reference and an ideal condition for achieving the three conditions, that is, freedom, justice, and efficiency. Bernácer does not doubt the virtuality of this hypothesis more than any other theorist.

The competitive market concept is undoubtedly ambiguous: it is probably different now than it was for the classics. The historical evolution of market structures is clear, and the atomicity of supply and demand, the aspatial and atemporal patterns of the hypothesis are excluded from the contemporary concept of competition. However, this ambiguous concept is not currently meaningless: the EEC, the EU legislation for intra-community agreements, national regulations, and opinion campaigns against barriers to free trade, international negotiations for lowering tariffs, and the elimination of quantitative restrictions on trade illustrate the relevance of this concept of competition.

Nevertheless, we must not judge all theories that reference the competitive structure of the market to varying degrees. Like Marx, Keynes, and most contemporary theorists, Bernácer makes an implicit reference to the competition structure even though he explicitly endeavours to show the problems of monopolies in his criticism of capitalism.

Spatial Home Structure of the Rational System: The Transnational Market

Bernácer's liberalism also appears, of course, in his definition of the economic and political living space. Bernácer sees three obstacles to international development:

- Powerlessness to prevent the spread of crisis,
- Ability to maintain a permanent state of unemployment on a world scale,
- Likelihood of stimulating belligerency by worsening economic crises.

Moreover, the author notes the contradiction between technical progress and the narrow definition of economic space. Autarky, which allegedly protects the national economy, limits the necessary vital space for the implementation and development of economic progress, which is possible thanks to the amplification of scientific and technical progress. His argument goes beyond the strict economic framework and makes an unreserved apology to people united in solidarity to achieve progress. Nevertheless, Bernácer does not believe in the need to match the large transnational economic space to an integrated political space. He undoubtedly believes it is easier to integrate economic structures than mental and socio-political structures; nevertheless, he does not believe that the latter can hinder the former.

Fixed Capital Formation

Two kinds of capital formation are suggested: savings as a first condition for private investment and public investment.

The increase in production capacity depends on the amount of savings, i.e., the proportion of labour applied to produce not consumer goods but production goods. The savings amount does not depend on the interest rate but on production volume, that is, overall income. Savings are not money: they are non-consumed products, and product growth results from a good combination of savings volume and employment. Savings is a natural phenomenon and therefore is not generated by the interest rate. Nevertheless, savings can be hindered by inflation. To increase savings, the potential investor must find, when he or she desires, the amount of purchasing power that he or she does not achieve today on the production market.

From this point of view, saving is an adventure under the current system, which explains why, in its current state of disequilibrium, the economy does not spontaneously produce all the savings necessary for its stability and growth because the saver is not sufficiently prompted to save and investment in the production circuit is not attractive because, from this disequilibrium perspective, it involves risks.

It is therefore necessary that the New Economic Regime (NER) include a purchasing power guarantee mechanism, which should result from a widespread stabilization of the economy:

- Stability in the general level of prices,
- Stability in the general level of wages,
- Disappearance of fluctuations,
- Disappearance of unemployment,
- Disappearance of the rate of interest.

We saw earlier that this stabilization will be achieved through two conditions:

(a) All saved income is invested in fixed capital formation,
(b) Production growth financing is achieved through money creation.

This process can result in stability and growth; it is not enough to "open the taps of money and of the Government budget deficit to achieve full employment" (Bernácer 1916, p. 324).

Public Investment

Generally, in the current system, we observe savings surplus compared to private investment. Collective needs (particularly in infrastructure) that are generally always under public authority can be matched to this surplus. Even so, this surplus is likely to be stronger due to the elimination of investment opportunities on the financial market.

We assume, on one side, public service investment, and, on the other side, a surplus of disposable private savings. Taking historical evolution into account, Bernácer notes that the Government or a parastate-controlled body can perform this function. An action plan would be developed to define a programme of useful achievements. This programme would be completed in the time available for this purpose, which would depend on the volume of excess savings. What is the difference between this project and the current reality? Bernácer finds two differences:

(a) In public achievements

The only criterion must be usefulness and not, as is currently the case, one-off political opportunity. With a long-term continuous rational forecast, from overall criteria, we will avoid the inconsistent pointillism of improvised actions that are said to be acyclical.

(b) On the effects of public expenditure terms and conditions

Current achievements are often doubly inflationary: by their cost and by their financing method (fiduciary issue). In a rational system, real savings fund public projects, not money creation.

Therefore, Bernácer does not reject all Government action. He simply assigns the Government a specific role in the field of its own public goods. He rejects Government intervention in the economy and other areas.

6.2 Circulation and Distribution

As the financial market would disappear and the money market would be restructured, the distribution system would be impacted.

The Disappearance of the Financial Market and the Organization of the Money Market

It's important to define what we called disappearance of the financial market, leading to a reorganization of savings and business financial management.

Absence of the Financial Market in a Rational System

The existence of a speculative financial market stimulates hoarding in anticipation of good investments. Otherwise, dishoarding is possible when speculator expectations are unfavourable. Hoarding and dishoarding are the causes of disequilibrium on the financial market.

The best way to stabilize the system is to remove sources of disequilibrium and, therefore, the main structure of hoarding: the financial market. The elimination of the financial market first consists of establishing the inalienability of the property of previously unearned income-yielding assets. Then, it consists of replacing the different structures of the financial market (mainly the stock market) by a registry of movable property, as is required for real estate, with the maintenance of all contracts relating to such property with the exception of sales (inheritance, donation, usufruct, lease, mortgage, or pledges).

Recall that the financial market, as defined by Bernácer, includes real estate transactions. In this respect, it should be noted that land speculation will disappear with the collectivization of the bare ownership of the land. The lack of a financial market will require a reorganization of the production financing circuit.

Collection of Household Savings

Savings collection can be achieved in a way similar to the one we currently know. Households deposit their disposable funds into bank accounts, and these unpaid deposits are disposable on demand. For statistical reasons, to better identify the money supply for consumption and for savings, banks offer two kinds of accounts: current accounts and savings accounts.

In this system, withdrawals would only have a purpose of either consumption or real capital formation, that is, overall effective demand and the acquisition of contemporary production assets.

Companies can achieve fixed capital formation either by self-financing or by loans. We could conceive of a capital increase system by incorporating undistributed profits to workers and distributing newly issued capital securities between them in accordance with their profit rights. The self-financing mechanism of self-employed entrepreneurs seems consistent with the system conceived by Bernácer.

Workers therefore have the ability to allocate their savings to the company in which they work for a shorter or longer term, which would have a doubly beneficial effect:

- The worker's direct participation in the development of the production unit in which he or she works and from which he or she is able to expect increased income from labour: this is effect income;
- The worker's participation in management, at least in business monitoring: this is effect education, with the development of his or her professional, intellectual and social qualities contributing to the overall development process.

Companies in which employees' direct savings do not ensure that all production unit development financing would use public savings through banks managing savings surplus. Banks would grant loans following the standard warranty offered by the borrower and the real prospects for business development. There is nothing extravagant about this: Bernácer simply advocates a system in which interest disappears and only the effectiveness criteria should guide financial institutions' loan decisions. Exceptions for interest often occur under the current regime.

Business Financial Management

Companies are subject to financial normative prescriptions because the general stability of the economy depends on their financial management.

Fixed Capital Formation Financing

Net investment will be achieved through the issuance of securities either by the staff, by the public, or by the bank. The product of these issuances will be credited to the company's special account: the "disposable account for fixed investment". This account will also receive depreciation expenses and provisions made at the end of each financial year.

At the overall level, these amounts will be added to household accounts, forming disposable aggregate savings. In no case will these amounts be used to finance working capital because it could cause demand and production contractions.

Working Capital Financing

Companies' bank accounts will be credited with the amount of their sales and debited by their purchase amount on one hand and distributed income on the other. When business growth requires an increase in working capital, the credit needed to finance this capital will be increased.

It is of the utmost importance that bank accounts are managed according to very precise presentation standards, showing all operational aggregates at the overall level, which will highlight violations of the new financial system and detect warnings of crisis or inflation.

With its senior, each bank will have a credit quota to undertake the aforementioned working capital financing. The bank, as a unit production among many, will sell its financial intermediation services by collecting commissions that will cover its business expenses, staff salaries, and possibly a profit maintained at a normal level, thanks to competition.

6.3 Distribution

Distribution refers to labour, profit, and transfers

Labour, a Unique Source of Income

Labour—the only activity that legitimizes product ownership—is also the only main source of income.

Salary

Salary is the pre-determined income from productive activity. It is fixed in the early period, taking into account the average productivity of the industry, the production unit's past results, and the worker's individual aptitude. It represents a kind of base pay for individual effort, with rather stable characteristics.

Profit

Shared among all workers in a self-managed unit, profit is a type of excess salary that sanctions the production unit's collective efficiency during the productive concert. It takes into account, among other factors, the compensation for a firm's special ability to increase its productivity regarding other units at a spatial level and productivity in the previous period at a temporal level.

Transfers

Bernácer sometimes evokes equalization procedures and mutual insurance, which aim to share the risks inherent to particular situations or events among the community. Nevertheless, we believe that these practices are hostile to subsidies because they distort the market mechanism and impose tax burdens or inflation costs.

Bernácer's philosophy regarding the recommended economic system is based on three principles related to changes in production, circulation, and distribution processes.

6.4 Parameters of Bernácer's Economic Thought

Bernácer's economic thought and doctrinal options emerged from some parameters, such as his growing environment: family, political, social, and economic context.

Environment, Foundations of Bernácer's Personality

All personalities develop from two components: genetics and psychology. Bernácer's genetics have not previously been investigated, while psychology is a privileged field of economic anthropology.

The psycho-sociological component of Bernácer's personality must be examined through two lenses: family privacy and the perception of the social environment. The author fails to explain either; does that mean that neither of these concepts is reflected in his works? Should we neglect the search for an infrastructural explanation of his thought, confining ourselves only to report what he explicitly wrote? This attitude seems unsatisfying, and we aimed to explore the mysterious maze that founds personality.

We sought help in eyewitness testimony from Bernácer's family, friends, and colleagues. We also conducted an exegesis of his allusions to the concrete economy and, finally, we tried to build a logical (and therefore likely insufficient) explanation of Bernácer's personality from a brief reconstruction of the history of Spain.

Modesty of the Origin and Life of Bernácer

Bernácer was born to a modest family of very small traders in a medium-sized town, Alicante. It was the capital of the province and home to a port with medium amounts of traffic, with a hinterland at least predominantly—if not exclusively—agricultural. His life (1883–1965) covers a period with a wealth of discoveries, inventions, scientific, and technical applications, and political, military, social, and economic events in world history. The nineteenth century featured industrial revolution, which may seem trivial, given the period that followed and the acceleration of events that occurred within it.

The conjunction between his family's modesty and the rudimentary state of technology in his childhood—there was no electricity in Alicante and communications were difficult—likely contributed to Bernácer's intellectual humility and wonder of science and technology and their potential.

Despite an exceptional career as a teacher and senior official, Bernácer never lived very comfortably. He not only failed to make a fortune but also lived with minimal material comfort for his whole life; his only luxury was his house, beautifully situated on a hill facing the sea, on the beach of San Juan in Alicante. He acquired it at a time when rural land was sought only for agrarian purposes and when touristic attractions did not exist, at least in this part of the Spanish Mediterranean coast. His wife said that, at the end of his life, she encouraged him to buy a small apartment in downtown Alicante where he could spend the winter, but his family had a hard time convincing him because he believed it was superfluous and iniquitous to have two homes for his family.

Throughout his life, he was most willing to spend money on scientific, literary, or artistic books and on his children's education. Furthermore, he spent his own money to equip the School of Commerce of Alicante with a physics and chemistry laboratory and, later, through tenacity, he obtained financing for a large laboratory in the School of High Commercial Studies of Madrid.

Due to his lack of financial means and his desire to not personally profit from his position at the Bank of Spain, Bernácer did not travel as much as he wished. Thanks to a scholarship, he travelled one year (1911) in the main European countries while still single and teaching in Alicante. Forty-one years later, he left Spain again at the invitation of François Perroux to speak at a conference in Paris. Additionally, he met world-renowned economists in Madrid.

This careful management of his limited resources was certainly facilitated by his life experience; at 14 years of age, his father's business went bankrupt, and he had to leave school and work and study alone at home.

His attachment to his family was great; he was very close to his mother, and he left Alicante only after getting married and as he approached middle age. Even after placing first in the competitive examination for recruitment at the age of 23, he preferred an appointment in Alicante—despite a lack of physical and academic infrastructures—even though he would have been able to begin his career in Madrid.

The Influence of Spain's Contemporary, Political, Social, and Economic History

Spain has some features that have impacted Bernácer's life: religion, political, and social institutions as well as people he met all life long.

Catholic Tradition: A "Very Catholic" Spain

Recall that the monarchs of Spain always bore the title of "Most Catholic Majesty". The moral influence of the Catholic Church in Spain was and remains very strong. The vast majority of the population practiced the religion, especially women. Religion was present in all areas of life—political, official, and even commercial—and in the civil and social calendar, with a large number of paid religious holidays. The current Spanish Church has advanced political and doctrinal attitudes; it plays and will play, it seems, an important role in the evolution of social policy. Nevertheless, here, we do not refer to this post-conciliar Church, which is mainly the result of a significant fraction of the hierarchy and clergy being located in regions that feature fast industrial development.

Instead, we focus on the presence of the Church in Spanish daily life in order to sketch Bernácer's religious background. One of two important elements of this presence that we have not yet mentioned is the Church's hold on education. It was well-known, even among the low and middle classes that the only good-quality secondary schooling was public, and religion was long a compulsory subject in Government teaching and examinations from primary school to higher education.

Two anecdotes illustrate this situation:

- Francisco Ferrer, founder of laic education, was executed in 1909, perhaps because he was an anarchist. Nevertheless, his execution and its consequences—mourning throughout Europe and the fall of the tough Maura Government—demonstrate the importance of this conflict.
- More recently, in 1932, one year after the Republic proclamation—which was made without bloodshed—one of the most important laws first enacted by Azaña was the suppression of religious education. The consequences were such that Parliament was dissolved by the President of the Republic, Alcalá Zamora, and elections gave victory to the right, which was favourable of the Head of Government.

Another important aspect of the Church's stranglehold was the ramifications of its involvement in the Spanish economy in various industries, including agriculture, industry, commerce, and banking. The problem was severe at the beginning of the century; in 1910, the Liberal prime minister under Alfonso XIII, Canalejas, fought against the Church being involved in economic activity. His struggle was short: Canalejas was assassinated two years later.

These two aspects of the Church's power over education and economy persist. Perhaps the evolution of the post-conciliar Church made the Church lose some of its traditional prerogatives. Nevertheless, Spain is profoundly marked by Catholicism. Bernácer, despite being a practicing Catholic, was very critical of Church activities in secular areas and was apparently torn between his private religion and the exteriorizations of Spanish Catholicism.

Political and Social Institutions

Bernácer grew in an instable environment with violence that led to several dictatorship periods. His work was influenced by this context.

Half a Century of Government Instability

Without returning to the struggles between royal dynasties, the history of the final years of the nineteenth century and of the early twentieth century was marked by the birth of Republican power and by the inability of monarchy Governments to address the problems created by emerging industrialization, land reform, and the end of decolonization.

In 1893, violent social upheaval followed the challenges posed by the absence of land reform. Nevertheless, in 1904, Government instability began with an upsurge period starting in 1918 and ended with the fall of the monarchy in 1931. During the 21 years preceding the republic, 33 Governments assumed power, many of them dictatorships.

In addition, every year between 1907 and 1926, inclusively, the Government contracted at least one to finance the war in Morocco, the "latest" Spanish colony, leaving public finances in a deplorable situation. Bernácer denounced the effects of public debt borrowing, but he did not refer to Spanish events, namely, monetary instability and unearned income paid to Government lenders in exchange for money to finance these wars.

Political and Social Violence Was Experienced at Both Individual and Collective Levels

At the Individual Level

The same period was also marked by a series of assassinations and executions. We will mention the most important, those of three Prime Ministers—Canovas (1897), Canalejas (1912), and Dato (1921)—that of the former Minister Calvo Sotelo (1936), whose murder was one of the instigators of the Civil War, that of the former dictator's son, José Antonio Primo de Rivera (1936), founder of the Phalange, and the martyrdom of the Spanish Phalangists, the first nationalist supporters of General Franco during the Civil War (1936–1939). As the founder of laic education, Francisco Ferrer's execution in 1909 illustrates the power of violence in shutting down democratic aspirations.

At the Collective Level

The violence that marked this period developed progressively in collective forms: popular uprisings, repression, military putsches, and wars.

Various uprisings occurred, including the aborted Republican uprising of 1883; the general strike of 1917, caused by the UGT Central for a Demo-Socialist Republic; the revolutionary strikes throughout Spain in 1931, which led to the fall of Alfonso XIII; and last but most serious, the 1935 unrest (burning of churches and vendettas) that sparked the Civil War.

In response to popular uprisings, repression, which was commonly individual, also took collective forms; in 1912, the military apprehended railroad strikers by force; in 1935, riots were followed by bloody repression.

Military political arbitration played an important role in Spain in the early twentieth century. In 1916, defence armies—or "juntas"—formed to challenge the Government were considered too soft. In 1923, General Primo de Rivera rebelled against the Liberal Government. In 1929, other generals plotted to overthrow him. Finally, the military coup by the generals on July 18, 1936, under Franco's leadership, unleashed a real war and completed the infernal cycle.

During the naval war in 1898, Spain fought the United States off the coast of Cuba, its last American colony. The Spanish defeat caused a real civil crisis, whose most enduring event was a generation of writers strongly traumatized by Spain's collapse: the so-called *98 generation.*

The Morocco war was supposed to end in 1927 through a so-called pacification that was the result of a collaboration with France. Nevertheless, this war lasted two decades and ended with a Spanish military disaster in 1921.

Nevertheless, the Civil War, which lasted almost three years (1936–1939)—during which future World War II protagonists furnished their weapons and experimented with men and materials—affected more Spanish people than World War II. One million people died: almost as many as the victims of the First World War and three times more than French victims of the second.

Bernácer, a powerless spectator of these struggles and fratricidal strife, always proclaimed nonviolence. His underlying reasons for this are, we believe, twofold:

- He was intimately opposed to all forms of violence and could not acknowledge this option;
- He observed that violence generally leads to the opposite of the desired effect: there are cumulative processes of violence that usually end with the worst, most underhanded violence, dictatorship, regression, and abolition of freedoms.

According to Bernácer, violence, the exacerbation of conflict, is neither fair nor effective. His theoretical works show traces of this preference for non-violence in his recommended solutions and even in his analysis. Therefore, when Bernácer complains of unearned income unfairness—the opposition of interests between stakeholders in production—he hastens to add that the development of conflicts by the oppressed and the dispossessed cannot be an acceptable and effective solution.

In Spanish, "cacique" means a rich landowner who benefits from a kind of territorial monopoly through the concentration of a large amount of land located in a determined village, for example. He is the master of the local economy and, thus, of local policy. Additionally, he is a kind of integrated feudal lord in the representative political system via a straw man who assumes political and administrative functions on behalf of the cacique. A widespread phenomenon in the last century, caciquism still exists in some poor areas of central and southern Spain and in Spanish-American countries. As a character in many literary masterpieces of the late nineteenth and early twentieth centuries, the cacique embodies absolute, economic, political, and social power. Democrats—even those in the Government—often had to fight against both local feudalism and dictatorial forces—most often embodied by the army, which sometimes eliminated and supplanted politicians in power.

Even today, land distribution is a serious problem, especially in traditional farming areas and in the south. The old Spanish nobility still has huge dominion, and land reform was the economic stumbling block of the Second Spanish Republic. Its bankruptcy was the consequence of its inability to impose this land reform, which successive regimes have repeatedly promised in vain.

From Historical Facts to Economic Theory

In Bernácer's theoretical works and in almost all his popular articles, Spain is completely absent, except for some rare Spanish statistics, which serve as comparisons for matters as technical as the gold standard, as we reported in our money analysis. Even so, Bernácer, especially during the 24 years he spent in the Studies Department of the Bank of Spain, has been closely involved in economic life in his country. His book on Spain and European Communities is an essential work.

His preference for economic theory analysis is obvious, and he intentionally ignores the realities of the moment in his theoretical works. However, his works are part of a Spanish context and overall context that consists of cyclical crises and unemployment, and the first solution he recommends is the elimination of unearned income. A more direct link can be made in this regard within Bernácer's chosen field: normative economics. Behind unearned income, we must note the inequity in land distribution in Spain, parasitic financial activities, and causes of crisis and unemployment. Behind the condemnation of money issuance to finance public expenditures, the disaster of Spanish public finances must be noted. Given his distrust of Government intervention, Bernácer denounces his realistic analysis of structures, political power, political history, and seizure of private assets by the Government. Behind his rejection of violence, we observe not only a viscerally nonviolent individual but also an analysis of the dialectical political situation that leads to chaos. Therefore, is Bernácer a theorist, writing in his ivory tower? Precisely the opposite is true: the revolutionary aspect of Bernácer's economic analysis originates precisely from the fact that reality forced him, the self-taught economist, to refuse bookish teachings that were not in compliance with his observation and analysis.

Christian Humanism

Bernácer belongs to the great Christian humanist family, which from St Thomas Aquinas to François Perroux and Daniel Villey, emphasized the importance of economic doctrine for Christian thought, with its truths, eclipses, and regrettable silences.

Reading Villey's article "The Market Economy Before Catholic Thought" (1954, p. 936) inspired Bernácer to write an enthusiastic letter in which he emphasized his common views with the French scientist (January 17, 1955): "I want to express my agreement to you...... on compatibility between Catholicism and economic freedom. Even more, I believe that economic liberalism, the basis of political liberalism, is in the purest tradition of the Church... I think that capitalism as well as communism belongs, despite their apparent opposition, to a general trial of materialism in ideas, which doctrinally began from the Reform that replaced St Thomas Aquin's liberalism with a realism in contradiction with the roots of Catholic thought, and I believe also in opposition to the true goals of economic science. These goals are certainly directed towards obtaining material well-being not as an end in itself but as a step towards happiness, which is a moral purpose... Harmony between Economy and Ethics is the first necessary step for an agreement between economics and the Christian spirit".

Positive Aspect: Happiness Achievement

Extracts from Bernácer's letter show—better than exegesis of his works—what Figueroa denominated the *pillars* of Bernácer's thought. We will mention the tallest of these pillars: research on happiness, which is a moral purpose. Recall that the first of Bernácer's economic books was titled *Society and Happiness*; *Social Mechanics Essay* (1916). This ultimate goal of happiness that the author proposes for human society seems to be modelled on the concerns of his illustrious predecessor Sismondi, for whom the bicentennial of his birth was celebrated in 1973.

A very quick comparison between Sismondi's and Bernácer's thoughts reveals points of convergence. Concerns about scientific demonstration were highlighted by most participants in the symposium organized at Sorbonne in honour of Sismondi and his dynamic analysis Weiller (1973, p. 18): "He (Sismondi) sought to articulate demonstration differently and less to include there philanthropic concerns that a dynamic and perhaps even a dialectic… If Schumpeter appreciated Sismondi as the first theorist for dynamic analysis sequence, Henri Denis, followed also by Henri Guitton (in this regard, the convergence is striking) would make a convincing demonstration about it". Sismondi and Bernácer also share a refusal of orthodoxy and doctrine: "At a time when the history of Economics seems to hesitate, did Sismondi not already show the task that remains to be achieved: in-depth analysis of the connections that continue to operate within, perhaps, what we can call the 'FTP block' (facts, theories, policies)? And that in the name of what Sismondi called 'social economy'", as described by Walras.

Bernácer is therefore in line with economists from various intellectual and social origins, solicitous for their purposes and scientific consideration. Nevertheless, it is remarkable that these authors—heterodox in the sense of Weiller—were ignored or underestimated in their time and long after, but gained acclaim beginning in the middle of the twentieth century.

In this view, we would be inclined to judge marginalists to be hedonistic in the second half of the nineteenth century by showing how happiness can sometimes oppose pleasure, especially when these two concepts are promoted as social purposes. Nevertheless, if we insisted too much on parameters that are economically exogenous to Bernácer—even if they should be imposed on him—we would be driven too far from economics towards a science that Weiller called socioeconomic science, and we would give a false impression of Bernácer's economic thought.

In summary, according to Bernácer, economics—as fact, science, or policy—must be part of a set of structures that aim to achieve happiness. We have found no trace of an attempt by Bernácer to define "happiness", so it has the status of a scientific postulate.

Negative Aspect: Denunciation of Social Injustice

Social injustice is not natural; it is a product of human society. The scientist must discover the natural laws that form the body of its science. Thus, Bernácer, who is optimistic in a sense, rejects social organization and how humans designed and produced most of their social ills. Rousseau, who Bernácer does not quote, nevertheless appears to have left an impression on his mind.

Bernácer does not remotely believe that as long as a set of written laws is followed, all will go well. Conversely, he considers that any system, any action, and any human disposition commits the human being to a readjustment process from which a new order results. This order is, compared to the previous established order, more or less in line with a social ideal characterized by natural laws; but nevertheless, it results from the implementation of either antagonistic or convergent power, which worsens or improves social justice. Behind the order embodied by power structures looms the ideal of freedom that must govern any action related to social order. Thus, Bernácer supported German Ordoliberalism.

Social justice involves the problems of egalitarianism or elitism, of individual and social stimulation, of progress reports, and of the inequality of natural endowments. On all these points, we remain very cautious because they are just barely mentioned in Bernácer's works. The principle of social equality takes into account, we believe, a certain inequality in intellectual, psychological, or legal individual endowments, and these differences can be mitigated over time through progress and education expansion (solidaristic aspect) and with the implementation of stimulating structures that facilitate this expansion. In an economic order, decentralization, economic freedom, self-management, and collective profit sharing should promote social justice.

Nevertheless, the denunciation of social injustice as an established order should be the starting point, according to Bernácer's economic theory heterodoxy. His political economy only makes sense if it leads to a genuine economic policy.

Limit of Means: Moral Unity and Social Peace

Two rejections can be highlighted: ethical dualism and sociological dualism.

Rejection of Ethical Dualism or Integration of Morality in Economic Rationality

Based on the history of civilization, Bernácer observes that people have always sought privileged situations in which they could live without working through nobility privileges, from primitive tribal fighting to unearned income perceiver capitalist status. In all these historical regimes, the goal was the domination by a group of people who are inactive in the sense of production on other people who are active in production. This history of exploitation first took a violent form—wars, serfdom, or even slavery—and when money was involved, it often took more insidious forms. It allowed the ownership of certain assets that had the institutional and non-natural property to produce income. The historical forms of these assets are quite varied: loads granted by monarchs or purchased by bourgeois, land, buildings, and means of production.

The result of this economic and social organization is the cleavage of society into two opposing classes: a class that produces and pays unearned income and taxes, thievery or alienation, and a class which benefits from these revenues without working in return. It explains that people have always sought privileged situations as long as the system allowed it. The current means of this appropriation is money. In this way, people have tried to discover or invent systems to produce money: speculation in its various forms is, in this respect, the most productive of these systems.

Thus, society, especially Christian society, has generated the myth of ethical dualism. There is an extra-economic moral order with laws that must be observed scrupulously and an economic order in which everything is allowed, including letting unemployed people starve to death in an affluent society or propelling people who do not work but who have money to the highest level of social responsibility.

Bernácer (1956, p. 218) is in favour of moral monism: "money makes misfortune for the one who does not own enough and makes fortune for the rich. It is due to the fact that money falsely polarized human life. What humans must pursue is not money but happiness, which is a moral good with unity of consciousness as its first base … Even from the viewpoint of very strict economic efficiency, the spiritual dissociation of humans in moral order and economic order is false".

This morality unit is, moreover, consistent with the rationality of the economic system: nothing would be more economically efficient than the moral improvement of economic subjects. This improvement would decrease the monitoring cost and necessary control. Additionally, it would allow better combinations, which are impossible in a world based on mistrust. Conversely, human moral improvement would be favourably influenced by a rational economic system that would reward the most efficient person and therefore the one with the strongest ethics. This idea summarizes Bernácer's economic anthropology, which we describe as follows: the human being, who is naturally good, must create a social system that encourages his or her mental faculties to develop and thus his or her economic energy to thrive. We must formulate a set of operating laws to promote this thriving.

The current regime is the result of historical determinism in a descriptive order. Nevertheless, this determinism has no value in a normative order. It is the manifestation of Bernácer's heterodoxy regarding all the preconceptions of what we sometimes disparagingly call the political economy.

Rejection of Sociological Dualism and Refusal of Class Struggle

Bernácer was aware of the evidence of realism, but he rejected the dichotomous interpretation of social reality and the use of violence.

Evidence of Realism

Bernácer does not deny the existence of classes. At the end of his book (1956, p. 221), in the chapter on institutional history, he mentions "human struggles" and "serfdom" "from feudalism to historical plutocracy". These points are discussed in more detail in his first book.

Therefore, Bernácer perceives very well from experience the conflicts of interests embodied in class antagonisms. Bernácer observes that among primitive populations, the malnourished tried to appropriate the resources of neighbouring tribes by exterminating them. Later, cultured civilization rendered extermination unnecessary: land appropriation and producers' enslavement, which was apparently a less violent and more rational form, replaced it, perpetuated by the legal institution of property sanctioning. Individual or collective enfranchisement and financial reporting within feudal hierarchies are examples of money's role in medieval economic and political society. Additionally, the French Revolution did not end privileges: it transferred certain class benefits (clergy and nobility) to another class (bourgeoisie). "The aristocracy was replaced with plutocracy, a pushy class that came up due to speculation, even to smuggling and banditry, rather than work." This sentence marks the violent tone used by Bernácer to vilify the exploiting class and to demonstrate that at the origin of his analysis, he has a very firm grasp of political and social realities. The economic universe, described by Bernácer, or at least the basic data from which he develops his doctrine, is thus human in nature.

Refusal of the Dichotomous Interpretation of Social Reality

If the author refuses to make concessions about his observations of evidence, he does not draw the expected conclusions at the conceptual level. Bernácer says (1956, p. 214) that it is true that the mechanism of our economic system led to the creation of two classes: a class of possessors that is few in number and a great mass in the proletarian class. Nevertheless, "Marx's mistake is to regard class struggle as the pivot of economic mechanics and the result of the capitalists' will to exploit workers". Therefore, Bernácer (1956, p. 221) considers that in the social arena, there is a function of solidarity between employers and employees, and it functions against the individuals outside the production channel—that is, parasites—and it is legally supported, protected, and even encouraged by the system: "The fact is that class struggle is the fruit of all the evils that the flawed economic organization pours on society. The boss is a victim like the worker; both suffer from the same problem, although neither of them knows what it is". The author admits, of course, that "the boss enjoys more material goods, though he does not have the spiritual goods of tranquility, peace, and future security that everyone could have at the same time as material well-being if there were a more rational and fairer system".

To date, these difficulties have been solved by expedients in the political and social order. The advent of a certain political democracy in the world has introduced neither sustainable economic prosperity nor sustainable social peace. According to Bernácer, material (goods and services) and spiritual wealth have not achieved all the progress that science has seemed to promise. The underlying theory of economic and social entropy, waste, and degradation of energy implicitly returns to the author's thoughts. The solution lies not only in sharing the lean product generated by the current economic organization but also in business growth. Nothing is more urgent, despite the pioneering reserves that this concept produces, than this growth perspective.

The disappointments caused by political democracy that Bernácer (1916) does not condemn, of course, but rather considers powerless to promote economic progress by itself, are subject to a partial explanation. This concept illustrates what we perceive as a kind of elitism in the rational organization of society (to each according to his own intellectual and moral capacities). Bernácer notes the failure of these terms: "proletarian classes that seemed more interested in political conquests were disappointed that these democratic weapons were useless and they decided to do direct action either to achieve their demands or—in a more ambitious aim—to conquer power".

Then, he explains this failure: "making disposable to an illiterate mass, in rebellion against their fate and ignorant of the root causes from which their discomfort arises, the leadership of the nation is nonsense, it pretends that the flock guides the shepherd. Their fortunes are different, depending on the case, but their failure is obvious to all, creating the most diverse reactions developed against the eighteenth century democracy".

Refusal of Violence as a Means to Achieve Reform

As we have shown, Bernácer considers violence a source of social malaise and the origin of political, social, legal, and economic institutions at the end of a dialectical historical process. As a source of evil, violence is also a consequence of the current situation; it is both cause and effect. This dialectic is a logical consequence: violence cannot be a solution, as history and current events have shown. Because of a corollary or his sociological analysis, Bernácer's rejection of violence has a hypothetical status in building his rational system and in reform implementation, the transition from capitalism to the new regime.

Bernácer's approach seems logical so far. Nevertheless, since there is, on one hand, the latent or expressed situation of violence, and on the other hand, the reform he proposes, we fear that the latter is considered a real revolution and as a violent act *sui generis*. Is it possible to implement the reform without violence? If this reform is legitimate, is it desirable to implement it without the means to achieve it? Is it effective to renounce the use of certain means at the risk of completely sacrificing the purpose? These questions have to be asked regardless of the position we adopt.

Vigour of Solutions or "Radicalism" of the Reform Advocated by Bernácer

After reminding the reform pillars, this section focuses on the way Bernácer designed the reform implementation.

Reminder of the Reform Pillars

The pillars are the unearned reform deletion, the collective ownership of infrastructure assets, the self-management of entrepreneurial firms and tax elimination.

The Unearned Income Deletion

Bernácer advocates for the elimination of interest. Nevertheless, in light of his theory on the origin of the interest and his entire economic doctrine, it seems more accurate to speak of unearned income elimination. In its current meaning, interest is only a particular aspect of unearned income. To respect Bernácer's thought, we must generalize the concepts of interest and unearned income and simplify the question, setting it as a necessary and sufficient condition for the new economic regime to operate, where the only source of income is work. We will now call the rational system advocated by Bernácer the new economic regime (NER).

The regime does not exclude the possibility of organizing transfers to address specific individual situations (transfers qualified of social, insurance against all kinds of risks, and savings for retirement). Unearned income elimination involves financial market elimination or halting the bottomless pit of disposable funds, according to the case, i.e., the elimination of the structure or organization of exchanges between money and unearned income-yielding assets. This financial market, whose purpose was to facilitate the exchanges of such assets, must disappear so that these exchanges no longer occur.

The Collective Ownership of Natural Heritage

This market suppression does not necessarily mean the disappearance of all forms of ownership over goods, which currently produce unearned income. Bernácer makes a distinction between natural endowments—for which the only legitimate ownership is collective (land and natural resources)—and assets created by humans, which are therefore incorporated labour (buildings, housing, and production equipment).

These latter are private property, provided that this property does not give any rights to receive an income without productive work.

These goods that are likely to be privately owned may be transferred for a fee or cost, according to legal and administrative forms that discourage any speculation (imposed formalism) or freely, free of charge (donations, inheritance). In NER, the transmission of these properties that constitute incorporated labour would be totally free of tax.

Bernácer therefore responds to a social idea of justice and peace for which current events highlight a need felt at an overall level. He tracks unearned income and tackles one of its most insidious and odious forms:

capital gains. He also addresses this abuse of the right to absolute private property. His disposition aims to solve real problems that the modern world is increasingly facing: outrageously unfair land speculation, absurd monetary speculation that causes countless problems both inside and outside the country, the use of public domain (private beaches), expropriation of and problems with building land estimation, unconscionable weakness of wages, etc. We stop the list here, as concrete examples abound. We recall an article published in *le Monde* a few years ago, where a parallel was drawn between the utopian Proudhon predictions or suggestions and the abundant French law, which, since the late nineteenth century, has tried to solve the problems it denounced. We could do the same with Bernácer's NER.

Companies' Autonomous Management

Suggested by Bernácer in 1916, the self-management of companies by workers (managers, executives, employees, and labourers) was carried out in some countries with varying fortunes and somewhat sporadically. In Yugoslavia, the system seemed to fairly match the author's idea, although he never mentioned this example, probably because the macroeconomic environment he advocates—including freedom and the market—did not seem to be achieved there. In France, the idea of cooperation between workers had some doctrinal favours and some achievements that operate almost reasonably.

In light of contemporary events, conflicts, excessive spatial and functional concentrations, disequilibria and disorders between decision centres and concerned stakeholders, declaring that Bernácer addresses severe problems is an understatement. At an ideological level, decentralization is necessary and desirable, so we must imagine new relations between Governments and governed people. The company, the main cell of economic life, is the subject of many debates on its structures, and it seems that everyone would ideally admit that workers' participation in management is both a condition for progress and eventually inevitable.

The expansion of education, the need for efficiency in production units make the implicit or formal transfer of power indispensable and empirically realized in effective democratic organizations. Of course, this principle confronts established situations and anchored routines, and its implementation will not be without difficulties. Nevertheless, any active person knows that those who decide and direct this activity are bound to face difficulties and that this perspective should, under no circumstances, discourage attempts to restructure if necessary.

It seems that Bernácer was convinced of the determinism of structures on human behaviour, provided that the structures are themselves the consecration or the institutionalization of behaviour. This means that if some people are not considered able to currently fill certain positions of responsibility and initiative, it cannot be assumed that tomorrow, through stimulating structures, we cannot generally change their behaviours.

Affirming the contrary occurs under a pessimistic attitude that Bernácer condemns. Simple observation of companies operating under the current system demonstrates the importance of what Galbraith called the techno-structure, i.e., a decision-making complex that holds de facto if not *de jure* power in the company and, beyond, in any firm with some permanence to its decision-making structures. This technostructure is composed of humans who mainly come with recognized skills. Their profile is more that of skilled workers than that of capitalist unearned income perceivers. Why would these people be unwilling to use their skills to serve the cause of a self-managed production unit by holding their power in the virtue of their abilities and achievements in the same way they currently hold it by transferring it from the board of directors composed of their company owners?

Promoting self-managed production units—directed by a techno-structure held by workers but not necessarily exclusively by them—in a market economy and with a profit stimulus is doomed to failure; it is a pessimistic bet that Bernácer did not make.

Tax Elimination

Bernácer considers taxes to be the result of a historical process that the monarchs and later, public entities, needed to realize the community plans; these were resources that only individuals were able to provide under the pretext of obtaining, in exchange, protection by public authorities.

While collective needs undoubtedly exist, it is also undeniable that the community naturally owns a heritage: natural endowments, land, energy, and mineral resources. A part of their value—that exceeds any enhancement work—cannot be legitimately appropriated by any individual under the pretext that he has property rights. Therefore, while Bernácer recognizes the need for the Government and for local authorities to have a budget, he believes that this budget should not be unbearable; the Government's tasks should be selective; and the necessary revenues should come from collective heritage and not through the distorted and sometimes unfair collection of individual income. Agreeing that the community bears the expenditure of collective order, he argues that it is not preordained to charge the community on the fruits of their labour (tax); rather, the Government can collect from the fraction of income that does not match work (unearned income). This point of view is original but not totally unfounded, as we will analyse more thoroughly.

How Bernácer Perceives the Switch From Capitalism to the New Economic Regime (NER)

According to Bernácer, the transition should not be based on violence nor spoliation but through restructuring unearned income system.

Social Peace and Justice Requirements

In order for it to be effective and sustainable, Bernácer sets as a principle of the transition from the old to the new regime that it comply with social peace and justice.

We briefly recall that Bernácer, due to his personal temperament and the lessons from history, refuses violence—either physical or of any other form—as a means to achieve his reform.

Among the owners of the unearned income assets primarily targeted by the reform, some acquired such assets legitimately, that is, without any speculative motive. They invested their savings in these assets. Dispossessing them would amount to an outright theft.

Nevertheless, it is difficult and inappropriate to investigate the legitimacy of the way properties are acquired, so Bernácer, with a pragmatism worthy of Anglo-Saxons, offers not to seek to discriminate between genuine *innocent* savers and real *unearned income perceiving exploiters.* According to Bernácer, the future new order is most important. If ultimate wealth, which was sometimes illegitimately acquired in the past, is the price of social peace, society must agree to pay it, especially since the *institutional* elimination of unearned income tends to automatically reduce property values—which were formerly sought precisely for their ability to produce unearned income—at a cost value and even at an indexed cost.

Bet on the Success of Reform: The Optional Purchase of Unearned Income-Yielding Assets

One of the dangers of reform is that the owners of unearned income-yielding assets, who are traditionally inclined to panic, do not massively demand the purchase of unearned income-yielding assets by the community at the time of the reform. Bernácer believes that the fact that these goods no longer produce unearned income does not eliminate their intrinsic value, and the owner's inability to find cash-yielding assets would remove any attempt to transfer these assets for money since no other acquisition would be particularly attractive a priori because of the disappearance of interest and of unearned income.

Nevertheless, we cannot hide that Bernácer operates in an autarkic economy, as it would be enough, of course, for a single country to welcome that kind of capital, for money to escape and therefore for the owner's desire to sell the formerly unearned income-yielding assets to be realized by finding unearned income-yielding investments abroad. Bernácer's optimistic bet would therefore be unfounded. This reservation must be made because Bernácer's liberalism seems to contradict the only probable safeguard: the regulation of capital outflows. Nevertheless, we should not overstate this internal contradiction because the hypothesis we consider may be subject to temporary safeguards.

These asset transfers should therefore be normally achieved gradually along the natural needs experienced by the population, during special events at the individual level, such that a priori, there is no reason to believe in theory that owners will rush to sell their properties to a community. This hypothesis may have inflationary consequences that can be guessed because the Government would be forced to issue money.

Collection of Natural Unearned Income and Public Finance

Three main requirements are recommended: the collectivization of unearned income-yielding assets, the decreasing and selective role of Government as entrepreneur, and the planning of collective needs funded by public loans.

Collectivization of Unearned Incomes, Lands Unearned Incomes, to Finance Current Public Expenditure

Collective natural assets that are entrusted to private agents for their exploitation would provide society with permanent revenue. Unearned incomes and land unearned incomes are thus paid directly but precariously by the operators to the community, the exclusive and permanent owner of these assets.

Decreased and More Selective Role of the Government as Entrepreneur

Bernácer does not believe in the Keynesian panacea of public investment: substituting the market initiative with state initiative. Against the tide of past historical evolution, this position may wrongly appear as the survival of Bernácer's classicism. However, history is not continuous; we cannot predict today that the coming years will feature the same pattern as the years following the publication of the *General Theory*. Keynes promoted the theoretical principle of sporadic experiments (public works to aid companies that experience difficulties), which were attempted by Governments since the first-ever crises and extended only in very exceptional circumstances.

Until then, these interventions had been perceived as a temporary palliative; after Keynes'—and perhaps despite him—Government intervention as an entrepreneur was institutionalized, promoted to a dogmatic and lively degree.

Bernácer is aware that the Government and decentralized authorities have a vital role to play, but he is wary of planning (no higher intelligence can replace the role of the market), of statism (takeover of a governing fraction by a governed majority), and of bureaucracy (dissolution of responsibility and a lack of stimulant). The Government and communities have a natural role to play and specific functions to be performed. In the spirit of Bernácer, we believe that the economic game implies the previous distribution of roles and cards and that agents have a *sui generis* vocation to assume this or that function. Circumstances may amend the generic, but this opportunity to adapt to the circumstances we keep for ourselves, and we should not forget that distribution must eventually tend towards general satisfaction.

It should be noted that Bernácer's position is very defensible on the theoretical level:

(a) First, he is committed to economic efficiency and to its impact on the community, and, in this regard, observing the behaviour of the official producer, under different political climates, shocks him. Keynes did not appear to raise the question of effectiveness and, even at the theoretical level, his replacement of private expenditure with Government expenditure is based on a confused logic, as we have already denounced; the propensity to save slows a high level of activity and employment. We talked at length about the mistakes in Keynesian theory in the second part, and we will not dwell further on this subject. We simply recall that, in our view, the role of the Government in Keynesian theory

    - Is perfectly relevant to the premise of his analysis,
    - Is nevertheless based on mistakes in observation and analysis of economic facts,
    - May correspond to a necessary passage in economic history between the old failed capitalist system and a certain new regime.

(b) In NER, in which workers could implement their own work in the companies they create and where the market would generate collective profit at a reasonable level that is strictly shared between the active participants in production, profit sanctions the efficiency of the production unit, and unearned income should be appropriated by the Government, criticisms of capitalism that were used as a basis for the nationalization principle stand alone. The problem of nationalization is a burning issue that causes epidermal and passionate reactions. Leftist political parties evoke denationalization as heresy, and the political right suggests that nationalization regresses freedom because it violates the right to property. However, there was a nuanced position on this issue to which Bernácer certainly subscribed, promoted for a long time, and died without recognizing: the nationalization of the Bank of Spain.

Bourcier de Carbon (1972, p. 112) said, without nostalgia, it seems, "Indeed all nationalized activity is not subject to denationalization. Nevertheless, in all cases, the management system could be improved by adequate reforms and some of them are half way to a kind of denationalization". He concluded: "It takes as much to denationalize for social as for economic reasons. Whenever private industry can do as well as the Government, and naturally when it can do better, we must free the Government, take it back to its real task that it fulfils as bad as further unnecessary burdens are added. The Government's role as arbitrator continues to grow in the modern economy. Without this arbitrator, many opposing interests that lie in the nature of things cannot find peaceful solutions. Ultimately, freedom is threatened. Too often and unnecessarily, the Government wants to take responsibility".

Keynesianism took him to assume increasing responsibility, economically, and the Government took the credit to cope: hazardous acquisition that strongly exposes it to the onslaught of all clients; a weak situation that resulted in many sources of inflation against which the Government became weak after causing—and then fighting—them. In order, with the necessary steps, to take care to prepare public opinion for a proper understanding of reality from a multiplication of Nora style reports: "*Everything which normally comes under private area must be denationalized*" (author's emphasis).

Collective Needs Planning and Realization Through Loans

Bernácer recognizes the need for planning, given that it is at the level of decision-making units and thus decentralized. Companies must plan their activities and the Government must consider its specific burden: collective needs. The Government would therefore have a task list to complete according to the possibilities of economy financing. Borrowing—of course, without any interest charges—would be the normal mode of financing, and in exceptional cases, when the exigencies of the economic equilibrium require it, the Government could use money issuance, provided that the deficit is erased rather quickly after.

What is remarkable in Bernácer's argument is the evidence of the complementary characteristic of public expenditure in relation to private expenditure due to budget constraints:

$$\begin{aligned}&(\text{Public expenditure})(t_i)+(\text{Private expenditure})(t_i)\\&\leq(\text{Income})\,(t_i)+\text{ Unspent disposable funds at the end of }(t_{i-1})\end{aligned}$$

By neglecting this constraint, Keynesians are unable to theoretically and practically address the new situation of permanent inflation created after the Second World War. Keynes, meanwhile, demonstrated exceptional timeliness in writing *How to Pay for the War* in 1941, thus partially completing his insufficient analysis in *General Theory*. Nevertheless, did his writing greatly inspire his disciples?

Provisional Equilibrium Sheet for Reform

We proceed here as if the reform envisaged by Bernácer were carried out, and we attempt to project its consequences and results.

A Solution That Seems Very Positive: Collectivization of Unearned Income and Public Finance

The first consequence would be the compatibility between social justice and efficiency as well as the disappearance of speculation and tax inequity.

Compatibility Between Social Justice and Efficiency

Bernácer's system has the merits to meet the criteria of social justice and efficiency. In a world enmeshed in contradictory and dialectical relationships, it is comforting to think that there is a solution, albeit theoretical, that makes justice and efficiency compatible. Bernácer's reform is less utopian in absolute terms than some visionary theories that are strongly forthcoming on that matter. Nevertheless, these theories left deeper traces than we think. This reform also seems more feasible in the near future, given the progress achieved and the need to consider all costs that reforms eventually impose. Indeed, injustice and a lack of productivity are felt as increasingly unsustainable in the majority of the political spectrum.

Significantly, in the conclusion of his book, Stoléru (1967) cited passages from the encyclical Mater et Magistra by Pius XI: "It would be radically wrong to see either in the capital alone or in working alone the sole cause of everything producing their combined effort; it is unfair how one of the parties contesting the other in any efficiency would claim all the fruit for itself… this need for justice can be satisfied in many ways, as suggested by experience. One of them, and the most desirable, is to ensure that workers are able to participate in the ownership of companies in the most suitable forms and measures" (our emphasis).

Social and Financial Restoration Order: Disappearance of Speculation and Tax Inequity

In Bernácer's time, everywhere in the world, financial disturbances had annihilated the world economic equilibrium, speculation on the dollar dropped despite two devaluations in less than 18 months, and speculation on gold reached truly absurd prices, far exceeding the need for this form of money. Demand for durable goods reached an abnormal level, and we can wonder if Bernácer was pessimistic when he proposed the first condition for disequilibrium of the financial market.

In autumn 1968, France, after several abortive attempts at reform, began taxing capital gains in a striking example of political obstruction of the economic system; several times a year, the system reorganizes certain points of detail. Early or delayed elimination of some taxes, relief for savings, endless discussions on the mix between direct taxes and indirect taxes and on the opportunity—if not justice—to heavily tax certain high labour income while simultaneously uncapping sight deposits in tax-free savings. Once again, we do not aim to identify all concrete examples that prove taxes are not close to reaching a stable limit and content.

What is more natural for Bernácer than to denounce misdeeds in tax collection, while providing the community with the resources they need through natural unearned income collection? Again, Bernácer sensed that Governments are caught in a gear that has its own dynamics and leads to progressive nationalization, to stifling economic activity, and to a social welfare slowdown. Bernácer's position may now seem heretical, given the abundant use of the public revenue and expenditures. However, we are convinced that the future will prove Bernácer right, at least partially. Now note the absurdity of the current situation, which consists of proliferating painless taxes, specifically on goods with low price elasticity, which is justifiable in terms of financial science but not necessarily in terms of overall economic impetus.

Indeed, a tax on labour is, in a sense, absurd and unfair. Nevertheless, why do we collect more on labour income in France than on capital if, in reality, labour income is the more "certain" income; even if it is subject to taxation, it cannot succeed in tax evasion. We blame Governments not for wanting to penalize workers but for taxing income anyway, as we do not present the most drastic means, which consists of outright transferring unearned income from the individual to community by rule. In this regard, Bernácer's solution seems greater than the energy tax that we periodically evoke in France and that proceeds, in part, on the same premise but has many other disadvantages.

In contrast, the concept of public service may not necessarily be linked to the idea of gratuity. If we extend the author's reasoning, we observe that in a system where individual income from work (salary plus profit share) increases, the individual is likely to pay a number of public services of which he/she takes advantage individually, without prejudice for a development or exemption regime that is always compatible with NER. It indeed seems logical that the place given to the market in NER implies that this market is the best possible, raising the question about price and the terms of improving competition.

Bernácer is far from seeing in all these system improvements remnants of classicism or neoclassicism. In contrast, we believe that the author struggles against a common myth spread by supporters of the planned economy because Keynesians and Marx himself never truly denied the idea of economic competition. In a *normative* order, competition remains, for the economist, an ideal working hypothesis. In this regard, the unanimity of Western legislators not only in terms of regulation but also in action shows that competition—regardless of its confusion and ideals—remains a kind of model for the ideal market structure. The legislator should further strive to define and control the compliance to basic rules that govern the market—information, consumer protection, unfair competition, and advertising—than to just try, often in vain and sometimes at the cost of opposite effect of that intended, to influence market components and to sterilize resources that remain lacking for other purposes in the community.

Clouds on the Horizon: Will the Stability Objective Be Achieved in NER?

Bernácer insists that stability is an important goal of the economic system. Let us add, moreover, that this objective must be assessed as a condition for the primary objective of sustainability: full employment. Is NER a more suitable system than any other to ensure stability? Bernácer believes that the main cause of instability is investment—speculative or not—on the financial market.

Its elimination must be a system-stabilizing factor. Nevertheless, Bernácer neglects the real factor that leads to demand inflation: demand excess. Perhaps he would note that greater competition on the market due to the new structure of production units would make supply more fluid and responsive to demand incentives. Nevertheless, reasoning at the macroeconomic level, he neglects bottlenecks that can occur on labour and materials markets, i.e., the circumstances in which the probability of rapid adjustment is low enough to avoid a sustainable disequilibrium process. In this sense, Bernácer was an economist before 1950, and his synthesis between the real and the monetary in this regard seems less elaborate than that of Perroux, for example, whose essential contribution is in, we believe, highlighting the non-isotonic universe, that of mainstream economics.

NER certainly very significantly reduces the current system's instability. Nevertheless, it is unlikely to remove all the causes of instability. Bernácer is not fooled and admits that absolute price stability is eventually inconceivable and that stability must be relative, seemingly, characterized by the $\frac{\text{wages}}{\text{prices}}$ ratio.

Nevertheless, we must also insist on the need for a stability hypothesis not as a result but rather as a condition for the proper functioning of NER. Indeed, while certain stability in nominal prices is not met, it is feared that strong tensions occur for certain goods. These could rightly or wrongly be considered as subject to revaluation in the future, given the likely market trends. Then, they might produce a new generation of unearned income-yielding assets, with unearned income consisting exclusively of nominal gains. Some outflow of money would risk hastening the instability process.

Perhaps we might consider the indexation of loans as a solution to guarantee the purchasing power of money. Nevertheless, this process would not be without risks, and according to dialectical principles of repeatedly mentioned relations [system↔behaviour], it is feared that institutionalized indexation itself becomes a cause of instability.

There is evidence that even if it is not perfectly stable, NER would be more stable than the current system.

Conclusions on NER: Neglect of Political Efficacy Conditions

In theory, NER has few flaws, even in terms of political psychology. However, flaws appear in the historical conditions of the implementation of reform.

Theoretical Realism of NER Implementation

Bernácer mentions a few guarantees in the approach he suggests to apply the reform:

(a) Safeguarding acquired situations in regard to bare ownership. This aims to appease opposition between any refractory owners to empirically address the legitimate concern about depriving "legitimate" owners and savers.
(b) Maintaining company profit as a condition for a dynamic system. Bernácer responds to a need for a stimulus of productive activity and, subconsciously, he meets the aspirations of a certain class of individuals inhabited by entrepreneurship. This is a real challenge for the future, quite in line with the innovative spirit emphasized by Schumpeter that corresponds to a certain conception of the player in the production unit strategy.
(c) People's self-management or profound aspiration to the human dimension of their environment.

The human being is capable of accepting responsibilities or even risks to take initiative, to work as a team, and to participate in decisions that affect him. We all have memories in which nature instils these gifts in us. Some individuals are atrophied, while others are hypertrophied. Based on this potential that is more or less consciously experienced, it is easy to admit that individuals are more or less consciously willing to participate, to be stimulated, and to excel in creative activities, particularly the vital one: their jobs. There is, it seems, no happier individual and no more talented storyteller than the one who speaks of a business or profession that he/she likes. Bernácer, once again, excites this kind of anti-*homo economicus* that the human is: advocating self-management, he undertakes visionary work.

Flaws in the Implementation Programme for the Reform

(a) The lack of international environment consideration

Bernácer is in no way bothered to establish the international requisites that can enable the reform. Despite highlighting the international spread of the cycle, he did not imagine that the international environment could thwart NER's implementation or viability. It is all the more unfortunate that Bernácer's liberal doctrine does not allow him to use the principle of capital outflow regulation to isolate a potentially hostile or simply shifted international environment.

(b) Absence of genuine political strategy

Bernácer has no taste for politics and, in any case, the structure of his country did not instil it in him. Nevertheless, he realizes that NER is a revolutionary action plan that it is in itself a violent attack against thousand-year-old institutions—de facto or *de jure*—and that consensus will therefore not be achieved spontaneously.

We reproach him for totally neglecting three aspects:

– An analysis of the behaviour of living forces in a country, which should support the idea of NER.
– The difficulty of making a large part of the population, who have producer and unearned income perceiver functions and abandon a portion of their income (unearned income), although they must find it in the form of additional compensation.
– The difficulty of having political forces that truly accept the fight for decentralization. This implies that this force is favourable to other social objectives. Indeed, "Jacobinism" (as a hard centralization regime in France) is often the result of many politicians who, often in good faith, are obsessed with power and policy options to influence the community's destiny. In a letter dated November 9, 1953, Montgomery D. Anderson (op. cit. Above section *Testimonials*), of the University of Florida, wrote to Bernácer about his article written in French "The Monetary System and Collective Benefit" (in Économie appliquée): "I find that the remedies you offer for fluctuations are very original, though I am inclined to wonder if they are not too drastic to find any audience, with the parliaments of most countries still living under the regime of free enterprise, even if it is somewhat modified".

These reproaches correspond to Bernácer's personality: one of his friends qualified him as a seraphic man.

We do not believe that no current party would endorse the NER programme. However, we are convinced that NER could, on one hand, provide the basis for a real plan of progressive reforms, and on the other hand, to inspire, among a large majority of individuals, fertile reflection that could lead to consensus that would produce nonviolent political action. Even so, who would undertake the required political education campaign?

6.5 Liberalism

Bernácer's penultimate book title, *Free Economy, Without Crisis and Without Unemployment*, includes the economist's two main concerns—to prevent crisis and unemployment—and then the means he recommends to achieve it: economic freedom. Note that in all his writings, from his first book in 1916 until his final articles, and therefore in spite of significant events that occurred in the meantime, he has a constant concern to rehabilitate freedom in the economy, especially for a better future. This freedom he argues for economic activity does not have the same characteristics as the arguments of classicals or neo-liberals: he vigorously defends himself against them.

Freedom, a Condition for Individual and Collective Morality

The relevance of freedom requires to be explained through the economic history and the role of Government.

Freedom Vicissitudes in Economic History

Freedom has gradually disappeared in economics due to historical events and some failures that are presented below.

Economics Were Originally Free

In Rousseau's view, economic activity was a spontaneous phenomenon, free from any intervention. This perspective was maintained until an organized political power emerged. Bernácer fails to emphasize that this freedom was at least relative, as he notes that primitive humans already fought for food. Maybe he made an allusion to Eden?

People established social structures, which led to altering the freedom that was in the nature of things. These structures culminate in the heyday of old monarchy, when freedom is decreased to its simplest expression.

In a backlash against the ancient established order, and in the name of outrageous egalitarianism and liberalism, revolution destroyed nearly all the ancient structures. Thus, in late-eighteenth-century France, common lands, corporations, and any impediment to economic freedom were abolished all at once. Social structures of labour disappeared without being replaced, and thus a certain type of capitalism took hold and flourished in the Western world.

Failure of Capitalism

We can certainly say that freedom was then the rule. Nevertheless, this pseudo-freedom ignored the basic laws of the natural order and led to abuses in the social order and to crisis in the economic order. The Government was prompted, by pressure from certain groups, to initiate the proclaimed freedom. Sometimes, this freedom aimed to protect workers by giving them a way to fight within the law, strikes, and trade unionism, which fought monopolistic policies in the employment field. Sometimes, it also aimed to protect employers who then coalesced and called for a return to trade protectionism against foreign industries. This attitude was shared by workers' unions, which prohibited or fixed quotas on foreign worker immigration, even when these same unions called themselves the international labour movement. It is remarkable that despite professions that were at least partly liberal, this state of affairs still exists.

Paths Opened by Capitalism Failure

According to Bernácer, capitalism has since degenerated (in an etymological sense) in three directions. The first, which is totalitarian and consistent, was inspired by Marx's ideas. This revolution transferred to the

Government the means of production ownership and to replace the market with a planification mechanism of production and needs. Despite other economic conditions, it seems that Bernácer more strongly regrets the disappearance of means of production from the market rather than the ownership transfer to the Government. Bernácer says that no human intelligence can properly plan a complex economic activity and that the necessary corrections are therefore extremely expensive, as they are a posteriori. In this regard, an efficient economic system composed of cybernetics is too inert, as adjustments are delayed.

The second path of capitalism's evolution is Keynesian, including Governmental interventionism; it was pragmatic and therefore inconsistent. It was, according to Bernácer, more a political doctrine than an economic theory. No basic element of the system is distorted except all mechanisms, according to the interventions prompted by any observed disequilibria that we claim to fight. Without thinking that everything would be better without Government intervention, we cannot help but evoke the current contradictions of agricultural policy or of practices of certain subsidies. In this system, we hypocritically reaffirm a principle (freedom), a mechanism (the market), and an institution (private ownership of means of production), and yet we violate them all, gradually but surely and inevitably, by distorting the mechanism and hurting people. There was also a temporary third way, that of national socialism or fascism, which came about as an intervention around the same time as an analysis of the failure of capitalism and a refusal of Marxist totalitarianism. Bernácer did not insist on sanctioning this doctrine, at least in its most violent manifestations—German and Italian experiences—history dealt with it (but at what cost?). As for capitalism without Government intervention, Bernácer saw it disappear during the Great Depression of the 1930s.

Thus, economic history is a result of ebbs and flows, with liberal waves followed by interventionist waves. The latter coincided with exceptional periods, often of war or of preparation for war. The author nevertheless condemns the intellectual attitude taking the opposite view of a dysfunctional system, believing that the opposite system will work better. It is an antiscientific attitude that compromises in advance any possibility of theoretical and practical progress and results in an amplification of historical cycles because instead of correcting, we upset, and readjustment, if it occurs, is further delayed.

In his inaugural speech at the Academy of Economic and Financial Sciences, Bernácer advocates for the development of a liberal economy, which requires the mobilization of energies to build a true economic science, that is, a set of laws from the observation of economic activity. Quoting the example of François Perroux, who addresses Marxist criticisms of capitalism by highlighting the internal contradictions of the Marxist economy, Bernácer regrets that by criticizing the other systems, we forget our own. Especially when our system of economic organization fails, history shows that we strive to adopt from opposing systems techniques that are incompatible with our system.

We see that Bernácer does not share, at all, theorists' optimism on systems convergence, which is achieved through reciprocal borrowing from initially contradictory systems that are logically opposite. The author therefore does not have the same point of view as Schumpeter in *Capitalism, Socialism, Democracy*. Nothing, in fact, gives evidence that the natural course of history will make the systems sufficiently more similar and lead to rational and effective new systems.

Bernácer condemns both Marxism and Government intervention policy and abandons capitalism to its fate. His key idea is that of a certain ineffable liberalism; he does not always have defined outlines. In this regard, we can criticize his attitude, which is convenient and sometimes vague.

Refutation of the Legitimacy of Government Intervention

The idea of freedom in Bernácer's mind is first based on a negative argument, the historical conclusion, in which Government intervention proves pernicious. His hypothesis of freedom in the natural order of the economy will produce an authentic liberal economic system; he justifies its superiority and explains how it works.

History is marked by attacks by a dominant power against people's natural freedom. In economic orders, attacks on freedom have taken many different forms, from simple dispositions and corporate regulations to the Soviet imperative plan. History is, in this regard, a series of more or less unfortunate interventions that are both inconsistent and ineffective. From this failure, Bernácer calls for a genuinely liberal economic system, deliberately going against the tide of recent contemporary history in which, on the contrary, opportunities and forms of Government intervention increased since the Second World War. Bernácer's argument is simple: because intervention was sometimes helpless and sometimes pernicious, we should come back to basics, trying to find the laws that govern the world of economics in an unbiased fashion.

Intervention Is Exceptional by Nature

In the past, there has been a coincidence between the times of central Government intervention and periods of crisis, especially in times of war or preparation for war. In other words, the historical role of Government was to intervene in exceptional circumstances. Supposing that we admit the principle of these limited and episodic interventions, is it logical to postulate the need that intervention has, instead of a discrete and one-off characteristic, a continuous and widespread nature? In this respect, Bernácer's opinion—in which interventionism, that is, Government intervention, adopted as a *modus vivendi* with the economic world—is absolutely incoherent compared to the Marxist totalitarian system that he refutes or the liberal economy that he advocates. In his inaugural speech at the Academy of Economics and Finance entitled "*Freedom Against Interventionism*", he states (Bernácer 1959, p. 5), "War is par excellence a period of interventionism, because we do not care of the basic criteria of economic activity, namely, lower cost and maximum profit. On the contrary, everything is mobilized to achieve victory at any price".

Socio-Political Obstacles to the Effectiveness of Government Intervention

We do not want to imply that Bernácer totally ruled out a priori the possibility of beneficial Government intervention. In his first book, *Sociedad y felicidad* (Society and Happiness, p. 290), he theoretically foresaw the possibility for the Government to intervene in crisis situations to ensure full employment. Twenty years before Keynes, he sensed the potential role of the Government in this regard: "Precisely, the effect of our economic system is to create abundant reserve forces that would like nothing more than to be used to produce, since it provides them the means, one of these means being that Government collects amounts that would otherwise form the circulating money and launches them on the market as demand for goods and services, thus employing labour that otherwise would remain idle, as everyone knows. It is the way to overcome serious times of crisis. Therefore, there is no economic conflict in expenditure growth (of the Government); the conflict arises from the fact that classes that can form savings and hold it are not in favour of giving their consumption residual in tax form to the Government. Middle and humble classes unable to save are against it because, for them, to pay this additional tax would result in the destruction of public prosperity… Even so, the ruin of the classes of producers is national ruin; production, consumption, and incomes fall; plutocrat avarice kills the goose that lays the golden eggs… Governments of the plutocracy did not find another way to resolve the conflict, namely, the conflict that arises from the failure of public resources facing the need to increase public expenditures, to the taste of the dominant influences, than obtaining the necessary monetary resources from wealthy classes who hold them in the form of depreciable loans and not as a tax."

We better understand how, after noting the possibility of Government intervention to promote social justice and in contrast—given the history of Spain as of other countries—that the Government is dominated by classes who care only about their interests—the bourgeoisie in the capitalist system and political bureaucracy in so-called popular democracies—Bernácer rejects Government intervention as an aggravating cause of economic disequilibrium and social unease. This seems to be the explanation for his economic freedom hypothesis, as in all later works, he frequently speaks of freedom but never explains its precise content and no longer evokes the reasons that motivate his refusal of Government intervention.

Proposal of Freedom in the Natural Economic Order

This section defines what Bernácer means by liberalism that is not capitalism. Freedom seems to be a scientific postulate in Bernácer's mindset and pertains to natural economic order.

Liberalism Is Not Capitalism

Noting capitalism's failure, Bernácer (1922) separates liberalism from capitalism by elementary precaution, showing that the former does not necessarily imply the latter, and that capitalism was only inspired by the liberal doctrine. Additionally, liberalism, as understood by Bernácer, certainly never existed historically, as capitalism quickly rejected the liberal path, and its failure was due precisely to restrictive freedom, managerial, and trade-union practices (trade protectionism and immigration), with dominance effects on the market being the most exemplary events.

Bernácer wrote to François Perroux (letter, August 7, 1950), "… Even so, capitalism and liberalism are not synonyms or inseparable things as undoubtedly believe those who, to escape the evils of capitalism, offer solutions that include, even without their awareness, freedom repression. If capitalism failed, it is not because it applied freedom but because it wanted to apply it in conditions that basically deny freedom". This idea is shared by the French economist, as he talked of "capitalism operating wrong" (Perroux 1948).

Bernácer, while denying planning or interventionism as a solution, does not seek to "recover" capitalism or to rehabilitate it. On the contrary, he distanced himself from it beginning in 1916, seeking to rehabilitate the liberal economy, which was compromised by capitalism deviations and historical failure. There are also other reasons why liberalism should be distinguished from capitalism. The second is a materialist system, like Marxism, while the first is humanist or spiritual.

Freedom as a Scientific Postulate

According to Bernácer, freedom is a genuinely scientific postulate. He does not seek to demonstrate the superiority or necessity of economic freedom, as a postulate is not to be demonstrated. Euclidean geometry gives the example of logical construction that is coherent, useful, and sustainable based on a postulate or assumption.

However, freedom is an important landmark, as systems define themselves in relation to freedom. There is a kind of decreasing gradation from liberalism to communism through capitalism and interventionism. We would undoubtedly qualify this ordinal ranking by relativizing it to the different social groups; in each of these schemes, the freedom scale is different according to categories of individuals.

Finally, if we intend to contribute to economics science, we must still admit, as a logical starting point, that we can discover the laws that govern the world of economics, so there are phenomena that recur as a result of the same cause. Without this assumption, it is futile to speak of science; we would attain at most a partial and imperfect knowledge of a constantly changing reality. This context motivates Bernácer's idea of the existence of natural laws in the economic universe, without which the economy would be viable only through directed, necessarily arbitrary and permanent intervention.

Natural Order in the Economic Universe

Bernácer has a metaphysical intuition towards economic freedom. The universe is governed by pre-existing laws that the scientist seeks to discover, not invent (referring to intervention due to human will). This notion applies, for example, to the biological and physical sciences. Why does the same argument fail to apply to the economics field, and why do we believe that the scientist should strive to discover and formulate these natural laws and not attempt to achieve the natural order, that is, that freedom is achieved through interventions conceived by the scientist and effectively upsetting this natural order?

Because freedom is a divine essence, it would be the natural order of the universe. Bernácer sees in this freedom an extension of the Catholic Church doctrine. He writes (Bernácer's letter, January 17, 1955) in this sense to Villey, "I want to express my agreement with the general sense of your work, i.e., the compatibility between Catholicism and economic freedom. Even more, I believe that economic liberalism, the basis of political liberalism, is in the best tradition of the Church".

Finally, it seems that freedom is idealized by Bernácer: it is a kind of lost paradise that everyone should strive to rediscover.

6.6 Bernácer's Scientific Method

Bernácer's contribution in terms of the scientific method applied to the economy is not entirely original but historically important. It is characterized by methodological options to achieve a convergence of methods and by human weaknesses that we qualify as intra-personal conflicts that are poorly overcome. The analysis of these intra-personal conflicts, at the end of the book, does not symbolize our overall opinion on Bernacér's method, that is a deeply positive opinion. It merely confirms the incomplete condition of every human work, the assessment of which must reflect primarily the overruns it raises more than the perfection of the previously completed studies.

Bernácer's Methodological Options

Bernácer based his work on critical spirit, using empirical positism and scientific analogy.

Autonomy Regarding Conventional Wisdom or Triumph of the Critical Spirit

Bernácer, the economist, belongs to no school, had no teacher, and formed his thoughts by tackling his directly observed reality with the theories he found in books. Having never taken a political economics class, he spent his life writing and lecturing in the field of theoretical economics. Schools and theories that bloomed at the time of his birth and his youth had little control over his critical thinking. Thus, for example, he succeeded in keeping away the negative results of marginalism in our discipline. Recall the famous survey conducted by Hall and Hitch (1939), in which business leaders did not recognize anything equivalent to the concepts of cost and marginal income: they fixed their prices on the basis of a *full cost principle*. Also note the investigation in the United States, quoted by Marchal, as a result of which it became clear that labour demand did not depend on the marginal productivity of labour but on the extent of the expected market for products.

As a physicist and occasional mathematician, Bernácer remains indifferent to both the mathematical school of Walras and Pareto and the excesses of the Harvard "hyperstatistician" school. He mocks Böhm-Bawerk's theory on agio and remained fiercely opposed to the notion of time preference throughout his life. As a result of his business studies, he is very aware of accounting policy and was among the first to use it in his macroeconomic theoretical analysis.

All these factors explain the originality of Bernácer's economic thought system. Before becoming a famous economist himself, he freely and coldly judged, exogenously, the inconsistencies or shortcomings of the so-called—and sometimes disparagingly called—traditional political economy.

Empirical Positivism in the Approach to Economic Fact

*Bernácer's Anti-*homo Economicus *or Deductive Rationality Limitations*

It is currently common to denounce Robinsonades, who often act as precursors to the classicals and neo-classicals. However, some contemporary authors, especially when they initially isolate money from their analyses at a given time, fall under this kind of premise. Bernácer begins from a small number of basic rational economic principles but observes the whole economic subject immediately, in all its imperfection. Furthermore, Bernácer is particularly interested in the causes of irrational factors, such as disequilibria, crises, and cumulative movements. Bernácer is not a theorist of equilibrium, a nostalgic and passive observer of agents that he would wish to be more rational, nor a cold logician that highlights the inconsistencies of economic organization, with regard to an ultra-rational ideal model.

Thus, regarding the distribution without money that Bernácer considers, just for a moment, as a theoretical solution to the problem of hoarding, he says (1956, p. 15), "If this utopia is to be realized one day, we will make huge progress in morality. I will not say it will not be possible, one day, but that day is far away". Bernácer rejects considering economic solutions that do not take into account humans as they are, in his given historical state; he does not try to solve human problems by postulating an internal revolution of the latter. He is respectful of his free will and of the diversity among people, which explains his inclination for action on factors and structures.

The deductive method is not absent from Bernacér's analysis, even though it is absent from any properly theoretical work; it is simply a moment or a vector of analysis.

Refusal of Psychological Analysis and Consideration of Tangible Demonstrations of Psychology

Bernácer is keen to purify his economic analysis by avoiding the involvement of para-economic factors he senses or announces but considers uninvolved in the field of analysis. From this perspective, it seems that Bernácer belongs to the nineteenth century rather than to the twentieth century. In the nineteenth century, in fact, political economy was only a branch of philosophy; many economists were philosophers until that time. Gradually, they tried to break away from the mother-discipline and were able, thanks to the specialization advocated by Descartes (1668), to make effective progress towards economic analysis. Additionally, we note that Pareto's last work is itself a sociology book. In reality, Bernácer is really an author of the twentieth century, and his first and last theoretical books give great credence to sociological and historical analysis. Finally, remember that a fierce debate currently divides economists since one current of economists favour enrichment of this discipline with the contribution of other sciences, even psychosociological ones.

Indeed, Bernácer's refusal of psychological analysis translates into a distrust of abuse and the diversions it can cause, rather than denying its importance. This deficiency, if it exists, does so only on the surface, as we will see later. This attitude comes more as a reaction against marginalists, including the Vienna psychological school he knows well through Böhm-Bawerk and against the shortcomings or stalemates to which some Keynesian analyses are led. It is remarkable that Keynes founded his theory of interest on a psychological behaviour—liquidity preference—while Bernácer bases his theory on a more concrete structure, the financial market, although it is clear that it involves a psychological behaviour that Bernácer condemns.

Bernácer judges psychological variables to be elusive and, it seems, especially conducive to individual analysis; the author prefers variables that are more objective and more tangible and that belong to macroeconomic analysis, where individual psychology can contradict the conclusions of the overall analysis. If this is the reason that inspires Bernácer, we must object that progress in group psychology leads to inserting psychology in economic analysis.

Need for Structural Analysis or Objectivation for Economic Analysis

As a corollary about psychology, Bernácer feels the need to intervene in the economic analysis of structural variables and emphasizes those that are not self-mental structures. Thus, the actual price reveals—among other things—a complex of buyers' and sellers' psychological behaviours. Bernácer should have known that price movements conceal changes in behaviour, but the analysis of the past does not fall with his domain of analysis; we find multiple examples with the interest rate, the profit rate, etc. Regarding the price level, the comparison between Keynes's and Bernacér's analyses—which are quite similar at their core—is eloquent. According to Keynes, a price level change was due to the change in liquidity preference—but why does this latter change occur? Bernácer's explanation is more basic and provides an answer. Behind liquidity preference—a human behaviour—we find a particular structure—the financial market—where certain goods are organized and explain monetary behaviour. Bernacér's analysis is structural and, in this respect, it is not surprising that the author had personal contacts and intellectual affinities with Johan Ackermann (1957). We will mention two types of structures analysed by Bernácer.

Role of Institutions in Economic System Operations

It is difficult to classify Bernácer among institutionalists, especially because this American school, which stresses the need for economic relativity over institutional, legal, geographical, historical, and mental structures, commits us to giving up the discovery of great laws that govern the economic world. Nevertheless, Bernácer proclaims that there are such laws, without which the economy would not be a science. Nevertheless, in the descriptive order of his economic analysis, Bernácer attaches importance to concrete institutions as an explanation for economic system malfunctions. Thus, for example, the history of human struggles, crystallized in its current legal system, explains the existence of monopolies, unearned income, and interest.

Scientific Analogy

Economics, a young science, naturally developed from structures invented elsewhere and already available, which must be, given the diachronic evolution of science, physics, and mathematics. Economists also borrow from biology; nevertheless, according to Bernácer, biological borrowing has a casual characteristic and is at the metaphorical level. Therefore, he sometimes speaks of morphology and metabolism, for instance, about crises.

Perroux (1943, p. 27) is more reluctant than Piatier to use analogies: "analogy, he says, this human science danger… economist has too much succumbed to it". Marchal also had difficulty following André Piatier to full confidence in the mathematical method advocated by Harvard statisticians. In fact, the methodological opposition between these two types of economists is more apparent than real; in any case, nuances must be established. Piatier is aware of the limitations of Perroux's analogy, and Perroux is careful not to deny every analogy. While one is rather optimistic about its use, believing that analogy corresponds to a stage in the historical development of economics, the other is sceptical, noting the aberrations that guide economists when they try to formalize their theories.

Bernácer contributes to both of these trends and, of course, his works give the impression of the author's heartbreak between the concern for scientific rigor as embodied in exact sciences, which drives him to use analogical reasoning, and the very strong desire to contribute to building an autonomous economic science with its own laws free from all analogy, given the specificity of its object.

De Broglie (1951, p. 46) makes a very clear distinction between mathematical physics, which is a "thorough and critical examination of Physics theories by a mind trained in mathematical speculations to improve and make demonstrations more rigorous" and theoretical physics, which is a "construction of theories able to account for experimental facts and to guide the work of the laboratory people… it …is not ordinarily effective mathematicians' work; it requires a great knowledge of experimental facts and, above all, a kind of physical intuition that not all mathematicians have." This statement should reassure non-mathematician economists because it is "a commonly committed mistake… to imagine that the only truly scientific method applicable to this social science as political economy is the mathematical method" (Marchal 1952, p. 106). An economist mathematician, such as "Cournot was not mistaken about it, and refused to confuse mathematical demonstration and scientific demonstration".

Bernácer shares this opinion: the body of his economic theory forms a coherent whole, consisting of comments and proposals of scientific laws, without symbolic mathematical intervention. In his first book, *Society and Happiness* (1916), there are no equations; in his second book, *The Interest of Capital* (1925), the few equations he uses are found in the Appendix, and in his most recent "theoretical" book, *A Free Economy Without Crisis and Without Unemployment* (1955), he proceeds in the same manner. Only his third book, *Functional Theory of Money* (1945) concurrently uses the literary method and mathematical statements in support of his theory.

It must be said, in this regard, that the economics is favourable to mathematics and that Bernácer wanted to deliberately exploit mathematical tools, controlling them, of course, by assigning them a supporting role in the demonstration process. Thus, Rueff said that Bernácer was among the first to use an econometric approach. This assertion seems defensible, giving a broad sense to Bernacér's idea of econometrics, a science of the measurement of economic phenomena. Nevertheless, we do not find in his econometric essays any opposition to real statistics for the sake of mathematical analysis, which seems to characterize recent developments in econometrics.

Bernácer, a Physicist Doomed to Economics

We detect in Bernácer's economic research his physicist training through the rigor of his language and his observation of facts and through the logical analytic treatment to which he subjects his observation. The close combination of deduction and induction in all his research is certainly due to his physics training.

Physicist's Imagery

We found numerous images borrowed from physics simply served educational purposes, namely, a means to communicate the idea: these images are not the idea but only the expression of the idea. Most of the images were provided by electricity, mechanics, and hydrodynamics.

We have experimented with images from physics by introducing valves i_1 and i_2 in the hydraulic ram of crisis and by repeated mentions of entropy. Similarly, Viner spoke of the horror of vacuum among physicists alongside the horror of idle money among economists.

Mechanistic Aspect of His Economic Approach

For some authors, the mechanistic approach to economics would represent a classical resurgence, but we can interpret it differently. Durkheim's sociology, which has long dominated social sciences, including political economics, might be behind this analytical design for considering social realities from outside, as if they were inert.

According to Llau (1961, p. 221), like Bernácer, Allais has a mechanistic view of economic phenomena and advocates applying the method of solid or fluid mechanics, even saying that "economic science, we emphasize, is directly comparable to physics" (Allais 1947a, b, p. 468). Bernácer does not take as extreme a position. While his first book, *Society and Happiness*, is subtitled *Social Mechanics Essay*, we should not interpret this at face value. This subtitle is explained more by Durkheim's sociological conception than the desire to transpose physics methods. In particular, he justifies scrutiny in the examination of social mechanisms, i.e., generally, the analysis of group morphology and metabolic behaviour.

Nevertheless, it is true that the omnipresence of the time factor as a separate variable in his economic theory may be explained by the fact that he constantly keeps in mind the concept of mechanics (Fvt), which leads him to conduct economic analysis in terms of dynamics and circuits; the fact that we are now very familiar with these two concepts does not minimize the historical and current importance of Bernácer's contribution in this regard.

Mathematical Tool: Aptitude and Reluctance

Bernácer's mathematical ability must be assessed in three aspects. The author is a physicist, but physics was long the privileged field in which mathematical tools were utilized, to use the image of Piatier (1961). Thus, more than the vast majority of economists for the years 1920–1940, Bernácer used mathematics as a teaching support; his essay on the functional theory of money in 1945 can even be qualified as econometric theory because it falls under the category of technical modelling. Finally, Bernácer participated in founding the Spanish Society of Applied Mathematics alongside two great Spanish mathematicians and published a methodology article in one of the first issues of *Arquímedes*, the society's journal.

Bernácer's Use of the Mathematical Method Combined with Accounting

Bernácer (1955, p. 53) feels the need for mathematics in order to quantify phenomena. Rising vehemently against the "hollow expressions that clutter economy treaties", he adds, "What interests economists is that the mathematical expression provides us discriminating criteria of equilibrium and disequilibrium, and allows even by its magnitude, measure the degree of disequilibrium". Hansen argues in *A Guide to Keynes* (1953), "Economic analysis cannot move forward with truisms such as effective purchases (demand) are always equal to effective sales (supply)".

Mathematical tools are, according to Bernácer, auxiliaries of another tool that comes earlier in the analytical process: national accounting. Aggregates are characterized between them by the existence of accounting order relations, that is, the great discovery of macroeconomics. These aggregates and these relations are the preferred factors mathematical processes in macroeconomic analysis.

In terms of methods, it is futile to try to separate approaches through accounting, mathematics, and statistics, as they are strictly interdependent in overall analysis, as Bernácer perfectly noted. The last applied quantity theory, accounting, made a significant contribution to economics. Even so, Bernácer had already advocated this concept in his first book, 30 years before the first works on national accounting and nearly 40 years before the publication of the first French economy tables. Then, he used the same method to perfect it in all his subsequent theoretical writings, although Spain did not yet use overall statistics. It would be pointless to examine whether Bernácer was interested in macroeconomics because he used an accounting approach or whether accounting inspired him to pursue macroeconomics. Nevertheless, in retrospect, we fully conceive that his two innovations were concomitant.

Limits of the Mathematics Field

Bernácer was concerned about the fact that certain basic economic phenomena are not measurable. However, he assigns a strictly limited field to the mathematical method, that of acts capable of measurement. Therefore, he interprets the Swedish attitude as follows: "on supply and demand curves, the intersection point would correspond to the *ex-post* concept, while other points of the curves would correspond to the *ex-ante* concept. All these points are imaginary (*Ibid.* p. 55)...". Bernácer means that the only point that can be traced—because it is the only one to represent an effective measure—is the equilibrium point, while the other points are plotted from a projection starting from the simple hypothesis: the supply function is generally increasing over the price, and the demand curve is decreasing. Bernácer concludes that we can legitimately draw only the points corresponding to measurements on physical quantities and on real observed prices on the market. His positivism abounds: "it is certain that economics is not an objective science in the sense of physics; but it is neither metaphysics… although its phenomena are not realized as a physical body, they must nevertheless be facts, they must have a real objective existence outside of the subjects themselves that have generated them".

Reluctance to the Mathematical Method

Bernácer is afraid, we believe rightly, of abuses to which the use of mathematics may lead. His reluctance lies in two propositions:

- Any element of economic analysis that can be expressed as mathematics can be simply expressed in everyday language, and
- Not all elements of economic analysis are capable of mathematical expression.

This position may seem debatable, especially since mathematics is used as an instrument of calculation, particularly for predictive purposes.

Nonetheless, let us note that Bernácer's attitude—which seems to be shared by his two contemporaries, Robertson and Keynes—may correspond to a moment of economic science development in which the reaction against the mathematical school of the nineteenth century seems legitimized by marginalism's bad habits. Conversely, especially after 1950, quantity methods (mathematics, statistics, and accounting) gained a respectable place in economics through more precise definitions of their application areas and the development of statistical methods and overall or specific economic action.

Finally, we note that the search for interdependence relations, as opposed to causal relations and effect relations, advocated by Cournot (1838), did not really advance the search for order relations. Indeed, it is quite certain that talking about interdependence became almost commonplace, essentially arguing that everything is in everything. What

Cournot and, after him, neoclassical and too many contemporaries did not see is that introducing time into relations splits interdependence into two different consecutive times when phenomenon A is the cause of phenomenon B and the latter in turn causes a new manifestation of A. Thus, interdependence does not exclude the cause and effect; it implies both. From this point of view, Bernácer's temporal dynamics analysis represents a significant contribution to our economics because it explains *both historical irreversibility and interdependence.*

Triumph of the Synthesis or Combination of Methods

Bernácer's economic theories, including value theory, money theory, and interest theory, are all synthetic. His antimonism is also expressed through his methods.

Theory Dual Supremacy on Analysis Tools and Reality

Bernácer stressed the need for testing and observing without forgetting a strong base of theory.

Marks of Concern for Testing: Mathematical or Statistical Tools or Even of Pure Logic subordination to Theory

Bernácer feels the weakness, difficulty, or even impossibility of true testing in economic sciences. As a physicist, he does not feel a genuine frustration; in contrast, he constantly has this characteristic of economics in mind. He therefore tries to compensate for this deficiency in scientific treatment attributable to the permanent confrontation between factual observation and knowledge through logic that is alternatively mathematical and rarely statistical. He reasons most often at a high level of macroeconomic abstraction, which is less conducive to the application of the latter method.

Nevertheless, he is careful—unfortunately, unlike most mathematicians or statistical economists—to never become overwhelmed by logical conclusions from mathematical and statistical treatments. He never lets himself become diverted from observable reality. The field of economic phenomena must be studied with care, as it uses tools that are often borrowed from other sciences and therefore relatively inadequate. It goes without saying that Bernácer is well aware of the imperfection of the method, the lack of control of the economist over his discipline, and the need to advance science without leaping to a particular method.

Transcendence of Real Experience or Contempt for Applied Economics as a Minor Field

According to Bernácer, economics needs a strong body of perfectly demonstrated theories. Applied economics or at least what it has of descriptive economics includes time in the analysis. This element is required, included in either the data collection or results experimentation, with all the contingencies that it implies. This analysis is only a small element of economic science; it must result from a sublimation of the explanation for a basic, historical, and unique act.

The results of the inductive method must then be corroborated by deductive analysis and critical confrontation with reality. If one of these three elements is missing, there is no real scientific work. Bernácer's position, without agreeing with Walras or Pareto's ambitions to create a single theory that totally and completely explains reality, nevertheless goes against the attitudes of historicists, hyperstatisticians, and institutionalists.

Nevertheless, the concern about normative action, although discreet, is present throughout all of Bernacér's analyses. Therefore, real contempt does not drive Bernácer in his approach. Instead, it is for a "better" reality that Bernácer, transcending the explanation of current reality, will model the future. The title of René Dumont's most recent book, *Utopia or Death*, is especially expressive of this state of mind. Transposed to Bernácer, it means to try to imagine an economic universe in which the interest rate is absent; if the intended result is positive, do everything to change the current economic system. How many inventions or scientific discoveries appeared unachievable at first—was advocating their realization not scientific work? It is the contrary attitude—believing in the inevitability of predetermination—that is ascientific. It is true that, currently, we are inclined to believe that it is possible to discover or invent anything; exact sciences, from this point of view, benefited from significant mind mutation. When will social sciences follow the same evolution?

Basic research in economics, in the proper sense of the term—namely, the one that should lead to the discovery of solutions—is thus advocated by Bernácer.

The "Omnimethodological" Perspective or Opening Economics to All Methods

Bernácer was a precursor to multidisciplinary thinking. His vast cultural background, his curiosity about everything related to humans, together with his scientific training, led him to explore all aspects of economic action, the centre of his research.

Deductive Method, Common Denominator of Every Theory Abstraction

The deductive method has been much criticized and often used as a symbol of pure speculation without any real constraints. As part of the history of dialectic methods, this criticism is certainly justified because the deductive method, whether in exact or physiological sciences, has achieved significant scientific advances. Nevertheless, as in all things, the misuse or exclusiveness of the deductive method was rightly reviled. However, this method is the basis of all scientific knowledge in the way that we discussed the need to transcend basic fact to achieve knowledge of a phenomenon.

This method is inherent to basic research, so it is logical that Bernácer did not widely use this analysis for various economic realities because his aim was to contribute to economic theory. The author is well aware of the dangers or limits of the transition from pure economics to applied economics. What the economics student retains from Léon Walras or

Maurice Allais is neither the former's proposed land nationalization nor the latter's positivity theory of interest based on private ownership of land. Additionally, note that commentators are generally severely critical of pure economics theorists when they venture to formulate concrete proposals.

These censors make dichotomous judgements of their colleagues, with their typology endorsing the cleavage they establish between theorists—who would not have the right to address the concrete—and others who have every opportunity to proceed in applied, monographic, or other economics analyses. André Marchal's wish is nonetheless that every economist should alternately focus on pure economics and applied economics. These same critics would not fail to observe that the portion of Bernácer's works devoted to the concrete is significantly less developed than the theoretical portion. Nevertheless, it should be noted that Bernácer, as Director of the Studies Department at the Bank of Spain, made economic reality his daily lot for nearly thirty years, and this experience did not dissuade him from pursuing basic economic research.

Historical Method

To support his analytical findings, Bernácer frequently uses the results of observations, supported by mathematical methods or accounting approaches, and historical arguments found by adopting the dynamic approach. Most often integrated into various chapters or appendices, historical analysis seems to be the most concrete support for his deductions.

Bernácer exists in what is called the historical tradition of Lucien Febvre and Marc Bloch. The history on which he underpins his theories of unearned income and of monopoly or gold fetishism is the history of institutions and changes in social structures. Unearned income, monopoly, wage, labour, and unemployment are the result of violent historical evolutions that imply the domination of certain social groups over others, the victory of a certain condition, institutionalized by certain rights, for equity.

We argue that Bernácer is the opposite of institutionalists because he examines economic theory to determine what is permanent, common, and universal among economic phenomena. Nevertheless, his conception of history is such that a phenomenon such as interest is present universally in the historical context because land is universally (with very few exceptions) the subject of private ownership (legal structure), following the victory of unequal and oppressive individualism over a social organization, as advocated by Plato or Aristotle (historical evolution), in which interest exists. In a new historical sequence that could create different legal structures, in which a number of reforms advocated by Bernácer would triumph and the existence of interest would decrease to nothing. Nevertheless, without historical analysis, the origin of interest, according to Bernácer, has no basis. Interest's only legitimacy is historical. Similarly, we show that unemployment is only the fruit of a certain historical development enshrined by pernicious institutions (the financial market).

The pure inductive method is not only more satisfactory than the deductive method; the results of Harvard hyperstatisticism confirm it. Nevertheless, through this method of qualitative relations that can then undergo deductive and analytical treatment and then statistical trials, identification is an important element of economic methodology.

Considering the validation of his economic analysis, Bernácer focuses on the weighted critical confrontation of the results obtained through different methods. In this regard, all methods that are likely to provide a part of the answer must be applied, and it should be noted that among these, the accounting method, taken from National Accounts eight decades ago (an important moment for the evolution of our science and economic activity through the means of action it generates), has a special place that Bernácer and others have helped to promote.

Bernácer's Poorly Overcome Intrapersonal Contradictions

Bernácer, as we have argued, appeared to often be torn by inner contradictions, both doctrinally and methodologically.

Bernácer's Strong Criticisms of Concrete Reality and Refusal of Force as a Means to Impose Radical Reforms

Bernácer conducted a very firm and uncompromising analysis of the anomalies of the current economic system from both functional and social justice points of view. He usually uses moderate language, but sometimes it is quite strong, illustrating the strength of his point of view. Therefore, we can expect an unreserved condemnation of the system and drastic solutions. Nevertheless, according to Bernácer, the end does not justify the means. Given the options to either realize his reform by possibly violent means or to not carrying it out in order to preserve social peace, we believe he would likely choose the second option. This position—which is hypothetical, of course—may seem endearing. Nevertheless, is it relevant regarding his analysis of socio-economic fact.

Almost "Shameful" Emergence of Mathematics, Psychology, and Sociology in Bernácer's Thought

Bernácer, as shown previously, holds some contempt for mathematical and psychological modes. He undoubtedly has reasons to reproach both fields from the hedonic school: the mathematical school and the psychological school are based on the same premise and have the same neomarginalist mistakes. Nevertheless, he uses psychology, sometimes implicitly. He sometimes indulges in mathematical modelling and makes room for sociology and institutional history. The fact that sometimes he limits these extra-economic contributions to his book appendices is meaningless. In reality, these different approaches are perfectly combined and integrated—sometimes implicitly but often explicitly—at the heart of his analysis.

Nevertheless, we understand that Bernácer usually recommends a moderate use of mathematics for macroeconomic explanation. Similarly, we observe that macroeconomic explanatory models are not generally taken seriously because of their questionable educational value when they are used as anything other than tools of economic analysis. This approach would be quite different for forecasting—that is, for the quantified observation of economic facts—to create a more precise knowledge of reality and in view of economic praxis.

Additionally, we understand Bernácer's distrust of psychology and of its use by several generations of economists. However, he has less reluctance toward sociology and often mixes it with his economic analysis. For him, this discipline probably seems less conducive to scientific abuse.

Nevertheless, a partial or superficial reading of his publications implies contradictions in Bernácer's research, but, in reality, these are simply expressions of legitimate scientific doubts by a truly scientific man.

Bernácer's thought has influenced his prescriptive work dealing with capitalism. Three components compose his thought: *freedom, ethics*, and *efficiency*. His work has mainly been influenced by his environment such as his family, social, politic, and economic contexts. His methodology helps to enhance his conclusions. The way that he crossed the different methodological options in his work is positive and had impacted his results even if it has its limits.

This last chapter of the second part finalizes the criticism of *capitalism* by Bernácer. He focused on the value and place of money in the economic theory leading to the interest rate as one of the factors of economic disequilibria and crises. Finally, he suggested some improving actions to address the capitalism faults.

References

Ackermann, J. (1957). *Structures et cycles économiques* (Structures and economic cycles), t. 1 and 2. Paris: P.U.F.

Allais, M. (1947a). *À la recherche d'une discipline économique (In search of economic discipline)*, t. 1, « Économie et Intérêt » (Economy and interest). Paris: Imprimerie nationale.

Allais, M. (1947b). « La vie et l'œuvre d'Irving fisher » ("The life and work of Irving fisher"). *Revue d'économie politique*.

Bernácer, G. (1916). *Sociedad y felicidad – Ensayo de Mecánica Social* (Society and Happiness – Essay on Social Mechanics). Madrid: Ed. Beltrán.

Bernácer, G. (1922). La teoría de las disponibilidades como interpretación de las crisis y del problema social (The theory of disposable funds as interpretation of crisis and social issues). *Revista nacional de economía*, (40).

Bernácer, G. (1945). *La teoría funcional del dinero* (The functional theory of money). Madrid: Consejo Superior de Investigaciones Científicas, 2nd edition, 1956.
Bernácer, G. (1955). *Una economía libre sin crisis y sin paro* (Free economy without crisis nor unemployment). Madrid: Aguilar.
Bourcier de Carbon, L. (1972). Faut-ildénationaliser? (Is it necessary to denationalize?). In *Efficacité Sociale du libéralisme* (Social efficacy of liberalism). Paris: Albatros.
Cournot, A. (1838). *Recherche sur les principles mathématiques de la théorie des richesses* (Research on mathematical principles of wealth theory). Paris: Hachette.
De Broglie, L. (1951). *Savants et découvertes* (Scientists and discoveries). Paris.
Descartes, R. (1668). *Discours de la méthode* (Discourse of the method). Paris: Hachette.
Hall, R. L., & Hitch, C. J. (1939). Price theory and business behaviour. *Oxford Economic Papers, 2.*
Hansen, A. H. (1953). *A guide to Keynes*, New York; French translation: *Introduction à la Pensée keynésienne* (Introduction to Keynes' thought). Paris: Dunod, 1967.
Keynes, J. M. (1941). *How to pay for the war*. Londres: Macmillan and Company.
Llau, P. (1961). *La détermination des taux d'intérêts* (Rate of interest determining). Paris: Cujas.
Marchal, A. (1952). *Méthode scientifique et science économique; le conflit traditionnel des méthodes et son renouvellement* (Scientific method and economics; the methods traditional conflict and its renewal). Paris: Génin.
Perroux, F. (1943a). *Science de l'homme et science économique* (Human science and economics). Paris: Librairie de Médicis.
Perroux, F. (1943b, December). L'intégration de la théorie de la monnaie à la théorie de la valeur des biens (Integration of the theory of money to the theory of property value). *Economie contemporaine.*
Perroux, F. (1948). *Le Capitalisme.* Paris: Presses Universitaires de France.
Piatier, A. (1961). *Statistiques et observation économiques* (Statistics and economic observations), V. 1 & 2. Paris: PUF.
Savall, H. (1973, September). Germán Bernácer, économiste espagnol (1883–1965). Une thé oriegénérale de l'emploi, de la renteet de la thésaurisation (General theory of employment, unearned income and hoarding). PhD dissertation at the University of Paris II, 602 p. mimeographed.

Savall, H. (1975). *G. Bernácer: L'hétérodoxie en science économique* (G. Bernácer: The heterodoxy in economics). Paris: Dalloz, Collection Les Grands Économistes.

Savall, H., Péron, M., Zardet, V., & Bonnet, M. (2017). *Socially responsible capitalism and management*. New York: Routledge.

Villey, D. (1946). Doctrines et science économique (Doctrines and economics), in *Mélanges Gonnard, op. cit.*

Villey, D. (1954). L'économie de marché devant la pensée catholique (The market economy faced to Catholic thought). *Revue d'Économie Politique*.

Weiller, J. (1973, March 15). « Sismondi était à la recherche d'une économie politique: Science du bonheur » (Sismondi was in search of political economy: Science of happiness). *Le Monde*.

7

Conclusion: Advocacy for Bernácer's Rehabilitation

7.1 Summary of Bernácer's Contribution

In many ways, we have seen that Bernácer deserves the title of a modern economic founder, alongside a few others. This was, somehow, our historical theory. Nevertheless, we should offer a brief inventory of the shortcomings of his theoretical works and show the topicality of several issues they raise.

Shortcomings

In Terms of Scientific Research: Relative Solitude and Inadequacy of the Debate

Bernácer was a solitary researcher who built his theory by himself between 1905 and 1925 and perfected it until 1942. However, he only had exchanges with world-renowned economists after 1940. His isolation, which was commendable in many respects, also has issues. His works are those of a loner who did not benefit from the contributions that we would expect of a debate on his original, innovative ideas, either in his

H. Savall, *Radical Origins to Economic Crises*,
https://doi.org/10.1007/978-3-319-93366-5_7

country or abroad. Keynes, placed at the centre of the intense mix of facts and ideas that characterized the Anglo-Saxon world in the 1930s, found himself in a somewhat *opposite* situation: his strictly personal contribution is less clear than the string of ideas and syntheses that he realized and published with a remarkably effective timeliness.

Bernácer was not responsible for his isolation from international scholars during the development of his theory, as he began in 1922 to send his writings to the greatest economists of his time. Eighteen years later, Robertson (1940) recalled the indelible mark left on him by Bernácer's article on the theory of disposable funds.

Nevertheless, according to witnesses, Bernácer, director of the Studies Department at the Bank of Spain, published numerous articles on doctrine or popularization in Spain but did not do whatever it took to create a real school in Madrid. From this point of view, Bernácer's solitary work can be seen as a failure.

In-depth discussions with pragmatic Americans likely encouraged him to nuancc his macroeconomic point of view by diversifying levels of analysis. Exchanges with François Perroux on the dominant economy concept, for example, enabled him to more firmly support his theory with a further analysis of monopolies and to conceive a non-isotropic universe. A better understanding of Leontieff's works and national accounting in France provided him with elements of a more specific industry approach to the economy. Without fundamentally questioning his theory, we believe that such studies remarkably enriched Bernàcer's analysis and his dissemination.

Bernàcer's reform, which is based on an almost epidermal rejection of government action and an unreserved apology for the market, would have increased in quality if these two important points had been deepened. We would agree with his conclusions if these two premises were better supported. He always recommended scientific rigor and often applied it to his reasoning, but his approach appears inconsistent regarding these two weak points of his analysis. Bernácer tries his hardest to argue the merits of his dichotomous theory on the economic system. Busy convincing the reader of the highly poisonous nature of the *financial market*, he is naturally inclined to avoid further analysing the conditions for the solid operation of the production market. Therefore, he strives to integrate goods and services supply into his analysis, but this is not the true nature of a comprehensive analysis. This topic is almost completely absent from the inflation process, the analysis of which nevertheless has a very important place in his theory. As for government action, without compromising the general philosophical quality of the system advocated by Bernácer and without forgetting the criticism that should currently inspire us—that of government effectiveness—we should recognize that the author, who was likely intellectually isolated in Spain, did not think to weigh the pros and cons of such an action.

In Recommended Action: Reform "Appears" Less Directly Operational Than Keynes's Policy

We will not reproach the intrinsic quality of Bernácer's New Economic Regime (NER) reform, which seems to be more solid than Keynesian policy. Nevertheless, the obstacles it would face discourage its application. Everyone knows—though we must certainly deplore—that short-term policy wins more often for long-term forecasts and that the duality between the short and long horizons is one of the most poorly overcome conceptual and practical obstacles in the field. In a word, NER may seem utopian due to its attempt to solve basic and complex socio-economic problems globally and in depth.

Keynesian policy had the merit of being applied—or at least of inspiring concrete actions—for six to seven decades. This does not necessarily demonstrate the quality of Keynesian policy, but its application is undoubtedly a success for scientists, whose goal remains, we believe, to discover varying solutions to the problems of their time. Nevertheless, what is the role of Keynesian-inspired policies in the economic development of these seven decades? Did it not, by its shortcomings, cause new problems that it is powerless to solve?

As a result, we disagree with Bernácer that his structural reform proposals should be applied sensitively by considering human lives. Nevertheless, we do not consider this a basic flaw in his theory. Moreover, the future may contain more challenges than our current imagination can forecast. The recent turmoil and chaotic upheavals caused by the acute overall crisis of 2007–2012 created perspectives on political boldness that regulatory bodies and transnational cooperation might consider.

Bernácer's Collapse: The Relative Ignorance of His Work

In the 1940s, the biggest names in Economics entered into contact with Bernácer (1945, 1955). Haberler suggested that Bernácer could write articles or a book to be published in the United States in which his theory would appear more concrete and more operational, and he could compare his proposals to those of Keynes. Perroux (1948) requested his collaboration as an ISEA correspondent. Thus, we believe that Bernácer was guilty of either a lot of pride or detachment by failing to give a real response to these proposals. He repeatedly petitioned for the translation and publication of some of his works abroad, but he refused to make these works accessible through their conception or their writing. However, he could not claim that his views triumphed because he was a solitary Spanish economist. Quoted by Guitton (1974, p. IX), André Piettre notes, "Bernácer missed out on being Anglo-Saxon!" We believe that here the end justifies the means, that the legitimate desire to communicate ideas must have encouraged Bernácer to be concerned with the public and to market his theory, not in terms of the content, of course, but in terms of better dissemination.

Finally, we will not play devil's advocate against Bernácer because he never called his theory general. Frankly, the impression from his works does him credit: his shortcomings are largely offset by his ideas, which currently remain original, such as his dialectical conception of the economy, his theory of unearned income and double hoarding and, finally, the supreme materiality of his theoretical foundations, his refusal of the human cost notion, and even his concept of work and labour.

Topicality of Problems Raised and Solutions Outlined by Bernácer

Recognizing the value of Bernácer's theory is above all recognizing the current nature of the issues it raises, the pathways it opens, and the solutions and propositions it advocates (Savall and Zardet 2018).

Linking with the theory of economic crisis, the mainstream literature on liberal capital markets addresses financial and stock exchange practices and short-term regulations but only rarely addresses economic crisis given that these theories were mainly inspired by Keynesian thought. Here we discuss (Savall and Zardet 2018) a rare example from a contemporary author: Paul Krugman. He says (2014) that an extensive study of economic and financial crisis resurgence worldwide since the second half of the twentieth century has demonstrated that conventional economic remedies were ineffective, even counterproductive.

Krugman analyses the 2008–2009 crisis in the United States and the broader world that originated in the real estate sector. Prices increased so much that real estate purchases became inaccessible for many Americans. After 2006, sales slowed and quickly collapsed in 2008, particularly where prices were very high. A tragedy occurred when homeowners found it difficult to sell their property and loans were not repaid. One important difference between the 2008 crisis and the 1930s crisis is the fact that the shadow banking system was more involved than the conventional banks in 2008. Extremely complex financial instruments used to make subprime loans created legal obstacles that prevented any debt reduction. Krugman estimates that the real estate bubble destroyed €8000 billion of wealth, including €7000 billion due to losses to homebuyers and €1000 billion to investors. These losses caused the collapse of the "shadow banking system" and resulted in a global financial crisis.

The world economy remains a depression economy. There is limited demand for goods and private resources are not sufficient to fully exploit production capacities. This limits the enhancement of prosperity development in developed and developing countries. The question is how can one create sufficient demand? First, central banks must inject additional capital into local banks in the near term to restore banks' lending capacity. Second, central banks must also reduce interest rates significantly to support investment. This may require recapitalization of banks, a temporary nationalization of parts of the financial system, permitting federal officers to temporarily grant loans directly to the non-financial sector, and revitalizing the credit markets by implementing the fiscal stimuli advocated by Keynes.

To conclude, Krugman's analysis of financial crisis argues that the real problem is not insufficient resources because slack resources are available to create value. The real problem lies in the *limitations of current economic theories*. The important structural obstacles to economic prosperity are the *obsolete models* and doctrines of economics that obstruct our understanding.

Contemporary Evidence Supporting Bernácer's Theory

Bernácer defended the economic regime of social capitalism (or liberalism) that criticizes monopolies, redefines the role of the state in the economy, and advocates for an open and regulated international opened economy. The world economic system continues to show evidence of the processes and propositions uncovered by Bernácer's analyses.

Monopolies Restrict Fair Competition

Joseph Stiglitz (2012, 2016) argues that the economic activity of numerous industries (e.g., information technology, health care, and pharmaceuticals) is inconsistent with free enterprise capitalism if one considers this economic activity from the point of view of fair competition. The dominant type of competition in the contemporary world is oligopolistic competition, not the pure and perfect competition described in economic treatises. Economic advisors to US President Barak Obama have noted the high level of concentration of activities and profits in several industries and found that the market share of bank deposits of the ten largest US banks rose from 20% in 1980 to 50% in 2010. These values show that inequalities exist at all levels of the economy and not simply between individuals.

Limiting State Influence

The rise of an extensive public administration is inconsistent with the needs of the social liberalist economy and is in greater evidence in France than in Germany. There were more than 6,171,400 public administrators in France in 2016, some 500,000 more than in 2004. France has 90 state employees per 1000 inhabitants (21.9% of the working population) whereas Germany has only 50 state employees per 1000 inhabitants and the average for other member countries of the OECD is 15.5% (Delsol 2017). The centralist Welfare State (Olivier Babeau 2017) aims at normalizing our behaviour and seeks to change individuals, even unwillingly, to enhance common well-being. The Welfare State requires the dependence of the individuals towards it while the liberal State, as underlined by Tocqueville, aims to accustom people to take control of the state themselves.

Addressing Chronic Under and Unemployment Difficulties

The Spanish Government implemented measures of budgetary discipline to reduce unemployment in 2015. It experienced employment growth, unemployment fell by 8%, and three years later job growth in Spain reached 3.2%. Overall, Spain gained about 500,000 full-time equivalent jobs and unemployment fell from 26% to 18.5% (Morel 2016a, b). Thus, the implementation of budget discipline advocated by Bernácer was an effective way of managing unemployment.

De-emphasing Stock Prices and Reinvesting Profit in the Real Economy for Future Growth

BlackRock manages more than $5000 billion of investment in financial markets and asks client firms to de-emphasize the short-term market price of their firm's stock for the next months and reinvest this profit within the firm to finance future growth and longer term increases in share values. Larry Fink, the President of BlackRock, even favours new measures to reward companies for their long-term vision and efforts to insure a better pension system for their staff (Coffrini 2017): these are practices consistent with social liberalism.

Perverse Speculation

Bernácer has shown the perverse effects of hoarding that limits growth and condemns the economy to stagnation and perpetual poverty. An extreme example is the fraud committed by Bernard Madoff who swindled 20,000 investors out of their investments by promising fantastic yields. He used "double hoarding" mechanism to finance the process. So, recent payments by investors were used to pay prior investors until a 64 billion dollar gap unveiled the swindle (Lauer 2017).

Hoarding: A Defensive Against Future Economic Uncertainty

Robert Shiller (2015) anticipated the Internet Bubble in the early 2000s and the American real estate crisis of 2008. He argues that many people face unprecedented economic uncertainty because of the financial crisis cycle and also because of uncertainty about the side effects that new technologies have for workers.

Low or Null Interest Rates

Economies in the 2010s witnessed the emergence of very low interest rates. Yet in 1998, the prospect of interest rates of zero or less was only a theoretical curiosity. So when Mario Draghi began his career as a European Central Banker (ECB) low interest rates were not a concern. By acquiring massive amounts of debt on financial markets and by also lowering their interest rates to zero, Mario Draghi and his counterparts managed to lower the cost of the money to a negative level. These unconventional policies make it possible from now on for certain States

(Germany, Japan) or large companies to borrow on financial markets at negative interest rates. From now, the interest as a source of income for banking services can be replaced by the explicit sale of their services at a proper fixed price.

The average rate of property loan is unless 2%, something unheard of since the 1940s. Between January 2009 and March 2016, the average interest rate on property loans to private individuals declined from 4.75% to 1.97%. Banks do not hesitate to reduce their margins to obtain new customers and hold their sales objectives (*Les Échos*, April 6, 2016). Thus, Bernácer's "utopian" ideas of low or negative interest rates and service charges rather than interest have been shown to be possible and even feasible.

Current Major Issues: Speculation, Stability and Economic and Social Organization

Among non-Marxist contemporary authors, Bernácer most severely condemns the institution of *unearned income*. Recall that unearned income recovers both the *non-labour income* collected periodically and capitalized income in the form of capital gains. This second element is particularly important in this time of growth, of needs development, and, therefore, of demand. This form of unearned income has many problems, leads to social injustice, and is a serious element of economic instability. It is also multifaceted, affecting land, movable property, and even materials. Nevertheless, can the free market alone provide an instant solution to these price fluctuations? Is the market not also a structure that sometimes encourages the development of disequilibria and, currently, to inflation? However, is it desirable to distort market operations by any incentive measure? The debate remains open, and Bernácer deliberately avoids the first question.

Nevertheless, to his credit, Bernácer worries about stability, including monetary stability, while promoting a policy to ensure high levels of employment. He is right, we believe, not to separate the two aspects of the *ultimate goal: harmonized growth* and *high employment levels*. In this,

his theory is clearly superior to that of Keynes. Since the 2007–2008 global crisis, monetary disorder has started to be taken seriously, given the upheavals it causes in production and distribution and in internal and external circuits.

In the area of economic and social organization, the market economy—with self-managed production units, free access to the market, the free implementation of work by the worker in stimulating the production structure and developing individual faculties—responds to the current desires of the majority of the population, which is often clumsy in raising the issue or hesitant regarding how to understand and solve it. Given that these proposals were formulated a century ago, in Bernácer's first book published in 1916, we note the foresight and visionary capacity of the author.

General Philosophy of Recommended Solutions: An Original Form for Action Between Liberalism, Keynesianism, and Marxism

Therefore, are we currently in the third economic age of our civilization?

Without going into detail once again about the solutions proposed by Bernácer, we can characterize his praxis as remaining at an equal distance from what he calls *revolutionism* and *conservatism*, with the following two features:

- Confidence in humanity, that is, confidence in an individual's ability to ultimately improve his fate at whatever level he finds himself in the economic complex at a given moment. No entity can replace humanity's assessment of its needs and of what must be its productive effort.
- Confidence in certain, basic, economic mechanisms under certain reform conditions: the market, competition, and structures that support initiative and overtaking.

Confident in the future, provided that humans show imagination and ingenuity, Bernácer could have endorsed the phrase used by René Dumont (1973) to title his last published book, *Utopia or Death.* Indeed, where does utopia begin? What else must we do to discover solutions?

Will progress in the exact or natural sciences ever stimulate the social sciences? Aware of the difficulties of the latter, Bernácer remains an optimistic teacher.

We wish to give Germán Bernácer his rightful place in the history of economic thought as the founder of modern, heterodox, and innovative economic theory. If Keynes had the merit and the opportunity to be heard in his lifetime, Bernácer should have at least the same posthumous consecration as Wicksell.

References

Babeau, O. (2017). *L'horreur politique : l'État contre la société* (Political horror: State against society). Paris: Manitoba Les Belles Lettres.

Bernácer, G. (1916). *Sociedad y felicidad – Ensayo de Mecánica Social* (Society and happiness – Essay on social mechanics). Madrid: Ed. Beltrán.

Bernácer, G. (1922). La teoría de las disponibilidades como interpretación de las crisis y del problema social (The theory of disposable funds as interpretation of crisis and social issues). *Revista nacional de economía* (40).

Bernácer, G. (1945). *La teoría funcional del dinero* (The functional theory of money) (2nd ed., 1956). Madrid: Consejo Superior de Investigaciones Científicas.

Bernácer, G. (1955). *Una economía libre sin crisis y sin paro* (Free economy without crisis nor unemployment). Madrid: Aguilar.

Coffrini, F. (2017). BlackRock sermonne encore les entreprises américaines (BlackRock still sermonises the American companies). *Le Figaro Économie, 25-1*, 17.

Delsol, J.-P. (2017). Libéralisme économique (Economic liberalism). *Le Figaro, 25-1*, 16.

Dumont, R. (1973). *L'utopie ou la mort* (Utopia or death). Paris: Seuil.

Guitton, H. (1974). Preface to Savall (1975) *G. Bernácer, l'hétérodoxie en science économique* (G. Bernácer. Heterodoxy in economics). Paris: Dalloz.

Krugman, P. (2014). *Pourquoi les crises reviennent toujours?* (Why do crises keep-coming back?). Paris: Seuil.

Lauer, S. (2017). Madoff continue à faire des affaires en prison (Madoff is still conducting business in jail). *Le Monde, 25-1*, 15.

Les Échos (2016, April 6). *Tribune.*

Morel, S. (2016a). L'Espagne accélère les baisses d'impôts (Spain speeds up tax decrease). *Le Monde, 12-7,* 15.

Morel, S. (2016b). En Espagne, moins de chômage (In Spain, less unemployment). *Le Monde, 6-4,* 13.

Perroux, F. (1948). *Le capitalisme* (Capitalism), Collection « Que sais-je » (3rd ed., 1958). Paris: PUF.

Robertson, D. H. (1940, févr). A spanish contribution to the theory of fluctuations. *Economica, 16*(1), 50–65.

Savall, H., & Zardet, V. (2018). Bernácer's topical theory of crisis and unemployment. In R. P. Gephart, C. Chet Miller, & K. S. Helgesson (Eds.), *Risk, crisis and emergency management.* New York: Routledge. (publication in process).

Shiller, R. J. (2015). *Irrational exuberance.* Princeton/Oxford: Princeton University Presse.

Stiglitz, J. E. (2012, September 2). Interview. *Journal du Dimanche,* p. 17.

Annexes

Germán Bernácer's Publications

Economics Books (All Written in Spanish)

The distribution of these books was largely as follows: in Spain for books 3, 4 and 6 and in Latin America for books 3, 4 and 5 (testimony of a UNESCO expert and two South American economists, Rafael Olarra Jiménez and Orestes Popescu; see above Chaps. 1 and 2 *Contemporary economist testimonials*).

1. (1916) *Sociedad y felicidad. Ensayo de Mecánica Social* (Society and Happiness. Social Mechanics Essay), Madrid: Ed. Beltrán (exhausted), 582 pages.
2. (1925) *Interés del capital. El problema de sus orígenes* (Capital interest. Its origin issue), Alicante: Ed. Lucentum (exhausted), 252 pages.
3. (1945) *La doctrina funcional del dinero.* (Functional theory of money), Madrid: Consejo Superior de Investigaciones científicas (exhausted). Second edition in 1955, 365 pages. Our book references refer to the second edition.

H. Savall, *Radical Origins to Economic Crises*,
https://doi.org/10.1007/978-3-319-93366-5

4. (1953) *La doctrina del gran espacio económico*. (The doctrine of the great economic space), Madrid: Aguilar, 192 pages.
5. (1955) *Una economía libre, sin crisis y sin paro*. (Free economy, without crisis and without unemployment), Madrid: Aguilar, 316 pages.
6. (1961) *Estudios sobre la unidad económica de Europa*. (Studies on Europe's economic unity) Collective book, in which BERNÁCER wrote the chapter: "España y las comunidades económicas europeas" (Spain and European Economic Community), Madrid: Espasa-Calpe, 89 pages.

Journal Articles

In Spanish

7. *Revista nacional de economía*. Madrid, Barcelona, from 1919 to 1932: 11 cited articles, including:
   - « La moneda y las cuestiones sociales » ", 1919 (Money and social issues).
   - « La teoría de las disponibilidades como interpretación de las crisis y del problema social, n° 40, nov.–déc. 1922 (Theory of disposable funds as an interpretation of crisis and social issues). Robertson translated the essential passages in the British journal *Economica*, February 1940.
   - « El ciclo económico », n° 66, march–april, 1926 (Economic cycle).
8. *Economía española*. Madrid, from 1933 to 1936: 6 cited articles:
   - « Análisis de la demanda y síntesis del mercado», n° 9-1933 (Analysis of demand and market synthesis).
   - « Etiología de las crisis », 1934 (About crisis origin),
   - « La teoría del mercado financiero », 1935 (Theory of the financial market).

– « Moneda y ciclo económico », 1935 (Money and the economic cycle).

9. *Anales de economía*. Madrid:

   – «La teoría monetaria y la ecuación del mercado» (Monetary theory and the market equation), n° 1, march 1941. This article contains a response to Robertson's objections in his 1940 article in *Economica*.
   – «La expresión básica del valor del dinero», 1942 (Basic expression of money value).
   – «La ecuación monetaria en el mundo mercantilista», 1943 (Monetary equation of mercantilism).
   – « La ecuación monetaria de una economía capitalista», 1944 (Monetary equation of capitalism).
   – «El déficit presupuestario, la inflación y Mr. Kalecki », 1947 (Budget deficit, inflation and Mr. Kalecki).
   – « El profesor Pigou y el concepto de equilibrio económico », 1950 (Professor Pigou and the concept of economic equilibrium).
   – « El sistema financiero y las crisis », 1956 (Financial system and crisis).
   – « De la inflación crónica a la guerra social », 1962 (From chronic inflation to social struggle).

10. *Arquímedes*. Madrid, Journal of Econometrics: 2 articles in 1955.
11. *El eco de la industria*: 1 article in 1929.
12. *Trimestre económico*. México. In 1947 & 1948: 3 cited articles.

In German

13. *Weltwirtschaftliches archiv*. Kiel, from 1941 to 1944: 4 cited articles.
14. *Schmollers Jahrbuch*. Berlin (Directory Schmollers), from 1943 to 1956: 4 cited articles.

15. *Jahrbuch fur sozialwissenschaft*. Gôttingen: 1 article in 1950.
16. Zeilschrift fur die gesamte Staatswissenschaft. Tübingen: 1 article in 1952.
17. *Kyklos*. Berne (Cycle). « Sparen, Kapital und Zins (Eine kritische Betrachtung) », 1954 (Saving, Capital and interest).

In English

18. *Kyklos*. Berne. « Money and Freedom», 1950.
19. *Economica*. Cambridge (see Chap. 2: article of Robertson).

In Italian

20. *Moneta e credito*. Roma, from 1948 to 1953:4 cited articles.
21. *Rivista bancaria*. Milan, from 1955 to 1962: 5 cited articles, especially:

 – « Stabilità monetaria contro pieno impiego: una teoria dell'inflazione secolare » "(Monetary stability against full employment: a theory of secular inflation), March–April 1957.

In French

22. *Économie appliquée* (Applied Economy). Paris:

 – « Le circuit monétaire et l'avantage collectif » (Money circuit and collective advantage), 1952.
 – « Les tendances répressives dans l'économie capitaliste» (Repressive trends in the capitalist economy).

23. *Textes choisis*. Vol. 1, « Problèmes monétaires » (Monetary issues) (Paris):

 – Germán Bernácer: « Une théorie de l'inflation séculaire » (A theory of secular inflation).

Popularized Articles

Bernácer wished to help develop a Spanish public opinion that were aware of economic problems, so he occasionally collaborated with various newspapers and magazines when his theoretical work allowed.

24. *El economista*. Madrid, from 1940 to 1947: 26 articles.
25. *Economía*. Madrid, from 1941 to 1948: 24 articles.
26. *Economía mundial*. Madrid: 3 cited articles.
27. *Información*. Bilbao: 26 cited articles until 1959.

Conferences and Speeches

28. In Spanish. From 1920 to 1959: six conferences, and his inaugural speech at the Academy of Economic and Financial Sciences of Barcelona: "Libertad frente a intervención", April 1959 (Freedom against intervention).
29. In French:

    – « La notion d'intérêt général et le choix de la dimension du flux monétaire global» (The notion of general interest and the choice of overall cash flow size), Paris, ISEA, 1952.

Book Prefaces

A pioneer of modern economics in Spain, Bernácer was asked to write prefaces for many books, including those by Adam Smith and Robertson.

Three Handbooks for Use by Business School Students

Physics and chemistry books published between 1906 and 1936.

Unpublished Manuscripts

Treatise of Physical Methodology, written in approximately 1932, when Bernácer prepared his second physical aggregation contest in Madrid, and a handbook of physics and chemistry for business school students written in approximately 1950.

Bernacerprize.com
Bernácer Wikipedia.com

For Further Reading

Ackley, G. (1961). *Macroeconomic theory.* New York: Macmillan.

Algoud, J.-P. (1971). Les périodes de libéralisation en Union Soviétique (The liberalisation periods in Soviet Union), 1921–1928; 1953–1958, Essai de traduction cybernétique (Cybernetic translation essay). PhD dissertation, Université de Lyon.

Allais, M. (2008). Comment vivre ensemble: Conditions économiques et sociales pour la démocratie (How to live together: Economic and social conditions for democracy). In *XI° Journée François Perroux.* Écully: ISEOR.

Allen, R. D. G. (1969). *Théorie macroéconomique* (Macroeconomic theory). Colin.

Almenar Palau, S. (1983). Bernácer G., Robertson D. H., Keynes J. M. *Una encrucijada de la teoría del desequilibrio económico.* (Crossroads of the theory of economic disequilibrium). Working paper, Universidad de Valencia (Spain).

Almenar Palau, S. (2014). La evolución del pensamiento económico de Germán Bernácer (The evolution of G. Bernácer's economic thought). In S. Almenar Palau (Ed.), *Germán Bernácer y la edad de plata en Alicante* (p. 63). Canelobre: Instituto de Estudios Alicantinos.

Anderson, L. C., & Carlson, K. M. (1970, April). A monetarist model for economic stabilization. *Federal Reserve Bank of St Louis Review.*

H. Savall, *Radical Origins to Economic Crises*,
https://doi.org/10.1007/978-3-319-93366-5

Anderson, L. C. & Jordan, J. (1968, November). Monetary and fiscal actions: A test of their relative importance in economic stabilization. *St Louis Federal Reserve Bank Review*.

Ansoff, I. (1981). Preface to the English translation of the book by H. Savall. *Work and people. An economic evaluation of job-enrichment* (216p.). New York: Oxford University Press (2nd ed. Charlotte: Information Age Publishing, 2009).

Armand, L. (1972). L'État et l'Entreprise (The government and the company). In *Efficacité sociale du libéralisme* (Social efficacy of liberalism). Paris: Albatros.

Aron, R. (1958). Notes sur le pouvoir économique (Notes on economic power). *Revue Économique, VI*.

Aron, R. (1961). *18 leçons sur la société industrielle* (18 lessons on industrial society). Paris: Gallimard.

Association François Perroux. (2008). *Comment vivre ensemble: Conditions économiques et sociales pour la démocratie* (How to live together: Economic and social conditions for democracy). Écully: ISEOR.

Austruy, J. (1962). De la mémoire économique (About economic memory). In *Annales de la Faculté de droit de Lyon*.

Austruy, J. (1964). *Le scandale du développement* (The scandal of development). Paris: Rivière.

Bachelard, G. (1927). *Essai sur la connaissance approchée* (Essay on approximate knowledge). Paris: Vrin.

Bachelard, G. (1934). *Le nouvel esprit scientifique* (The new scientific spirit). Paris: PUF.

Barre, R. (1950a). La période dans l'analyse économique. Une approche à l'étude du temps (The period in economic analysis. An approach to the analysis of time). PhD dissertation, Université de Paris.

Barre, R. (1950b). Les critères modernes de la statique et de la dynamique (Modern criteria of static and dynamic). *Revue Économique, II*.

Barre, R. (1952). Dynamique économique et économique dynamique (Economic dynamics and dynamic economics). *Revue Économique, III*.

Barre, R. (1955). L'efficacité de la politique monétaire; quelques enseignements récents (Monetary policy efficacy; some recent teachings). Revue Économique, *VI*.

Barre, R. (1957). Éléments pour une analyse des récessions économiques (Elements for economic recession analysis). *Revue Économique, VI*.

Barre, R. (1965). *Économie politique* (Political economy), t. 2. Thémis. Paris: PUF.

Barre, R., Blardone, G., & Savall, H. (Coord.). (2005). *François Perroux: le centenaire d'un grand économiste* (François Perroux: The centenary of a great economist). Paris: Economica.

Barrère, A. (1959). Stabilisation et expansion (Stabilization and expansion). *Revue Économique, V.*

Barrère, A. (1965). *Économie financière* (Financial economy). Paris: Dalloz.

Bartoli, H. (1946). Le problème de la valeur chez les physiocrates (The problem of value with physiocrats). In *Mélanges Gonnard, op. cit.*

Bartoli, H. (1954). *Fluctuations économiques* (Economic fluctuations). Paris: Domat-Montchrestien.

Benetti, C., & Cartelier, J. (1973, January). *Profit et exploitation: le problème de la transformation des valeurs en prix* (Profit and operating: The problem of the transformation of values into prices), mimeographed.

Berger, P. (1966a). *La monnaie et ses mécanismes* (Money and its mechanisms). Paris: PUF.

Berger, P. (1966b, December 28). Les progrès de la régulation monétaire (The progress in monetary regulation). In *Le Monde.*

Bernácer, G. (1958). Riesgo y Ventura del mercado común (Risk and venture of a common market). *Revista «Información»*. Bilbao (Spain).

Bernadet, M. (1967). Les théories de l'utilité (Utility theories). PhD dissertation, Université de Lyon.

Bernard, R. (1974). Money quantity theory. PhD dissertation, Université de Lyon.

Bernard, H., & Petit-Dutaillis, G. (1964). *Le crédit et les banques* (Loan and banks). Paris: Sirey.

Blardone, G. (2013). Un nouveau monde et les zones d'échanges organisés. In Association François Perroux (2008). *Comment vivre ensemble: conditions économiques et sociales pour la démocratie* (How to live together: Economic and social conditions for democracy). Écully: ISEOR.

Blardone, G. (2014a). *La crise 2007–2014. Chronologie, analyse et perspectives: du capitalisme financier à l'économie solidaire et sociale de marché.* Écully: ISEOR.

Blardone, G. (2014b). Vers une gestion participative des entreprises et de l'économie. *Recherches en sciences de Gestion, 2*(101), 23–56.

Bloch-Lainé, F. (1963). *Pour une réforme de l'entreprise* (For a company reform). Paris: Seuil.

Blondel, D., Daloz, J.-P., & Jessua, C. L. (1970). *Essais sur la nouvelle théorie quantitative de la monnaie* (Essays on new quantity theory of money). Paris: PUF.

Boianovsky, M. (2007). Bernácer G. In L. E. Blume & S. N. Durlauf (Eds.), *The New Palgrave dictionary of economics* (2nd ed.). London: Palgrave Macmillan. Online: 2008.

Boianovsky, M., Dar, H., Presley, J. R., & Brañas Garza, P. (2006). Cambridge and the Spanish connection: The contribution of Germán Bernácer. *History of Political Economy, 38*, 3. Duke University Press.

Boje, D. (Ed.). (2015). *Organizational change and global standardization: Solutions to standards and norms overwhelming organizations*. London: Routledge.

Boje, D., & Rosile, G. A. (2003). Comparison of socio-economic and other transorganizational development methods. *Journal of Organizational Change Management, 16*(1), pp. 10–20. Emerald.

Bonnet, M., et al. (2003). Enhancing the efficiency of networks in an urban area through socio-economic interventions. *Journal of Organizational Change Management, 16*(1), pp. 72–82. Emerald.

Bonnet, M., Savall, A., Savall, H., & Zardet, V. (2018). The socio-economic approach to management: Preventing economic crises by harnessing hidden costs. In R. Gephart, C. Chet Miller, & K. S. Helgesson (Eds.), *Risk, crisis and emergency management*. London: Routledge.

Bourcier de Carbon L. (1972). *Essai sur l'histoire de la pensée et des doctrines économiques* (Essay on thought history and economic doctrines). Paris: Montchrestien; t. 1: « De Montéchrestien à Karl Marx ». Three main themes: Government, individual, and society, 1971; t. 2: « Aux sources du scientisme et de l'humanisme économiques modernes. Les origines d'une dichotomie fondamentale » (At the sources of scientism and modern economic humanism. The origins of basic dichotomy).

Braudel, F. (1950). Pour une économie historique (For historical economy). In *Revue Économique, I.*

Bresson, Y. (1969). Faut-il abandonner les courbes classiques d'offre et de demande? (Should we abandon the classic curves of supply and demand?). *Revue Économique, I.*

Brochier, H., & Tabatoni, P. (1963). *Économie financière* (Financial economy). Paris: PUF.

Buono, A. F. (2003). SEAM-less post-merger integration strategies: A cause for concern. *Journal of Organizational Change Management, 16*(1), pp. 90–98. Emerald.

Buono, A. F., & Savall, H. (Eds.). (2007). *Socio-economic intervention in organizations: The intervener-researcher and the SEAM approach to organizational analysis*. Charlotte: IAP.

Buono, A. F., & Savall, H. (Eds.). (2015). *The socio-economic approach to management revisited: The evolving nature of SEAM in the 21st century*. Charlotte: IAP.

Buono, A. F., Savall, H., & Cappelletti, L. (Eds.). (2018). *Intervention research: From design to publication*. Charlotte: IAP.

Cappelletti, L. (2010). Vers un modèle socio-économique de mesure du capital humain? *Revue Française de Gestion, 8*(207), pp. 139–152.

Cappelletti, L. (2012, December 19). La macroéconomie et l'imposture (Macroeconomics fake). *Les Échos.*

Cartelier, J., Cf. Benetti, C. (1969). Essai sur l'instabilité en économie monétaire (Essay on unstability in monetary economy). PhD dissertation, University of Paris.

Chaineau, A. (1968a). *Mécanismes et politique monétaires* (Monetary mechanisms and policy). Paris: PUF.

Chaineau, A. (1968b). Étude économétrique de la thésaurisation française (Econometric analysis of French hoarding), 1952–1966. In *Banque,* Juin.

Chaineau, A. (1970). *La demande d'encaisses monétaires* (Demand for monetary cash). Paris: Cujas.

Chaineau, A. (1971). *Monnaie et équilibre économique* (Money and economic equilibrium). Paris: Colin.

Cid, R. (2011). Bernácer G. y las crisis económicas. *Le Monde Diplomatique*, p. 17. Spanish edition.

Conbere, J., & Heorhiadi, A. (2011). Socio-economic approach to management. *OD Practitioner, 43*(1), pp. 6–10.

Cordebas-Nême, C. (1958). La notion de crise est-elle périmée ? (Is the notion of crisis outdated?). *Revue Économique, IV.*

Cordebas-Nême, C. (1972). *Organisations économiques internationales* (International economic organizations). Paris: PUF.

Cotta, A. (1969). *Théorie générale du capital, de la croissance et des fluctuations* (General theory of capital, growth and fluctuations). Paris: Dunod.

Coulbois, P. (1967). *Éléments pour une théorie de la politique des revenus* (Elements for a theory of income policy). Paris: Dalloz.

Courbis, R. (1970). Comportements financiers et développement économique (Financial behaviors and economic growth). *Économie et Statistique*, n° 12, pp. 27–44.

Datry, F., & Savall, A. (2015). Global-local (glocal) creation of value-added. In A. F. Buono & H. Savall (Eds.), *The socio-economic approach to management revisited: The evolving nature of SEAM in the 21st century*. Charlotte: IAP.

De Brunhoff, S. (1965). *Capitalisme financier public. Influence économique de l'État en France* (Public financial capitalism. Economic influence of the government in France): 1948–1958. Paris: SEDES.

De Jouvenel, B. (1958). *L'épargne* (Savings). Édition de l'Épargne.

De Montbrial, T. (1971). *Économie théorique* (Theoretical economics). Paris: PUF.

De Montbrial, T. (1973a). Reformulation et généralisation de la théorie néo-classique de l'intérêt (Reformulation and generalization of the neo-classical theory of interest). *Économie Appliquée.*

De Montbrial, T. (1973b). Intertemporal general equilibrium and rate of interests theory. *Économie Appliquée, 4*, pp. 160–185.

Delors, J. (1975). Preface to H. Savall « *Enrichir le travail humain: l'évaluation économique* » (Enriching human work: The economic evaluation). Paris: Dunod.

Denis, H. (1951). *La monnaie* (Money). Paris: Editions sociales.

Denis, H. (1967). *La formation de la science économique* (Economic science formation). Paris: PUF.

Denizet, J. (1950, November). Marché monétaire et conjoncture économique (Money market and economic cycle). In *Revue Économique.*

Denizet, J. (1967). *Monnaie et financement* (Money and finance). Paris: Dunod.

Derycke, P. H. (1966). Taux d'intérêt, taux d'actualisation et croissance économique (Interest rate, discount rate and economic growth). *Revue Économique, IV.*

Dieterlen, P. (1954). *Quelques enseignements de l'évolution monétaire française de 1948 à 1952* (Some lessons on French monetary developments 1948–1952). Paris: Colin.

Dieterlen, P. (1961, May–June). Monnaie et expansion: le rôle de la Banque Centrale (Money and expansion: The role of Central Banking). *Revue d'Économie Politique.*

Dieterlen, P. (1964). *L'idéologie économique* (Economic ideology). Paris: Cujas.

Dischamps, J.-C. (1960). *Comportements économiques et distorsions fiscales* (Economic and fiscal distortions behaviors). Paris: PUF.

Divisia, F. (1950). *Monnaie et intérêt* (Money and interest). *Revue d'Économie Politique.*

Dobb, M. H. (1971). *Études sur le développement du capitalisme* (Studies on capitalism development). Paris: Maspéro.

Dockès, P. (1969). *L'espace dans la pensée économique du XVIe au XVIIIe siècle* (Space in economic thought from the sixteenth to the eighteenth century). Paris: Flammarion.

Dockès, P. (1971). Preface in Ricardo. *Des principes de l'économie politique et de l'impôt* (On the principles of political economy and taxation). Paris: Flammarion.

Duesenberry, H. (1950, May). Income determination in open inflation. *Review of Economic Statistics.*

Duharcourt, P. (1970). *La fonction d'investissement* (Investment function). Paris: Sirey.

Falise, M. (1959). *La demande de monnaie* (Demand for money). Louvain.

Fan, H. (1939). Mr Keynes and Marx on the theory of capital accumulation; money and interest. *The Review of Economic Studies, 7*(1).

Fau. (1967). Équilibre et déséquilibre dans le processus productif national (Balance and disequilibrium in national productive process). *Banque, V.*

Faure-Soulet, J. F. (1970). *De Malthus à Marx* (From Malthus to Marx). Paris: Gauthier-Villars.

Fernández Díaz, A. (1983). Regards sur la pensée économique espagnole (Perspectives on Spanish economic thought). *Revue Économique, 4*, pp. 212–228.

Fernández Ruvalcaba, M. M. (2007). Socio-economic approach to management in Mexico. In A. F. Buono & H. Savall (Eds.), *Socio-economic intervention.* Charlotte: IAP.

Fourastié, J. (1973, February). Editorial. *L'Express.*

François-Poncet, J. (1970). *L'Allemagne Occidentale. Politique économique* (West Germany. Economic policy). Paris: Sirey.

Freyssinet, J., Hollard, M., & Romier, G. (1973). Note préliminaire pour un projet de recherches sur l'élaboration d'une comptabilité en temps de travail et le problème de l'agrégation (Preliminary note for a project of research on the elaboration of accounting in working time and aggregation problem), mimeographed.

Friedmann, M. (1962). *Capitalisme et liberté* (Capitalism and freedom), French edition. Paris: Robert Laffont, 1971.

Gaillard, Y., & Thuillier, G. (1965). Sur la thésaurisation (About hoarding). *Revue Économique, V.*

Garello, J. (1972). Les nationalisations et l'efficacité économique (Nationalization and economic efficacy). In *Efficacité sociale du libéralisme...* (Liberalism social efficacy ...). Paris: Albatros.

Gephart, R. P., & Smith, R. S. (2009). An invitation to ethnostatistics. *Revue Sciences de Gestion-Management Sciences-Ciencias de Gestión.*

Gephart, R., Chet Miller, C., & Helgesson, K. S. (Eds.). (2018). *Risk, crisis and emergency management.* London: Routledge.

Godelier. (1968). *Rationalité et irrationalité en économie* (Rationality and irrationality in economics). Paris: Maspéro.

Gonnard, R. (1946). *Mélanges économiques dédiés à M. le Pr René Gonnard* (Economics miscellaneous dedicated to Prof. René Gonnard). Paris: LGDJ.

Gonnard, R. (1948). Histoire des doctrines économiques (Economic doctrines history). Librairie générale de droit, new edition.

Granger, G. G. (1955). *Méthodologie économique* (Economic methodology). Paris: PUF.

Guillaumont-Jeanneney, S. (1969). *Politique monétaire et croissance économique en France* (Monetary policy and economic growth in France). Paris: Colin.

Guitton, H. (1959, March). La coexistence des âges différents dans l'économie. Les relations du vieux et du neuf (The coexistence of different ages in economy. The old and new relations). *Revue des Sciences économiques.*

Guitton, H. (1967). *Maîtriser l'économie* (Mastering the economy). Paris: Fayard.

Guitton, H. (1970). *À la recherche du temps économique* (In search of economic time). Paris: Fayard.

Guyenot, J. (1972). *Droit antitrust européen* (European antitrust law). Québec: Les Presses de l'Université du Québec. Diffusion l'École, Paris.

Haberler, G. (1937). *Prosperity and depression.* Genève; French translation: « Prospérité et dépression », 1942.

Heller, W. W. (1968). *Nouvelles perspectives de la politique économique* (New perspectives of economic policy). Paris: Calmann-Lévy.

Herzog, P. H. (1968). *Prévisions économiques et comptabilité nationale* (Economic forecasts and national accounting). Paris: PUF.

Hicks, J. R. (1956). *Valeur et capital* (Value and capital). Paris: Dunod.

Hicks, J. R. (1967). *Critical essays in monetary theory.* Oxford: Clarendon Press.

Hope, R. (1949, June). Profits in British industry from 1924 to 1935. *Oxford, Economic Papers.*

Hostache, R. (1958). *Le Conseil national de la Résistance* (The national council of the resistance).

Hurtado Jordá, J. (2014). El jóven Bernácer. Sociedad y felicidad, ensayo de mecánica social. In S. Monllor (Ed.), *Germán Bernácer y la edad de plata en Alicante* (pp. 311–325). Canlorbe, Instituto de Estudios Alicantinos.

Jacot, J. H. (1970). La surchauffe économique (Economic overheating). PhD dissertation, Université de Lyon.

Jacot, J. H. (1973). De quelques problèmes théoriques relatifs à la valeur (Some theoretical issues relating to the value), mimeographed.

James, E. (1955). *Histoire de la pensée économique au XXe siècle* (History of economic thought in the twentieth century) (2 vol.). Paris: PUF.

James, E., & Marchal, A. (1951). *La monnaie* (Money). Paris: Domat-Montchrestien.
Jean XXIII (Pape). (1961). *Mater et Magistra*, encyclique.
Keynes, J. M. (1923). *A tract on monetary reform*. Londres: Macmillan and Company.
Keynes, J. M. (1933a). *The mean of prosperity*. Londres: Macmillan and Company.
Keynes, J. M. (1933b, December 13). Letter to President Roosevelt. *New-York Times*.
Krier, H., & Le Bourva, J. (1968). *Économie politique* (Political economy). Paris: Colin.
Krugman, P. (2014). *Pourquoi les crises reviennent toujours?* (Why do crises keep coming back?). Paris: Seuil.
Lajugie, J. (1953). *Proudhon*. Paris: Dalloz.
Lajugie, J. (1957, 1974). *Les systèmes économiques* (Economic systems). Paris: PUF.
Lambert, D. C. (1959). Les inflations sud-américaines (South American inflations).
Lambert, D. C. (1970). *Terminologie économique et monétaire* (Economic and monetary terminology, French-English lexicon). Paris: Éditions ouvrières.
Le Bourva, J. (1962). Création de monnaie et multiplicateur de crédit (Creation of money and credit multiplier). *Revue Économique*, Janvier.
Lecaillon, J. (1950). Marx et Keynes devant la pensée économique contemporaine (Marx and Keynes to contemporary economic thought). *Revue Économique*.
Lecaillon, J. (1969). *Analyse macroéconomique* (Macroeconomic analysis). Paris: Cujas.
Leduc, G. (1955). *Inflation et épargne* (Inflation and savings). Paris: Édition de l'Épargne.
Lefournier, P. H. (1970, September). La France terre d'inégalité. La lourde machinerie des transferts sociaux ne parvient pas à redistribuer les revenus (France, land of inequality. Heavy machinery of social transfers cannot redistribute income). *L'Expansion* magazine.
Leprince Ringuet, L. (1973). *Science et bonheur de l'homme* (Science and humanity happiness). Paris: Flammarion.
Lhomme, J. (1966). *Pouvoir et société économique* (Power and economic society). Paris: Cujas.
Lindhal, E. (1939). *Studies in the theory of money and capital*. New York: Farrar & Rinehart, French translation. Paris: Génin.
Lindsay, R. M., Lindsay, L. M., & Irving, V. B. (1996). Instilling ethical behaviour in organizations: A survey of Canadian companies. *Journal of Business Ethics, 15*(4), 393–407.

Llau, P. (1963). Taux d'actualisation et taux d'intérêt dans la décision d'investissement de la firme (Discount rates and rate of interests in the investment decision of the firm). *Revue Économique, VI.*

Llau, P. (1966). La rationalité du taux d'actualisation. Réflexions sur l'actualisation des valeurs dans le Ve plan (The rationality of the discount rate. Reflections on updating values in the fifth plan). *Revue Économique, IV.*

López Moreno, M. J. (1983). Sobre mis recuerdos de Germán Bernácer Tormo. *Hacienda Pública Española, 81*, 19–28.

Marchal, J. (1946). Les fondements de la valeur. Critique de la théorie de la valeur fondée sur l'utilité marginale (The foundations of value. Criticism of the theory of value based on marginal utility). In *Mélanges Gonnard, op. cit.*

Marchal, A. (1950). L'économie politique mathématique (Mathematical political economics). *Revue Économique.*

Marchal, J. (1955). Esquisse d'une théorie moderne des salaires et d'une théorie générale de la répartition (Outline of modern theory on wages and general theory of distribution). *Revue Économique, IV.*

Marchal, J. (1964). Les conditions de l'équilibre macroéconomique dans la stabilité des prix (The conditions for macroeconomic equilibrium in price stability). *Revue Économique, VI.*

Marczewski, J. (1956). La rationalité économique du socialisme (Economic rationality of socialism). *Cahiers de l'I.S.E.A.*, G-3.

Marjolin, R. (1941). *Monnaie, prix et production* (Money, price an production). Paris: Librairie du Recueil Sirey.

Martín Aceña, P. (2000) El servicio de Estudios del Banco de España 1930–2000 (The Banco de España Department of Surveys). Madrid: Banco de España.

Martínez García, E. (2009). *Bernácer G. «Functional doctrine of Money»*, Federal Reserve of Dallas.

Martínez García, E. (2016, December 14). Apuntes para una Relectura Actual de la Obra de Germán Bernácer Tormo (1883–1965), Federal Reserve of Dallas, paper, Conference on Bernácer.

Mendès-France, P. (1945). Lettre au Général de Gaulle du 18 janvier 1945 (Letter to General de Gaulle of January 18th, 1945) (quoted by Bourcier de Carbon in *Economic analysis*, op. cit.).

Mendès-France, P. (1962). *La République moderne* (The modern Republic). Paris: Gallimard.

Mifsud, P. (1973). Modèle de Léontieff et valeur travail (Léontieff model and value work), mimeographed.

Miró, G. (1944). *Les cerises du cimetière* (The cherries of the cemetery). French translation, Paris: Sorlot.

Mockers, J. P. (1969). *Croissances économiques comparées: Allemagne, France, Royaume-Uni, 1950–1967; Essai d'analyse structurale* (Compared growing economies: Germany, France, UK, 1950–1967; Essay of structural analysis). Paris: Dunod.

Monteil, J. (1962). Coûts certains et coûts aléatoires (Certain costs and random costs). In *Méthodes quantitatives au service de l'entreprise*. Paris: Dunod.

Monteil, J. (1968). *Les théories des surplus* (Theories of value-added). Paris: Gauthier-Villars.

Monteil, J. (1974). Une politique pour mieux vivre (A policy for better living). Paris: Éditions Marcel Rivière.

Nême, J., & Nême, C. (1970) *Économie* européenne (European economy). Paris: PUF.

Nicolaï, A. (1962). L'inflation comme régulation (Inflation as adjustment). In *Revue Économique, IV.*

Olarra-Giménez, R. (1965). *El dinero y las estructuras monetarias.* (Money and monetary structures). Buenos-Aires: Aguilar.

Ortega, Y., & Gasset, J. (1929). *La révolte des masses* (The revolt of the masses). French translation (1937). Paris: Editions Gallimard.

Page, A. (1959). Objectifs actuels de la théorie du salaire (The current objectives of wage theory). *Revue Économique, I.*

Parly, J. M. (1966). Fondement d'une analyse structurelle des liquidités (Basis of liquidity structural analysis). PhD dissertation, Université de Paris.

Pen, J. (1966, février). La controverse entre l'école monétaire et l'école des dépenses: quelques contributions récentes (The controversy between the monetary school and expenditure school: Some recent contributions). *Bulletin de la Banque nationale de Belgique.*

Perlstein, J. (1967). Information et concurrence parfaite (Information and perfect competition). PhD dissertation, Université de Lyon.

Péron M., & Péron, M. (2003). Post-modernism and Socio-economic approach to organizations. *Journal of Organizational Change Management.* Emerald, *16*(1), pp. 49–55.

Perroux, F. (1952, Décembre) La croissance du revenu national français depuis 1780 (The growth of French national income since 1780), *Economie et Sociétés, 7.*

Perroux, F. (1925). *Le problème du profit* (The problem of profit). Paris.

Perroux, F. (1931). L'or et la politique de la Banque de France (Gold and the policy of Bank of France). *Revue Économique Internationale.*

Perroux, F. (1939). Pour un approfondissement de la notion de structure (For a deepening of the structure concept). In *Mélanges Witmeur.* Paris: Sirey.

Perroux, F. (1940). Les banques d'émission et l'État (The issuing banks and the government). *Revue d'Économie Politique*, 4 & 6.
Perroux, F. (1946). Libéralisme et liberté» (Liberalism and freedom). In *Mélanges Économiques dédiés à R. Gonnard, op. cit.*
Perroux, F. (1948, 1958). *Le capitalisme* (Capitalism). Paris: PUF.
Perroux, F. (1949, July). La généralisation de la General Theory (The generalization of the general theory). University d'Istanbul.
Perroux, F. (1957a, November). Le profit et les progrès économiques (Profit and economic progress). *Revue d'action populaire.*
Perroux, F. (1957b). Structural inflation and the economic function of wages; the French example: The theory of wage determination. *Proceedings of a conference held by the International Economic Association.* London: Macmillan.
Perroux, F. (1958a). La recherche de la stabilité: facteurs réels (The search of stability: Real factors), *Économie Appliquée*, 1 & 2. Translated in English in *Stability and progress in the world economy.* London: Macmillan.
Perroux, F. (1958b). *La coexistence pacifique* (Peaceful coexistence) (3 vol.). Paris: PUF.
Perroux, F. (1964). *L'économie du XXe siècle* (The economy of the twentieth century). Paris: PUF.
Perroux, F. (1972a, September 26). Le pouvoir a droit de cité en science économique (The power has citizenship rights in Economics). *Le Monde* magazine.
Perroux, F. (1972b). *Pouvoir et économie* (Power and economics). Paris: Dunod.
Perroux, F. (1973). Review of « La croissance française... by J.-J. Carré, P. Dubois, E. Malinvaud » (French growth, *op.cit.*). *Mondes en développement, 2*, 274–279.
Perroux, F. (1979). L'entreprise, l'équilibre rénové et les coûts «cachés» (Company, updated equilibrium and "hidden" costs). Preface to H. Savall *Reconstruire l'entreprise. Analyse socio-économique des conditions de travail* (Reconstructing the firm: Socio-economic analysis of working conditions). Paris: Dunod.
Perroux, F. (Ed). (1947) Le revenu national (The national income), Paris: PUF.
Piatier, A. (1962). L'entreprise et la prévision (Company and forecast). In *Méthodes quantitatives au service de l'entreprise.* Paris: Dunod.
Piatier, A., Austruy, J., et al. (1964). *Les formes modernes de la concurrence* (Modern forms of competition). Paris: Gauthier-Villars.
Piatier, A., Cahuzac, P., & Chambadal, L. (1965). *Économie et Mathématiques* (Economics and mathematics). Paris: PUF.

Piettre, A. (1947). *Économie dirigée d'hier et d'aujourd'hui: du Colbertisme à notre temps* (Yesterday and today steered economy: From Colbertism to now). Paris: Médicis.

Piettre, A. (1950). *Humanisme chrétien et économie politique* (Christian humanism and political economy). Strasbourg: Le Roux.

Piettre, A. (1955). *Les trois âges de l'économie...* (The three ages of economy). Paris: Éditions Ouvrières, Économie et Humanisme. (3rd ed. Fayard, 1967).

Piettre, A. (1957a). Les deux aspects de la dynamique des structures (The two aspects of structures dynamics). *Revue d'Économie Politique.*

Piettre, A. (1957b, 1966). *Marx et le marxisme* (Marx and marxism). Paris: PUF.

Piettre, A. (1969). *Histoire économique, les faits et les idées* (Economic history, facts and ideas). Paris: Cujas.

Pina, A. (2002, November 10). El español y la ciencia económica, Keynes (1883–1946) en Madrid. Boletín Económico ICE 2746.

Pirou, G. (1939). *Traité d'économie politique* (Treatise on political economy). Paris: Sirey.

Pirou, G. (1946). La monnaie en économie libre et en économie dirigée (Money in free economy and in steered economy). In *Mélanges Gonnard, op. cit.*

Ponsard, C. (1958a). L'actualité de la théorie quantitative de la monnaie (The topical of quantity theory on money). *Études et Conjonctures.*

Ponsard, C. (1958b). De l'action de la banque centrale sur le taux d'intérêt à court et à long terme (The action of the Central Bank on the rate of interest in the short and long term). *Revue Économique.*

Presley, J. R. (1989, November). Keynes J. M. & Robertson D. H.: Three phases of collaboration. *Research in the History of Economic Thought and Methodology, 16,* 31–49.

Rist, C. H. (1936, 1938). *Histoire des doctrines relatives au crédit et à la monnaie* (History of doctrines related to credit and money). Paris: Sirey.

Robert, P., & Rey, A. (2007). *Le Robert & Collins.* Paris: Dictionnaires Le Robert.

Robertson, D. H. (1922). *Money.* Londres: Nisbet and Company.

Robertson, D. H. (1926). *Banking policy and the price level.* Londres: P. S. King & Son.

Robertson, D. H. (1940). *Essays in monetary theory.* London: P. S. King & Son.

Robertson, D. H. (1952). *Utility and all that, and other essays.* London: Allen & Unwin.

Robinson, J. (1971). *Essai sur l'économie de Marx* (Essay on Marx economy). Paris: Dunod.

Rueff, J. (1929). *Une erreur économique: l'organisation des transferts* (An economic mistake: The organization of transfers). Paris: Gaston Doin.

Rueff, J. (1931). L'assurance-chômage, cause du chômage permanent (The insurance-unemployment, cause of permanent unemployment). *Revue d'Économie Politique.*

Rueff, J. (1947). Les erreurs de la théorie générale de lord Keynes (Lord Keynes general theory mistakes). *Revue d'Économie Politique.*

Rueff, J. (1949a). *L'ordre social* (Social order). Paris: Génin-Médicis.

Rueff, J. (1949b). *Épître aux dirigistes* (Epistle to interventionists). Paris: Gallimard.

Rueff, J. (1953). *La régulation monétaire et le problème institutionnel de la monnaie* (Monetary management and institutional problem of money). Paris: Sirey.

Ruiz, G. (1983, July–December). El sistema de pensamiento de Germán Bernácer Tormo (The way of thinking of Germán Bernácer Tormo (1883–1965)). *Pensamiento Iberoamericano: Revista de Economía Política.*

Ruiz, G. (1984). *Germán Bernácer: Un economista anticipativo.* Madrid: Pirámide.

Sánchez Monllor, M. (2002). Bernácer: el economista-humanista. In M. Sánchez Monllor (Ed.). (Coord.) (2005) *En torno en la Obra y Figura del Economista Germán Bernácer.* Alicante: CAM.

Sauvy, A. (1951). Réformateurs économistes et prophètes (Economist reformers and prophets). *Revue Économique, 1.*

Sauvy, A. (1952). Pouvoir, possession, propriété (Power, possession, ownership). *Revue Économique, IV.*

Sauvy, A. (1965). *Histoire économique de la France entre les deux guerres* (Economic history of France between the World Wars). Paris: Payot.

Savall, H. (1974, 1975). *Enrichir le travail humain: l'évaluation économique* (Enriching human work: The economic evaluation). PhD dissertation at the University Paris IX-Dauphine; integral text published at Dunod; 4°th edition increased, Economica, 1989. Translated in English: *Work and people: an economic evaluation of job enrichment.* New York: Oxford University Press (1°.Ed 1981); 2°Ed. Charlotte: IAP (2010); in Spanish: *Por un trabajo más humano.* Madrid: Tecniban, (1°Ed 1977); 2° Ed. Charlotte: IAP (2012).

Savall, H. (1978a). Article « Bernácer » In *Encyclopédie de l'Économie.* Paris: Larousse.

Savall, H. (Coord.) (1978b). Aspects humains et sociaux de l'économie industrielle (Human and social aspects of the industrial economy). *Revue d'Économie Industrielle.*

Savall, H. (1979). *Reconstruire l'entreprise. Analyse socio-économique des conditions de travail* (Reconstructing the firm. Socio-economic analysis of working conditions). Preface by François Perroux. Paris: Dunod.

Savall, H. (1983). *Germán Bernácer. La heterodoxia en la economía* (Germán Bernácer. The heterodoxy in economics). Alicante: Instituto de Estudios Alicantinos.

Savall, H. (1987). Les coûts cachés et l'analyse socio-économique des organisations (Hidden costs and socio-economic analysis of organizations). In *Encyclopédie du management*. Paris: Economica.

Savall, H. (2003). An update presentation of the socio-economic management model and: International dissemination of the socio-economic model. In Savall, H. (Ed.), *Socio-economic approach to management. Journal of Organizational Change Management, 16*(1), pp. 33–48. Emerald.

Savall, H. (2010). Bouleversement des normes et pilotage stratégique des organisations: menaces et opportunités (Disruption of norms and strategic management of organizations: Threats and opportunities). In D. Bessire, L. Cappelletti, & B. Pigé (Coord.) *Normes: origines et conséquences des crises*. Paris: Economica.

Savall, H. (2016, December 14). Superando la crisis: actualidad de la teoría de Germán Bernácer y eficiencia de la gestión socioeconómica de las organizaciones (Overwhelming crisis: Topicality of Germán Bernácer' work and socio-economic approach to management). Paper, University of Alicante Conference.

Savall, H., & Zardet, V. (1987, 2008, 2015). *Maîtriser les coûts et les performances cachés. Le contrat d'activité périodiquement négociable.* Prix Harvard l'Expansion de Management Stratégique (Harvard-L'Expansion Award in Strategic Management, 6th edition, 2015), Paris: Economica. Translated in English *Masterring hidden costs and performance.* Charlotte: IAP (2008).

Savall, H., & Zardet, V. (1992). *Le nouveau contrôle de gestion. Méthode des coûts-performances cachés* (The new management control. Method of hidden costs-performances). Paris: Éditions comptables Malesherbes-Eyrolles.

Savall, H., & Zardet ,V. (1994). Performance économique et engagement social de l'entreprise: jusqu'où est-ce compatible? (Economic performance and social commitment of the company: How far is it compatible?). *Stratégies Ressources Humaines, 9*, pp. 30–38.

Savall, H., & Zardet, V. (1995a, 2005). *Ingénierie stratégique du roseau, souple et enracinée* (Strategic engineering of the reed, flexible and rooted). Paris: Economica.

Savall, H., & Zardet, V. (1995b). Management socio-économique de l'entreprise: ou comment régénérer confiance et performances (Company socioeconomic

Management: Or how to regenerate confidence and performances). In *Confiance, entreprise et société*, collective book. Paris: Eska.

Savall, H., & Zardet, V. (2004). Recherche en sciences de gestion, approche qualimétrique: observer l'objet complexe (Research in management, qualimetric approach: Observing the complex object). Preface by David Boje. Paris: Economica.

Savall, H., & Zardet, V. (2005). *Tétranormalisation, défis et dynamiques* (Tetranormalization, challenges and dynamics). Paris: Economica.

Savall, H., & Zardet, V. (Coord.) (2007). Evaluación de desempeño y gestión socioeconómica (Assessment of performance and socio-economic management). Mérida: Gobierno de Yucatán, UAM, ISEOR.

Savall, H., & Zardet, V. (2008a). *Mastering hidden costs and socio-economic performance*. Charlotte: IAP.

Savall, H., & Zardet, V. (2008b). Le concept de coût-valeur des activités. Contribution de la théorie socio-économique des organisations (The concept of cost-value activities. Contribution of organization socio-economic theory). *Revue Sciences de Gestion-Management Sciences- Ciencias de Gestión, 64*, pp. 61–90.

Savall, H., & Zardet, V. (2008c). Tétranormalisation et nouvelles règles du jeu: contribution de la théorie socio-économique (Tetranormalization and new rules of the game: Contribution of socio-economic theory). In XI° Journée François Perroux, ISEOR.

Savall, H., & Zardet, V. (2009). *Ingeniería estratégica. Un enfoque socioeconómico*. México: UAM.

Savall, H., & Zardet, V. (2010). Tétranormalisation: origine, cheminement et portée du concept (Tetranormalization: Origin, progression and scope of the concept). In D. Bessire, L. Cappelletti, & B. Pigé (Coord.) *Normes: origines et conséquences des crises* (Standards and norms: Crisis origins and consequences). Paris: Economica.

Savall, H., & Zardet, V. (2011a). Contribution de la théorie socio-économique des organisations à la poursuite et valorisation de l'œuvre de François Perroux au XXI° siècle (Contribution of organization socio-economic theory to the continuation and enhancement of François Perroux's work in the XXI century). In E. d'Hombres, H. Savall, & E. Gabelieri (Coord.) *Humanisme et travail chez François Perroux* (Humanism and labor in François Perroux's work). Paris: Economica.

Savall, H., & Zardet, V. (2011b). Le management de la responsabilité sociale de l'entreprise par les indicateurs. In Trébulle et Uzan *Responsabilité sociale des entreprises: Regards croisés Droit et gestion* (Corporate social responsibility: A new look law and management). Paris: Economica.

Savall, H., & Zardet, V. (2011c). *Qualimetrics approach: Observing the complex object*. Charlotte: IAP.

Savall, H., & Zardet, V. (Coord.) (2011d). *Réussir en temps de crise: stratégies pro-actives des entreprises* (Succeeding in times of crisis: Proactive business strategies). Paris: Economica.

Savall, H., & Zardet, V. (2013). RSE, lien entre l'individu, l'organisation et la société: nouvel énoncé de la théorie socio-économique (CSR, linking individual, organization and society: New statement of socio-economic theory). *Management et sciences sociales.*

Savall, H., & Zardet, V. (2017). *Strategic engineering of the reed*. Charlotte: IAP.

Savall, H., Zardet, V., & Bonnet, M. (2000, 2008). *Releasing the untapped potential of enterprises trough Socio-Economic management;* see also French version: *Libérer les performances cachées des entreprises par un managemnt socio-économique*, and Spanish version *Mejorar los desempeños ocultos de las empresas a través de una gestión socioeconómica*). Genève: ILO-BIT.

Savall, H., Zardet, V., & Bonnet, M. (2009). Théorie socio-économique et tétranormalisation: perpétuer l'œuvre de François Perroux (Socio-economic theory and Tetranormalization: Perpetuating the work of François Perroux). In M. Kalika (Coord.) *Les hommes et le management: des réponses à la crise* (People and management: The responses to the crisis). Paris: Economica.

Savall, H., Zardet, V., & Bonnet, M. (2011a). RSE et développement durable, fondements de la théorie socio-économique des organisations. In N. Barthe & J. J. Rosé (Coord.) *RSE entre globalisation et développement* durable (CSR between globalization and sustainable development). Bruxelles: De Boeck.

Savall, H., Zardet, V., & Péron, M. (2011b). The evolutive and interactive actor polygon in the theater of organizations. In D. Boje (Ed.), *Storytelling and the future of organizations. An antenarrative handbook*. New York: Routledge.

Savall, H., Péron, M., Zardet, V., & Bonnet, M. (2015). *Le capitalisme socialement responsable existe (Socially responsible capitalism and management)*. Paris: EMS.

Savall, H., Péron, M., Zardet, V., & Bonnet, M. (2017). *Socially responsible capitalism and management*. New York/London: Routledge.

Say, J.-B. (1803). *Traité d'Économie Politique* (Treatise on political economics).

Schneider, E. (1968). *Money, income and employment*. London: Allen and Unwin.

Schumpeter, J. (1942, 1965). *Capitalisme, socialisme, démocratie* (Capitalism, socialism, democracy). French translation. Paris: Payot.

Selden, P. (1965, October). La théorie quantitative de la monnaie contre l'optique des dépenses et du revenu » (The quantity theory of money against expenditure and income view). *Bulletin de la Banque Nationale de Belgique.*

Sevilla, M., & Torregrosa, T. (2014). *El pensamiento económico de Bernácer y la doctrina funcional del dinero* (pp. 337–349). Alicante: Canelobre, Instituto de Estudios Alicantinos.

Shackle, G. L. S. (1971). Les théories récentes sur la nature et le rôle du taux d'intérêt (Recent theories about the nature and the role of interest rate). In R. S. Thorn (Ed.), *Théorie monétaire.* Paris: Dunod.

Shiller, R. J. (2015). *Irrational exuberance.* Princeton/Oxford: Princeton University Press.

Simiand, F. (1929–1930). *Cours d'économie politique au Conservatoire National des Arts et Métiers* (Political economics course at the National Conservatory of Arts and Crafts). Paris: CNAM.

Sorensen, P. F., Yaeger, T. F., Savall, H., Zardet, V., Bonnet, M., & Péron, M. (2010). A review of two major global and international approaches to organizational changes: SEAM and appreciative inquiry. *Organizational Development Journal, 28*(4), pp. 31–39.

Sraffa, P. (1970). *Production des marchandises par des marchandises* (Production of goods through goods). French translation. Paris: Dunod.

Stoléru, L. (1969). Taux d'intérêt et taux d'actualisation (Interest rate and discount rate). *Économie et Statistique, 5*. pp. 3-11.

Tabatoni, P. (1954). Notes sur la politique monétaire de stabilisation aux États-Unis depuis 1950 (Notes on stabilization monetary policy in the US since 1950). *Revue Économique, V.*

Taddeï, D. (1968). *Plein-emploi ou stabilité des prix* (Full employment or price stability). Paris: Cujas.

Teilhac, E. (1953). Fluctuations de l'économie politique (Political economy fluctuations). *Revue Économique, III & IV.*

Thorn, R. S. (1971). *Théorie monétaire* (Monetary theory). Paris: Dunod.

Van Praag-Chantraine, J. (1959). *Gabriel Miró ou le visage du Levant, terre d'Espagne*. Paris.

Varga, E. (1967). *Essais sur l'économie politique du capitalisme* (Essays on capitalism political economy). Paris: Éditions du Progrès.

Velarde Fuertes, J. (1984). Notas bibliográficas. Crónica del homenaje español a Germán Bernácer (Bibliographical notes. Spanish tribute to Germán Bernácer). *El Trimestre Económico, 51, 203*, 670–680.

Ventejol, G. (1972). Les nationalisations et la condition ouvrière (Nationalization and workers' conditions). In *Efficacité sociale du libéralisme, op. cit.*
Vigreux, P. (1947). *Turgot, textes choisis* (Turgot, selected texts). Paris.
Villacís González, J. (1983). La Teoría del Interés y el Dinero en Germán Bernácer. *Revista de Hacienda Pública.*
Villacís González, J. (1984). El Paralelismo entre Prados Arrarte y Germán Bernácer en la Macroeconomía. *Revista de Pensamiento Iberoamericano, 6.*
Villacís González, J. (1986a, July). La Macroeconomía de Germán Bernácer. *Boletín ICE.*
Villacís González, J. (1986b, November). El Error de la Ecuación de la Macroeconomía y de la Teoría Cuantitativa. *Boletín ICE.*
Villacís González, J. (1986c). Macroeconomía y Política Fiscal en la Teoría de las Disponibilidades. *Revista de Derecho Financiero y Hacienda Pública, XXXVI*(186).
Villacís González, J. (1987, March). Una Teoría de los Ciclos a la Luz de la Teoría de las Disponibilidades. *Boletín ICE.*
Villacís González, J. (1988, March). Una Teoría del Interés a la Luz de la Teoría de las Disponibilidades. *Boletín ICE.*
Villacís González, J. (1992). Análisis Macroeconómico Histórico y Actual de la Teoría de las Disponibilidades en Germán Bernácer. *Revista de Derecho Financiero y de Hacienda Pública, XII.*
Villacís González, J. (1993). *Germán Bernácer, el origen de la macroeconomía en España. Polémica Keynes-Bernácer.* (Germán Bernácer, the origin of the macroeconomy in Spain. Argument Keynes-Bernácer). Madrid: Paraninfo. Translated into English and preface by Samuelson P.
Villacís González, J. (2009). Dynamic theory of the money market, disposable money and interest. *Journal of Business and Economics Research, 7*(9), pp. 78–97.
Villey, D. (1966, 1967). *Cours de doctorat d'histoire de la pensée* (Doctoral course in the history of thought). Paris: Les cours de Droit.
Villey, D., & Cordebas-Nême, C. (1973). *Petite histoire des grandes doctrines économiques* (Short history of major economic doctrines). Paris: Génin.
Wallich, H. C. (1947). Review of *La doctrina funcional del dinero*, by Germán Bernácer. (Review of the functional doctrine of money). *Review of Economic Statistics, 29*(1), 65–66.
Webb, S. & B. (1898).. – Histoire des Trade-Unions (History of trade-unionism). Reviewed by A. Boggiano, *Rivista Internazionale di Scienze Sociali, 18*-72, pp. 645-648.
Wicksell, K. (1893). *Uber Wert, kapital und Rente.* London: G. Fischer.
Wicksell, K. (1896). *Finanz-theoretische Untersuchungen.* London: Allen & Unwin.
Wicksell, K. (1898). Geldzins und Güterpreise. Stockholm: Capital Buch.

Worley, C., Zardet, V., Bonnet, M., & Savall, A. (2015). Becoming agile: How the SEAM approach to management builds adaptability. Jossey Bass: John Wiley and Sons.

Ybarra (Ed.). (2014). Presentation of new edition of Germán Bernácer's book *Sociedad y felicidad.* Ensayo de mecánica social. Universidad de Alicante.

Yvars, B. (2000). *La pensée économique espagnole dans l'Espagne autarcique (1939–1959)* (Spanish economic thought in autarkic Spain (1939–1959)). Working paper, Centre d'Économie du Développement, Université Montesquieu Bordeaux IV, 51.

Zardet, V. (2010). Développement du potentiel humain et création de valeur économique (Human potential development and economic value creation). In Association François Perroux (2008). *Comment vivre ensemble: Conditions économiques et sociales pour la démocratie* (How to live together: Economic and social conditions for democracy). Écully: ISEOR.

Zardet, V., & Bonnet, M. (2008). Partenariat Public-Privé, (Public-private partnership) in Association des Amis de François Perroux. *Comment vivre ensemble: conditions économiques de la démocratie* (How to live together: Economic conditions for democracy). Écully: ISEOR.

Zardet, V., & Bonnet, M. (2010). Intensification actuelle de la tétranormalisation: Risques et bonnes pratiques émergentes (Current intensification of Tetranormalization: Risks and emerging good practices). In D. Bessire, L. Cappelletti, & B. Pigé (Eds.), *Normes: Origines et conséquences des crises* (Norms, origin and consequences of crises). Paris: Economica.

Zardet, V., & Voyant, O. (2003). Organizational transformation through the socio-economic approach in an industrial context. *Journal of Organizational Change Management.* Emerald, *16*(1), pp. 56–71.

Zarka, C. (1963). Sommes-nous à l'âge de l'inflation? (Are we in the age of inflation). *Revue Économique, IV.*

Zeghni, S. (2014). Note de lecture sur le livre de Savall H; (2012) Origine radicale des crises économiques: Germán Bernácer, précurseur visionnaire. *Mondes en développement, 42*(2), 166.

CD-Rom on the Archives of Bernácer, Caja de Ahorros del Mediterráneo, University of Alicante.

ISEOR Website: http: www.iseor.com

Website on Bernácer: http: www.euce.es/g_bernácer.htm

Miscellaneous

Newspaper Articles About Bernácer

ABC de Madrid. (1973, March 2). Una economía libre sin crisis et sin desempleo (A free economy without crisis and without unemployment).
ABC de Séville. (1973, January 30),
Información de Alicante, 4 et 5 juin 1965.
La Verdad de Murcia, 16 juin 1965 et juin 1966.
Revue Le Management (1972, November). 25 ans de participation (20 years of participation). *Journal officiel,* 5 janv. 1973, pp. 228–229.

Other Sources

Cahiers de l' ISEA, « Économie et Société » (Economy and Society), Série H.S., n°14, août 1972.
Communications on the conference on Value, organized by Y. Bouchut and P. Dockès at the Institut des Études économiques (Analysis-Epistemology-History Department) of the Economics Department of University of Lyon, January 1973.
Dictionnary Robert.
Encyclopaedia Britannica, t. 21, p. 131 à 147, Spain.
Encyclopaedia Universalis, vol. 6, Paris, 1970; vol. 11, Paris, 1971.
Encyclopedia Universal ilustrada europeo-americana, Ed. Espasa, Calpe, Madrid, 1970.
Higino París Equilaz, *Desarrollo económico español* (1906–1964). Madrid: Ed. Sucesor de J. Sánchez de Ocaña y Cía.
Salvador de Madariaga, Spain, London, 2nd ed., 1942.

Index

H. Savall, *Radical Origins to Economic Crises*,
https://doi.org/10.1007/978-3-319-93366-5

The manufacturer's authorised representative in the EU is Springer Nature Customer Service Centre GmbH, Europaplatz 3, 69115 Heidelberg, Germany. If you have any concerns regarding our products, please contact ProductSafety@springernature.com

Printed and bound by CPI Group (UK) Ltd, Croydon, CR0 4YY
05/10/2026
02228140-0013